CAMPAIGNS & ELECTIONS

CAMPAIGNS & ELECTIONS
Rules, Reality, Strategy, Choice

2012 ELECTION UPDATE

John Sides
GEORGE WASHINGTON UNIVERSITY

Daron Shaw
UNIVERSITY OF TEXAS, AUSTIN

Matt Grossmann
MICHIGAN STATE UNIVERSITY

Keena Lipsitz
QUEENS COLLEGE, CITY UNIVERSITY OF NEW YORK

W. W. Norton and Company
New York • London

W. W. Norton & Company has been independent since its founding in 1923, when William Warder Norton and Mary D. Herter Norton first published lectures delivered at the People's Institute, the adult education division of New York City's Cooper Union. The firm soon expanded its program beyond the Institute, publishing books by celebrated academics from America and abroad. By midcentury, the two major pillars of Norton's publishing program—trade books and college texts—were firmly established. In the 1950s, the Norton family transferred control of the company to its employees, and today—with a staff of four hundred and a comparable number of trade, college, and professional titles published each year—W. W. Norton & Company stands as the largest and oldest publishing house owned wholly by its employees.

Editors: Ann Shin, Peter Lesser
Associate editor: Jake Schindel
Editorial assistants: Caitlin Cummings, Sarah Wolf
Project editor: Kate Feighery
Production managers, College: Benjamin Reynolds, Diana Spiegle
Design director: Rubina Yeh
Designer: Lissi Sigillo
Photo researcher: Michael Fodera
Marketing manager: Sasha Levitt
Composition: TexTech, Inc—Brattleboro, VT
Manufacturing: Courier—Westford, MA

The Library of Congress has cataloged another edition as follows:

Library of Congress Cataloging-in-Publication Data

Campaigns and elections : rules, reality, strategy, choice / John Sides . . . [et al.]. — 1st ed.
     p. cm.
  Includes bibliographical references and index.
  ISBN 978-0-393-93262-1 (pbk.)
  1. Political campaigns—United States.   2. Elections—United States.   I. Sides, John.
  JK1976.C333 2011
  324.70973—dc23

This edition: 978-0-393-92365-0

                                                                              2011037180

W. W. Norton & Company, Inc., 500 Fifth Avenue, New York, NY 10110
wwnorton.com
W. W. Norton & Company, Ltd., Castle House, 75/76 Wells Street, London WIT3QT

CONTENTS

8

Presidential Campaigns   214

9

Congressional Campaigns   250

10

State and Local Campaigns   280

11
Voter Participation   308

12
Voter Choice   342

13
Democracy in Action or a Broken System?   374

This book aims to present a comprehensive treatment of political campaigns in the United States. It is structured around four key components that shape American campaigns: the *rules* that govern the electoral process; the *reality* that candidates confront when a campaign begins; the *strategies* employed by important campaign actors, including candidates, parties, interest groups, consultants, and the media; and the *choices* made by voters, which are themselves a response to the rules, reality, and strategies.

The rules that govern the electoral process include institutions such as the Electoral College, as well as the laws that govern campaign finance. The reality that parties and candidates confront consists, in part, of current events, the state of the economy, the presence of an incumbent in the race, and the partisan leaning of their constituents. The importance of rules and reality is augmented by the fact that candidates cannot easily change them. Instead, they structure candidate strategy in important ways. The strategic choices made by candidates comprise the familiar elements of modern campaigns, including message development, television advertising, fund-raising, and voter mobilization. These choices mesh with rules and reality to create the "outputs" of campaigns that are manifest to voters. The response of voters to these outputs goes a long way toward answering the question, "Do campaigns affect voters?" We contend that any good answer to that question is a version of "it depends," and we devote significant attention to what magnifies or diminishes the effects of campaigns.

Throughout the book, we also draw attention to the *democratic functions* of campaigns. We discuss debates about the roles campaigns should play in our democracy and how well contemporary campaigns achieve those goals. We focus on four standards. The first, free choice, means that citizens can participate free of coercion or manipulation. The second, political equality, means that laws cannot disadvantage certain groups of citizens—as, for example, Jim Crow laws disadvantaged southern blacks before the civil rights era. The third, deliberation, refers to the quality of the information that citizens receive from the candidates, the media, and other political actors. Is it sufficient to ensure that citizens can make an informed choice? Of course, deliberation also requires that citizens have the time and motivation to think about electoral choices. The fourth standard, free speech, refers to the constitutional protections that affect whether and how the government might regulate political campaigns. Could, for example, the government require that opposing candidates spend identical amounts of money, so that neither candidate will dominate the airwaves? In discussing such debates, we do not promote any one viewpoint, but instead seek to describe how these values can inform both why campaigns are the way they are, and whether we should attempt to reform them. We emphasize the difficulty of meeting all of these standards simultaneously. It is more likely that making campaigns "better" by one standard will make them "worse" by another. For example, ensuring that citizens receive certain kinds of information may violate the candidates' right to free speech.

This book aims to be comprehensive. We discuss electoral rules and realities not only at the national level but also in the fifty states. We focus on campaigns at all levels of office, including presidential, congressional, state, and local. Doing so illuminates both similarities and differences. For example, although state elections and local elections mimic national elections in key respects—such as by having election dates fixed on the calendar, rather than occurring at the discretion of elected officials themselves—any individual state may differ in the specifics, such as the precise date that elections are held. Similarly, although candidates at all levels of office have the same basic goal—to craft a compelling message and thereby win the election—they do so with vastly different levels of resources and thus with very different kinds of campaign strategies. A presidential campaign spends more on catering in a week than many local campaigns spend in total.

We also seek to be comprehensive in another respect: by including the perspectives of both campaign professionals and academics. We take into account the views of professionals who work "on the ground" during campaigns and who usually believe that their efforts are consequential. The instructor resources that accompany this book—available at wwnorton.com/nrl—include exercises that simulate some of the decisions that campaign professionals must make.

We also take into account the views of political scientists, who have traditionally been more skeptical about the effects of campaigns, and the views of political theorists, who debate the democratic functions of political campaigns. Ultimately, we hope to provide an insider's perspective on the choices that political actors face in campaigns while simultaneously offering a judicious account of the impact of campaigns on voter attitudes and electoral outcomes.

Perhaps above all, we hope that the book engages readers as citizens. Most Americans experience political campaigns primarily as spectators and profess to dislike what they see. Thus, we want to help readers think critically about two things: what campaigns actually do and what campaigns should do. The former entails identifying when, how, and for whom campaigns matter. With this knowledge, readers will have a more sophisticated view of campaign effects—one that does not attribute great significance to every twist and turn but does not rule out influence entirely. The question of what campaigns should do is meant to engage readers in a broader conversation about the ideals that underpin the electoral process, and whether the process can be reformed to better approximate those ideals.

Resources to accompany this book

The following resources, developed specifically to accompany this book, are available to students and instructors:

Student StudySpace Web site (wwnorton.com/studyspace). This free and open site includes materials for study and review, as well as exercises that ask students to apply what they have learned from the text to understanding real-life campaigns.

- **Practice quizzes** let students test your knowledge of the chapter.
- **Chapter outlines** provide an overview of the chapter.
- **Flashcards** help students review the key terms from each chapter.
- **Video exercises** provide opportunities to use the concepts from the text to analyze real-world examples, such as campaign ads and other clips.

Instructor Resource Web site (wwnorton.com/nrl). Accessible to confirmed instructors only, this site includes:

- **PowerPoint slides** of all figures and tables from the text. These are also provided in JPEG format.
- **Test questions** for every chapter.
- **Activity modules**, with detailed instructions for in-class and outside assignments, as well as materials for these activities. These modules allow students to apply what they have learned in the text as they work through hands-on simulations of several aspects of campaigns.

Acknowledgments

We are grateful to those who have assisted us in writing this book. Many scholars read portions of the book at various stages: Scott Adler, Brian Arbour, Suzanne Chod, David Dulio, Philip Habel, Danny Hayes, Valerie Hyman, Phil Jones, Ray LaRaja, Mingus Mapps, Seth Masket, Nate Persily, Andrew Reeves, Travis Ridout, Joe Romance, Wayne Steger, Jessica Trounstine, and Jonathan Winburn. We thank Jake Haselswerdt for providing research assistance. We also thank W. W. Norton for supporting and nurturing this project—including our editor, Ann Shin, for her expert guidance and feedback; associate editor Jake Schindel; editorial assistant Caitlin Cummings; e-media editor Lorraine Klimowich; project editor Kate Feighery; copy editor Jodi Beder; and production manager Ben Reynolds.

John Sides
Daron Shaw
Matt Grossmann
Keena Lipsitz

CAMPAIGNS & ELECTIONS

<table>
<tr><td>**CHAPTER**</td><td>**1**</td></tr>
</table>

Introduction

On November 2, 2004, President George W. Bush was elected to a second term and the Republican Party retained control of both the U.S. Senate and House of Representatives. At a press conference two days later, Bush seemed empowered by his victory. He said, "I earned capital in the campaign, political capital, and now I intend to spend it." A week after Bush's election, his chief political strategist, Karl Rove, was eager to describe the scope of Bush's victory:

> This was an extraordinary election. [Bush won] 59.7 million votes, and we still have about 250,000 ballots to count. Think about that—*nearly 60 million votes!* The previous largest number was Ronald Reagan in 1984, sweeping the country with 49 states. We won 81 percent of all the counties in America. We gained a percentage of the vote in 87 percent of the counties in America. In Florida, we received nearly a million votes more in this election than in the last one.[1]

Some commentators, even liberal ones, agreed with Rove and believed there had been a fundamental change in American politics, one that would lead to continued Republican dominance.[2] This was, by all accounts, Rove's goal all along.

The post-election euphoria of Bush and Rove proved short-lived. The war in Iraq, which had begun in March 2003, dragged on and on. Following the U.S.-led invasion, protracted sectarian violence engulfed Iraq and U.S. military casualties continued to mount. The American economy also began to weaken, a trend has-

---

[1] Joshua Green. 2007. "The Rove Presidency." *The Atlantic*, September. www.theatlantic.com/magazine/archive/2007/09/the-rove-presidency/6132/ (accessed 5/20/10).

[2] One example was Michael Lind, writing at the blog *Talking Points Memo*: http://tpmcafe.talkingpointsmemo.com/2005/08/11/1896_and_2004/ (accessed 5/20/10).

tened by the financial crisis that shook both Wall Street and Main Street in the fall of 2008. In the months that followed, the United States would experience the deepest economic downturn since the Great Depression. In the last month of his presidency Bush's approval rating dropped to about 30 percent. The capital he apparently earned in 2004 was long gone.

In the 2006 midterm election, the Democratic Party struck its first blow, taking back control of the House and Senate. This was the first time since 1994 that the Democrats controlled both chambers. The Democrats elected the first female Speaker of the House, Nancy Pelosi of California, and quickly sought to make good on their campaign promises — specifically, a six-point agenda that they called "A New Direction for America," or, for short, "Six in '06." In her speech after being elected Speaker, Pelosi said, "The election of 2006 was a call to change — not merely to change the control of Congress, but for a new direction for our country."

That new direction got a further boost on November 4, 2008, when the Democratic nominee, Barack Obama, won the presidency — a victory all the more noteworthy because he became the first African American to hold this office. In his victory speech, Obama was no less ambitious than Bush: "This is our time — to put our people back to work and open doors of opportunity for our kids; to restore prosperity and promote the cause of peace; to reclaim the American Dream and

Core of the Analysis

Focusing on four aspects of campaigns — rules, reality, strategy, and citizens — helps us understand the outcomes of American elections:

- The *rules* refer to laws and constitutional doctrines that govern the electoral system and affect how campaigns are carried out and ultimately who wins elections.
- Broader economic and political *realities* shape the tenor of public opinion and often place limits on how much campaigns can affect opinion.
- The *strategies* employed by candidates, political parties, interest groups, and the media reflect their unique interests and agendas and can, when circumstances are right, affect public opinion as well.
- The *choices made by citizens* — whether and how to vote — depend on a mix of longstanding habits, current realities, and new information from the campaign itself.
- The democratic values of free choice, equality, deliberation, and free speech help us evaluate campaigns.

TABLE 1.1 Percent of Popular Vote Won by Presidential Candidates, 1856–2008*

Year	Democrat	Republican	Independent Candidates or Third Parties	Year	Democrat	Republican	Independent Candidates or Third Parties
1856	**45.3%**	33.1%	21.6%	1936	**60.8%**	36.5%	2.7%
1860	29.5%	**39.7%**	30.8%	1940	**54.7%**	44.8%	0.5%
1864	45.0%	**55.0%**	0.0%	1944	**53.4%**	45.9%	0.7%
1868	47.3%	**52.7%**	0.0%	1948	**49.6%**	45.1%	5.4%
1872	43.8%	**55.6%**	0.6%	1952	44.3%	**55.2%**	0.5%
1876	**50.9%**	47.9%	1.2%	1956	42.0%	**57.4%**	0.7%
1880	48.2%	**48.3%**	3.5%	1960	**49.7%**	49.6%	0.7%
1884	**48.9%**	48.3%	2.9%	1964	**61.1%**	38.5%	0.5%
1888	**48.6%**	47.8%	3.6%	1968	42.7%	**43.4%**	13.9%
1892	**46.0%**	43.0%	11.0%	1972	37.5%	**60.7%**	1.8%
1896	46.7%	**51.0%**	2.3%	1976	**50.1%**	48.0%	1.9%
1900	45.5%	**51.6%**	2.8%	1980	41.0%	**50.8%**	8.2%
1904	37.6%	**56.4%**	6.0%	1984	40.6%	**58.8%**	0.7%
1908	43.0%	**51.6%**	5.4%	1988	45.7%	**53.4%**	1.0%
1912	**41.8%**	23.2%	35.0%	1992	**43.0%**	37.5%	19.6%
1916	**49.2%**	46.1%	4.6%	1996	**49.2%**	40.7%	10.1%
1920	34.2%	**60.3%**	5.5%	2000	**48.4%**	47.9%	3.8%
1924	28.8%	**54.0%**	17.1%	2004	48.3%	**50.7%**	1.0%
1928	40.8%	**58.2%**	1.0%	2008	**52.9%**	45.6%	1.5%
1932	**57.4%**	39.7%	2.9%				

* Winner's percentage in bold.
Source: Dave Leip's Atlas of U.S. Presidential Elections. www.uselectionatlas.org/ (accessed 5/20/10).

reaffirm that fundamental truth — that out of many, we are one." Working with his large congressional majorities, Obama moved swiftly to act on those ambitious goals. He and congressional Democrats succeeded — over nearly unanimous Republican opposition — in passing a stimulus package intended to help the economy, a climate change bill in the House, and, most notably, health care reform in March 2010.

But once again, the success of the party in power proved short-lived. By the next midterm election, in November 2010, the economy was no longer in a tailspin, but it was only limping toward recovery. Obama's approval rating was about 45 percent — 20 points lower than when he was inaugurated. All of these facts spelled trouble for the Democrats in Congress. In the 2010 elections, the party lost six seats in the Senate and a whopping 63 seats in the House of Representatives. The number of seats lost in the House was the largest experienced by the president's party since 1938. In a press conference after the election, Obama acknowledged that the Democrats had taken a "shellacking."

These six years from 2004 to 2010 brought important changes in party power and tempered the ambitions of two presidents. Table 1.1 shows that frequent shifts between the Democratic and Republican parties have been the norm across presidential elections in the past 150 years. These shifts point toward one of the central questions of this book: *What explains the outcomes of American elections — presidential, congressional, and state and local?* Addressing this question entails attention to others. Why do some candidates choose to run and others do not? Why do some candidates win and others lose? There are many interpretations of elections, but far fewer solid answers to these questions.

An obvious answer might be the campaign itself. A political campaign combines elements of two other, nonpolitical types of campaigns. In some ways, it is like a military campaign, with the goal of winning a contest and vanquishing an opponent. It is also like an advertising campaign, with the goal of persuading citizens to buy a product. One might think that political campaigns are always consequential, with millions of dollars being spent, professional strategists scheming, advertisements blanketing the airwaves, and armies of volunteers pounding the pavement. But this is not necessarily so. Elections depend on the overall state of the country, which even brilliant campaigning cannot change. Hence the second central question of this book: *How much does the campaign itself matter?*

It is easy to imagine how campaigns might matter. Campaigns could convince citizens to support one candidate or oppose another, or motivate them to go to the polls on Election Day. Professional campaign operatives frequently argue that campaign strategies accomplish these things. Indeed, it is hard to see how they could believe otherwise: their livelihoods depend on it! Political scientists, however, approach the question differently: rather than relying on personal experience, they use different kinds of research designs and evidence to determine how much the campaign actually matters. This entails acknowledging that the campaign's impact, however meaningful, could prove secondary to that of other events. For example, what was more important for Obama's victory in 2008: the $730 million that he spent campaigning or an unpopular George W. Bush and a tanking economy?

The fact that Obama spent so much money raises the third central question of this book: *How should we evaluate the American electoral process?* One complaint is that American campaigns are just too expensive, and the incessant fund-raising distracts and possibly corrupts politicians. People wonder whether the system allows the best candidates to emerge. They question whether campaigns are fair, informative, truthful, and engaging. They worry that citizens fail to learn what they need to know in order to make political decisions, or that constant mud-slinging alienates citizens and leads them to stay home on Election Day. It is important to think through these complaints analytically — to ask, for example, whether negative campaigning really turns citizens off. But it is also important to think critically about what elections and campaigns *should* be like. Then we will understand not only how much campaigns affect citizens but also how much they help or hurt our democracy.

A Framework for Understanding Campaigns and Elections

In this book, we use a simple framework to understand **campaigns** and **elections** in American politics. This framework emphasizes four aspects of campaigns and elections:

- The *rules* that govern elections.
- The broader *reality*—economic, political, and historical—that parties and candidates confront as they decide whether to run or how to campaign.
- The *strategic choices* that various actors make, including candidates, the media, political parties, and interest groups.
- The *choices of citizens*, who will ultimately decide the outcome.

The goal of this framework is to identify the major features of the American electoral system that ultimately influence the actual outcomes of elections—who wins and who loses. We will also see how the elements of the framework depend on each other. For example, the strategic choices of candidates depend on both the electoral rules and the broader reality that candidates confront. Similarly, the choices of citizens, especially in the voting booth, may depend on rules and reality, but also on the strategies of candidates, parties, the media, and others, all of whom broadcast information that may influence citizens' feelings about the candidates. In the following sections, we elaborate on each element of this framework.

Rules

Any sports fan can see that the rules of the game matter. When college and professional basketball created a longer-distance shot worth three points, it changed the game, making sharpshooting players more valuable and helping teams who had more such players. Although we cannot replay history, it seems likely that teams have won numerous games that they otherwise would have lost if not for three-point shooting.

Elections are no different. Rules affect their every aspect: who is qualified to run for office, when the election is held and thus when the campaign begins, the size and characteristics of constituencies, how much money can be donated and spent, who is eligible to vote, and, ultimately, who wins the election. All of the actors involved in the election—citizens, candidates, parties, interest groups, the media—find themselves subject to rules. For example, sixteen-year-olds cannot vote. Thirty-year-olds cannot be president.

In 2010, voters elected a new Republican majority — led by Speaker John Boehner — to the House of Representatives. Why were the Republicans so successful in 2010? Did smart campaigning enable them to win 63 additional seats in the House? Or were other factors more important than campaign strategy?

Candidates and parties cannot accept unlimited amounts of money from a wealthy donor. Interest groups cannot coordinate their campaign spending with the candidates it would benefit. Television stations cannot sell advertising time to one candidate but refuse to sell it to the opponent.

The rules of elections are important because, in many cases, they cannot be changed easily. Changing a rule may require legislation or a Supreme Court decision—at the extreme, a constitutional amendment. Even in the simplest cases, changes typically do not happen during the campaign itself. Thus, as the campaign gets under way, the rules constitute a hand that all the candidates are dealt and thereby constrain candidate strategy in important ways. Consider some of the basic rules about campaign finance. Existing laws limit the amount of money that any individual can donate but do not limit the amount of money that any candidate can spend. The former means that candidates must devote a lot of time to fund-raising as they try to amass campaign funds from many individual donors. The latter means that some wealthy people will be tempted to run for office and spend their own money to finance their campaigns. The challenges of financing a campaign under the existing rules also seem to discourage potential female candidates. In a survey of women and men in professions, such as law and business, that frequently lead to political careers, women were less likely than men to say that they had contemplated running for office, and many women cited the challenges of raising money as a dissuading factor.[3]

Reality

The context in which an election occurs—what we call "reality"—also strongly affects a candidate's success or failure. In 2004, Barack Obama ran for U.S. senator in his home state of Illinois. His opponent was Jack Ryan, a wealthy former businessman who was working as a volunteer at a local Catholic school. Early polls gave Obama a substantial lead, but many respondents described themselves as undecided. Ryan had been divorced from the actress Jeri Ryan in 1999, and in June 2004, after a lawsuit by the *Chicago Tribune* and other media outlets, a judge unsealed the court proceedings from that divorce. In those proceedings, Jeri Ryan alleged that her husband asked her to have sex with him in sex clubs in New Orleans, New York, and Paris. When this information became public, Ryan withdrew from the race. In his place, Alan Keyes stood as the Republican candidate. Keyes was a staunch conservative who had run and lost handily in several other elections, including two ill-fated attempts at the Republican presidential nomination, in 2000 and 2004. He established residency in Illinois only days before he began running for this Senate seat. Obama trounced him by 43 points.

To take another example, in early 2008, when Barack Obama ran for the Democratic nomination for president, there was an unpopular war in Iraq, an unpopular Republican president, and the beginnings of a deep recession. After Obama became the nominee, the economic crisis worsened, with several large banks failing or nearly failing—requiring extraordinary government action to save them and prop up both the financial system and the larger economy. Obama again beat his opponent, this time Senator John McCain of Arizona, by a decisive margin.

Both of these stories illustrate the importance of the broader reality candidates face. Here, "reality" refers to several factors in particular: the candidates' biographies, the records of the political parties, and recent and current political and economic events, such as a war or recession. These elements of the broader context are similar in one crucial respect: they are rarely under the control of the candidates themselves. Ryan's divorce, the nomination of Keyes, the war in Iraq, the economic recession: Obama made none of these

---

[3] Jennifer L. Lawless and Richard L. Fox. 2008. "Why Are Women Still Not Running for Public Office?" *Brookings Institution Issues in Governance Studies*, May.

events happen. They happened to him or to his opponents or to the public and arguably increased his chances of winning his Senate seat and then the presidency. Ultimately, the things that candidates can control, such as their campaign strategy, may not overcome the effects of events that conspire against them.

A first important component of reality is the background of the candidates themselves. This may involve their personal lives—for Jack Ryan, his divorce—or their professional lives, including prior service in elected office. Candidates cannot rewrite their biographies from scratch. What they have done or said in the past will follow them, including both the good and the bad. Candidates try to capitalize on the best aspects of their biography, such as a happy family, service to the community or country, and support of popular policies. Opponents bring up the worst aspects, such as lies, unpopular actions, and scandals.

A second component of reality involves the legacies that political parties bequeath to candidates. The major parties have each developed reputations for giving attention to specific key issues as well as for their positions on those issues. The Democratic Party has traditionally favored using government resources to help people. The Republican Party has favored lowering taxes, in part in an effort to shrink the size of government. An anti-tax Democrat or a pro-welfare Republican are at odds with these legacies and can have difficulty convincing citizens that their positions are sincere. The parties have also developed coalitions of supporters from different groups in society. The Democratic Party's early commitment to civil rights, despite the resistance of Southern Democrats, earned it the lasting loyalty of African Americans. The Republican Party's conservative position on social issues, such as abortion and gay rights, garnered the support of many evangelical Christians. Candidates find it difficult to make inroads with groups that have not traditionally supported their party.

Another component of reality is current or recent events that are directly connected to government policies and the formal powers of political office. For example, foreign-policy crises and wars are particularly important for the electoral prospects of presidents and presidential candidates. The terrorist attacks of September 11, 2001, led the public and Congress to rally behind President Bush. The Republican Party even picked up seats in the 2002 midterm elections, despite the fact that the president's party typically loses seats in midterm elections. By 2004, Bush had lost the goodwill of many Democrats, but September 11, as well as the Iraq War, still loomed large over the campaign. War and national security issues were central to Bush's message and that of his opponent, Senator John Kerry, in 2004. Ongoing wars can help or hurt the **incumbent** president. Consider Lyndon Johnson, who decided not to run for re-election in 1968 because the long, costly Vietnam War had become so unpopular. Foreign affairs and war may not be completely outside politicians' control, in that presidents help decide how to conduct foreign relations and whether and how to wage war. But presidents cannot control other countries and their armies, and they often confront the unexpected. The same is true for other elected officials and for events related to other policy areas.

A final and especially important component of reality is the economy. Just as the public tends to prefer peace over war, it prefers prosperity to poverty. And the public holds incumbent officeholders responsible for economic conditions, particularly the president. As we will discuss in more detail in later chapters, incumbents presiding over a robust economy will typically win a larger share of the vote than those presiding over a weak economy. As with foreign affairs and war, elected officials often have some influence on the economy. For example, as happened during the recession that confronted Barack Obama when he took office, the president and Congress can pass bills that attempt to stimulate the economy or that provide government support to unemployed Americans. These types of measures can be important, but

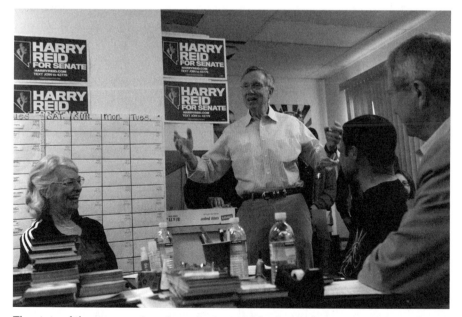

The state of the economy is an important part of the "reality" campaigns face, and voters often punish incumbents during economic downturns. In 2010, Senate Majority Leader Harry Reid faced an unusually tough campaign for re-election in Nevada.

they are often less effective than politicians and the public would like. The ups and downs of the economy depend on many factors outside any politician's control.

Taken together, the elements of reality affect candidate strategies, the decisions of citizens, and, ultimately, election outcomes. Their impact on election outcomes makes it difficult to credit campaign strategy for every victory and blame it for every defeat. Incumbent candidates running during a time of peace and prosperity may win easily, even if their campaigns were full of strategic miscalculations. These same candidates running during an unpopular war and a weak economy may lose, no matter the brilliance of their campaign strategy.

Strategy

The impact of rules and reality can lead to doubts about the effects of campaign strategy. But campaign strategies do matter. One need look no further than the fluctuations in the candidates' poll numbers during the campaign. In 2008, Bush's unpopularity and the weak economy advantaged Obama, but had the election been held in early September, McCain, basking in the glow of the Republican National Convention, would have won, according to the polls. Why did McCain's lead dissipate? Why did Obama's lead continue to grow throughout the rest of September and October? Questions like these draw our attention to the potential impact of campaign strategy.

Campaigns involve a variety of actors. Most visible are the candidates. Their strategic choices involve every facet of a campaign: whether to run in the first place, what issues to emphasize, what specific messages or themes to discuss, which kinds of media to utilize, and which citizens to target. Candidates' personal campaign organizations, sometimes with paid professionals on board, create much of the visible campaign activity, from yard signs and bumper stickers to television advertising and YouTube videos. Political parties engage in similar strategic debates about the best agenda, message, and targeting strategy. Parties also deploy resources on behalf of their candidates, including ads, voter registration drives, and get-out-the-vote operations on Election Day. The same is true of interest groups, who raise and spend money in support of favored candidates. And, throughout the campaign, the news media are crucial. Although candidates can communicate directly with citizens through advertising, citizens receive a lot of information from news media outlets. Thus, the news media's coverage of the campaign may also matter.

All of these actors are in part following their own strategies and in part responding to others. Candidates routinely try to "stay on message" but often respond to their opponents' claims. Parties and interest groups often structure their campaign activity to complement that of their favored candidates, but at times the strategies of the candidates and those of parties and interest groups diverge. Interest groups, for example, are far more likely than candidates to air negative advertisements. The media depend on political parties, interest groups, and, especially, candidates for news but often impose their own definition of newsworthiness. The media's agenda frequently diverges from those of the candidates; in short, the media are talking about something different than the candidates.[4] This is one reason candidates frequently criticize the coverage they receive.

Campaign strategy is the element of elections that candidates and other actors can control. They may not be able to end a war or make the economy grow, but they can craft a slogan, produce a television advertisement, give a speech, and kiss a lot of babies at a campaign rally. Much money is spent doing all of these things. The ultimate question is how much difference it makes.

Citizens

In any democratic political system, an election's outcome depends on the people. Eligible American citizens have two choices to make in an election: *whether* to vote and *how* to vote. Rules and reality affect these choices. Campaign strategists aim to influence these choices as well, by convincing people to support a particular candidate and encouraging supporters to vote on Election Day. The central question is: How susceptible are citizens to campaign influence? Answering this question also means determining how much citizens are affected by broader realities such as the state of the economy, which might matter more than the campaign itself.

Citizens are not blank slates. They have preexisting political habits and opinions. Some vote in every election. Others never vote. Some tend to vote for Democrats, and some for Republicans. Habits put limits on what a campaign can accomplish. No matter how much money candidates spend, or how catchy and engaging their advertisements are, they will not be able to persuade some citizens to support them or to vote. Moreover, at times campaigns struggle simply to command the public's attention. Some people do not follow politics closely and are not interested in watching the news, candidate debates, or political advertisements. Simply put, many votes are not up for grabs, and those that are may not easily be won with the tools of modern

---

[4] Danny Hayes. 2009. "The Dynamics of Agenda Convergence and the Paradox of Competitiveness in Presidential Campaigns." *Political Research Quarterly* 63, 3: 594–611.

campaigns. Indeed, undecided citizens may respond more to "reality" than to campaign messages.

Journalists often describe campaigns as important, as do campaign consultants, naturally enough. Victorious candidates are presumed to have run skillful campaigns. The day after the 2008 election, the front page of the *New York Times* had this headline adjacent to a victorious Obama: "Near-Flawless Run from Start to Finish Is Credited in Victory." The losers are presumed to have run flawed campaigns. Neither presumption is warranted, absent scientific evidence of how much the campaign mattered. Gathering this evidence and demonstrating its persuasiveness are difficult tasks.

Evaluating Campaigns and Elections

Thinking about rules, reality, strategy, and citizens helps illuminate what actually happens in campaigns. The next question is: What should happen? Here, "should happen" does not mean "my candidate should win." Rather, we mean what is good for the democratic political system in which we live?

In democratic systems, campaigns are crucial processes. They are a time during which citizens typically pay the most attention to politics. They also provide a level of interaction between leaders and citizens that is rarely attained at other times. Thus, a lot is at stake in getting this process "right." However, a large majority of the public professes not to like campaigns very much. In a 2006 poll, 80 percent of respondents thought that campaigns had gotten worse in the past 10 years. The public routinely complains that campaigns are too long, too costly, and too negative. In the public's eyes, much can and should be done to reform campaigns.

But campaign reform is not a simple matter. There may be good reasons for the status quo, however objectionable it is to some Americans. Moreover, any reform is likely to involve trade-offs, improving things by one standard but worsening them by another. It is helpful, then, to establish a set of standards by which we can evaluate campaigns. Each of these standards represents a potential goal of a democratic political system. Together they may not capture every conceivable goal, but they do represent a starting point. We will refer to them in many subsequent chapters, as we seek not only to understand how campaigns and elections operate but also whether they can or should be improved.

The first standard is *free choice*. For elections to be truly democratic, citizens must be free from coercion or manipulation. To facilitate their choice, they must also have adequate information about the contending candidates and parties. Campaigns that involve violent intimidation of opposition party supporters do not meet this standard, nor do campaigns in which the incumbent regime controls all major news outlets. In the United States, such behavior is rare but is known to occur. For example, during the 2006 election, a letter was sent to approximately 14,000 residents of Orange County, California, all of whom had Latino surnames or foreign birthplaces. The letter, written in Spanish, suggested that immigrants might go to jail for voting, with the apparent intent of discouraging Latino citizens from voting and thereby hurting the re-election prospects of the Latina incumbent, Representative Loretta Sanchez. Sanchez's Republican opponent, Tan Nguyen, was convicted in 2010 for lying to federal investigators about whether he played any role in sending the letter.

Even if such dramatic attempts at coercion are rare, we may ask if the information that citizens receive in American campaigns is sufficient to ensure free choice. What if, for example, a well-funded incumbent is competing against a poorly funded challenger? Chances are, citizens will hear much more from the incumbent than the challenger. Is this a problem? What if the situation is even more lopsided, and there is no challenger for this incumbent? For example, in the 2008 election, 65 percent of House incumbents had no opposition in their party's primary. Does it violate the standard of free choice when there is only one choice?

A second standard is *political equality*. Citizens must, by this standard, be equal in the eyes of the law. Laws that disadvantage certain citizens violate this standard. One example is Jim Crow laws in the South. These laws, which were in effect in many Southern states from 1876 until 1965, effectively disenfranchised blacks using a variety of means, such as literacy tests and poll taxes. (Blacks, who were often less educated and less affluent than whites, were more likely to fail these tests and be unable to afford the tax.) Although Jim Crow laws were eventually abolished, voter eligibility requirements continue to have implications for political equality. For example, requiring potential voters to supply identification, such as a driver's license, will disproportionately affect those without such identification, who tend to be elderly or members of racial minorities.

The standard of political equality could be applied to candidates as well. The example of the rich incumbent and the poor challenger may violate this standard. But this standard also raises some challenging questions. Must every pair of opposing candidates have identical amounts of money to spend campaigning? What if a challenger has raised little money because he or she seems to lack important qualities or qualifications, leaving potential donors reluctant to give?

A third standard is *deliberation*. Deliberation speaks not just to the quantity but also to the quality of information available to citizens. The interaction between the opposing candidates can be evaluated by this standard. For example, in a truly deliberative interaction, the candidates highlight points of similarity and difference between them. This helps citizens decide whom they prefer. Media coverage of the campaign can be evaluated by this same standard. Does the news give citizens this information? Critics often complain that it does not, because campaign reporting is more focused on the latest polls than on the policy proposals of the candidates. The 2008 election provides but one of many examples. A study by the Project for Excellence in Journalism found that more than half of campaign news stories in 2008 were framed around strategy, tactics, and polling.[5] Only 20 percent were framed

One democratic value is equality — but what does this mean in the context of elections? Should rich candidates be prohibited from outspending poorer opponents? In the 2010 California gubernatorial race, Jerry Brown was vastly outspent by Meg Whitman, who drew on her personal fortune to spend $160 million, as compared with Brown's $25 million. (Nonetheless, Brown won.)

---

[5] Project for Excellence in Journalism. 2008. "Winning the Media Campaign: How the Press Reported the 2008 Presidential General Election." www.journalism.org/analysis_report/winning_media_campaign (accessed 4/7/11).

around discussions of policy. Is the public learning enough about the real differences between the candidates when their views on issues are so rarely discussed? Before we are too quick to criticize the media, we must also ask: Does this focus on strategy rather than policy merely reflect the desires of news consumers, who are happy to read about polls but not so interested in long articles about the candidates' views on complicated aspects of policy?

A fourth standard is *free speech*. This is a linchpin of the American political system, one enshrined in the Bill of Rights. Upholding free speech may in fact complicate attempts to promote equality or deliberation. Eliminating disparities between incumbents and challengers in the interest of equality entails limiting the amount of "speech" that incumbents have—for instance, by restricting how and how much they campaign. One way to do this is with campaign finance laws, which affect how much candidates can raise and spend. Ensuring deliberation would place restrictions on what the candidates and news media talk about, perhaps by forcing candidates to engage each other on specific issues, even if they would rather not discuss those issues. Either could be said to violate the standard of free speech.

Designing the ideal campaign or election is a difficult task, especially because the four standards discussed here are not always compatible. But these standards are still useful ways by which to evaluate the rules and institutions that govern the electoral process—such as the Electoral College and campaign finance laws—as well as the strategies pursued by candidates. Americans commonly complain when candidates attack their opponents. Is this always a bad thing? These standards can help us address that question. They also help us evaluate the behavior of citizens. Does the attention Americans pay to the campaign and their knowledge of the candidates live up to democratic ideals?

Conclusion

To understand and evaluate campaigns, we take into account the perspectives of both political professionals and political scientists—who, as we noted in the beginning of this chapter, often have quite different perspectives on how much campaigns affect elections. Professional campaign operatives and consultants are focused on the nuts and bolts of campaigning—the how-to's—and tend to believe that campaigns have important effects on citizens. Political scientists formulate broader theories of campaigns and elections and then test those theories with empirical research on public opinion, media coverage, and campaign activity. They tend to be more cautious in attributing significance to campaign strategy. Our goal is to provide a sense of what happens on the ground in campaigns, and also whether it ultimately matters—to individual voters and to election outcomes.

The next chapter outlines the basic rules of the electoral process in the United States. Chapter 3 describes how American political campaigns have evolved throughout history. Chapter 4 describes how contemporary campaigns are financed—another aspect of the rules that has important consequences for strategy. Chapter 5 discusses the major elements of modern campaign strategy, drawing on political science theories and evidence as well as the thinking of political consultants; much of this chapter focuses on the behavior of candidates. Chapters 6 and 7 consider the specific roles played by other actors: political parties, interest groups, and the media.

Chapters 8–10 delve into three specific categories of campaigns: presidential, congressional, and state and local. An important theme throughout the book is that the rules, realities, and strategies inherent in campaigns may differ across levels of office. Thus, it is important to examine how each type of campaign typically unfolds. Chapters 11 and 12 turn the focus to citizens, including their decision to participate in elections and their decision to support a particular candidate. These two chapters devote particular attention to how much campaigns affect each decision. Finally, Chapter 13 evaluates contemporary American campaigns by the standards presented above. Some discussion of these standards also appears in other chapters, but this final chapter provides a broader perspective on whether American campaigns and elections reflect a "broken system" or effective "democracy in action."

KEY TERMS

campaign (p. 7)
election (p. 7)
incumbent (p. 11)

FOR DISCUSSION

1. What are the central differences in how political consultants and political scientists think about the impact of campaigns?

2. Why do the rules constrain candidates when they are campaigning? Why don't candidates simply change the rules to benefit their campaigns?

3. What are several dimensions of "reality" that might affect campaign strategies and election outcomes?

4. Why would the standards of deliberation and equality potentially come into conflict with the standard of free speech?

 Visit StudySpace for quizzes and other review material.
wwnorton.com/studyspace

CHAPTER 2

The American Electoral Process

In the spring of 2001, Barack Obama, a state senator in Illinois, was a year removed from his most stunning political defeat. In the 2000 Democratic primary for a U.S House seat, he had challenged another black Democrat, the incumbent congressman Bobby Rush, and lost by 31 points. Obama had struggled to win votes in some parts of Rush's district, particularly black neighborhoods where professors at the University of Chicago — even African American professors like Obama — were viewed with suspicion. Obama had more appeal in South Side neighborhoods around the university, and also North Side neighborhoods closer to downtown, including the so-called Gold Coast along Lake Michigan. The Gold Coast is home to many wealthy (and mostly white) Chicagoans, an ideal group from which to raise money for a political campaign. The problem was that as a state senator Obama did not represent the North Side and its Gold Coast; his district was on the South Side.

One day that spring, Obama went to a room in a downtown building in Springfield, a room guarded with fingerprint scanners and coded keypads. Inside the room were computers on which a select few employees of the Illinois Democratic Party worked. Their job was to draw legislative districts. The Democrats had won control of the Illinois House and now, the year after the 2000 census, were drawing up a new set of state legislative districts — as was the Republican majority in the Illinois Senate. Obama sat with a Democratic consultant, John Corrigan, and drew himself a new district, one that started in the South Side and then stretched north to the Gold Coast. It was a "radical change," said Corrigan.

After a protracted battle, the Democrats succeeded in implementing their districts. This gave Obama a new district well suited to funding his political ambitions, and it also helped the Democrats win a majority in the Illinois Senate in the 2002 elections. This majority helped Obama by allowing him to more easily establish a record of legislative accomplishments. With this newfound potential for raising money and promoting legislation, Obama was poised to run for the U.S. Senate in 2004.[1]

This chapter is about the rules of campaigns and elections, the first part of the framework introduced in Chapter 1. All democracies depend on rules to govern political life. The anecdote from early in Obama's political career illustrates their importance. Obama was lucky: he had some influence over redistricting, which determined who his constituents would be. Most of the time, political leaders, candidates, and parties do not have this luxury. Rules are often fixed by law, sometimes even by the Constitution itself, and cannot be changed quickly or easily to benefit a party or candidate.

The rules of the American electoral process help us to answer many crucial questions pertaining to campaigns. This chapter explores five of them: who can run for office, when elections are held, where to run, who can vote, and who wins. For each, we first explore what the rules are. The answers are not always straightforward, due in part to a second consideration: who makes the rules. The Constitution, Congress, state legislatures, and political parties all have some say. The rules are not the same for every level of office or in every state. But even general answers are informative.

Knowing what the rules are and who makes them leads to the "why" question: Why these rules and not others? Rules reflect ideals or values — that is,

Core of the Analysis

- Elections are conducted according to rules that determine who runs, when elections are held, where candidates run, who can vote, and who wins.
- The rules often vary across states and levels of office because they are designed by multiple decision makers, including the framers of the Constitution, Congress, state legislatures, local officials, and political parties.
- The rules reflect values about what constitutes a "good" election, but they often further certain values at the expense of others.
- Many rules are largely outside of the control of candidates, political parties, and voters, especially once the campaign has begun.
- The rules strongly affect the decisions of every relevant actor during a campaign, including candidates, parties, interest groups, the media, and voters.

[1] This anecdote comes from Ryan Lizza. 2008. "Making It: How Chicago Shaped Obama." *The New Yorker,* July 2.

When Barack Obama was a member of the Illinois legislature, the rules for redistricting determined who his constituents were. Advantageous district boundaries helped set Obama up for a successful U.S. Senate campaign in 2004.

conceptions of what is a good or fair electoral process. For example, a good electoral process might feature a vigorous competition between two candidates — one that provides information to citizens and motivates them to vote. But competitive elections are also more expensive, as candidates have an incentive to raise more money so that they can effectively communicate with citizens. Many people wish that elections were not so expensive and fear that soliciting campaign contributions corrupts candidates. So whether one favors increased competition might depend on what one considers more important: informing voters or mitigating the potential for corruption. Inevitably, electoral rules reflect compromises and almost never fully codify any particular value, reflecting instead trade-offs among competing values. Small wonder, then, that electoral rules are often so controversial.

We turn now to the major rules of American elections. In this chapter, we will see that perhaps the most important aspect of electoral rules, especially from a candidate's or party's point of view, is their consequences for campaign strategy and for whether they are likely to win or lose. Perhaps Barack Obama had philosophical objections to a system in which his party got to redraw the Illinois political map to help both him and his party. But ultimately he did not try to change the rule; he merely tried to make it work in his favor.

Who Can Run

Who is eligible to run for office? In the American political system, the qualifications usually involve a minimum age, American citizenship, and a minimum time living in the community one seeks to represent. For federal office,
the Constitution spells these requirements out. A candidate for the House of
Representatives must be at least 25 years old, a citizen for seven years, and
an "inhabitant" of the state the district is in. The qualifications for senator are
similar, except that the candidate must be at least 30 years old and a citizen
for nine years. These more restrictive qualifications are because the framers of the Constitution believed that the Senate demanded more from its
members than did the House. James Madison wrote, "The propriety of these
distinctions is explained by the nature of the senatorial trust, which, requiring greater extent of information and stability of character, requires at the
same time that the senator should have reached a period of life most likely to
supply these advantages."[2]

The requirements for president are even more restrictive. Candidates must
be at least 35 years old and U.S. residents for at least 14 years (although
the Constitution does not specify when that period of residency must have
occurred). Moreover, they must be native-born citizens of the United States.
Naturalized citizens may run for the House and Senate.

Candidates for state and local offices typically must meet requirements
for minimum age and residency, although different localities have different
rules. For example, in Louisiana, candidates for governor need to be at least
25 years old, and citizens of the United States and Louisiana for at least the
five years before the election. In Minnesota, candidates for governor must
also be at least 25, but need only have lived in the state for the year before
the election. Candidates for the Louisiana state legislature must be at least
18 years old, state residents for the preceding two years, and residents of
their legislative district for at least the preceding year. Candidates for the
Minnesota legislature must be at least 21 years old and must be residents of
the state for one year and of the district for at least six months immediately
preceding the election. Other states have their own stipulations about age
and residency.

Despite these differences, federal, state, and local qualifications for office
reflect a common set of values. One is competence. Age requirements help
ensure that candidates have the intellectual and emotional maturity to handle

---

[2] *The Federalist Papers*, no. 62.

the job. To be sure, age is an imperfect measure of competence. Consider Luke Ravenstahl: at the age of 26, he was elected the mayor of Pittsburgh in 2006. If he is mature enough to be mayor of a major American city, he is probably mature enough to be a U.S. senator. There have also been cases where older politicians, due to age or infirmity, lost a significant degree of competence but still held office. In 1919, President Woodrow Wilson suffered a debilitating stroke. His wife, Edith, took over and saw to it that important tasks were delegated to the proper cabinet secretaries—all of whom were kept in the dark about the president's condition.[3] But although any age threshold is somewhat arbitrary, it would be foolish to have no thresholds whatsoever. Whatever the talents of thirteen-year-olds, they are probably not ready to be leaders of the free world.

A second value reflected in these qualifications is loyalty. Requiring candidates to be citizens of the United States helps to ensure that they will work for its interests and not those of another country. Residency requirements for state offices reflect a similar concern—the desire to have representatives who will work for their constituents' interests and not those in some other district or state. Residency requirements also imply a third value: familiarity with those a candidate seeks to represent. Having lived among his or her constituents could help a candidate better understand their needs. Of course, citizenship does not ensure loyalty and residency does not ensure good representation, but both kinds of requirements may foster these ideals

Outside of age, citizenship, and residency, there are relatively few requirements in widespread use. Two more deserve brief mention, however. First, although it is not codified in the U.S. Constitution or state constitutions, the dominance of political parties in American elections virtually requires candidates to be party members in order to seek office. Party membership does not necessarily imply years of loyal service, and often parties will accept defectors from a competing party with open arms. That said, candidates cannot credibly hopscotch back and forth among parties, and this leads most of them to commit to a single party. This commitment is valuable to parties, who want to ensure that candidates represent the views of party members. **Independent candidates**—those unaffiliated with a party—often face significant challenges in simply getting on the ballot, as do candidates from smaller political parties. States typically require candidates to collect a certain number of signatures from voters to get on the ballot. In some cases, this

---

[3] August Heckscher. 1991. *Woodrow Wilson*. New York: Scribner.

requirement is not too onerous; for a potential candidate for the U.S. House of Representatives, Tennessee requires only 25 signatures from registered voters who reside in that House district—a tiny fraction of the 700,000 or so residents in a district. But in Texas, a potential candidate for governor must get a number of signatures equal to a larger fraction (1%) of all voters in the previous gubernatorial election. One percent may not sound like a lot, but for a candidate in the 2010 gubernatorial election, that entailed about 44,000 signatures.

Second, politicians can sometimes be disqualified from seeking re-election if they have already served in an office for a specified length of time. The shorthand phrase for such a rule is **term limits**: limits on the number of terms politicians can serve in a particular elected office. For example, because of the Twenty-second Amendment (1951), the president can serve only two terms. Members of Congress have no term limits; laws passed by some state legislatures to impose term limits on members of Congress were overturned by the Supreme Court in 1995.[4] However, term limits on governors and state legislators are not prohibited. Thirty-eight states limit the number of consecutive terms a governor may serve, typically to 2.[5] Fifteen states limit the number of terms a state legislator may serve.[6] Term limits imply a certain vision of representation: good representatives are closer to the people, and this can best be achieved with frequent turnover. Otherwise, representatives may go to their respective capitals, spend years in office, and lose perspective on what their constituents want. Critics of term limits tend to emphasize a different ideal: good representatives are more experienced and more knowledgeable about public policy. Under term limits, the argument goes, legislators have little incentive to develop expertise because they will soon be out of a job. Note the tension between the values underlying minimum age and residency requirements on the one hand, and term limits on the other. Minimum age requirements are intended to ensure basic competence, and residency requirements to ensure a better connection with constituents. But to the extent that a longer tenure in office builds representatives' competence and their connection to their constituents, term limits will harm both.

---

[4] *U.S. Term Limits, Inc. v. Thornton* 514 U.S. 779 (1995).

[5] National Governors Association. "Term Limits." www.nga.org/portal/site/nga/menuitem .9e1238065e726e63ee28aca9501010a0/?vgnextoid=3d252b (accessed 4/8/11).

[6] National Council of State Legislatures. "The Term Limited States." www.ncsl.org/default .aspx?tabId=14844 (accessed 4/8/11).

In some respects, the rules regarding age, citizenship, and residency are rarely a constraint on candidates. Most potential candidates are not motivated to run for office until they are older. Nearly all meet the necessary requirement for U.S. citizenship, with the exception of naturalized citizens, such as former California governor Arnold Schwarzenegger, who are not eligible to run for president. Residency is only occasionally an issue, and this is usually not because candidates fail to meet the letter of the law but because opponents claim that although they maintain a home in the state or district, they really live elsewhere (for example, in Washington, D.C.), or that they arrived too recently in a state to represent it well (as the earlier example of Alan Keyes illustrates). In fact, party membership and term limits probably have a larger impact on "who can run." The advantages that come with party membership discourage candidates who do not identify with either major party. Term limits regularly force elected leaders to leave office or run for a different office, even when they would prefer to run for re-election to the same office.

The natural criticism of eligibility requirements hinges on the standard of free choice that we discussed in Chapter 1. One might argue that such requirements restrict the choices that citizens have by eliminating candidates who might otherwise be qualified but for one characteristic. Some critics of term limits make precisely this argument: it should not be a law that requires politicians to leave office but the will of the voters as demonstrated by the election of another candidate. The same might be said of other requirements. For example, citizens might also be able to evaluate whether a candidate is mature enough to hold office even without a law that sets a minimum age. The implication is not that eligibility requirements are inherently unnecessary, simply that imposing them tends to prioritize other values (competence, loyalty) over free choice.

The standard of deliberation is relevant here as well. Any requirement that restricts the candidates who can run for office might degrade the quality of deliberation by giving voters less information and possibly limiting the variety of information. This is easiest to see when considering the plight of many independent candidates, who face an uphill battle even to be listed on the ballot. Critics argue that ballot access laws deny voters the ability to consider alternative candidates, particularly those not affiliated with the Democratic or Republican parties. With fewer candidates running, there is less information in circulation, especially information that might come from perspectives different than those offered by the two major parties. Of course, some hurdle for ballot access may be necessary simply to prevent unserious candidates from throwing their names on the ballot. The question is how high that hurdle should be.

When Elections Are Held

When do candidates start campaigning for office? At the federal level, the timing of elections is set by the Constitution. Elections for the House of Representatives are held every two years; for the Senate, every six years; for president, every four years. These terms in office vary in part because the framers of the Constitution envisioned a different kind of representation from each type of office. House members were meant to be in closer contact with the people, and shorter terms help ensure more frequent interaction. By contrast, senators were expected to be more insulated from public opinion and thus better able to deliberate about public policy. George Washington said that "we pour legislation into the senatorial saucer to cool it."[7] For all federal offices, the date of the general election is, by law, the first Tuesday after the first Monday in November.

States typically follow the same practices, with similar terms in office for legislators (typically two or four years) and governors (typically four years). They use the same November election date. States do vary in what year they elect governors—some hold gubernatorial elections during years with a presidential election, others during even-numbered years (without a presidential election), or, in Virginia and New Jersey, in every other odd-numbered year. Many local elections are not held concurrently with federal elections.

General elections are actually the second stage of the process. Most candidates must first secure the support of their party. This is typically determined in a **primary election**, where candidates compete with others from their party for the nomination for a particular office. States have a great deal of leeway in setting the date of their primary, although for the presidential nominations process (discussed further in Chapter 8), the parties pressure states to obey a particular calendar. Candidates in some states thus face an earlier primary than candidates in other states. Only after a primary election victory do candidates then compete in the general election.

Not every country has fixed election dates. In many parliamentary systems, there are only minimum requirements for when elections are held. For example, in Great Britain, they must be held at least every five years, but the head of the government, the prime minister, can call for an election at any point. Once an election has been called, the candidates have roughly six weeks to campaign before Election Day. The incentive this creates is obvious: whenever possible, prime ministers prefer to call elections when their party is likely to win.

---

[7] U.S. Senate. "Senate Legislative Process." www.senate.gov/legislative/common/briefing/Senate_legislative_process.htm (accessed 4/8/11).

The timing of American elections creates different incentives and power-fully affects candidate strategy. Because politicians and potential candidates at every level of office know when the next election is scheduled, they can begin preparing for it well in advance. This creates a campaign that is longer than in many other countries and that requires extraordinary effort from candidates. Presidential candidates often begin campaigning for the nomination years before the November general election—in preparation for the 2008 election, Senator Joseph Biden (D-Del.) announced his candidacy for president in March 2006. They then spend many months raising money and giving speeches, often on the road and away from their families.

Politicians routinely express their dislike for this life. After announcing his retirement from the Senate in 2010, Evan Bayh (D-Ill.) wrote, "raising in small increments the $10 million to $20 million a competitive race requires takes huge amounts of time that could otherwise be spent talking with constituents, legislating or becoming well-versed on public policy."[8] But most politicians appear unwilling to take chances on letting opponents get a jump on them. They raise money constantly. They travel to their states or districts

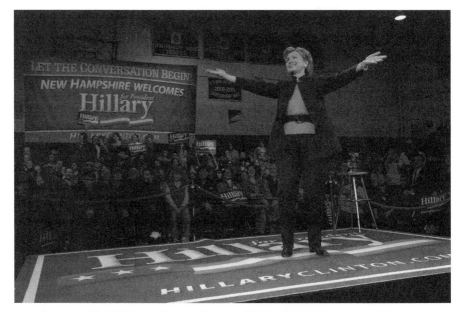

American presidential campaigns are long and typically start as many as two years in advance of the election. As a candidate for president in the 2008 election, Hillary Clinton held her first rally in New Hampshire in February 2007.

---

[8] Evan Bayh. 2010. "Why I'm Leaving the Senate." *New York Times*, February 20.

nearly every week to interact with constituents. They conjure up creative ways to appear in the news media whenever possible.

What is good and bad about a **permanent campaign**? On the one hand, a permanent campaign may help improve the quality of deliberation in the campaign. The longer the candidates campaign, the more information citizens receive because news coverage and advertising persists for weeks if not months. A permanent campaign can also improve the quality of representation because such a campaign keeps politicians in constant contact with citizens and perhaps better aware of their needs and interests. Critics respond that much of this effort is for naught: citizens often do not pay much attention until the election is close at hand; all of the early campaigning may be a waste of time and money. Candidates seem to agree in that they intensify their campaigning as the election approaches.

A permanent campaign may also hurt the ideal of free choice by dissuading some good candidates from running. Some talented people, faced with the prospect of endless fund-raising and nights away from home, will simply opt out. And for those who do run, campaigning takes time away from learning about policy or writing legislation. The permanent campaign may therefore detract from good governance. This is all the more true if the permanent campaign keeps politicians focused only on short-term electoral benefits even though the country's problems demand long-term solutions.

Where to Run

Where do candidates run for office? For some offices, such as president, senator, and governor, the boundaries of the constituency are easily determined and do not change. The president represents the country as a whole—although, as discussed in Chapter 8, candidates focus their campaigns on "battleground states." Senators, governors, and any other statewide officeholders represent their states. But for others, notably members of the House of Representatives and state legislatures, the answer to this question is more complicated.

Single-Member Districts

With a few exceptions, federal and state legislators are elected in **single-member districts**. That is, each state is subdivided into districts and each district is represented by one legislator. In a handful of states with small populations, such as Alaska and Wyoming, there are no subdivisions and the state is represented by one member of the U.S. House of Representatives. A system of single-member districts contrasts with a system in which each district is represented by multiple representatives. This is the case in **at-large elections**. For example, for elections to its House of Delegates, Maryland is divided into 47 districts, each of which elects three representatives. Vermont's House of Representatives is composed of some districts represented by one state legislator and some represented by two legislators. Nevertheless, single-member districts are the norm.

Reapportionment

The number of U.S. House districts in each state is proportional to the state's population. The actual number of districts is determined by the process of **reapportionment**. After the decennial census, the number of representatives in each state may be adjusted depending on changes in state populations.[9] For example, after the 2010 census, Georgia, South Carolina, Utah, Arizona, Nevada, and Washington each gained a seat in the House, while Florida gained two seats, and Texas gained four seats. A number of states lost a seat—mainly Midwestern states such as Michigan, Illinois, Iowa, and Missouri—while New York and Ohio lost two seats. Occasionally, reapportionment generates controversy. After the 1920 census, representatives from rural areas blocked reapportionment because they feared that it would shift power to rapidly expanding urban districts, with potential policy consequences such as the repeal of Prohibition.[10] In 2000, Utah came up 857 residents short of earning an additional seat, which went to North Carolina. Utah representatives were upset because the census did not take into account the number of Utah residents who were traveling abroad as Mormon missionaries—even as the census counted military personnel living overseas, which advantaged states like North Carolina that are home to large military bases. In 2009, two Utah representatives introduced legislation to require the census to count all Americans living overseas; as of yet, no such requirement has been passed.

Redistricting

Far more controversial than deciding the number of seats is the process of drawing district boundaries, known as **redistricting**. Redistricting affects both state legislative and U.S. House district boundaries. As a state senator,

---

[9] For additional detail on how this is done, see Brian J. Gaines and Jeffery A. Jenkins. 2009. "Apportionment Matters: Fair Representation in the US House and Electoral College." *Perspectives on Politics* 7, 4: 849–57.

[10] Daniel Okrent. 2010. *Last Call: The Rise and Fall of Prohibition.* New York: Scribner.

FIGURE 2.1 Who Does Redistricting?

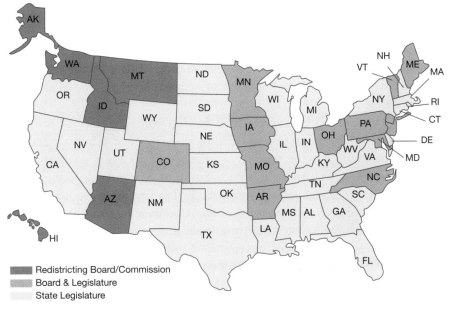

Source: State Legislative Council.

Obama was involved in redistricting his state legislative seat. The fights over U.S. House district boundaries are usually more visible in the news media. In most states, these boundaries are drawn by the state legislature, often with the governor's approval required (Figure 2.1). Less frequently, states use independent commissions, although in some states the legislature picks the members of the commission, making it something less than independent and neutral between the parties.

Malapportionment and "One Person, One Vote"

The major requirements for U.S. House and state legislative districts are two. First, districts must have nearly equal numbers of residents. This prevents **malapportionment** and ensures that representatives each have essentially the same number of constituents. It was not always this way. Prior to a series of Supreme Court decisions in the 1960s, malapportionment was widespread in both congressional and state legislative districts. Typically, urban areas had grown in population relative to rural areas, but due to the influence of rural legislators, districts had not been redrawn, leaving rural districts with far fewer constituents per representative. In the mid-twentieth century, rural areas held the majority of seats in state legislatures even though more than two-thirds of Americans lived in urban areas.[11]

The Court's dismantling of this system began in the 1962 with the case *Baker v. Carr*.[12] In this case the Court established that issues regarding reapportionment and redistricting were justiciable—meaning that the courts could intervene even though these issues had historically been the domain of legislatures. Without *Baker v. Carr*, the subsequent decisions would not have been possible.

The next important case was *Gray v. Sanders* (1963).[13] The case involved Georgia's "county unit" system of deciding the winner of primary elections. The candidate who won the majority of votes in each county unit was awarded that unit, and the candidate who won the most units was declared the victor. The problem was that the units were not equal in size, which sometimes led to bizarre outcomes. In 1946, for example, one winning candidate actually received 16,000 fewer votes than the loser, but won the vast majority of county units. In rejecting this system, the Court established the important principle of "**one person, one vote.**" Because the Fourteenth Amendment (1868) guarantees equal protection under the law, states must have electoral systems in which each person's vote counts equally. Under the county unit system, the vote of a person in a sparsely populated county unit counted more than the vote of someone in a more populous unit.

The Court noted, however, that the Constitution allows deviations from this principle in two important cases. One is the U.S. Senate, which is famously malapportioned. According to the 2010 census, California had 37.2 million residents, or about 18.6 million for each of its two senators, while Wyoming had about 563,000 residents, or only about 281,500 residents for each senator. The other involves the Electoral College, which is the institution that formally elects the president. Each state is assigned a number of electors equal to its number of representatives and senators combined. The inclusion of senators in this tabulation makes the votes of the residents of less populous states count a bit more.

The "one person, one vote" rule had implications for drawing district boundaries. First, these Court decisions made redistricting actually happen. Previously, many state legislatures simply failed to redistrict after the decennial census even when their state constitution required it. As long as redistricting

---

[11] Stephen Ansolabehere and James M. Snyder, Jr. 2008. *The End of Inequality: One Person, One Vote and the Transformation of American Politics.* New York: W. W. Norton.

[12] 369 U.S. 186 (1962).

[12] 372 U.S. 368 (1963).

was left entirely up to the state legislatures, there was no means of forcing them to do it, and naturally the parties in power that were advantaged by existing arrangements were reluctant to do so. Second, the Court's decisions mandated that districts had to be roughly equivalent in population. In two 1964 cases, *Wesberry v. Sanders* and *Reynolds v. Sims*, the Court invalidated Georgia's congressional districts and Alabama's state legislative districts, respectively.[14] In each state, the districts were drawn so that they had dramatically different populations. Subsequent Court decisions have established a strict standard of equivalence: today, even small deviations among U.S. House districts might be held unconstitutional, while greater leeway is given to deviations among state legislative districts. For state legislative districts, deviations of 10 percent or less are typically accepted, although that standard is not set in stone and deviations under 10 percent may be considered suspect in some cases.[15]

The "one person, one vote" rule transformed American elections, legislatures, and public policy. As Stephen Ansolabehere and James Snyder write in their history of this rule, "all states eradicated gross disparities in legislative district populations within five years. The American states began in the 1960s as the most unequal representative bodies in the world, and they finished the decade adhering to one of the strictest standards of equal representation."[16] Although it did not eliminate the ability of self-interested politicians to influence legislative district boundaries—see the discussion of gerrymandering below—the application of the rule did produce state legislatures that were much more representative of state populations in their partisan and ideological complexion. It also led to a more equitable distribution of government spending within states. Equal votes really did result in more equal power.

Racial Minorities and Voting Rights

The second requirement for congressional districts involves racial minorities. After Reconstruction, southern states took various steps to dilute the voting power of African Americans. One way was to draw district boundaries so as to split up black communities, placing a small number of blacks into each district and thereby limiting their ability to elect a candidate reflecting their background and preferences. In 1960, the Supreme Court took a step toward prohibiting this practice, arguing that a redrawing of the Tuskegee,

---

[14] *Wesberry v. Sanders* 376 U.S. 1(1964); *Reynolds v. Sims* 377 U.S. 533 (1964).

[15] See *Cox v. Larios* 542 U.S. 947 (2004).

[16] Ansolabehere and Snyder, *End of Inequality,* pp. 187–88.

Alabama, city boundaries to exclude most black voters violated the Fifteenth Amendment (which gave the right to vote to citizens regardless of race).[17] In 1965, Congress addressed this issue by passing the **Voting Rights Act**, which forbade states from intentionally diluting the voting power of minorities, including not only blacks but also Native Americans, Asians, and Hispanics. In 1982, amendments to the Voting Rights Act established an even stricter standard: the voting power of minorities could not be diluted even as an unintentional by-product of some other action. The Voting Rights Act also singled out as "covered" jurisdictions specific states and counties with a history of persistent discrimination, including virtually every county in several southern states. Those counties have to submit any change in voting procedures or electoral laws to the Department of Justice for "pre-clearance." Only after the Department of Justice signs off on the change can it be implemented.

How would we know if district boundaries dilute the voting power of minorities? The Supreme Court took up this question in *Thornburg v. Gingles* (1986).[18] A group of African Americans claimed that the redistricting plan passed by the North Carolina General Assembly would have prevented blacks from electing representatives of their choosing. (Lacy Thornburg was the attorney general of North Carolina at that time; the named plaintiff was Ralph Gingles.) The Court ruled in favor of the plaintiffs, and in so doing established three criteria for demonstrating that district boundaries dilute minority voting power. First, the minority must be both sufficiently large and geographically concentrated to comprise a majority in a single district. Second, the minority must be politically cohesive, meaning that members tend to have similar political preferences. Third, racially polarized voting, wherein the majority typically votes as a bloc for a candidate other than the one the minority prefers, must be present. The decision has been interpreted as a broad endorsement of the Voting Rights Act as amended in 1982.[19]

Besides these two rules—"one person, one vote" and the prohibition on diluting minority voting power—there is little else that formally constrains the drawing of district boundaries. Districts are often drawn to be relatively compact and also contiguous. Contiguity means that a district is not comprised of "islands" of territory within a state, as would be the case for a district that was made up of a couple neighborhoods in San Francisco, a couple in Los Angeles, and nothing in between. Districts are also often drawn to correspond

---

[17] *Gomillion v. Lightfoot* 364 U.S. 339 (1960).

[18] 478 U.S. 30 (1986).

[19] See T. Alexander Aleinikoff and Samuel Issacharoff. 1993. "Race and Redistricting: Drawing Constitutional Lines after *Shaw v. Reno*." *Michigan Law Review* 92, 3: 588–651.

to **communities of interest**, such as existing towns or cities. These guidelines are not codified as formal rules at the federal level; however, some states require that districts respect community boundaries.

Gerrymandering

Without more explicit rules, those drawing the district boundaries can engage in **gerrymandering** (with the resulting set of districts constituting a "gerrymander"). Gerrymandering is the deliberate manipulation of district boundaries for some political purpose. Its results are most evident in oddly shaped districts. The term was coined in response to a redistricting plan that

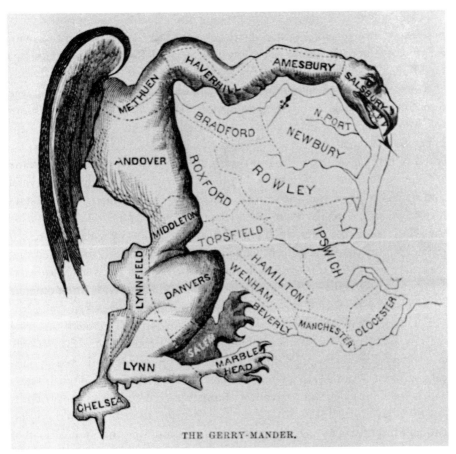

THE GERRY-MANDER.

The term *gerrymander* comes from a strangely-shaped district designed under Governor Elbridge Gerry in Massachusetts in 1812. Gerry's goal—and the goal of many gerrymanders since—was to give an electoral advantage to partisan allies. However, gerrymanders may also have other purposes.

was implemented under Massachusetts governor Elbridge Gerry in 1812. The plan included a district that some thought resembled a salamander, and "Elbridge Gerry's salamander" begat "gerrymander."

Gerrymandering can serve multiple aims. It can create districts that maximize the number of voters who are racial minorities, thereby helping to ensure the election of representatives who are racial minorities themselves. Districts in which racial-minority voters make up the majority of voters are sometimes called **majority-minority districts**. Gerrymandering can also protect incumbents by ensuring that their districts are populated with voters likely to support them. Gerrymandering frequently has a partisan motivation. The party in control of the redistricting can try to maximize the number of seats it can win. To do so, it may "pack" voters from the opposite party into as few districts as possible. It may "crack" apart an existing district where the opposite party has been dominant, forcing that district's incumbent into a new district with many constituents who do not know him or her. "Kidnapping" forces two incumbents from the opposite party to compete against each other.

Much about gerrymandering seems objectionable on its face, but the Supreme Court has let many gerrymanders stand. It has raised objections to some redistricting plans geared toward empowering African Americans under the auspices of the Voting Rights Act, however. The most famous case was a North Carolina plan that included a district (the 12th District) some 160 miles long, which was drawn to include black communities in several different cities and was sometimes scarcely any wider than the interstate highway that connected these cities (Figure 2.2). In *Shaw v. Reno* (1993),[20] the Court's majority described this district as "highly irregular," expressed considerable discomfort with racial gerrymanders in general, and argued that they were subject to the Court's highest standard of review, known as "strict scrutiny," because they could in theory violate the Fourteenth Amendment's equal protection clause. This district was then subject to years of court battles, including three further Supreme Court cases, as well as much tinkering with its boundaries.[21] Ultimately, the Supreme Court upheld the district only after North Carolina successfully argued that its boundaries reflected a political goal—to create a safe Democratic seat—rather than a racial goal. These and other Court decisions have not eliminated race-conscious redistricting, but they have forced states that draw such districts to justify them on different, and more demanding, terms. It is also worth noting that in nearly all of

---

[20] 509 U.S. 630 (1993).

[21] Those decisions were *Shaw v. Hunt* 517 U.S. 899 (1996) and *Hunt v. Cromartie* 526 U.S. 541 (1999 and 2001).

FIGURE 2.2 North Carolina's 12th Congressional District

Source: National Conference of State Legislatures. "North Carolina Redistricting Cases: the 1990s." www.senate.leg.state.mn.us/departments/scr/redist/redsum/NCSUM.HTM (accessed 5/16/11).

these cases, the Court was narrowly divided, five to four, signaling that there was hardly a consensus on racial gerrymandering.

The Court's concern about racial gerrymandering does not extend to other forms of gerrymandering. In 1973, the Court upheld a Connecticut plan that created separate Democratic and Republican strongholds and thereby provided considerable protection for incumbents.[22] The Court saw benefits in the plan because it provided a legislative body that mirrored the partisan composition of Connecticut voters. Subsequent decisions confirmed that incumbent protection was not necessarily problematic in the view of the Court.[23] The Court has also refused to declare partisan gerrymanders unconstitutional. The Court has confirmed that the questions raised by partisan gerrymanders are justifiably the domain of the courts under the Equal

---

[22] *Gaffney v. Cummings* 412 U.S. 735 (1973).

[23] See Nathaniel Persily. 2006. "The Place of Competition in American Electoral Law," in *The Marketplace of Democracy: Electoral Competition and American Politics*, eds. Michael P. McDonald and John Samples. Washington, DC: Brookings Institution Press, pp. 171–95.

Protection clause,[24] but in that case and in later cases, it has not sought to define or apply a standard by which partisan gerrymanders could be evaluated. This was evident most recently when the Court considered, but did not invalidate, Pennsylvania's partisan gerrymander.[25] However, in that case several justices indicated the need for such a standard, suggesting that the constitutionality of partisan gerrymanders is far from settled.

Reapportionment and especially redistricting constrain political candidates in an important way: they have only limited control over who their constituents are. Their input is limited by the timing of redistricting, which occurs only every ten years following the census. The ten-year cycle is not set by law. In 2003, the Republicans in the Texas state legislature initiated a new round of redistricting, taking advantage of the fact that Republicans had won control of the legislature in 2002. The resulting plan shifted the Texas congressional delegation from 17 Democrats and 15 Republicans as of 2002 to 11 Democrats and 21 Republicans after the 2004 elections. This example is, however, the exception rather than the rule; most states adhere to the norm of redistricting after the decennial census. Moreover, candidates may be constrained by the process by which district boundaries are drawn. In those states where the state legislature decides on the district boundaries, politicians in the minority party may have little if any input. Constituencies are thus somewhat fixed and constitute part of the reality that candidates must face.

How does limited control over the constituency affect candidate strategy? In some cases it may forestall a candidate's political career: in a district strongly skewed toward one party, a candidate of the opposite party is unlikely to win and, perhaps, to run for office in the first place. At the same time, a particular redistricting cycle may endanger or even end the career of someone already in office, particularly if district boundaries change dramatically and the incumbent must confront large numbers of new constituents who are not supporters. Campaign messages also reflect the realities of district boundaries and constituent demographics. The issues that candidates emphasize, the groups they target, and actions they take if elected to office all reflect the nature of their constituency. For example, Democrats who represent conservative-leaning districts — the so-called Blue Dog Democrats — are typically quick to highlight their conservatism. One Blue Dog, Representative Heath Shuler of North Carolina, titled a section of his 2010 campaign

---

[24] *Davis v. Bandemer* 478 U.S. 109 (1986).

[25] *Vieth v. Jubelirer* 541 U.S. 267 (2004).

The Technology behind Redistricting

The process of redistricting involves precise decisions about where to draw district boundaries. No matter whether the goal is to promote competition, protect incumbents, or favor a political party's candidates, the architects of the new map scrutinize neighborhoods down to the city block and street — looking for any potentially favorable adjustment. How do they do this?

Years ago, the process of redistricting could be extraordinarily labor-intensive. It involved teams of people poring over paper maps, often with calculators in hand to tabulate past voting results and figure out the partisan complexion of particular areas. District boundaries would be sketched in different colored markers. Contemporary redistricting, however, draws heavily on computer technology. Geographic information systems (or GIS) can store enormous amounts of data about geographical units, allowing users to draw new boundaries with clicks of the computer mouse. These systems first came to prominence in the 1991 redistricting, when all but four states used GIS in their congressional or state legislative redistricting.[1] Some states also relied on consulting firms who could provide specialized expertise in GIS.

By the next round of redistricting, in 2001, there had been further innovation. Computers were more powerful and redistricting software was widely available. Essentially, anyone with a laptop could purchase this software, download geographical data from the U.S. Census Bureau or a state government agency, and draw their own district boundaries. Some software packages will automatically draw district boundaries based on a particular criterion — making the process even easier. It is more difficult, however, for software to take account of all relevant criteria — such as the need to make districts that have equal populations, are somewhat compact, abide by the Voting Rights Act, and so on. Thus, the participants in the redistricting process — such as state legislators — must do more than simply approve the district boundaries the software has produced.

Computer software remains an imperfect tool, and its increasing prominence has troubled some observers. They fear that because politicians can rely on more precise data and more powerful computing, they can draw even better gerrymanders. For example, in his dissenting opinion in the *Vieth v. Jubelirer* (2004) decision, Supreme Court justice David Souter cited concerns about the use of technology in redistricting and wrote, "[T]he increasing efficiency of partisan redistricting has damaged the democratic process to a degree that our predecessors only began to imagine."

At the same time, there are limitations on what computers can do. Moreover, many controversial gerrymanders — including Elbridge Gerry's original in 1812 — preceded the development of computers. If politicians want to create oddly-shaped districts, they probably do not need a computer to do so. In fact, the widespread availability of redistricting software actually allows people besides politicians — including interest groups and citizens — to try their hand at redistricting. If you are interested, see: www.publicmapping.org/

---

[1] Micah Altman, Karin Mac Donald, and Michael McDonald. 2005. "From Crayons to Computers: The Evolution of Computer Use in Redistricting." *Social Science Computer Review* 23, 2: 334–46.

Web site "Faith and Family Values," and within that section emphasized that he was opposed to abortion and believed that "all life was sacred."[26]

The redistricting process and the prevalence of gerrymandering raise philosophical questions as well. Gerrymandering can limit the competitiveness of legislative elections and instead favor an incumbent legislator or a particular party, leaving opposing candidates or parties on very unequal footing. Their underdog status makes it difficult for opposing candidates to raise money and effectively advertise their candidacy. The resulting election may fall short of the ideals of both free choice and deliberation. Although voters are not being coerced into making a choice, their choices may be limited because gerrymandering makes it difficult for certain candidates to run. In such cases, citizens receive less information than they would if the election were competitive, and thus find it harder to deliberate about the candidates' relative merits.

At the same time, gerrymandered districts may actually make elections more representative. Districts drawn to guarantee that a particular party wins usually have a large majority of voters from that party. Most voters in that large majority will typically feel well represented by their representative. Compare that to a district where voters are divided 51–49 percent between the two major parties. If the majority always wins with 51 percent of the vote, a much larger fraction of voters than in the gerrymandered district—possibly even 49 percent—will feel poorly represented. Partisan loyalties are not the only relevant loyalties either. Gerrymandered districts can also give racial minorities a chance to elect the representative of their choice. None of this means that competitiveness is unimportant or undesirable, simply that it must be balanced against alternative considerations.

The debate over redistricting involves other concerns as well. For example, critics argue that in gerrymandered districts, the favored party's candidates will cater only to that party's base, becoming more ideologically extreme and further polarizing the parties in the state legislature or Congress. Concerns about redistricting's effects on competition and polarization have led a number of states to reform their redistricting process, for example by placing responsibility in a commission rather than the state legislature and by instituting more detailed rules about how districts can be drawn. Washington state, for instance, requires that its commission exercise its powers "to provide fair and effective representation and to encourage electoral competition." There is evidence that redistricting processes that involve courts and commissions

---

[26] Heath Shuler. "Faith and Family Values." www.heathshuler.com/release_details.asp?id=7# (accessed 5/17/10).

produce a larger number of competitive districts than processes involving only the state legislature.[27]

At the same time, even as redistricting often advantages the party that controls the process, political science research suggests that its effects are not always as large as critics suggest. It does not necessarily advantage incumbents, reduce competitiveness, or exacerbate political polarization.[28] Furthermore, there are limits to how much redistricting reforms can increase competition. In some areas of the country, preexisting residential segregation naturally produces politically homogeneous communities. It would be difficult, for example, to carve out a Republican congressional district in Berkeley, California—unless one were willing to draw some pretty contorted salamanders.

Who Can Vote

Electoral rules affect not only candidates but also citizens. The central question concerning citizens is who is eligible to vote. The qualifications for voting have changed a great deal throughout American history. Early restrictions based on race were invalidated by the Fifteenth Amendment (1870) and, perhaps more consequentially, by the 1965 Voting Rights Act. Restrictions based on sex were invalidated by the Nineteenth Amendment (1920). Restrictions based on wealth were invalidated by the Twenty-fourth Amendment (1964), which banned **poll taxes**, fees that one had to pay in order to vote and that were also used to disenfranchise black voters in the South. Restrictions based on level of education were invalidated by the Voting Rights Act, which banned the use of **literacy tests**—another way by which southern blacks were disenfranchised. Restrictions based on age were relaxed by the Twenty-sixth Amendment (1971), which lowered the voting

---

[27] Jamie Carson and Michael Crespin. 2004. "The Effect of State Redistricting Methods on Electoral Competition in United States House Races." *State Politics and Policy Quarterly* 4, 4: 455–69.

[28] The evidence with regard to the incumbency advantage and polarization is fairly clear. There is more debate about the effects of redistricting on competitiveness. See Alan I. Abramowitz, Brad Alexander, and Matthew Gunning. 2006. "Incumbency, Redistricting, and the Decline of Competition in U.S. House Elections." *Journal of Politics* 68, 1: 75–88; John N. Friedman and Richard T. Holden. 2009. "The Rising Incumbent Reelection Rate: What's Gerrymandering Got to Do With It?" *Journal of Politics* 71: 593–611; Andrew Gelman and Gary King. 2004. "Enhancing Democracy through Legislative Redistricting." *American Political Science Review* 88, 3: 541–59; Michael P. McDonald. 2006. "Drawing the Line on District Competition." *PS: Political Science and Politics* 39, 1: 91–94; Nolan McCarty, Keith Poole, and Howard Rosenthal. 2009. "Does Gerrymandering Cause Polarization?" *American Journal of Political Science* 53, 3: 666–80.

	Date of Examination_____
Name of Applicant_____	
Address of Applicant_____	

QUESTIONS	ANSWER	ANSWER OF APPLICANT
1. Who is President of the United States?	Harry S. Truman	
2. What is the term of office of the President of the United States?	four years	
3. May the President of the United States be legally elected for a second term?	Yes	
4. If the President of the United States dies in office who succeeds him?	Vice-President	
5. How many groups compose the Congress of the United States?	Two-The Senate and House of Representatives	
6. How many United States Senators are there from Georgia?	Two	
7. What is the term of office of a United State Senator?	Six years	

Literacy tests, like this one used in Georgia in 1949, limit who can vote. Laws that require literacy tests were invalidated by the Voting Rights Act in 1965.

age from 21 to 18. These reforms dramatically expanded the size of the American electorate.

Two remaining restrictions are in place nationwide: the minimum voting age of 18 and the requirement that eligible voters be native or naturalized citizens. Other restrictions vary across states. States differ in how they treat criminals and the mentally ill. Although nearly every state bans convicted felons from voting while in prison—only Maine and Vermont permit inmates to vote—states differ in whether they allow convicted felons to vote while on parole or probation. They also differ in whether they deny convicted felons the right to vote after their sentence is served and in the process by which felons can regain the right to vote.[29] These laws have become increasingly consequential, as the number of convicted felons has grown over time. State laws about the mentally ill are similarly wide-ranging, although it is not clear how often any restrictions related to voting by the mentally ill are actually enforced.

States also differ in whether they require citizens to register as a member of a political party in order to participate in primary elections. In a **closed primary**, only citizens registered with the party can vote in that party's primary. In a **semi-closed primary**, both unaffiliated voters and those registered as members of the party can vote in that party's primary. In an **open primary**, all voters can vote in either party's primary, but not both. In a **blanket** (or **jungle**) **primary**,

[29] The Sentencing Project. 2010. "Felon Disenfranchisement Laws in the United States." www .sentencingproject.org/doc/publications/fd_bs_fdlawsinusMarch2010.pdf (accessed 5/17/10).

there is a single ballot with the candidates for each party listed, and citizens can mix and match, voting for a Democratic nominee for senator, a Republican candidate for governor, and so on. This form of primary was invalidated by the Supreme Court in 2000.[30] The Court argued that it violated the parties' First Amendment right of association because a party's nominee could be chosen in part by people who do not affiliate with that party and who even actively oppose it. The blanket primary survives only in a nonpartisan form. For example, in Louisiana, all candidates are listed on the ballot, and if a candidate wins 50 percent of the vote, he or she is elected to that office. If no candidate wins 50 percent of the vote, the top two vote-getters for any office go on to the general election, regardless of their party affiliation. In Washington and California, the same ballot structure is used, but there is no possibility of winning the election outright at the primary stage. The top two vote-getters go on to the general election no matter how much of the vote the front-runner received.

All of these requirements are enforced via a system of voter registration. In every state except for North Dakota, citizens must register to vote and provide evidence that they meet the necessary criteria. Among the states that require registration, there are further differences about when citizens must register in order to be eligible to vote—ranging from 30 days prior to the election to the day of the election itself. The nine states in this latter category have **same-day (or election-day) registration** (Idaho, Iowa, Maine, Minnesota, Montana, New Hampshire, North Carolina, Wisconsin, and Wyoming). States are also currently debating the identification that voters must show to prove their identity: 26 states require identification and eight of those require photo identification.[31]

All of these requirements affect campaign strategy by affecting the number of citizens who actually vote. The more onerous the requirements, the more likely it is that some eligible citizens cannot or will not register to vote or turn out on Election Day.[32] For example, in 2008, voter turnout in states that did not have election-day registration was, on average, eight points lower than in states with election-day registration, although there is some debate about how much of that gap was actually caused by other factors.[33]

---

[30] *California Democratic Party v. Jones* 530 U.S. 567 (2000).

[31] National Conference of State Legislatures. "Voter Identification Requirements." www.ncsl .org/LegislaturesElections/ElectionsCampaigns/StateRequirementsforVoterID/tabid/16602/ Default.aspx (accessed 5/18/10).

[32] See Raymond E. Wolfinger and Steven J. Rosenstone. 1980. *Who Votes?* New Haven: Yale University Press.

[33] Demos. "Voters Win with Same Day Registration." www.demos.org/pubs/voterswin_ feb032010.pdf (accessed 4/8/11). See also Craig Leonard Brians and Bernard Grofman. 2001. "Election Day Registration's Effect on U.S. Voter Turnout." *Social Science Quarterly* 82, 1: 170–83; Michael Hanmer. 2009. *Discount Voting.* Cambridge: Cambridge University Press.

Some countries, such as Brazil and Australia, make voting compulsory. Unlike in countries with compulsory voting, the American system leaves the responsibility up to citizens, and many eligible citizens choose not to vote. This leads to a second consequence for campaign strategy, one that reflects both an opportunity for and a burden on candidates and parties. They have the opportunity to mobilize citizens to vote, including perhaps some who otherwise would not have participated. Successful mobilization can help a candidate win. The burden arises simply because mobilization efforts demand time, energy, and money.

Rules about voter registration affect campaign strategy a third way: by affecting the types of citizens who are eligible or likely to vote. For example, who is eligible to vote in the primary has implications for the content of campaign messages. Candidates competing in an open primary are more likely to campaign on moderate or centrist themes than those in a closed primary. Some research suggests that making it easier for felons to vote helps Democratic candidates: in part, because felons and ex-felons are disproportionately African American, they are more likely to vote Democratic than is the population as a whole.[34] Finally, election-day registration seems to encourage the participation of two groups, young people and nonwhites, who are both more likely to vote Democratic than Republican.[35]

For these reasons, candidates and parties naturally tend to resist reforms that they fear will increase voter turnout among members of the opposite party. That said, most such reforms would not necessarily lead to a vastly different political landscape. The predicted changes in turnout among particular demographic groups are not always large; moreover, many elections are won by such large margins that changes in turnout would probably not affect the outcome.[36] Predicting the effects of election reforms is fraught with uncertainty, and this uncertainty, along with concerns about adverse effects on their own and their party's electoral prospects, makes politicians wary of reform.

Perhaps the primary value considered throughout the history of voting rights is political equality. Much of the battle for voting rights, such as those

---

[34] Jeff Manza and Christopher Uggen. 2004. "Punishment and Democracy: Disenfranchisement of Nonincarcerated Felons in the United States." *Perspectives on Politics* 2, 3: 491–505.

[35] R. Michael Alvarez, Stephen Ansolabehere, and Catherine H. Wilson. 2002. "Election Day Registration in the United States: How One-Step Voting Can Change the Composition of the American Electorate." Caltech/MIT Voting Technology Project Working Paper. www.vote .caltech.edu/drupal/files/working_paper/vtp_wp5.pdf (accessed 4/8/11).

[36] Jack Citrin, Eric Schickler, and John Sides. 2003. "What If Everyone Voted? Simulating the Impact of Increased Turnout in Senate Elections." *American Journal of Political Science* 47, 1: 75–90.

for women and African Americans, was about changing laws that denied voting rights to a particular group even as other groups had that right. As noted in Chapter 1, ongoing debates about voting rights still concern political equality. If members of some groups are less likely to possess a particular form of identification, such as a driver's license, and voter identification laws require would-be voters to show a poll worker this identification, does this violate the standard of political equality?

A second relevant value is the level of participation. For many people, "good" elections are ones in which large percentages of eligible citizens vote—and, in their view, turnout in the U.S. is too low. If so, then rules about voter qualifications should be structured to ensure that as many people as possible can and will participate. Compulsory voting would even be a reasonable step, from this perspective.

But maximizing equality and participation may not be the only relevant goals. It may be justifiable to limit participation, even if those limits fall disproportionately on certain groups. Restrictions with regard to age and mental illness imply a concern about competence; very young people or people who are mentally ill are assumed, correctly or incorrectly, unable or unready to vote. Requiring citizenship implies a concern about loyalty; the people choosing a country's leaders should be "members" of that country themselves. Disenfranchising felons reflects the belief that the right to vote depends on a willingness to obey the law. Requiring party registration for a primary election reflects a belief that a party's candidates should be chosen by voters loyal to that party. Requiring voters to register ahead of the election, or provide identification on Election Day, is intended to prevent such fraud as impersonating another voter or attempting to vote more than once. All of these rationales can be critiqued. For example, opponents of voter identification laws argue that cases of voter fraud are rare.[37] The broader point is that electoral rules are geared not simply toward promoting strict equality before the law or encouraging citizens to participate; they are intended to further other goals as well.

Who Wins

Once candidates have campaigned and citizens have voted, a crucial question arises: How are votes counted to determine a winner (or winners)? In the United States, most elections adhere to a simple winner-take-all principle.

---

[37] Justin Levitt. 2007. "The Truth About Voter Fraud." Brennan Center for Justice at New York University School of Law. http://brennan.3cdn.net/c176576c0065a7eb84_gxm6ib0hl.pdf (accessed 4/8/11).

That is, the person with the most votes (a plurality of votes) wins the election. For example, in order for a presidential candidate to win a state and therefore receive all of that state's Electoral College votes, the candidate need only win more votes than any other candidate in that state. A plurality is not necessarily a majority, more than half of the votes. **Plurality rule** is more common than majority rule in American elections, although some states do have rules in place to ensure that for certain offices the winning candidate does get a majority. This often entails a runoff election between the top two vote-getters, as in the Louisiana system discussed earlier.

The American system of plurality rule in single-member districts differs from that of many other democracies. A helpful contrast involves those countries whose legislatures are chosen by **proportional representation**, such as Israel (see Box 2.1 on p. 47). In these systems, seats are allocated to parties in proportion to the percentage of the vote they received. A party that wins 20 percent of the vote can expect to receive 20 percent of the seats, although many countries have a threshold such that a party must win at least some minimum percentage of the vote to gain any seats. To achieve proportionality, these systems often do not have single-member districts but either nationwide elections or districts with multiple winners. Voters vote for a slate of candidates chosen by the party, rather than for an individual candidate nominated via a primary election. To be sure, proportional systems differ from each other in their specific rules, and some countries combine features of both kinds of systems. But this general description highlights the major points of contrast between these systems and the American system.

A candidate competing in a plurality election must get the most votes; second place, even by a margin of only one vote, gives the loser nothing. One implication of this was spelled out by the French political scientist Maurice Duverger, in what became known as **Duverger's Law**: In a system with single-member districts and plurality voting, there is a strong tendency for only two parties to emerge, and candidates not affiliated with either of those parties face serious obstacles. This is because in an election with more than two candidates, voters in a plurality system often engage in **strategic voting**—voting for a candidate who is not their first choice but has a better chance of winning. Some supporters of independent candidates or candidates from minor parties do not want to "waste" their vote on a candidate who has little chance of winning a seat. And so they end up defecting to whichever of two major-party candidates they like better (or dislike less). Third-party or independent candidates typically fare poorly. Duverger's Law helps explain why the American party system is characterized by long periods of two-party dominance. In contrast, in a system that uses proportional representation, candidates from smaller parties may still win some seats, even if they have no chance of winning the most votes, so their supporters are less likely to defect.

The use of plurality rather than proportional rules in the United States gives candidates a strong incentive to affiliate with a major party. It also gives parties and candidates the incentive to invest significant effort only in competitive races. For example, political parties raise money that they can then spend on behalf of any of their candidates. Where is that money best spent: in an uncompetitive district where it might help the party's candidate win, say, 30 percent of the vote instead of 15 percent? Probably not. In a winner-take-all election, 30 percent of the vote earns nothing more than 15 percent. Instead, parties will likely target more competitive districts where this money might

---

BOX 2.1

Proportional Representation in Israel

Unlike election to the U.S. Congress, election to the federal legislature in Israel, called the Knesset, relies on a system of proportional representation. A brief overview of this system provides some useful contrasts with the American system.

First, the Israeli system does not have districts. Representatives to the Knesset are elected in nationwide elections and do not represent any specific districts.

Second, voters in Israel are voting for party lists, not for individual candidates. Party leaders compose these lists, as opposed to having voters nominate candidates via primary elections. The order of candidates on the party list determines who ultimately gets a seat. If a party wins only one seat, then the first person on that party's list joins the Knesset.

Third, parties are given seats in the Knesset in proportion to the number of votes they receive, with one stipulation: to be given any seats, the party must receive at least two percent of the vote. This relatively low threshold is quite favorable to small parties. In the Israeli election in 2009, 12 different parties won seats in the legislature. As an example of how proportional the allocations of seats are, consider the top vote-getter, the Kadima Party: it received 22.47 percent of the votes and 23.3 percent of the seats (28 out of 120). By contrast, in the 2010 U.S. Senate elections, Republican Senate candidates received about 50 percent of all votes nationwide but substantially more— 62 percent—of the seats up for election. The 2010 House elections were somewhat more proportional: Republican candidates received 51.6 percent of the vote nationwide but 55.6 percent of seats.

make the difference between winning and losing. The same logic applies to presidential candidates, given the winner-take-all nature of the Electoral College. It makes little sense for candidates to campaign in states where they are virtually guaranteed to win or to lose. They go instead to the "battleground" states where the outcome is in doubt and additional campaign dollars may make the difference.

The dominance of the two major parties is one criticism of the American system and is frequently cited as a reason for favoring a system of proportional representation instead. Proportional representation, the argument goes, enhances free choice by providing more options for voters. These increased options may also enhance the deliberative potential of elections, as a wider range of issues and policy proposals are likely to be discussed. Fewer votes are "wasted" because more citizens are encouraged to select their first choice. In particular, minorities—whether political, racial, or otherwise—may find it easier to elect representatives of their choice under a proportional system. Some supporters also argue that citizens are more likely to vote because they have an option that truly represents their preferences, although there is not much evidence that turnout is higher in proportional systems.[38]

On the other hand, proportional representation is sometimes criticized for promoting a multiparty system that often results in elections lacking a clear winner. In a proportional system, it is common for no one party to win a majority of seats in the legislature. Then two or more parties must form a coalition to achieve a majority and govern the country. Critics argue that negotiations among parties may produce coalitions that voters did not anticipate or intend. To take a hypothetical example, imagine that a country had three parties, Left, Right, and Center, and none got the majority of the vote. It turns out that most voters of the Center Party prefer the Left Party to the Right Party. But after the election, Center and Right form a coalition. Is this what Center Party voters want? If they had known that this coalition would result, might they have voted for the Left Party instead?

A second criticism is that proportional representation produces less stable government. Coalitions can be fragile. If one party leaves the coalition, the coalition may fall apart, necessitating a new election. Finally, proportional systems often lack the personal form of representation that can be provided

---

[38] André Blais. 2007. "Turnout in Elections," in *Oxford Handbook of Political Behavior*, eds. Russell J. Dalton and Hans-Dieter Klingemann. Oxford: Oxford University Press, pp. 621–35.

in single-member districts, where representatives have a long history in the community and know their constituents well.

Supporters of proportional representation have answers for all of these criticisms, noting that instability is far from inevitable and that personal representation may provide little consolation to constituents who sharply disagree with their homegrown representative. The larger point, however, remains: any set of rules will promote certain values over other values.

Conclusion

This chapter has discussed the basic rules of the American electoral system—rules that govern nearly every aspect of the electoral process. Even in this brief overview, it is clear that the American system reflects no grand logic. It is the result of many compromises that are guided by multiple decision makers, including the framers of the Constitution, the Supreme Court, and federal, state, and local lawmakers. As such, the rules can change over time and vary across states and localities. The rules are also products of contending values about what a "good" election looks like. Whether rules strike observers as fair or unfair will depend in part on which values they hold dearest. Moreover, it is challenging to construct electoral rules that uphold all these values simultaneously. Trade-offs are inevitable. Voter identification laws may help ensure clean elections by mitigating fraud, but they may also discriminate against eligible voters who may lack the appropriate identification.

The rules that govern elections affect all of the actors whose roles we describe in later chapters. The rules provide the framework for the decisions of candidates, parties, and citizens alike. They are rarely as newsworthy as a candidate's gaffe or a hard-hitting campaign advertisement, but they are important nonetheless. Electoral rules are all the more important because they are not easy to change and remain largely outside of the control of candidates, parties, and citizens. Passing new laws and amending the Constitution are difficult. Candidates instead adapt. The rules then become part of the hand that candidates are dealt, at least once the campaign is under way.

Even seemingly arcane rules can be consequential. The adoption of the new district that Obama helped draw as a state senator literally came down to a piece of paper that was picked out of a hat. The Democrats, who controlled the Illinois House, had drawn up one set of districts. The Republicans, who controlled the Illinois Senate, had drawn up another. The two parties could not agree, and a redistricting commission composed of four Democrats and four Republicans was convened to select the new map. When it, too, failed to reach agreement, the Illinois Supreme Court submitted the names of one Democrat and one Republican to break the deadlock. One of those names was to be drawn from a hat—a hat made to resemble Abraham Lincoln's stovepipe hat, no less—and that person would then be the tie-breaking vote on the commission. The Democrat's name was drawn and his vote enacted the Democrats' map and thus Obama's new district. The rest, as they say, is history.

KEY TERMS

independent candidates (p. 24)

term limits (p. 25)

primary election (p. 27)

permanent campaign (p. 29)

single-member districts (p. 29)

at-large elections (p. 30)

reapportionment (p. 30)

redistricting (p. 30)

malapportionment (p. 31)

one person, one vote (p. 32)

Voting Rights Act (of 1965) (p. 34)

communities of interest (p. 35)

gerrymandering (p. 35)

majority-minority districts (p. 36)

poll taxes (p. 41)

literacy tests (p. 41)

closed primary (p. 42)

semi-closed primary (p. 42)

open primary (p. 42)

blanket/jungle primary (p. 42)

same-day/election-day registration (p. 43)

plurality rule (p. 46)

proportional representation (p. 46)

Duverger's Law (p. 46)

strategic voting (p. 46)

FOR DISCUSSION

1. What are arguments for and against term limits?

2. What formal rules and informal norms govern the drawing of U.S. House districts during redistricting?

3. How might different rules about who can vote in primary elections affect how candidates campaign?

4. How does the American system's combination of single-member districts and plurality rule disadvantage minor political parties and independent candidates?

 Visit StudySpace for quizzes and other review material.
wwnorton.com/studyspace

CHAPTER 3

The Transformation of American Campaigns

On September 15, 2008, political scientist Darrell West published an article entitled "2008 Attack Ads Hit an All-Time Low."[1] After acknowledging that past presidential campaigns have often been brutal, West argued that the 2008 presidential campaign was marked by particularly ugly and misleading rhetoric and allegations:

> In past years, the only upside of attack ads was that they generally contained more issue content than other types of ads. Since reporters police campaign appeals, the ads generally stick to the issues and rely on factually-accurate information. Ad sponsors and candidates realize they will be held accountable for unfair ad content. However, commercials run this year represent a break with this general pattern. Attack ads broadcast in recent months have twisted the truth, lied about personal background, taken statements out of context, and clearly sought to manipulate voter sentiments.

There may be some truth to West's characterization of 2008. The 2008 election was, in many ways, an unprecedented and historic election. And clearly the presence of an African American at the head of a major party ticket created an unusual dynamic, one that produced some explosive charges and story lines. But did 2008 constitute an "all-time low"? In fact, negativity has always been a central feature of American political campaigns. Indeed, negativity occurred in 2008 pales in comparison to that seen in some previous campaigns. For example, in the election of 1828, a local newspaper printed this attack against Democratic candidate Andrew Jackson: "Gen. Jackson's mother was a common

---

[1] Darrell M. West. 2008. "Commentary: 2008 campaign attack ads hit an all-time low." CNN Politics, September 15. http://articles.cnn.com/2008-09-15/politics/west.negative_1_attack-ads-worst-ads-john-mccain/ (accessed 12/27/10).

prostitute brought to this country by the British soldiers. She afterwards married a mulatto man, with whom she had several children, of whom Gen. Jackson was one." In 1860, Abraham Lincoln was attacked as "a fourth-rate lecturer, who cannot speak good grammar and who, to raise the wind, delivers his hackneyed, illiterate compositions at $200 a piece." As if that were not enough, Lincoln was also characterized as "a horrid wretch . . . Sooty and scoundrelly in aspect, a cross between the nutmeg dealer, the horse swapper, and the night man, a creature fit evidently for petty treason, small stratagems, and all sorts of sports."[2]

This chapter focuses on the lessons past campaigns teach us about contemporary American campaigns. Are there certain patterns and characteristics that appear time and time again? Or have the American electorate and its candidates evolved so that the essential nature of campaigns is dynamic and shifting? In this chapter we argue that the rules and the broad reality that drive election campaigns change infrequently, producing continuity in most aspects of American campaigns. But when these factors do change, they tend to do so abruptly, producing periods in which campaigns innovate and campaign strategies evolve. There have been at least four major eras of American political campaigns: 1788–1824 ("Pre-Democratic Campaigns"), 1828–92("Mass Mobilization Campaigns"), 1896–1948 ("Progressive Era Campaigns"), and 1952–2010 ("Candidate Campaigns"). Each is distinct enough from the others to warrant its own category, but each also contains elements common to the other eras.

Core of the Analysis

- Many aspects of modern campaigns can be seen in campaigns throughout American history.
- Changes in the conduct and content of campaigns have been produced by changes in rules, reality, strategy, and the electorate.
- Campaigns can be sorted into roughly four eras, each of which is distinguished by distinct forms of campaigning.
- There are also commonalities across these eras, particularly in the length, expense, and content of American campaigns.
- The increasingly competitive and polarized party system and the penetration of the Internet may or may not signify a new era for campaigns.

---

[2] These examples come from Paul Boller. 1984. *Presidential Campaigns*. New York: Oxford University Press.

We will also see that the American campaign, as we know it today, has roots in the 1950s but really took on its current characteristics around 1972, with (1) changes in campaign finance and party nomination rules, (2) a new political reality driven by social upheaval and the Vietnam War, (3) changes in strategy driven by the rise of the survey and marketing industries and the expansion of television, and (4) the expansion of the electorate to include previously disenfranchised blacks (who were protected by the Voting Rights Act of 1965 from discriminatory voting practices, especially in southern states) and 18–20-year-olds (who were granted the right to vote by the Twenty-sixth Amendment in 1971). Some observers have argued that in more recent years the increased competitiveness of elections, the polarization of the parties, and new technological advances — most notably, the development of the Internet — have ushered in a new era. As we will see, it is unclear whether we are currently in a new period of campaigning that differs significantly from previous eras. We will explore this question toward the end of the chapter.

The First Campaign Era: Pre-Democratic Campaigns, 1788-1824

In some ways, the earliest era of campaigning is unique. The first two presidential contests, which resulted in unanimous elections of George Washington, were like no others in American history. Washington was considered the logical choice for the job—indeed, there are some who believe the Constitution would not have been ratified had lawmakers not assumed Washington would serve as the first president—and there was no serious campaign against him. Unsurprisingly, the sum total of Washington's campaign in 1788 was to provide two casks of Virginia spirits for electors.[3] Similarly, the election of John Adams as Washington's successor in 1796, though contested, involved only trace elements of the partisan effort, conflict, and machinations that emerged a scant four years later.

The 1800 election marked a turning point within the first era in American election campaigns (Figure 3.1), which we refer to as the **era of pre-democratic campaigns**. Adams's first term as president was marked by the

FIGURE 3.1 Four Major Eras of Political Campaigns

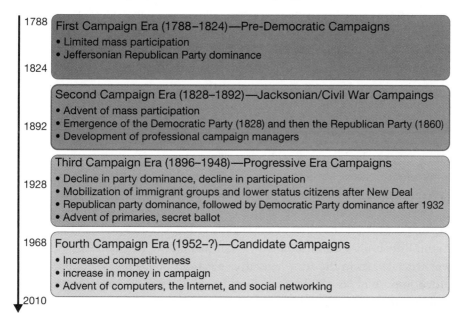

1788
First Campaign Era (1788–1824)—Pre-Democratic Campaigns
• Limited mass participation
• Jeffersonian Republican Party dominance
1824

Second Campaign Era (1828–1892)—Jacksonian/Civil War Campaigns
• Advent of mass participation
1892 • Emergence of the Democratic Party (1828) and then the Republican Party (1860)
• Development of professional campaign managers

Third Campaign Era (1896–1948)—Progressive Era Campaigns
1928 • Decline in party dominance, decline in participation
• Mobilization of immigrant groups and lower status citizens after New Deal
• Republican party dominance, followed by Democratic Party dominance after 1932
• Advent of primaries, secret ballot

1968 **Fourth Campaign Era (1952–?)—Candidate Campaigns**
• Increased competitiveness
• increase in money in campaign
• Advent of computers, the Internet, and social networking
2010

---

[3] Boller, *Presidential Campaigns*.

unraveling of the uneasy truce that had marked Washington's tenure. In its place, two camps emerged. On one side was the **Federalist Party**. The Federalists believed in a strong federal government, preferred allying with Great Britain, and were enormously suspicious of the radicalization of the French Revolution. The Federalists, who were especially numerous in New England and the mid-Atlantic states, were led by many of the architects of the Constitution, including John Adams and Alexander Hamilton. On the other side was the **Republican-Democratic Party**. The Republican-Democrats distrusted the expanding federal government and suspected that it only served the commercial interests of the northeastern states. They preferred an alliance with France, even in the face of the French Revolution, to an alliance with Great Britain and its monarchy. Republican-Democrats, who were numerous in the southern states, were led by Thomas Jefferson and his trusted ally James Madison.

The actions of these two camps as the presidential election of 1800 approached illustrate one of our major themes: the importance of the rules that govern campaigns and elections. At that point in time presidential electors were chosen by state legislators and not by ordinary citizens. In fact, citizens did not come to dominate the presidential election process until the 1820s, which is why we characterize this era as one of "pre-democratic campaigns." Because state legislators were so consequential, presidential candidates sought their support and attempted to influence the composition of state legislatures. They also tried to get legislatures to adopt rules that would give them more votes in the Electoral College. Jefferson's Republican-Democrats, for example, worked hard to win a majority of districts in Pennsylvania's lower house in early 1800 and then attempted to change Pennsylvania's rules so that all of the state's electors would go to the candidate whose party commanded a legislative majority. The Pennsylvania Senate, where Adams's Federalists had a majority, blocked the move. This state-by-state effort to craft favorable electoral rules offers the earliest glimpse of the emphasis on "battleground states" that dominates contemporary presidential campaigns.

The importance of state legislators also led to another innovation in strategy: the first organized attempts to get eligible citizens to the polls. In New York, Aaron Burr built a political network that helped the Republican-Democrats win crucial seats in the state legislative elections of 1798—seats that would prove important in 1800, when Burr became Jefferson's running mate. In building this network, Burr employed several strategies that later became staples of political campaigns, including identifying sympathetic citizens and turning them out to vote on Election Day.

The 1800 election also featured the kind of negative campaigning that pundits today sometimes bemoan. There were attack ads, many of which centered on Jefferson's sympathies with the French Revolution as well as his religious faith (or lack thereof). Here is one passage from a Federalist newspaper, attacking Jefferson and other members of the "anti-federal junto":

> Citizens choose your sides. You who are for French notions of government; for the tempestuous seas of anarchy and misrule; for arming the poor against the rich; for fraternizing with the foes of God and man; go to the left and support the leaders, or the dupes, of the anti-federal junto. But you that are sober, industrious, thriving, and happy, give your votes for those men who mean to *preserve the union* of the states, the purity and vigor of our excellent Constitution, the sacred majesty of the laws, and the holy ordinances of religion.[4]

The central difference between the 1800 election and contemporary presidential elections is how little campaigning the candidates themselves actually did in the earliest presidential campaigns. For the most part, the organizational activity and the negative campaigning were carried out by surrogates. Adams did some campaigning during a trip from Massachusetts to Washington, D.C., in the spring of 1800. But it was mainly Hamilton and other Federalists who worked to influence legislative elections and wrote letters and articles excoriating Jefferson and his Republican-Democratic allies on every issue of the day. Jefferson stayed mainly in his Virginia home, Monticello, communicating by letter with Madison, Burr, and other Republican-Democratic leaders.

The election of 1800 culminated in Jefferson's victory. Discontent over the prospect of higher taxes and more intrusive government worked against Federalist arguments. Moreover, the Federalists made several key mistakes, such as supporting the Alien and Sedition Acts, which had been passed in 1798 under the Adams administration and which made it illegal for the press to publish "false, scandalous, and malicious writing" about the government or its officials.

The next twenty-five years brought relative stasis to American political parties and campaigns. Federalist presidential candidates attempted to hold electors in their New England base while winning over electors in the mid-Atlantic and southern states by emphasizing the need for greater national government

---

[4] Edward J. Larson. 2007. *A Magnificent Catastrophe*. New York: Free Press, p. 93.

support of commercial development and infrastructure. Meanwhile, Madison and James Monroe maintained—and in ways expanded on—the coalition established by Jefferson. Candidates continued to campaign behind the scenes, writing letters, encouraging supporters, dictating strategy, and suggesting lines of argument and attack. The brutality of 1800 abated somewhat, but campaigns were marked by substantive differences as well as personal attacks.

However, conditions were changing even as Jefferson assumed the presidency in the spring of 1801. Most notably, the states began changing their rules so that presidential electors would be chosen by a statewide popular vote. Moreover, they also began changing their standards for citizenship in ways that significantly expanded the eligible electorate. This would set the stage for a more democratic mode of campaigning.

The Second Campaign Era: Mass Mobilization Campaigns, 1828–92

The two decades between 1820 and 1840 saw the development of the first mass democratic electorate. Politicians began to campaign to this electorate, thus changing the nature and meaning of campaigning. The 1828 presidential campaign was particularly important in setting the tone for all subsequent American campaigns. Although the level and sophistication of campaigning varied over time and from place to place after the 1828 election, its innovations became increasingly widespread.

The campaign arguably began four years earlier, when a political slight against Andrew Jackson produced a personal vendetta. In the presidential election of 1824, Jackson was easily the most popular candidate running— he received 41 percent of the national vote, winning 7 states worth 99 electoral votes. Unfortunately for Jackson, there were 261 total electoral votes, and a candidate needed 131 for the majority necessary to win the presidency outright. His competitors, John Quincy Adams (84 electoral votes), William Harris Crawford (41 electoral votes), and Henry Clay (37 electoral votes) had more than enough electoral votes among them to prevent the race from being decided in the Electoral College. Because Jackson did not secure an Electoral College majority, the election was thrown into the U.S. House of Representatives, where each statewide congressional delegation casts a single vote. In this case, a reputed deal between the Speaker of the House, Henry Clay, and supporters of John Quincy Adams resulted in the election of Adams. Jackson was outraged. Perhaps more significant, so were his supporters.

Jackson and a handful of confidants, stung by the "stolen" election of 1824, began to lay plans to avoid what they felt would be another "theft" in 1828. As in modern presidential campaigns, all of this began well in advance of the election itself. Jackson's message centered in part on his status as a war hero. (Jackson had won fame by defeating the British army at the Battle of New Orleans in 1815.) It also centered on his promise to "clean house" and fight northeastern commercial interests that had become entrenched in Washington and who, Jackson argued, enriched themselves at the expense of the country's "common folk."

Jackson's campaign operation provided the template for all subsequent American campaigns, and especially presidential campaigns. The first element of that template was its structure. The campaign was led by a small group of friends and supporters who were motivated by their personal loyalty to Jackson. These individuals recruited political operatives in important counties. The operatives were not paid, but Jackson's promise to "clean house" led them to (reasonably) expect that they would receive jobs in a Jackson

In the nineteenth century, candidates were more likely to engage personally in campaigning when the election was expected to be close. When Stephen Douglas ran for the U.S. Senate in 1858, he campaigned vigorously against Abraham Lincoln in a closely fought race, as this cartoon depicts.

administration. This expectation—that working on the campaign could lead to a government job—remains to this day.

The second element of the template was the emphasis on organizing voters. This may seem like an obvious strategy, but in fact it was an important innovation. It was made possible by the changes in state voting laws that enfranchised a larger segment of the electorate and thus created more eligible citizens to target. Jackson's operatives were in charge of mobilizing eligible voters in their counties.

The third element of the template concerns how these voters were organized. As in previous campaigns, Jackson's followers promoted his candidacy with a sustained public relations campaign in local newspapers, writing letters and enlisting the aid of sympathetic editors. But the need to appeal to a mass electorate necessitated a new tactic: entertainment. This and subsequent campaigns featured rallies, public speeches, picnics, torchlit parades, songs, slogans, and bombastic rhetoric. Policy issues took a backseat to partisan allegiances and personalities. This is an important point: anyone criticizing modern campaigns for their dearth of substance is displaying a lack of historical knowledge. American campaigns have been long on style and somewhat short on substance since the beginning of mass politics in the United States.

This emphasis on mass politics gave rise to a further innovation: candidates themselves increasingly campaigned for office. To be sure, many candidates were still reticent about campaigning, but as early as the 1840s it was no longer an entirely unheard-of concept. For example, when Stephen Douglas ran for the U.S Senate in 1858, he campaigned tirelessly on his own behalf, making dozens of speeches across the state of Illinois. During the course of this campaign, Douglas participated in seven public debates with his opponent, a state legislator named Abraham Lincoln. As was often the case for candidates in this era, Douglas's actions were influenced by his expectation that the election would be close. It seems that candidates were more likely to embrace electioneering when facing tough competition.

All of these elements pioneered in 1828 were visible in many subsequent campaigns during this era. The 1840 election is a good example. After Jackson's victory in 1828, his supporters formed the core of what was to become the **Democratic Party**. Beginning in 1832, the Democrats faced stiff competition from the newly formed **Whig Party**, which favored congressional authority over presidential, and supported a program of modernization and economic protectionism. This competition came to a head in 1840, when Whig candidate William Henry Harrison attempted to unseat Jackson's successor, incumbent Democratic president Martin Van Buren.

When the Democrats claimed that William Henry Harrison was the type of man who would live off his pension, sitting on his porch drinking hard cider, Harrison's supporters turned the charge around to portray Harrison as a man of the people. In this 1840 engraving, Harrison is depicted welcoming a veteran with his "hard cider hospitality."

Just as Jackson's campaign did in 1828, Harrison's campaign emphasized his war record, particularly his role in the battle of Tippecanoe, a famous victory for U.S. forces against an American Indian Confederation in the Indiana Territory in 1811. The Democrats charged that Harrison was the sort of fellow who would just as soon live off his pension, sipping hard cider on the porch of his log cabin. Harrison's campaign countered by turning this into a virtue, presenting Harrison as a man of the people—just as Jackson had done 12 years earlier. Meanwhile, the emphasis on mobilizing eligible voters continued apace. More citizens voted in 1840 than in any previous presidential contest, thanks in part to the surfeit of campaign rallies, parades, and other hoopla. Harrison won relatively easily.

Even the growing disagreements over slavery and the Civil War itself did not create striking changes in political campaigns. As the Whig Party split up over the issue of slavery, a series of abolitionist parties emerged: the Free

Soil Party, the Liberty Party, and (finally) the **Republican Party**. Although the Republicans were a party dedicated to the preservation of the Union and the abolition of slavery, they adopted the campaign tactics and copied the campaign strategies of the Whigs. In the 1860 election, fought on the eve of the Civil War, the Republicans chose not to emphasize the policies of their nominee, Abraham Lincoln. Instead, in almost every broadside and campaign missive they spoke of Lincoln's honesty and his connection with the common man. After the end of the Civil War, campaigns continued to focus on pageantry, personality, and symbolic (rather than substantive) issues. In the presidential elections of 1868 and 1872, for example, the newly dominant Republicans nominated General Ulysses S. Grant, and focused their campaigns on reminding Americans who had been on the winning side in the war.

The 1876 presidential election provides a striking example of campaigning from this period. By 1876, the Republicans were faltering after the scandal-plagued second term of President Grant. In the election for his successor, Rutherford Hayes, a Republican, faced off against Samuel Tilden, a Democrat. Hayes and Tilden agreed on almost all of the major issues of the day, but, once again, the campaign was rancorous. Republicans continued to link the Democrats with the South's secession during the Civil War. One supporter of Hayes said this: "Every man that endeavored to tear the old flag from the heavens that it enriches was a Democrat. Every man that tried to destroy this nation was a Democrat. . . . The man that assassinated Abraham Lincoln was a Democrat. . . . Soldiers, every scar you have on your heroic bodies was given you by a Democrat!"[5] For their part, Democrats thought up some bold lies, too. Hayes was said to have stolen the pay of dead Civil War soldiers in his regiment, cheated Ohio out of vast sums of money as governor, and shot his own mother.

Perhaps more important, the resolution to the 1876 presidential election brought about one of the major changes that would contribute to a new era of political campaigns. Four states—Oregon, South Carolina, Louisiana, and Florida—had disputed election results, and Hayes needed all four of them to win, while Tilden needed only one. An election commission was appointed, with five senators, five representatives, and five Supreme Court justices. Seven of the members were Republicans, seven were Democrats, and one was independent. But the independent—Justice David Davis—was elected

---

[5] Boller, *Presidential Campaigns*, p. 134.

The 1876 presidential race, between Republican Rutherford Hayes and Democrat Samuel Tilden, brought up bitter rivalries from the Civil War. The election was so close that it was decided (controversially) by an election commission. This 1877 cartoon calls for an end to the rancor surrounding the election.

to the Senate by the Illinois legislature before the commission completed its work and had to be replaced by Justice Joseph Bradley, a Republican. Bradley voted with the Republicans on all disputes, and Hayes ended up winning the election. As part of their efforts to appease outraged Democrats, Hayes and the Republicans agreed to pull federal troops out of Louisiana and South Carolina, hastening the end of the **Reconstruction**-era efforts to enfranchise African Americans in the South. The end of Reconstruction meant an end to widespread black participation in southern politics and essentially delivered the South to the Democrats for the next 100 years.

In a second change that affected campaigning, the latter half of the 1800s saw the gradual weakening of the partisan press. Candidates and parties had helped create and fund reliably supportive newspapers for nearly a century, but that was changing. During the American Revolution and in the days after the ratification of the U.S. Constitution, most newspapers were essentially party organs, writing stories that promoted a particular political agenda. By the 1830s, some East Coast cities—with their burgeoning middle- and working-class populations—began to see the development of the "penny press": for one cent (more traditional newspapers cost six cents) people could get information on crime, gossip, and adventure. By the late 1800s, many newspapers had become more financially independent, thanks in part to sensationalized coverage of people and events, such as that evident in the newspapers of publishing moguls William Randolph Hearst and Joseph Pulitzer. Newspapers did not need the funds provided by political parties, and so their connections to those parties began to weaken. At the same time, journalism was becoming increasingly professionalized, with an emphasis on objectivity and impartiality. This was, for example, the approach emphasized in elite metropolitan newspapers such as the *New York Times*. The norm of impartiality began to crowd out the openly partisan journalism of earlier periods.

A third and final change that influenced the conduct of campaigns was that political party organizations, which had been growing stronger during the nineteenth century, were about to be challenged. Their growth was particularly notable in such cities as New York and Boston, where waves of immigrants became the loyal foot soldiers of local party organizations and were often rewarded with government jobs and services. The parties functioned as **political machines**—a uniquely American combination of mass politics and government programs, with more than a whiff of money and corruption. In the urban campaigns of the 1800s, issues were almost incidental, particularly when compared to party performance and loyalty. Similarly, candidates were often irrelevant; their personal background and qualifications were less important than their party membership. Political power was wielded by party bosses, who never stood for election.

Although machine politics were never as pervasive as is sometimes assumed, they were still controversial. The crushing economic depression of the 1890s helped usher in a new era, one that would hamstring the parties, elevate the importance of individual candidates, and demobilize segments of the American electorate.

The Third Campaign Era: Progressive Era Campaigns, 1896–1948

The third era of campaigns, which began with the 1896 presidential election, had two important features: the continued trend toward more personal campaigning, with candidates increasingly involved in day-to-day electioneering, and reforms that weakened political parties and their ability to mobilize potential voters, resulting in a dramatic decline in voter participation.

FIGURE 3.2 Contemporary Map of Bryan's Campaign Travels, 1896

Candidates for the House of Representatives and Senate had routinely campaigned on their own behalf throughout the 1800s, giving speeches, writing letters, and frequently meeting their opponents in debates. Even a few presidential candidates took their turns on the campaign trail, openly seeking the support of American voters.

But the 1896 election was different. The Democratic nominee for president, William Jennings Bryan, ran a campaign that was especially aggressive in its appeal to Americans. He traveled over 18,000 miles by train, made more than 600 speeches (sometimes 10 or 20 in a day), and addressed 5 million people over the course of the campaign (Figure 3.2). His campaign speeches were filled with religious imagery, and his entire effort took on the aura of an evangelical crusade.

Bryan's Republican opponent, William McKinley, ran a much quieter but no less energetic campaign. After the Democratic National Convention, in which Bryan delivered his famous "Cross of Gold" speech, appealing to farmers and factory workers by proclaiming support for easing the money supply and rejecting close adherence to the gold standard, Republican strategists were worried. But McKinley refused to mimic Bryan's efforts.

. . . I cannot take the stump against that man . . . If I took a whole train, Bryan would take a sleeper; if I took a chair car, he would ride a freight train. I can't outdo him and I am not going to try . . . If I should go now, it would be an acknowledgement of weakness. Moreover, I might just as well put up a trapeze on my front lawn and compete with some professional athlete as go out and speak against Bryan.[6]

Instead, McKinley emulated Benjamin Harrison's 1888 **front-porch campaign**, conducting business from his home in Canton, Ohio. His manager, Mark Hanna, arranged for hundreds of delegations representing different interest groups and demographic groups to visit McKinley, whereupon the candidate would deliver a short speech that was often reprinted in the newspapers. McKinley also raised and spent $7 million and enlisted 18,000 speakers across the country on his behalf. Bryan spent only $300,000 and, lacking the support of many influential Democrats, largely spoke on his own behalf. These differences between McKinley and Bryan illustrate how reality—in this case, the backgrounds, connections, and abilities of the candidates—influenced their campaign strategies. Despite Bryan's efforts, McKinley beat him by five points.

In the 1912 presidential election, the candidates were even more involved in their campaigns. This election featured an unusual three-way dynamic. The candidates included not only the incumbent president, Republican William Howard Taft, and his Democratic opponent, Woodrow Wilson, but also Theodore Roosevelt, who ran for president as the nominee of the **Progressive** (or **"Bull Moose") Party** after being denied the Republican nomination by Taft's forces.

Taft mostly sat on the sidelines, giving few speeches and almost no interviews. But for the first time, two major presidential candidates—Wilson and Roosevelt—campaigned vigorously and personally. Roosevelt toured the country by rail, made hundreds of speeches, and worked the press with intensity and candor. Wilson also spent extensive time on the campaign trail. The passion of the campaign was embodied in the events of October 14, when Roosevelt was shot at close range before a speech in Milwaukee. Refusing to be driven to the hospital, Roosevelt insisted on giving his speech, which lasted for well over an hour. Later, doctors found that the bullet had fractured his fourth rib and lodged near his lung. He took two weeks off from the campaign, while Wilson and Taft halted their own activities out of a sense of fairness and respect. But Roosevelt was soon back on the trail, and

---

[6] Boller, *Presidential Campaigns*, p. 173.

by Election Day he had utterly exhausted his voice. With increasingly few exceptions, this was to be the new style of presidential campaigns: personal, aggressive, and relentless.

The second major development of this era was the reforms that weakened political parties. Up until the turn of the century, the Republican and Democratic parties had been extremely effective at mobilizing citizens to vote. But the Progressive movement—a loose association of activists dedicated to reforming government—believed that strong party organizations were often corrupt and empowered party bosses at the expense of ordinary citizens. The Progressives helped institute or advance three significant strands of reform.

One important reform built on the creation of the federal **civil service** in 1872.[7] The civil service gave federal government jobs to individuals on the basis of their professional qualifications and not party loyalty, which was naturally the important criterion when party organizations controlled government jobs. At the turn of the century, the number of civil service positions in the federal government expanded considerably. This undermined the parties' abilities to incentivize and compensate campaign workers.

Two other strands of reform concerned elections. One was ballot reform, in particular, the adoption of the **Australian ballot**, which protects the secrecy of voter preferences and prevents parties from monitoring voters and rewarding or punishing them accordingly. Second was the use of primary elections to determine nominees. Primaries, which were adopted in a small number of states during this era, took power out of the hands of party leaders, who typically selected candidates for office, and gave it to voters.

These reforms once again provide examples of how rules affect campaign strategy and the subsequent behavior of voters themselves. In this case, the reforms reduced the control parties had over candidates and voters. Individual candidates could then tailor messages to fit specific constituencies rather than simply adopting the positions of their party. Voters, now more anonymous because of the secret ballot, were freer to defect from the party line.

Perhaps most important, these reforms had an unintended chilling effect on voter participation and turnout. In major cities such as New

---

[7] The term *civil service* has two distinct meanings: (1) A branch of governmental service in which individuals are employed on the basis of professional merit as proven by competitive examinations, or (2) The body of employees in any government agency other than the military. We are referring to the first of these definitions.

York, Boston, and Philadelphia, reforms that limited the benefits that parties could offer to encourage campaign workers crippled the mobilization and outreach efforts of parties. At the same time, in the South, ballot reforms were used as a means to disenfranchise eligible black voters. For example, the secret ballot served as a de facto literacy test: many blacks could not read, and because their vote was now to be secret, no person could assist them in the voting booth. As a consequence, turnout plummeted. Even in the wild and woolly election of 1912, turnout was 20 points lower than in the 1896 election. Subsequent national events like the Great Depression and World War II also failed to increase turnout to its previous levels. Turnout in the presidential elections between 1932 and 1948 averaged 58 percent—compared to 74 percent in the second era of campaigns (1828–92).

This third era of campaigning came to a close amid more important transformations in the nature of news media. The continued movement away from the partisan press toward a more professional style of reportage created the need for candidates and parties not only to counter the negative stories in the outlets of the partisan opposition but also to shape how journalists reported on the campaign.

At the close of this era, important technological innovations also began to change campaign strategy. The days of torchlit parades and four-hour speeches were passing into history. A more complete continental rail system, soon to be followed by air travel and a national network of interstate highways, gave candidates greater ability to travel. Campaigns could adjust strategies more quickly as the telephone replaced telegrams and letters. Even something as simple as the microphone allowed candidates and their surrogates to address larger crowds. Finally, the radio emerged as a revolutionary way for people to reach mass audiences, although its campaign potential would not be realized until the 1940s and '50s. But all these changes taken together were not as transformational as the technology that would inaugurate the fourth era of campaigns: television.

The Fourth Campaign Era: Candidate Campaigns, 1952–?

Since the 1950s, the American campaign has been defined by television. The development of broadcasting technology and the proliferation of television sets across the United States in the 1950s ushered in a new age of political communication. Although campaigns continued to revolve around **retail** politics—door-to-door canvassing, speeches to crowds by the candidates and their supporters, and other in-person interactions—well into the 1960s, presidential and senate candidates of the 1950s began to develop detailed strategies for producing and placing television and radio advertisements. Dwight Eisenhower's 1952 and 1956 presidential election campaigns purchased advertising in specific time slots in selected media markets in battleground states. The New York advertising agency Doyle Dane Bernbach devised similar strategies for both John F. Kennedy in 1960 and Lyndon Johnson in 1964.

The rise of television had four important consequences for campaign strategy: it elevated the role of fund-raising, shifted power from parties to individual candidates, messaging, and changed the geographic unit for targeting and measuring the effects of the campaign. First, the allure of reaching millions of potential voters through television ads was something few campaigns could resist. But the cost of television advertising dwarfed the expenses of candidate travel, campaign literature, and wages for staff and workers. As a result, parties and candidates had to shift more and more time and effort to campaign fund-raising. Indeed, the need to raise money in order to produce and air campaign ads on TV has become one of the most prominent features of American politics today. As we note in Chapter 4, many House candidates report spending as much as half of their day raising money during election years. These fund-raising demands increased the pressure on office-holders (and candidates) to recruit and train more staffers, and to do so early in the campaign cycle. The demands also meant that accountants and lawyers became commonplace in campaigns.

Second, the rise of television shifted the focus away from political parties and onto individual candidates. We have noted that American campaigns have always tended to focus on personalities rather than policies. But this tendency was magnified with the advent of a mass communication medium that put candidates into the living rooms of American voters. Television made politicians stars in a more personal and immediate way than ever before.

Third, television changed the content of political communication, further emphasizing the sloganeering that had dominated American campaigns since the 1830s. The restricted length of television commercials—political ads usually last no more than 30 seconds—makes it imperative to communicate a message quickly and memorably. Moreover, political ads compete not only against other campaign ads but also against expensively produced, and often very entertaining, commercial product ads.

Finally, the rise of television has shifted the strategic focus of consultants away from precincts, cities, and counties and onto media markets. The fundamental unit of analysis in campaigns had long been the county. But television advertisements are bounded by signal reach and are measured at the level of the media market. These media markets have become the fundamental units of political and campaign analysis. Consultants are constantly evaluating media market demographics—the characteristics and loyalties of the voters—calibrating and recalibrating the cost per persuadable voter (see Chapter 5) of advertising in certain markets based on TV ad rates and how many swing voters there are in a specific locale.[8]

More generally, the logic and sequencing of a television advertising campaign has come to dominate the strategy of most high-level political campaigns. The itinerary and the talking points of any candidate on a given day often reflect the television advertising strategy, as candidates visit the markets in which their advertisements are running and repeat the messages contained in those advertisements. Campaigns thus look to reinforce their TV advertisements with other sorts of campaign activity.

A separate development of the fourth campaign era rivals the rise of television in its effect on campaigns: the rise of primary elections as the dominant means for selecting candidates. The nominating conventions that marked the 1800s and the first half of the 1900s were still the method of choice for choosing candidates well into the 1960s. But the exclusion of black voters from selection processes throughout the South and the dramatic protests at the Democratic National Convention in 1968 by voters who felt excluded from the nomination system resulted in reforms that led states to opt for primary elections. By the mid-1970s, over 40 states were using primary elections of some sort to select candidates.

The move to primary elections reinforced some of the effects of television's rise. Candidates often needed to raise and spend money to compete in both the primary and the general election. This necessitated raising money earlier, which in turn necessitated building an effective campaign organization as much as eighteen months before Election Day. Primary elections also changed how candidates thought about their campaign message, as they needed to develop a message that distinguished themselves from other candidates in the same party. Some observers argue that this meant taking more ideologically extreme positions in order to appeal to presumably more par-

---

[8] The rise of television has affected campaigning in other countries, as well. But in many of these other countries, political advertising is restricted. In some countries, laws limit (or prohibit) commercial advertising. Elsewhere, television stations are owned by the government and there is little or no advertising on the public airwaves.

tisan and ideological primary voters.[9] Others argue that primary elections make campaigns more focused on biography and personality because candidates have no other way to distinguish themselves from competitors within their party, most of whom share their views on issues. For example, in the 2008 Democratic presidential primary, Hillary Clinton and Barack Obama differentiated themselves from each other mainly in terms of who had the most experience (Clinton's argument) or who would best bring about change (Obama's argument).

While not as significant as the rise of television or the move to primary elections, the proliferation of polling is also a noteworthy development of the fourth campaign era. Campaigns have always attempted to craft popular messages and present the most appealing side of their candidate. But the application of a branch of mathematics called probability and statistics to mass markets turned guesswork into a science. George Gallup, among others, pioneered the field of **survey research** in the 1930s and '40s, in which representative samples of populations were drawn in order to estimate public opinion. The commercial applications of this science were obvious, but political practitioners soon discovered its utility for candidates for office.

Widespread polling by campaigns did not occur until the 1960s and especially the 1970s, when telephones became sufficiently widespread to ensure both representativeness and cost-effectiveness. Since that time, polling has become a staple of campaigns, and top pollsters have become famous and sought-after individuals. Polls have also increased our understanding of what citizens think and how they will react to issue positions and messages. Some claim that polls and pollsters have effectively trivialized and cheapened political discourse as candidates simply advocate whatever message appears popular with citizens. Regardless of whether that is true, polling has particular relevance in an era where television advertising is central. Polls help candidates formulate and test messages before spending millions of dollars to broadcast them.

A final change in this fourth era speaks to an important reality that candidates confront: the balance of partisanship in the electorate as a whole. This era began with the Democratic Party somewhat dominant in national politics. Despite Republican success in presidential elections—the GOP won nine out of fifteen presidential elections between 1952 and 2008—the

---

[9] This, in turn, could create difficulties for candidates who take more ideologically extreme positions to win primary elections, but then have to reposition themselves as more centrist for the general election (see Chapter 12).

How Technology Has Changed Campaigns

In the 1990 election for Texas governor, Republican Clayton Williams ran against Democrat Ann Richards. Williams, seeking to become only the second Republican governor of the Lone Star state since Reconstruction, spent freely from his personal fortune on television advertisements. In October and early November, Williams's campaign called potential supporters at their homes, and sent literature through the mail. He did not, however, have a Web site. Neither he nor his staff used e-mail. Needless to say, the campaign did not have Facebook or Twitter accounts. They did not post videos to YouTube. Even in the context of 1990, there was little innovation or excitement associated with the Williams campaign.

Twenty years later, in the 2010 election for Texas governor, Republican Rick Perry was running for an unprecedented third term. Perry did not have a personal fortune to spend. He did not have lawn signs or billboards. He chose not to debate his Democratic opponent, the former Houston mayor Bill White. Instead, Perry deliberately relied on a small set of campaign techniques that he and his staff — most notably, chief consultant David Carney — believed to be effective based on research they had conducted from 2006 to 2008. Computers and technology were critical to both the research and their preferred campaign techniques.

The Perry campaign set up Facebook and Twitter accounts for the governor early in 2009, and posted frequently thereafter. Sometimes Perry highlighted articles or speeches of note, sometimes he offered commentary. The campaign assiduously monitored "likes" and "dislikes" on Perry's Facebook postings, as well as his "friends" on Facebook and his "followers" on Twitter. They also used Facebook and Twitter to drive traffic to Perry's Web site and to collect e-mail addresses for additional outreach.

The governor's Web site became the focal point of his campaign effort. Perry's Web page guru, Jordan Root, constantly tinkered with the site based on feedback he received from visitors and from quantitative analyses. For example, Root found that links on Perry's site to interviews with newspapers like the *Wall Street Journal* were counterproductive because people would not return to Perry's site once they had linked to the original article. He also decided that every page on the Perry site needed a prominent "CONTRIBUTE/VOLUNTEER" icon so that visitors wouldn't forget about rendering such support.

In addition, the Web site emphasized Perry "home headquarters." Visitors could establish a Perry home headquarters by doing three things: (1) publicly identifying oneself as a Home Headquarters, (2) identifying 12 pro-Perry voters from among their friends, family, and coworkers, and (3) turning those 12 voters out to vote during early voting. Perry was not the first candidate to do this, but the particular emphasis placed on this effort shows how the Internet has become critical in the recruitment, organization, and direction of volunteer activity.

Democrats largely controlled the U.S. Congress until the 1994 election. Their advantage stemmed in part from the simple fact that since FDR's New Deal, more people have identified themselves as Democrats than as Republicans. The allegiance of many to the Democratic Party was an apparent result of the perceived success of the Roosevelt administration.

But by the 1990s, the Democrats' advantage began to diminish. The Democratic Party's support of civil rights reform, a woman's right to an abortion, and gay rights cost them support among several groups, such as white southerners and Catholics, that had been linked with the Democratic Party. Their gains among other groups, especially blacks, were not enough to make up the difference (Table 3.1). For example, in 1952, much more of the public identified with or leaned toward the Democratic Party (59 percent) than the Republican Party (36 percent). But by the 1990s, the Democrats' 23-point edge had shrunk by half—to an average of 12 points over the period between 1990 and 2008.[10] This slimmer margin, combined with the wholesale

TABLE 3.1 Average Democratic Margin in Presidential Elections among Key Social Groups

	1940s–1950s	1990s–2000s
Northern white Protestants	–15	–2
Whites of lower socioeconomic status	+36	+29
White Catholics	+40	+3
White southerners	+60	–22
Blacks	+33	+80
Hispanics	—	+34
Jews	+64	+72
TOTAL	+26	+2

Sources: Gallup Poll, 1940–48 Gallup Year Books; American National Election Studies, 1952–2008.

---

[10] These data are from the American National Election Study, www.electionstudies.org/nesguide/toptable/tab2a_2.htm (accessed 5/13/11).

transformation of the South from solidly Democratic to largely Republican, produced a series of very competitive elections and ultimately allowed the Republicans to take control of the House of Representatives in 1994 for the first time in 40 years. (See Chapter 12 for the demography of the 2008 presidential vote.) It's not surprising that a more competitive electoral environment creates even greater incentives for candidates to raise and spend money. Moreover, with the presidency or control the Congress much more in play, candidates and parties focus even more on a handful of competitive districts and battleground states.

The innovations of technology and polling, combined with the shift to primary elections and the increasingly narrow divide between Democrats and Republicans, have made modern campaigns qualitatively different from their forebears. At the same time, there is continuity between the past and modern campaigns. The need to raise money to run a campaign is nothing new; this fourth era simply made it a much more significant task. Similarly, the personalized campaigns of the modern era—where candidates take to the airwaves to present themselves to potential voters—merely magnify a tendency that has always been present in American campaigns. Indeed, despite the many dim opinions of modern campaigns, it is not clear that they are less substantive or any more negative than campaigns were in the past. Table 3.2 provides a review of the main characteristics of campaigns in the four major eras.

What About Today?

The new technologies that have been crucial to this fourth era are beginning to sound anachronistic today. After all, campaigns no longer rely exclusively on television. What about the Internet, including YouTube, Facebook, and Twitter? Have we moved into a new era of electioneering—one dominated by electronic communication and social networking? Have these new technologies, and other recent developments, transformed campaigns? Let us consider the ways in which campaigns today both differ from and resemble previous campaigns. Ultimately, it would appear that new developments, however important they may be, do not outweigh the ways in which contemporary campaigns resemble their ancestors.

New Developments

Clearly, technological innovations have influenced campaign strategy. For example, innovations in the measurement of public opinion, such as **focus groups** (in which small groups of people are asked their detailed impressions

TABLE 3.2 Characteristics of the Four Major Eras of Campaigns

Campaign Era	Focus of Campaigns	Campaign Method/Style
First (1788–1824)	Limited electorates for most races; state legislatures choose presidential electors.	Candidates do not campaign themselves, but encourage, cajole, and direct from behind the scenes. Use of friends, surrogates, and a partisan press.
Second (1828–92)	Mass electorates for all races. Campaigns seek to expand the participation of supportive groups, and reach out in attempts to persuade unaffiliated groups.	Some candidates campaign personally and directly, but many still emphasize indirect campaigning that relies on party organizations and personal relations. Campaigns are taken to the people. Many characteristics of contemporary campaigns emerge, e.g., slogans, songs, parades, conventions.
Third (1896–1948)	Campaigns tend to be fought over peripheral issues, while personalities and broad appeals dominate. Parties continue to use labor-intensive methods to mobilize eligible voters, but they no longer control the jobs or the ballot. Mass communication technologies begin to change the style and nature of campaigns by the end of the era.	Personal campaigning becomes the norm by the time of FDR. The general election campaign lasts from early October until Election Day.
Fourth (1952–?)	Campaigns focus on raising money in order to pay for television advertisements. They also attempt to position candidates to win the support of their party base (to protect against a primary-election challenge) as well as the general electorate.	Candidates campaign personally for both money and votes. Mass communication efforts dominate and one-on-one outreach fades, at least until the 2000s. Campaign supporters work to "spin" media to present their interpretation of news and events.

of candidates, advertisements, etc.) and dial groups (in which people are asked to use a 0–100 dial to rate their reactions to what they are seeing on a screen) have allowed campaigns to estimate more precisely who they should be talking to and what they should be saying.

Moreover, campaigns no longer have to rely on the information they can collect via polls or other indirect means. Both parties have constructed enormous databases with information on the vast majority of Americans.[11] These databases build on the information in state voter files, which record addresses, whether people actually vote, and, sometimes, party registration. The data are then merged with data from census reports as well as from private marketing firms. A typical profile for any individual might include name, age, address, phone, voting history, political donations, estimated income, race, family structure, mortgage data, magazine subscriptions, and other indicators. This enables campaigns to engage in more sophisticated targeting strategies, using this information to identify people's political views and the likelihood that they will turn out to vote. Campaigns can even target special interest groups—say, subscribers to *Guns & Ammo* magazine versus *Mother Jones*.

New developments in the media have multiplied the ways candidates can disseminate their message and target viewers. The rise of cable television and talk radio is one such development. Both have increased opportunities to target advertisements at relatively small but demographically distinct audiences. For example, conservative candidates can reach a large and like-minded audience through the talk-radio shows of hosts like Rush Limbaugh and Sean Hannity. The development of cable news networks such as CNN, Fox News, MSNBC, and HLN (formerly Headline News) also presents new opportunities (or possibly burdens) for candidates. Because these networks broadcast news virtually 24 hours a day, it means that candidates can put out a new message and see it picked up and rebroadcast almost instantly. At the same time, continuous news can create distractions for candidates, who may also feel compelled to respond to stories that quickly circulate on these networks even though they would prefer to talk about other issues entirely.

Then there is the computer revolution, accompanied by the development and popularization of the Internet, the attendant emergence of political, candidate, and social networking Web sites, and the rise of fax, e-mail and text-messaging technologies, all of which facilitate the widespread and instantaneous transmission of information. Although larger proportions of people still consume traditional media like television and newspapers, consumption of information online is growing quickly—a trend we discuss in Chapter 7.

So rather than simply air television advertisements and send out generic mail pieces, campaigns today engage in a variety of more targeted, personal

---

[11] Jon Gertner. 2004. "The Very, Very Personal Is the Political." *New York Times Magazine*, February 15. www.nytimes.com/2004/02/15/magazine/15VOTERS.html (accessed 8/12/10).

campaign activities. They post videos for the subscribers to their YouTube pages. They send out e-blasts to raise funds from small groups with similar issue interests. They direct volunteers from a community to visit specific households, where they will talk to potential voters and make specific appeals driven by polling information, and send their responses back to the campaign using smartphones.

The narrowing gap between numbers of self-identified Democratic and Republican voters has been accompanied by another trend: the ideological sorting and polarization of the parties. **Sorting** means that people's partisan preferences have become more closely aligned with their political views. Liberals have moved to the Democratic Party, while conservatives have moved to the Republican Party. In the past, parties were not so ideologically homogeneous. This trend has the potential to reshape campaign strategy. It may become harder for candidates to find ways to persuade voters who identify with the opposing party to support them; after all, it is unlikely that they will have enough common political ground. Instead, candidates may focus even more on mobilizing their own party's faithful, "the base." The expansive databases of information about individual citizens helps make this possible, as candidates can more accurately locate those people who are already likely to support them. Once candidates have identified likely supporters, they can then take advantage of such media as cable television, the Internet, and text-messaging to communicate with those supporters.

Other demographic changes are afoot in the American electorate. As noted earlier, the electorate has expanded in key ways as a result of the enfranchising of 18- to-20-year-olds and the removal of impediments that had made it difficult for some blacks to vote. But an even more important transformation may be at work. More specifically, there is the nation's growing ethnic diversity. Immigration and high fertility rates have greatly increased the share of the American population that identifies as Asian or Latino. For example, the Census Bureau projects that by 2050 whites will make up less than 50 percent of the population; Latinos will make up 30 percent, compared to 16 percent in 2010.[12] Campaign strategists are already seeking ways to reach these populations. Spanish-language political advertisements have become commonplace. In 2010, the California gubernatorial candidate Meg Whitman produced an advertisement in Chinese. It will be even more interesting to see whether the agendas and opinions of these populations lead candidates

---

[12] The projections are available at www.census.gov/population/www/projections/files/nation/summary/np2008-t6.xls (accessed 5/13/11).

to develop different messages. For example, a candidate who seeks to appeal to Latinos may need to talk about immigration differently than a candidate who seeks to appeal to whites.

The Case for Continuity

These changes in technology, the media, and demography are no doubt important, but they do not necessarily make campaigns today significantly different from the campaigns of the fourth era. In fact, some apparent innovations are modern-day versions of campaign strategies from centuries past. For example, the rebirth of partisan or ideological media on talk radio and cable news harks back to the partisan press of the 1800s. Similarly, sending volunteers door-to-door to mobilize potential voters, even if they are carrying Blackberrys, is fundamentally similar to the campaigning of old-school party organizations. Indeed, these recent trends in campaigns make them look like updated versions of nineteenth-century campaigns rather than the slick, mass-media-obsessed campaigns of the 1980s.

In other respects as well, contemporary campaigns have not changed that much. For example, the proliferation of primary elections in the 1960s and '70s was most responsible for lengthening campaigns—today's campaigns are not significantly longer than campaigns were in the 1980s. Presidential campaigns in 1988 and 1992 began in earnest during the late summer of the year before the election; in 2011, none of the presumably major Republican challengers to Barack Obama declared their candidacy before May 1 (Tim Pawlenty and Mitt Romney announced exploratory committees on March 22 and April 11, respectively).

If campaigns have not gotten significantly longer of late, have they gotten more expensive? As we will show in Chapter 4, the open race for the presidency in 2008 set all-time records for candidate fund-raising and expenditures. In fact, federal election campaigns in the United States in 2008 cost over a billion dollars. But it is unclear whether this spike in 2008 will be sustained, especially because there are unlikely to be such competitive presidential primaries in both parties in the immediate future. The overall trend in American campaign spending is a more gradual increase, with no indication that fund-raising and spending have been transformed. Moreover, the economic recession that began in 2008, coupled with popular disaffection with the federal government, may reduce the amount of money contributed to campaigns in the next few cycles. Other frequent complaints about recent campaigns concern their content: they don't focus enough on policy, they lack substance, they are too negative, and so on. As we have suggested throughout this chapter, American political campaigns have always focused on personality more than policy. Even now, with the political parties taking increasingly distinct positions on the issues, this polarization is not always reflected in how candidates campaign. They show little sign of sacrificing electoral appeal in favor of party-driven ideological purity. Partly this emphasis is driven by the reality of elections: candidates who focus on goals besides winning elections tend to be defeated by those who focus more exclusively on supremacy at the ballot box. And partly this is driven by the institutions and rules that exist in the United States. Officeholders represent single geographic districts and are elected through simple plurality elections, reducing incentives to work with other members of the party from faraway districts. Policies matter, of course, for candidates and voters. But you cannot implement a policy or represent a constituency if you do not win the election.

Thus, in American campaigns issue positions are often ambiguous (see Chapter 12). Candidates say they are for "middle-class tax cuts," or "saving Social Security," or "strengthening American defense." The logic here is straightforward: candidates know that specific issue positions involve costs and trade-offs, that may alienate some voters, so they tend to endorse broadly popular goals rather than any specific means of achieving those goals. Of course, present and past campaigns have involved clear and specific policy differences. Nevertheless, there is a venerable tradition of policy ambiguity in American campaigns.

Similarly, negative campaigning is hardly a recent invention. American political campaigns have been negative ever since Federalists were calling Thomas Jefferson an infidel. This does not mean that negative campaigning is necessarily more common or more important to vote choice than positive campaigning, now or then. It means that American campaigns have always involved contrasting the relative merits of the candidates, which typically necessitates providing unflattering information about one's opponent. But are contemporary campaigns any more negative than those of earlier campaign eras? It is difficult to say. No one has conducted a study comparing what kinds of information typical Americans in 1840 and in 2008, for example, were exposed to. If such a study were done, it seems likely it would reveal that today's voter would get substantially more information and a similar ratio of positive to negative information.

Conclusion

In this chapter, we have made the case that the United States has seen substantively different campaign eras. These differences have arisen for a variety of reasons, but chief among them is the transformation in information and communications technology, particularly with the development of broadcast media such as television. At the same time, campaigns throughout U.S. history have shared common qualities, including a focus on the candidates' biographies and personalities and a willingness to attack opponents. Thus, although most Americans believe that campaigns have gotten "worse," it is difficult to prove that this is true. As we noted in Chapter 1, the quantity and quality of information provided to citizens is an important criterion by which to judge campaigns. We are quite certain that more information is available to Americans today than 200 years ago, and it is far from clear whether that information is less useful or more superficial. This does not make contemporary campaigns "good" in any absolute sense, and there are reasonable arguments about how they might become better. Still, a historical perspective can be important in making such assessments.

KEY TERMS

era of pre-democratic campaigns (p. 55)

Federalist Party (1796–1828) (p. 56)

Republican-Democratic Party (1796–1824) (p. 56)

Democratic Party (1828–present) (p. 60)

Whig Party (1832–1852) (p. 60)

Republican Party (1860–present) (p. 62)

Reconstruction (p. 63)

political machines (p. 64)

front-porch campaign (p. 66)

Progressive/"Bull Moose" Party (1912–1914) (p. 66)

civil service (p. 67)

Australian ballot (p. 67)

retail politics (p. 68)

survey research (p. 71)

focus groups (p. 74)

sorting (p. 77)

FOR DISCUSSION

1. In what ways are today's campaigns similar to those of the second campaign era (1828–92)?

2. Thinking back to the second and third campaign eras, under what circumstances were candidates more likely to campaign personally for elected office? Why would this have been the case?

3. How did the rise of television and primary elections influence campaigns?

4. Some have argued that the Internet and the computer revolution have reinvigorated the more personal approach to campaigning that characterized earlier campaign eras. Do you agree or disagree with this argument?

 Visit StudySpace for quizzes and other review material.
wwnorton.com/studyspace

CHAPTER 4

Financing Campaigns

Every election year, commentators and citizens bemoan the amount of money spent in American elections. The 2012 presidential election was no different. Together President Obama and Mitt Romney spent more money than any other presidential candidates since 1976, when the Federal Election Commission instituted a comprehensive system for documenting fund-raising. Obama spent $684 million and Romney spent $433 million.[1] Whereas the combined spending of all presidential candidates in the primary and general elections was $66.9 million in 1976—the equivalent of $272 million in 2012 dollars (Figure 4.1)—the presidential candidates spent a stunning $1.4 billion in 2008 and 2012. Small wonder, then, that 75 percent of respondents in a May 2012 poll said that there is too much money in politics.[2]

To be sure, 2008 and 2012 were somewhat unusual elections. In 2008, both parties had contested primaries. The Democratic primary was especially long and expensive thanks to the tight battle between Obama and Hillary Clinton. Several primary candidates in 2008 and all of the serious ones in 2012 shunned **public funding**, funds provided to candidates by the federal government in exchange for their agreeing to restrictions on fund-raising from private donors. In 2008, Obama was the first general election candidate to refuse such funding, which is why he was able to spend more than double what McCain spent. In 2012, both Obama and Romney declined public funds. The main reason spending did not increase between 2008 and 2012 is because Obama had no serious primary challengers.

---

[1] Open Secrets. 2012. "2012 Presidential Race." www.opensecrets.org/pres12/index.php (accessed 3/27/13).

[2] Patricia Zengerie. 2012. "Most Americans Think Campaign Money Aids Rich." Reuters, May 24. www.reuters.com/article/2012/05/24/us–usa–campaign–spending –idUSBRE84N1RB20120524 (accessed 3/21/13).

FIGURE 4.1 Presidential Candidate Spending, 1976–2012

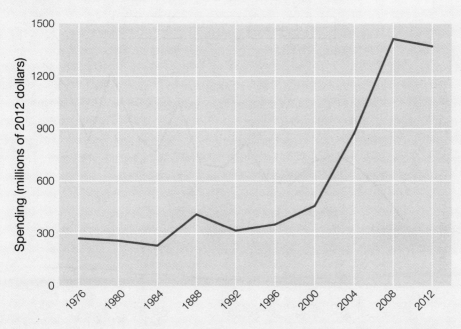

Source: Center for Responsive Politics. www.opensecrets.org/pres08/totals.php?cycle=2008 and www.opensecrets.org/overview/index.php (accessed 3/21/13).

Core of the Analysis

- The rules governing campaign finance place caps on donations but not on spending, which has allowed the cost of American campaigns to increase.

- These rules have an important implication for strategy: candidates and parties must raise the money necessary to fund their campaigns. Private donations are more important than public funding provided by the government.

- Campaign finance rules also allow independent groups, corporations, and labor unions to raise and spend money to try to elect or defeat candidates of their choice.

- These rules reflect a fundamental philosophical trade-off between two competing values: the right of donors and candidates to free speech and the need to guard against the potentially corrupting influence of money.

Spending in congressional elections has increased as well, albeit less steeply than in presidential elections. The average candidate in a general election for the House of Representatives spent about $427,000 in 1980 but about

FIGURE 4.2 Congressional Candidate Spending, 1980–2012

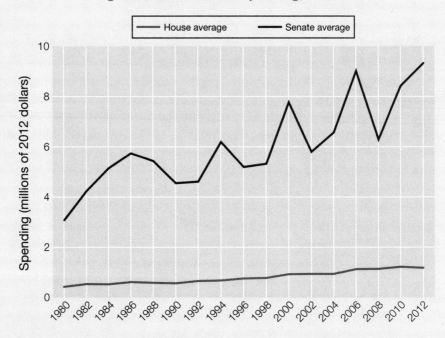

Source: Campaign Finance Institute. House: www.cfinst.org/pdf/vital/VitalStats_t2.pdf; www.cfinst.org/pdf/vital/VitalStats_t5.pdf (both accessed 3/21/13); and Michael Malbin.

$1.2 million in 2012.[3] The trend in Senate races is more variable, in part because it depends on which states have Senate races in any given year, but spending has still increased over time. The average general election candidate for Senate in 1980 spent about $3 million; the average Senate candidate in 2012 spent $9.3 million (Figure 4.2).

Candidates are not the only ones raising and spending more money. The political parties are also raising much more money in congressional elections, which they donate to candidates, spend on behalf of candidates, and use to mobilize voters—among other things. In the 1992 electoral cycle, the Republican and Democratic parties raised about $620 million dollars. In the 2012 cycle, they raised $1.3 billion (Figure 4.3).[4]

What does all this money buy? More than half of the average campaign's expenditures go to efforts to persuade and mobilize voters. One study of a

---

[3] These figures are in 2012 dollars.

[4] These figures are in 2012 dollars and include all fund-raising by the Democratic and Republican national committees, as well as by their respective campaign committees for the House of Representatives and the Senate.

FIGURE 4.3 Political Party Spending in All Federal Races, 1992–2012

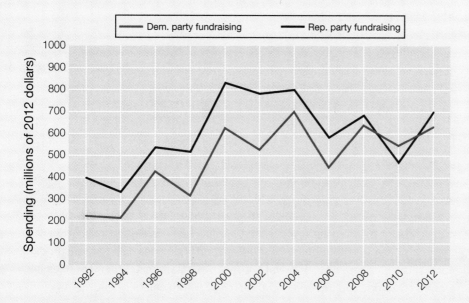

Source: www.cfinst.org/pdf/vital/VitalStats_t13.pdf (accessed 3/22/13) and Michael Malbin.

typical House campaign found that candidates spent about 22 percent of their budget on television ads, 16 percent on mail sent to voters and other campaign literature, 13 percent on radio and newspaper ads, and 1 percent on voter registration and get-out-the-vote drives. The bulk of the rest went to staff salaries (18 percent), office supplies and rent (11 percent), and fund-raising (9 percent).[5]

Despite their cost, it is not obvious whether American political campaigns are "too" expensive. By some metrics, they are cheap. For example, in the 2010–11 fiscal year, Proctor and Gamble spent $9.3 billion on advertising—six times as much as the 2012 presidential candidates spent on every aspect of their campaigns.[6] Some even wonder why American campaigns are not more expensive; given the value of government policies to interest groups and corporations, they contribute remarkably little money to political candidates and parties.[7] Ultimately, it may not be necessary to determine whether American political

[5] Paul Herrnson. 2008. *Congressional Elections*, 5th ed. Washington, DC: Congressional Quarterly Press, p. 84.

[6] Jim Edwards, "How P&G's Ad Budget Grew to $10B, Accomplishing Less and Less as It Went." CBS News, September 11. www.cbsnews.com/8301–505123_162–42750058/how–pgs–ad–budget–grew–to–10b–accomplishing–less–less–as–it–went/(accessed 3/21/13).

[7] Stephen Ansolabehere, John M. de Figueiredo, and James M. Snyder, Jr. 2003. "Why Is There So Little Money in U.S. Politics?" *Journal of Economic Perspectives* 17, 1: 105–30.

campaigns are too costly. The important question for political scientists is *why* American elections cost what they do. Much of the answer lies in the rules of American campaign finance.

As we discussed in Chapter 2, electoral rules govern crucial aspects of political campaigns. Campaign finance rules affect both sides of campaign finance: donors, including individuals and interest groups, and spenders, including political candidates, parties, and interest groups. With regard to donors, the rules determine who can give, to whom they can give, and how much they can give. With regard to recipients, the rules determine whether, how much, and when they can spend. As with the electoral rules discussed previously, there is no single set of campaign finance laws. Federal law governs federal elections, but state and local laws govern state and local elections. Any state's campaign finance laws may differ from federal law and from the laws of other states.

As noted in Chapter 2, campaign finance rules affect candidate strategies, most notably by allowing (or, perhaps, forcing) candidates to raise money for their campaigns. Although systems of public financing exist, American campaigns largely depend on private donations. Campaign finance rules also empower parties and interest groups, each of whom can raise and spend money on behalf of the candidates they favor or against candidates they oppose. As we discuss below, recent Supreme Court decisions have allowed a greater role for interest groups, including corporations and labor unions, which has in turn raised some fears that they will have too powerful an impact on elections.

Campaign finance rules are controversial. Like all rules, they reflect particular values. The challenge is that more than one value is relevant in political campaigns. One is the right of citizens and candidates to express themselves: without money, certain modes of expression are impossible. Another is the need to insulate candidates from the potentially corrupting influence of money: we want leaders to make decisions based on what is good for the country, or at least their constituents, not simply what is good for donors to their campaign. The trade-offs are evident: limiting the money raised and spent on campaigns might mitigate the potential for corruption, but it might also infringe on the right to free expression. In this chapter, we begin by explaining the rules central to financing federal campaigns. In the process, we describe the important legislation and Supreme Court decisions that have shaped these rules. We also describe how state campaign finance laws differ from federal law. We will once again see that the central consequence of these laws, from the perspective of candidates, parties, and interest groups, concerns campaign strategy and each candidate's chances of winning. It is usually not possible for candidates to change the rules, only to make them work to their advantage.

Rules for Donors

The rules for donors involve two basic questions: who is allowed to give and how much they can give. The central feature of this aspect of campaign finance law is the limits placed on donors and particularly on the amount of money that they can give to candidates and parties.

Who Can Give?

There are two main types of donors in American political campaigns: individuals and organized interest groups. Individual Americans are free to donate to a candidate, political party, or interest group, provided that they are either citizens or permanent residents. And while Americans have to be eighteen to vote, there are no restrictions as to the age of political donors. Minors can give, as long as it is their money and they do so voluntarily. Early in the 2008 presidential campaigns, a number of children in the extended family of Elrick Williams donated to Obama, including Williams's two-year-old niece, Carlyn, who gave Obama $2,300 of her hard-earned money. After queries from a *Washington Post* reporter, an Obama spokesperson stated that the campaign did not accept donations from children under 15 and that Carlyn's donation would be returned.[8]

Organized interest groups can also donate, as long as they are not themselves tax-exempt groups. (Otherwise, the federal government would be indirectly subsidizing political campaigns by allowing groups to keep money they would have paid in taxes and then give it to particular candidates.) Potential donors therefore include corporations and labor unions but not charities and churches. Neither corporations nor unions, however, can donate simply by giving some of their revenue directly to candidates or parties. Corporate donations were banned in 1907 with the passage of the **Tillman Act**. Instead, corporations and labor unions must establish separate **political action committees (PACs)**, which are groups that directly work toward the election of candidates, to pass or defeat a piece of legislation, or to advance a political agenda. Some small amount of corporate revenue can be spent to set up the PAC, but thereafter the PAC must raise money on its own. The PACs that give the largest amounts to political campaigns typically represent labor unions or industry associations (for example, the National Association of Realtors or the National Beer Wholesalers Association).

---

[8] Matthew Mosk. 2007. "As Campaigns Chafe at Limits, Donors Might Be in Diapers." *Washington Post*, October 24.

Membership organizations (groups with members who pay dues) must also establish PACs in order to give to candidates. Thus, there are PACs that represent groups with issue-oriented or ideological agendas, such as the National Rifle Association and Planned Parenthood. Political parties and political leaders can establish their own PACs as well. Political party organizations with PACs include the Democratic Senatorial Campaign Committee and the Republican Congressional Campaign Committee. The PACs of political leaders, sometimes called "leadership PACs," raise money and donate to candidates whom those politicians favor. For example, Representative Nancy Pelosi (D-Calif.), showing affection for terrible puns, has her "PAC to the Future." Sarah Palin's is simply called "SarahPAC."

Campaign donations by PACs have increased sharply over time. PAC donations to congressional candidates grew from $120 million in 1978 to $426 million in 2012 (Figure 4.4). But this increase conceals an important fact: individuals donate more money to campaigns than do PACs. This is somewhat counter to the impression fostered by media coverage, which exaggerates PAC contributions.[9] In 2009–10, individuals contributed

FIGURE 4.4 PAC Contributions to Congressional Candidates, 1978–2012

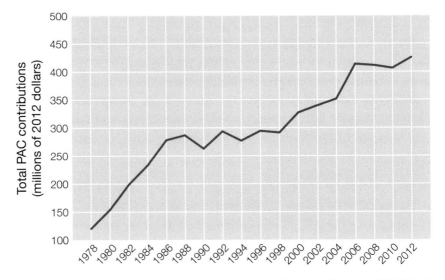

Source: Campaign Finance Institute. www.cfinst.org/pdf/vital/VitalStats_t10.pdf (accessed 3/21/13) and Michael Malbin.

[9] Stephen Ansolabehere, Erik C. Snowberg, and James M. Snyder, Jr. 2005. "Unrepresentative Information: The Case of Newspaper Reporting on Campaign Finance." *Public Opinion Quarterly* 69, 2: 213–31.

57 percent of the funds raised by House candidates, while PACs contributed 33 percent.[10] The remainder came from donations from parties, the candidates themselves, and a few other sources.

Campaign finance law also provides for the disclosure of donors. New rules about disclosure were established in 1971 by the **Federal Election Campaign Act (FECA)** and then revised by amendments to this act in 1974. Candidates, parties, and PACs must each maintain a central committee where all donations are received. They are then required to file quarterly reports with the **Federal Election Commission (FEC)** identifying anyone who has given them at least $200, with additional reports filed immediately before and after the election. In the final days of the campaign, any donation of $1,000 or more must be reported within 48 hours. In turn, the FEC maintains a searchable database of campaign donors. One can see that, for example, Ben Affleck, identified in the database as an actor living in Santa Monica, California, has given money to various Democratic presidential candidates, including General Wesley Clark, Congressman Dennis Kucinich (D-Ohio), and Barack Obama. Another actor, Chuck Norris of Dallas, Texas, has given money to a wide array of Republican candidates, including Senators John Cornyn and Kay Bailey Hutchison of Texas, George W. Bush, and Mike Huckabee (with whom Norris campaigned extensively in 2008).

How Much Can They Give, and to Whom?

Under federal campaign finance law, there are limits on campaign donations. These limits were established by the amendments to FECA in 1974 and remained unchanged until 2002, when new legislation, the **Bipartisan Campaign Reform Act (BCRA)**, adjusted the limits upward and indexed them to inflation, meaning that the limits will continue to increase in the future.[11] The limits are imposed on individuals, political party committees, and PACs, and affect what they can give to candidates, parties, and PACs, and, in some cases, their total giving to all candidates and parties. Table 4.1 summarizes the limits in effect for the 2011–12 election cycle. As of 2012, individuals can donate $2,500 to any candidate per election, for a maximum of $5,000 over the primary and general elections combined.

---

[10] The Campaign Finance Institute. 2009. *Campaign Funding Sources for House and Senate General Election Candidates, 1984–2012.* www.cfinst.org/pdf/vital/VitalStats_t8.pdf (accessed 3/25/13).

[11] This, and all of the major provisions of BCRA, were upheld by the Supreme Court in *McConnell v. Federal Election Commission* 540 U.S. 93 (2003). However, as we discuss below, a 2010 decision, *Citizens United v. FEC*, overturned some provisions.

TABLE 4.1 Contribution Limits in the 2011–2012 Election Cycle

	To Candidate	To National Party Committee	To State, District, and Local Party Committee	To Other Committee (e.g., PAC)	Overall Limits
Individual	$2,500 per election	$30,800 per year	$10,000 combined per year	$5,000	$117,000 overall every 2 years: $46,200 to candidates $70,800 to all PACs and parties
National party committee	$5,000	No limit	No limit	$5,000	$43,100 to Senate candidates per campaign
State, district, and local party committee	$5,000	No limit	No limit	$5,000	No limit
PAC	$5,000	$15,000	$5,000 combined per year	$5,000	No limit

Source: Federal Election Commission. "How Much Can I Contribute?" www.fec.gov/ans/answers_general .shtml#How_much_can_I_contribute (accessed 4/9/11).

Individuals are also limited to $117,000 worth of giving in every two-year election cycle, with separate limits on giving to candidates ($46,200) and to parties and PACs ($70,800). PACs can give no more than $5,000 to any candidate within an election cycle.

Most states follow federal law in imposing limits on contributions for gubernatorial and other state-level races. Only four states—Missouri, Oregon, Utah, and Virginia—have no such limits. The actual limits of the other states, however, vary widely. As of 2012, individual donors to a candidate for the Montana state legislature could give only $310 total for both the primary and general elections, while in Ohio, donors to a state legislative candidate could give up to $18,233. State restrictions on donations by PACs and parties are similarly diverse.

Political Parties and Soft Money

Current federal restrictions on contributions are now more far-reaching than they were before BCRA passed in 2002. Before 2002, political parties, such as the Democratic National Committee and Republican National Committee, could raise **soft money**. These were donations that were not subject to contribution limits or disclosure provisions. Donations subject to these rules are **hard money**. During the 1990s, the parties became increasingly successful at raising soft money: in 2000, the Democratic and Republican parties raised a combined $457 million.[12] A 1996 Supreme Court decision, *Colorado Republican Federal Campaign Committee v. Federal Election Commission*,[13] struck down spending limits on parties, enabling the parties to take further advantage of larger sums of soft money.

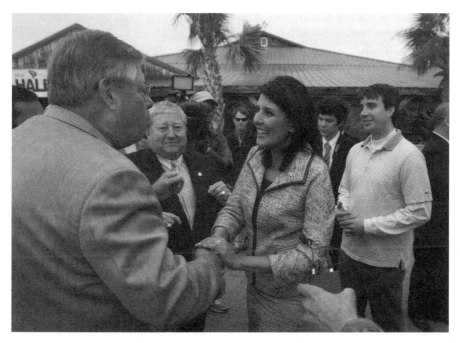

The limits on how much individual donors can contribute mean that candidates have to spend much time and effort amassing enough contributions to fund their campaigns by attending fund-raisers, wooing potential donors, and soliciting contributions. Here, Nikki Haley, who won the 2010 race for governor of South Carolina, attends a campaign event.

---

[12] OpenSecrets. "Soft Money Backgrounder." www.opensecrets.org/parties/softsource.php (accessed 4/9/11).

[13] 518 U.S. 604 (1996).

Soft money contributions could be spent on registering and mobilizing voters and on some kinds of political advertisements, but not on **express advocacy**—that is, directly advocating for a particular candidate. Spending on ads that stopped short of express advocacy was permitted; the key was whether an ad used words like "vote for" or similar **magic words**. Parties found ways to craft ads that conveyed a clear partisan message anyway, often by merging criticisms of a candidate from the opposite party with **issue advocacy**, or arguments for positions on a particular issue. Consider this ad from a 1998 Wisconsin congressional race, in which a party organization, the Democratic Congressional Campaign Committee, targeted Mark Green, the Republican candidate:

> Mark Green has taken over $22,000 from the healthcare industry's lobbyists. It's no wonder that he voted against keeping our medical records private, allowing HMOs and insurance companies to make our records public. It's no wonder he wanted to let negligent healthcare providers off the hook, even when they operated under the influence of drugs or alcohol. Tell Mark Green our healthcare isn't for sale. Support HMO reform.

The ad avoids the magic words and is ostensibly about an issue, namely reform of health maintenance organizations (HMOs) and insurance companies. Nevertheless, the partisan intent is clear. Citizens are not fooled, either. In a 2000 study, participants watched several party-sponsored ads that were intended as issue advocacy but which included critical statements about the opposing presidential candidates. The vast majority of participants, about 80 percent, said that the primary objective of the ad was to "persuade you to vote against a candidate," not to "present an issue."[14]

The ability of parties to raise soft money was a big loophole in the rules. A labor union or corporation could not give a million dollars directly to a candidate but could give it to party committees. Critics argued that this created the appearance of, and perhaps the reality of, corruption. And so BCRA banned soft money. The only money that national parties can raise is hard money that is subject to contribution limits. Although critics of BCRA feared that it would impoverish the parties, this has not come to pass. In fact, the Democratic and Republican National Committees raised $726 million in 2012, significantly more than they raised before BCRA.[15]

---

[14] David Magleby. 2000. *Dictum without Data: The Myth of Issue Advocacy and Party Building.* Provo, UT: Center for the Study of Elections and Democracy.

[15] OpenSecrets. "Political Parties Overview." www.opensecrets.org/parties/index .php (accessed 3/21/13).

Independent Groups

BCRA did not close a second loophole, however. Independent groups, who are unaffiliated with political parties or candidates, are able to raise soft money without contribution limits (Table 4.2). As we discuss below, this money is not given to candidates. Rather, it is spent independently of them on things such as political advertising, although the goal is still to help elect or defeat candidates. Spending by these groups increased dramatically after BCRA's passage and then again after the 2010 *Citizens United* decision, which we discuss below. Thus, their spending in presidential elections increased from $13 million in 1992 to $321 million in 2008, then climbed dramatically to $1.1 billion in 2012 (Figure 4.5).

There are three main legal categories of independent groups, some identified by a confusing array of numbers and letters that correspond to designations under the federal tax code, as administered by the Internal Revenue Service. The crucial differences among them involve federal laws about whether they must disclose their donors and whether and how they can be involved in campaign activity.

The first category of groups is **independent expenditure committees**—a type of actor that only came into existence during the 2010 campaign. These are PACs that pool donations from various sources and then use the funds to advocate explicitly for or against candidates. Because these PACs are not associated with a specific political party, corporation, or interest group, but gather contributions from multiple sources—individual donors, corporations, unions, and so on—they have been termed **super PACs.** Unlike ordinary PACs, they can collect unlimited amounts of donations as a consequence of a 2010 Supreme Court decision, *Citizens United v. Federal Elections Commission*, which we discuss below. They are required to disclose their donors.

The second category of independent groups are **527 organizations**. (The number 527 refers to a specific section of the tax code.) 527s are officially designated as political organizations under the tax code and are also required to disclose their contributors to the Internal Revenue Service. These organizations came to the fore in 2004, the first election after BCRA's ban on soft money for parties. 527s like America Coming Together (ACT), MoveOn.org, and the Swift Boat Veterans for Truth raised and spent a substantial amount of money—over $600 million.[16] ACT, perhaps most

---

[16] OpenSecrets. "527s: Advocacy Group Spending in the 2010 Elections." www.opensecrets .org/527s/index.php (accessed 4/9/11).

TABLE 4.2 A Donor Taxonomy

	Candidate Committee	Political Party Political Action Committee (PAC)	Federal PAC
Example	McCaskill for Missouri	Democratic Congressional Campaign Committee	American Meat Institute PAC
Description	Committee formed by the candidate to raise and spend money during the campaign	PACs formed by the parties that donate money to the candidates or spend it for other purposes, such as get-out-the vote efforts	PACs organized by interest groups that collect contributions from members or employees and then donate to candidates, parties, or other PACs
Limits on contributions to the group	Individuals: $2,500 per election PACs: $5,000 per election Corporations: cannot give except via a PAC	Individuals: $30,400 per year to a national party committee PACs: $15,000 Corporations: cannot give except via a PAC	Individuals: $5,000 per year PACs: $5,000 per year Corporations: cannot give except to their own PAC
Limits on how the group can use its money	A candidate committee cannot contribute more than $2,000 to another candidate committee or $5,000 to a PAC	A political party PAC can give no more than $5,000 a year to a candidate committee or another PAC. (A party PAC can also give no more than $43,100 to all Senate candidates combined.)	A federal PAC can give $5,000 per election to a candidate, $5000 per year to another PAC, and $15,000 per year to a party PAC.
Are donors disclosed?	Yes, to the Federal Election Commission	Yes, to the FEC	Yes, to the FEC

TABLE 4.2 (continued)

	Independent Expenditure-Only Committee	527	Nonprofits 501(c)4, (c)5, (c)6
Example	American Crossroads	American Solutions Winning the Future	Crossroads Grassroots Policy Strategies, U.S. Chamber of Commerce
Description	A PAC that pays for communications that can support or oppose a candidate by name.	A tax-exempt group that raises money for political activities, including voter mobilization and issue advocacy. These groups haven't typically supported or opposed a candidate by name, but are beginning to.	Tax-exempt groups that can engage in political activity, but it cannot be their primary purpose. These groups haven't typically supported or opposed a candidate by name, but are beginning to.
Limits on contributions to the group	Unlimited	Unlimited	Unlimited
Limits on how the group can use its money	These groups cannot donate to a candidate or PAC or coordinate their spending with parties or candidates.	These groups cannot donate to a candidate or PAC or coordinate their spending with parties or candidates.	These groups cannot donate to a candidate or PAC or coordinate their spending with parties or candidates.
Are donors disclosed?	Yes, to the FEC	Yes, to the Internal Revenue Service	No, Unless the contributor gives money for a specific political advertisement

Source: Adapted from "A Donor Taxonomy." *New York Times*, September 21, 2010. www.nytimes.com/imagepages/2010/09/21/us/politics/21money-graphic.html?ref=politics (accessed 4/10/11).

FIGURE 4.5 Independent Expenditures, 1990–2012

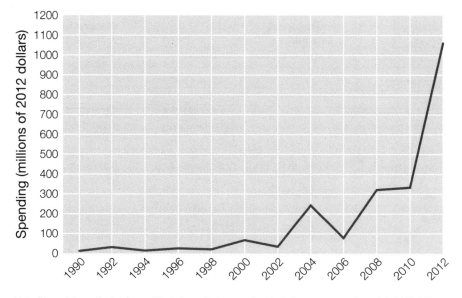

Note: These data are the totals spent by independent groups (not including party committees), in 2012 dollars.
Source: Center for Responsive Politics. 2012. "Total Outside Spending by Election Cycle, Excluding Party Committees." www.opensecrets.org/outsidespending/cycle_tots.php (accessed 3/27/13).

famous for sponsoring an ad featuring the actor and comedian Will Ferrell lampooning George W. Bush, spent over $78 million. As we will discuss in Chapter 5, the Swift Boat Veterans for Truth aired perhaps the most controversial ads of the 2004 campaign. Because donations to 527s are not subject to contribution limits, wealthy Americans give them large amounts of money; the financier George Soros gave $24 million to nine different left-leaning 527s in 2004.[17] In 2008, 527s played less of a role. MoveOn.org shut down its 527, partly because the Obama campaign asked it not to use its 527 to support Obama. Nevertheless, 527s still spent about $490 million in the 2008 election. In the wake of the *Citizens United* decision, many interests turned to super PACs as their preferred vehicles for raising campaign funds because they can openly support or oppose a candidate by name. As a result, 527s spent just $416 million in the 2012 election.[18]

---

[17] OpenSecrets. "Top Individual Contributors to Federally Focused 527 Organizations, 2004 Election Cycle." www.opensecrets.org/527s/527indivs.php?cycle=2004 (accessed 4/9/11).

[18] Open Secrets. "527s: Advocacy Group Spending." www.opensecrets.org/527s/index.php (accessed 3/25/21).

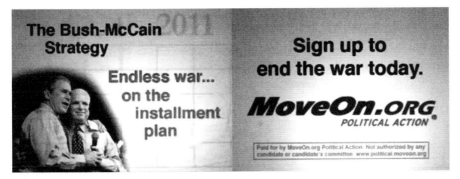

In 2008, the Obama campaign asked MoveOn.org to close its 527 organization due to concerns about the ethics of raising money through such groups. However, MoveOn continued to use its PAC to raise money for ads and other initiatives aimed at defeating presidential candidate John McCain and other Republicans, and supporting Barack Obama.

The third category of independent groups is known as **501(c) organizations**. These groups are designated as nonprofit organizations, are not required to pay taxes, and are not required to disclose their donors. There are various kinds of 501(c) organizations that are further designated with an additional number. For example, 501(c)3 organizations include charities, churches, and educational institutions. An example would be the March of Dimes. 501(c)4 organizations, such as the League of Women Voters, are designated as "social welfare" organizations under the tax code, meaning that their goal is to "operate primarily to further the common good and general welfare of the people of the community (such as by bringing about civic betterment and social improvements)."[19] 501(c)5 organizations include agricultural, horticultural, and labor organizations. For the purpose of U.S. campaigns, the most important 501(c)5 organizations are labor unions. 501(c)6 organizations include business leagues and chambers of commerce—most important among them the U.S. Chamber of Commerce.

Tax laws place restrictions on the campaign activities of 501(c)3 and 501(c)4 organizations. Organizations with 501(c)3 status are prohibited from participating in political campaigns, although some occasionally attempt to bend or skirt the law.[20] For example, a 501(c)3 organization might post a

---

[19] Internal Revenue Service. 2010. "Social Welfare Organizations." www.irs.gov/charities/nonprofits/article/0,,id=96178,00.html (accessed 4/9/11).

[20] Internal Revenue Service. "Final Report: Project 302, Political Activities Compliance Initiative." www.irs.gov/pub/irs-tege/final_paci_report.pdf (accessed 4/9/11).

sign on its property endorsing a candidate. By contrast, 501(c)4 organizations are allowed to participate in campaign activity as long as that activity is not their "primary purpose." During the 2010 election, 501(c)4 organizations became prominent, particularly those working to support Republican candidates. These organizations, which like many 527s used nondescript names like Crossroads Grassroots Policy Strategies, attracted some donors, particularly corporations, who did not want their identities revealed. Crossroads was estimated to have spent almost $9 million on television advertising between September 1 and October 20, 2010. Some questioned whether groups like Crossroads were flouting the law by making campaign activity their primary purpose, although it appears unlikely that these groups will be investigated, due to limited staffing and funding at the Internal Revenue Service.[21] Critics were perhaps even more concerned that such groups could raise and spend money without ever having to disclose their donors.

Rules for Spenders

The spenders in American political campaigns include candidates, parties, PACs, and independent groups. The rules for spenders involve three basic questions: how much they can spend, and when and how they can campaign. These rules, particularly with regard to independent groups, are among the most controversial aspects of campaign finance law.

How Much Can They Spend?

Central to American campaign finance law is this principle: contributions are limited, but spending is not. The federal government cannot limit how much candidate campaign committees, party committees, PACs, or independent groups such as 527s spend on campaign activity. And candidates can spend an unlimited amount of their own money on their campaign—that is, they can "self-finance."

Originally, FECA contained both spending and contribution limits. But when the FECA provisions were challenged in the Supreme Court in the 1976 case **Buckley v. Valeo**,[22] the Supreme Court upheld only the contribu-

---

[21] Michael Luo and Stephanie Strom. 2010. "Donor Names Remain Secret as Rules Shift," *New York Times*, September 20. www.nytimes.com/2010/09/21/us/politics/21money.html (accessed 4/9/11).

[22] 424 U.S. 1 (1976).

tion limits. The Court reasoned that although donating to candidates was an act of speech subject to First Amendment protections, the federal government had a compelling interest in preventing the possibility of corruption, which might arise if a candidate could raise large amounts of money from a few donors. Thus, contribution limits were declared constitutional. However, the Court ruled that there was no compelling interest in limiting spending, and thus the spending limits violated the free speech clause of the First Amendment. We revisit the logic of the *Buckley* decision below.

At the federal level, spending can be limited only in presidential races, and then only with the agreement of the candidates. FECA set up a system of public financing for presidential elections, which was upheld by the Court in *Buckley* and remains in place today. Public financing comes from tax dollars; there is, in fact, a box on federal tax forms that taxpayers can check if they want to give a small amount of money to help finance federal campaigns. In the nomination phase, public financing comes in the form of matching funds. If candidates have raised a certain amount in a certain number of states, the federal goverment will give them funds equal to the contributions from individuals, up to $250 for any single contribution. Thus, if an eligible candidate received 1,000 donations of $250, or $250,000, she would receive an additional $250,000 in matching funds. The requirement to raise at least some money helps to ensure that only viable, serious candidates qualify for matching funds. If candidates accept matching funds, however, they must then agree to a spending limit. In 2012, the limit was approximately $46 million overall, with specific limits by state depending on population size.[23] Again, the public-funding system is voluntary and some candidates refuse matching funds in the primaries because they want to raise and spend more than this limit. In 1996, Steve Forbes was the first primary candidate to take this step. By 2012, it had become accepted practice, with every Republican candidate refusing matching funds.

Presidential general elections also have a public financing option. After each party holds its nominating convention, the nominee for that party can receive a fixed amount of money from the federal government. This amount is indexed for inflation and varies from election to election. In 2012, it was $91.2 million. The candidate must then agree to spend only that amount—although, of course, party committees and independent groups may also be spending money in ways that help the candidate. Until 2008,

---

[23] Federal Election Commission. "Presidential Spending Limits for 2012." www.fec.gov/pages/brochures/pubfund_limits_2012.shtml (accessed 3/25/13).

every major-party presidential candidate accepted public funds for the general election.[24] That year, Obama refused public funding, allowing him to spend more than McCain. In 2012, both Obama and Romney spurned public funds.

Public financing systems also exist in about half of the states. As in the presidential system, all are optional and come with strings attached, such as minimum fund-raising requirements, pledges to limit or refuse private donations, and spending limits. For example, in New Jersey, gubernatorial candidates must, as of 2009, raise $340,000 to be eligible for public financing. The state will then match every $3,400 in private contributions with $6,800 in public money—up to $3.1 million for the primary election campaign and $7.3 million for the general election campaign. However, participating candidates may not spend more than $5 million in the primary campaign and $10.9 million in the general campaign.

Six states have gone further and established full public funding, also known as **clean elections systems**. Maine's system will illustrate. To be eligible, candidates for state offices must gather a certain number of $5 contributions: 50, 150, and 2,500 for state house, state senate, and gubernatorial candidates, respectively. Once candidates decide to accept public financing, they receive a grant from the state and may not receive any further private donations. For example, state senate candidates in Maine in 2008 each received $7,746 for the primary election and $20,082 for the general election. These amounts were set at 75 percent of the average expenditure in the two previous elections, and thus reflect the further goal of reducing the amount of money spent on campaigns.

When and How Independent Groups May Campaign

A final set of rules applies to when and how campaigning can take place. In line with the lack of limits on campaign spending, the American system also imposes few restrictions on when and how candidates may campaign. In stark contrast, some other democratic countries restrict televised political advertising. For example, in Belgium, France, Great Britain, and Spain, candidates and parties cannot buy broadcasting time on either commercial or public television. In lieu of purchased time, these countries provide free air time either on commercial or public television, albeit with substantial

---

[24] Minor-party and independent candidates are not eligible for federal funds unless they met the vote threshold from the previous election. If they adhere to FECA regulations, they can retroactively apply for public money.

restrictions on when and how much advertising can be aired.[25] The lack of such restrictions in the American system is one reason why campaigns are so expensive: the largest category of candidate spending is for television advertising, and that advertising can be aired at any point and in whatever amount. It is not surprising that in competitive races, this makes for long campaigns with seemingly endless advertisements.

The American system places more restrictions on independent groups than on the candidates or parties. A first rule is that if these groups want to spend their resources to support a candidate or the candidates of a party, they cannot consult with, coordinate with, or receive help from the candidates or the party. If a labor union PAC wants to help a Democratic candidate, neither that candidate nor her staff can assist with PAC fund-raising, the production of a television advertisement sponsored by the PAC, or the PAC's decision on when and where to air the ad.

Second, there are restrictions on the content of advertising by independent groups. When BCRA was passed in 2002, its proponents were not only concerned with soft money donations to political parties. They worried that, with a soft money ban for political parties, even more soft money would flow to independent groups, who would use these contributions to engage in issue advocacy, including ads that lacked the "magic words" but were essentially endorsements of (or attacks on) a candidate. BRCA established new rules. First, it defined a new and expanded category of "electioneering communications": ads that referred to a clearly identified candidate for federal office (regardless of whether the magic words were mentioned), that occurred up to 60 days before a general election or 30 days before a primary election, that were publicly distributed on radio or television, and that were broadcast to an electorate of at least 50,000 people. BCRA then stated that electioneering communication could not be funded with corporate or union treasury funds—that is, the revenue that corporations or unions raise as part of their regular operations. In order to engage in electioneering communication, these groups would have to establish PACs and raise hard money subject to contribution limits and disclosure provisions. Of course, BCRA's rules on electioneering communication contained exceptions. They did not regulate ads that occur outside the 30- or 60-day windows, or other forms of campaigning such as direct mail, online ads, or telephone calls.

---

[25] Christina Holtz-Bacha and Lynda Lee Kaid. 2006. "Political Advertising in International Comparison," in *The Sage Handbook of Political Advertising*, eds. Christina Holtz-Bacha and Lynda Lee Kaid. Thousand Oaks, CA: Sage.

Subsequent Supreme Court decisions have weakened these BCRA provisions substantially. The most important decision, **Citizens United v. Federal Election Commission**,[26] was handed down in 2010. Citizens United is a nonprofit organization that received corporate funding to produce a documentary film, *Hillary: The Movie*, which was critical of Hillary Clinton. The group wanted to run commercials advertising the film and to air it on cable television during the 2010 presidential primaries. The FEC considered this to be an electioneering communication—essentially, an argument that Clinton should not be elected—that could not be aired 30 days before a presidential primary. Citizens United asserted that the documentary was factual and politically neutral.

The more conservative justices on the Court took the unusual step of going beyond the narrow questions surrounding the documentary to consider a more fundamental issue: whether corporations and unions could be banned from spending their general treasury funds for electioneering communication. Commentators assumed that this signaled the conservatives' willingness to overturn the ban, and, indeed, that was correct. In a 5–4 decision, the Court ruled that the ban was unconstitutional. While corporations and unions are not literally people, the majority argued that "associations of persons" also have a right to free speech. The Court's decision opened the door to advertising by corporations and labor unions—not simply their PACs—that both targeted specific candidates (express advocacy) and was aired within the 30- and 60-day windows. The decision called into question the laws in 24 states that had imposed similar restrictions or bans on independent expenditures by corporations or unions. It also provoked criticism by President Obama in his 2010 State of the Union address, a speech made in front of members of both houses of Congress and the Supreme Court. We discuss this debate further below.

Some commentators feared that the *Citizens United* decision would lead to a flood of spending and advertising by independent groups. Analyses in the wake of 2010 suggested that these concerns might have been overblown. Indeed, in the 2010 election, there was a substantial increase in the amount of money spent by independent groups relative to the previous midterm election in 2006 (see Figure 4.5). However, the spending of other actors, including the candidates and parties, also increased, particularly in Senate races, where the fraction of advertisements that were sponsored by independent groups, as opposed to candidates or political parties, was no greater in 2010 than in 2008. In U.S. House races, this fraction doubled, from 6 percent

---

[26] *Citizens United v. Federal Election Commission*, 558 U.S. 08-205 (2010).

in 2008 to 12 percent in 2010, but even the 12 percent figure was a much smaller fraction than in 2000, when interest group advertisements constituted 17 percent of all advertisements in House races.[27]

In many ways, it was the election of 2012 that confirmed the worst fears of those who believed the *Citizens United* decision would open the floodgates of spending in campaigns. Outside groups spent $1.1 billion on independent expenditures and election communications for all federal candidates in the primary and general elections of 2012. This was nearly as much as the combined total of what they had spent in every federal election between 1990 and 2010 ($1.2 billion, adjusted for inflation). Thus, the 2012 election featured nearly as much outside group spending as the previous 20 years of elections.[28]

If party and candidate spending in 2012 had also increased dramatically then there would be less cause for concern, but as Figures 4.1, 4.2, and 4.3 demonstrate, that was not the case. As a result, the percentage of all Senate ads sponsored by independent groups doubled from 15 to 30 percent between 2010 and 2012. The percentage of presidential ads sponsored by such groups increased from 19 percent in 2004 to 31 percent in 2012. In House races, there was no notable increase in the proportion of ads sponsored by these groups.[29]

Commentators have also speculated about whether independent spending decides elections, especially because it favored Republican candidates more than Democratic candidates in 2010 and 2012. Outside groups typically target the most competitive races, where candidates and parties are also campaigning heavily. This means advertisements sponsored by independent groups may be drowned out in the general din of the more numerous advertisements from candidates and parties. Indeed, in 2010, Democratic candidates' disadvantage in terms of independent group spending was largely compensated for by their advantage in spending by candidates and party organizations. Similarly, in 2012, Obama compensated for Romney's 3-to-1 advantage in outside group spending by raising significantly more than his opponent in individual contributions.

---

[27] Michael M. Franz. 2010. "The *Citizens United* Election: Same As It Ever Was?" *The Forum 8(4), Article 7.*

[28] Center for Responsive Politics. 2012. "Total Outside Spending by Election Cycle, Excluding Party Committees." www.opensecrets.org/outsidespending/cycle_tots.php (accessed 3/27/13).

[29] Michael M. Franz. 2013. "Interest Groups in Electoral Politics: 2012 in Context." *The Forum 10(4), pp. 62–79.*

Does this mean outside group spending does not matter? Absolutely not. In 2012, if one excludes ads sponsored by interest groups, for every 53 ads that Romney aired in a media market, Obama aired 100 ads in the same media market. When one includes ads by independent groups, for every 82 ads favoring Romney in a media market, there were 100 Obama ads.[30] In other words, it can be argued that outside group spending kept Romney in the game and enabled him to mount a strong challenge against an incumbent president. Thus, an advantage in independent spending does not guarantee that a candidate will win an election, but it certainly improves their chances.

Campaign Finance Rules and Political Strategy

As we discussed in Chapter 2, understanding electoral rules is important because they profoundly influence the actions of citizens, candidates, parties, and interest groups. This is true with regard to campaign finance law as well. Below we identify some of the implications of the campaign finance system for each category of actors.

Citizens

Consider first the strategies pursued by individual citizens. By making private donations central to campaign fund-raising, the American system allows private citizens another avenue by which to express their political voice, one distinct from voting and writing to a member of Congress, for example. As with other forms of political participation, donating provides citizens another means by which they can establish a tie with candidates and hold elected leaders accountable for their performance in office. Donations are a particularly powerful way to encourage accountability: the central goal of any candidate is to be elected, and it is virtually impossible to do so without the resources provided by donations.

How do citizens decide what candidates to support with donations? In some cases, the decision is straightforward: a donor may give to a candidate who shares her values and goals. But the decision is often strategic as well. Consider, for example, primary elections, in which there are often few differences between the candidates. How might donors decide then? One important factor is whether donors expect a candidate to win. If two

---

[30] Franz, "Interest Groups."

candidates have similar platforms, donors often prefer to support the likely winner rather than "waste" their money on a likely loser. Potential donors will thus look to various indicators of candidates' viability, including polls, news coverage, and donations by other individuals and interest groups.[31]

Candidates

Campaign finance rules profoundly affect political candidates. By not limiting spending, the American system gives candidates the incentive to raise and spend as much as possible. By limiting the amount of each donation, the system makes it particularly onerous to raise money because candidates must raise it from a larger number of donors. If there were no limits on the size of donations, a candidate could conceivably fund his campaign with money from a single rich donor. Instead, candidates ask for contributions from thousands of donors, with phone calls, at receptions and dinners, and so on. One study of House candidates in the 1996 and 1998 elections found that a substantial fraction (42 percent) reported spending at least a quarter of their time engaged in fund-raising. Almost a quarter of these candidates (24 percent) reported spending at least half their time fund-raising.[32] Given this reality, candidates must seek out efficient ways to raise money. The Internet is helpful, as fund-raising online does not require receptions or dinners. Another strategy is to recruit "bundlers," relatively wealthy donors who can also enlist a set of friends and acquaintances to donate. Bundlers are so valuable that campaigns use catchy names to recognize them. For the 2000 and 2004 Bush presidential campaigns, bundlers were called "Pioneers," "Rangers," and "Super-Rangers" if they supplied $100,000, $200,000, and $300,000, respectively, in donations.

Candidates will likely face even greater incentives to raise money in the wake of the *Citizens United* decision. The increase in independent spending in 2010 may heighten candidates' fear of an advertising blitz sponsored by independent groups, much of which is likely to attack them.

Fund-raising takes considerable time and energy and will continue to do so. But not every candidate faces the same burden. The American system of campaign finance advantages incumbents to a significant degree. As we

---

[31] Diana Mutz. 1995. "Effects of Horse-Race Coverage on Campaign Coffers: Strategic Contributing in Presidential Primaries." *Journal of Politics* 57: 1015–42.

[32] Paul S. Herrnson and Ronald A. Faucheux. 2000. "Candidate Devote Substantial Time and Effort to Fundraising." www.bsos.umd.edu/gvpt/herrnson/reporttime.html (accessed 4/10/11).

Donor Maintenance

In 2008, Obama raised $745 million in campaign contributions of less than $4,600, which was the most an individual could give directly to a candidate that year. Yet many individuals also supported Obama indirectly by donating tens of thousands, if not millions of dollars, to independent groups, such as MoveOn.org. In 2012, however, many of these wealthy supporters were nowhere to be found. The reason cited over and over again in accounts of the campaign was something quite simple: poor donor maintenance.

Donor maintenance refers to how candidates and their staff cultivate relationships with contributors. For a president, it might include smaller gestures such as handwritten thank-you notes or larger ones such as tickets to the inauguration. As one Democratic donor says, "People want to be kissed. They want to be thanked. . . . You have to suck up."[1]

Many donors have felt snubbed by the president, but perhaps one of the best examples is George Soros, a financier who has contributed heavily to the Democrats. In 2004, he donated over $20 million—unheard of at that time—to independent groups with the goal of defeating George W. Bush. During Obama's first term he repeatedly requested a meeting to discuss the economy but, according to a senior advisor, was told the president "was very busy."[2] This may be why in 2012 he gave just $1 million to Priorities USA, the main super PAC supporting Obama.

One might attribute Obama's inability to attract large donations in 2012 to the fact that as a liberal, he is hostile to the "one percent." Yet, in 2008, Obama attracted more donations from Wall Street than John McCain, his Republican opponent.[3] It is true that Romney was a more natural ally of Wall Street in 2012, but Obama's main problem was not that his 2008 mega-donors had switched sides, it was simply that they were not opening their wallets for anyone.

Some attribute Obama's poor donor maintenance to the fact that he is a "dreadful schmoozer" who would rather talk policy with close confidants than attend parties.[4] Another explanation is ideological. Obama has long supported campaign finance reform and been highly critical of the *Citizens United* decision. As a result, it is difficult for him to pursue large donations without feeling hypocritical.

While many of his supporters understood this dilemma in 2012, Romney's ability to attract outside money scared them. "We concluded we couldn't play touch football if they were playing tackle," said David Axelrod, Obama's chief campaign strategist.[5] Despite a late push to go after large donations, Romney's independent group support trounced Obama's by a ratio of 3 to 1 in the end. Obama may have felt vindicated by his win in November, which was due in large part to his ability to attract smaller, direct contributions. Yet his administration will be held up as an example of how not to treat one's biggest supporters.

---

[1] Jane Mayer. 2012. "Schmooze or Lose." *The New Yorker*, August 27. www.newyorker.com/reporting/2012/08/27/120827fa_fact_mayer (accessed 3/25/13).

[2] Jo Becker. 2012. "The Other Power in the West Wing." *The New York Times*, September 1. www.nytimes.com/2012/09/02/us/politics/valerie-jarrett-is-the-other-power-in-the-west-wing.html?_r=1&pagewanted=all (accessed 3/25/13).

[3] Nicholas Confessore. 2012. "Obama's Not-So-Hot Date with Wall Street." *The New York Times*, May 2. www.nytimes.com/2012/05/06/magazine/obamas-not-so-hot-date-with-wall-street.html (accessed 3/25/13).

[4] Richard Cohen. 2012. "Obama, Enigma in Chief." *The Washington Post*, September 5. www.washingtonpost.com/opinions/richard-cohen-barack-obama-enigma-in-chief/2012/09/04/2ce8270c-f6b5-11e1-8b93-c4f4ab1c8d13_story.html (accessed 3/25/13).

[5] Mayer, "Schmooze or Lose."

discuss further in Chapter 9, incumbent members of Congress are typically much more successful than challengers in raising money. They are better known. They already have the status and power that makes them valuable to donors and interest groups. They are usually perceived as the likely victor. All of this stacks the deck against challengers.

The campaign finance system may also benefit wealthy candidates. The lack of spending limits means that candidates can fund their own campaigns, potentially giving wealthy individuals a significant advantage over the less wealthy. Thus, American elections often feature candidates who spend large amounts of their personal wealth to get elected. For example, in the 1992 presidential campaign, Ross Perot spent about $65 million of his own money running as an independent candidate. Self-financing can discourage some potential opponents from running against a wealthy, self-financed candidate.

However, the experiences of self-financed candidates also suggest that personal wealth does not guarantee victory. First, it is important to remember that many candidates spend their own money because they are forced to: because they are facing strong opposition and could easily be defeated if they only use what they raise from other donors, or because they are languishing in the polls and desperately need to give their campaign a jolt. In the 2004 presidential primaries, Senator John Kerry mortgaged his house so that he could loan $6.4 million to his campaign, which was struggling at that time. Second, dollars raised from other donors appear to produce more votes than dollars provided by the candidate. This may reflect the additional benefits of cultivating a network of supportive donors. Private donations signal the strength of the candidate to the media and political elites. It will surprise no one that a candidate would give his or her own campaign $3 million; after all, it is the candidate's money, and the candidate wants to win. But if 3,000 people give the candidate $1,000 each, it may convince others that the candidate is a serious contender. Moreover, the act of fund-raising may generate local media coverage of fund-raising events and may strengthen a candidate's ties to crucial interest groups and blocs of voters. Thus the possibility of self-financing entails a complex series of strategic calculations.[33]

As we discussed earlier, in presidential elections, candidates may accept public funding. But this necessitates another strategic calculation, because the public funding comes with a spending limit. For a lesser-known candidate

---

[33] See Jennifer Steen. 2006. *Self-Financed Candidates in Congressional Elections.* Ann Arbor: University of Michigan Press.

in the presidential primaries, accepting the money may be an easy decision. Unfamiliar candidates struggle to raise private donations and may be able to spend far more if they accept matching funds, despite the accompanying spending limit. Better-known candidates will be tempted to rely on private donations because they believe that there are many individuals and interest groups who will donate to them, and thus more money to be raised from private rather than public funds. Many believe that the fact that no candidates in the 2012 primary or general elections accepted public funds signaled the death knell of the public financing system for presidential elections. This is very likely true unless the level of public funding is raised high enough to make it attractive to candidates once again.

By accepting private donations, candidates face another strategic imperative: keeping donors happy. Donors can withhold their money to ensure accountability, and it is up to the candidate to make sure they are not disappointed. Here is the problem, however. As we describe further below, donors are not at all representative of voters as a whole. What donors want may not match up with what voters want. Thus, candidates may find themselves forced to take one position to please donors but another position to please voters—a difficult balancing act and one that often attracts criticism if contradictory positions become public knowledge.

Political Parties and Interest Groups

Under the current rules, political parties and interest groups, including corporations and unions, can raise and spend their own money on campaign activities. BCRA's ban on soft money has not hindered the parties in this regard. The Supreme Court's decision in *Citizens United* gave interest groups even freer reign to spend independently. This poses both an opportunity and a challenge for candidates. On the one hand, they may benefit from the campaign activity of their party and of interest groups who support them. On the other hand, they may find that their party and ostensibly supportive interest groups are not interested in helping them. They may also be attacked by the opposing party and its aligned groups. Thus, the presence of parties and interest groups can both facilitate and complicate the efforts of candidates.

A dispute within the Democratic Party during the 2006 election illustrates the complex ways in which the strategies of candidates and parties interact. The chair of the Democratic National Committee, the former Vermont governor and 2004 presidential candidate Howard Dean, advocated a "50-state strategy"—one that would invest the DNC's money in building up the Democratic party organization in every state, even in states where the party rarely won elections. This was a boon to many Democrats in such states, who typically did not attract much support from the party. At the same time, the chair of the Democratic Congressional Campaign Committee, Rahm Emanuel, had a very different strategy: he sought to use DCCC money to bolster Democratic House candidates in competitive races, and thought it was wasteful to spend party money in states where the party had little chance of winning. This was a boon to Democrats in hard-fought campaigns, but not to Democrats in Republican-dominated states. No matter which strategy the party pursued, some Democratic candidates would benefit more than others.

Like political parties, interest groups must make strategic decisions about which candidate to support, through either donations or independent expenditures. This will depend on their agenda. Groups that find their interests well served by current officeholders will pursue an "access" strategy, working to support incumbents of both parties and, via their contributions, guarantee access to these incumbents so that they can press their agenda. This creates an incentive for incumbent candidates to be responsive to groups to ensure their support during the campaign. Groups that tend to have a more ideological agenda, one further from the average officeholder, will pursue a "replacement" strategy, seeking to replace incumbents with new representatives who share this agenda. These new representatives will typically come from one party or even one ideological faction within the party.[34] The Club for Growth, a group that promotes conservative economic policies, is famous for targeting incumbent "RINOs"—"Republicans in Name Only"—that it considers too moderate. Of course, incumbent candidates will not sit idly by if they are threatened with such a challenge. They may take new steps to placate the interest groups and convince them not to support the challenger. If that is unsuccessful, they may adjust their own positions on issues to be more in line with their challenger's, thereby negating some of the rationale for replacing them. In the 2010 Arizona Senate race, John McCain, the incumbent, faced a conservative challenger, J. D. Hayworth, in the Republican primary. Hayworth's presence led McCain to take more conservative positions on several issues. McCain soft-pedaled his earlier advocacy for campaign finance reform and BCRA, even though he had been one of its staunchest advocates.

The agendas of candidates and their interest group supporters may not be well aligned—a very plausible scenario, given that under current campaign

---

[34] See Michael M. Franz. 2008. *Choices and Changes: Interest Groups in the Electoral Process.* Philadelphia: Temple University Press.

finance law, candidates and interest groups are not permitted to coordinate their campaign activities. A supportive interest group may emphasize different issues or themes or adopt a different set of tactics than the candidate it supports. For example, parties and interest groups tend to air far more negative campaign ads than do candidates. At times this may not bother candidates, who can take the high road and let others do the dirty work. But at other times, candidates may have to disavow a particularly aggressive ad aired by a supporter. In the 1988 presidential election, the National Security Political Action Committee (NSPAC) aired an ad attacking the Democratic candidate, Michael Dukakis, for a Massachusetts program that allowed prisoners to leave jail temporarily for furloughs as part of a rehabilitation effort. The ad focused on one prisoner, William Horton (the ad called him "Willie"), who, while on furlough, raped a woman and assaulted her fiancé. The ad featured a photograph of Horton, who was black, and became controversial after critics argued that it played on racial fears. The campaign of Dukakis's opponent, George H. W. Bush, ultimately requested NSPAC to withdraw it, although some have argued that the Bush campaign knew about the ad in advance and delayed their request for its withdrawal to give the ad time to have an impact.[35]

Ultimately, candidates may find that much of the campaigning that takes place, even on their behalf, is out of their control. As such, it may both help and hurt their campaign, at least as they see it. By expanding the number of actors eligible to raise and spend money, the American system of campaign finance creates loose alliances among candidates, parties, and interest groups that contain significant tensions even as these players seek a common goal.

The Debate over Campaign Finance Reform

The American system of campaign finance is perennially controversial, as the debate over the *Citizens United* decision illustrates. To understand this controversy, it is worth considering the values that underlie the campaign finance system, discussing the tensions among these values, and evaluating

---

[35] The Federal Election Commission conducted an investigation into whether there was illicit cooperation between the Bush campaign and the independent group that produced the ad. The Commission was deadlocked 3–3 on the question (not surprising given the presence of three Republicans and three Democrats on the Commission) and thus did not produce a conclusive ruling. www.insidepolitics.org/ps111/independentads.html (accessed 4/10/11).

proposed reforms to the system. As noted earlier, two important values underlying campaign finance law are freedom of speech, as discussed in Chapter 1 and as enumerated in the First Amendment; and guarding against corruption, and in particular the corrupting influence of money. Debate about campaign finance also engages other values discussed in Chapter 1, especially free choice and political equality.

The Supreme Court has weighed those values in different ways when considering the rules imposed on donors and spenders. In *Buckley v. Valeo*, the Court argued that donations to a candidate poses a significant threat of corruption, but that spending on behalf of a candidate (for example by an interest group) does not. It also argued that donations are not as meaningful as spending in terms of their communicative content. Donations serve only to convey general support but not the reasons for that support. Spending, on the other hand, is central to communicating one's ideas during a campaign. Both of these arguments buttressed the Court's decisions to limit donations but not spending. Concerns about free speech also led to the Court's decisions in *Citizens United v. FEC*, which struck down laws that restricted the spending of independent groups.

The Case against the Status Quo

The chief objection to these legal decisions (and to the American system in general) is that they allow money to have too much influence on politics. This has at least four possible negative consequences. First, it is hard on candidates, who must raise money incessantly, even to the detriment of other, possibly more beneficial activities, such as policy making. It may also discourage some talented individuals from running in the first place, especially ones who have no ability to self-finance as an alternative to raising private donations. In a 2008 survey of potential political candidates, 29 percent of women and 21 percent of men said that the prospect of soliciting campaign contributions would "deter them from running for office."[36]

Second, critics fear that money simply buys elections, meaning that whoever can spend the most wins. They point to the fund-raising disparities between incumbents and challengers and to the extraordinarily high rate at which incumbents win. This criticism is based on the values of free choice and political equality. Voters do not really have a choice, the argument goes, when a well-funded incumbent can scare off many potential challengers and

---

[36] Jennifer Lawless and Richard Fox. 2008. "Why Are Women Still Not Running for Office?" *Issues in Government Studies* 16. Washington, DC: Brookings Institution Press.

then easily defeat the poorly funded challenger who decides to run. Is it fair that campaign finance rules create such inequality, whereby some candidates have vastly more resources to spend than others?

Third, critics argue, the campaign finance system favors those wealthy enough to donate, giving them a greater voice in politics than those who cannot donate and violating the value of political equality. It is certainly true that wealthy individuals are far more likely than the poor to donate to candidates. In the 2008 American National Election Study, only 11 percent of respondents reported donating to a candidate or party. While people at or above the U.S. median income of $52,000 made up 49 percent of the overall sample, they made up 67 percent of those who reported donating. And that does not take account of how much they gave. Naturally, wealthier donors tend to give more. One 1990 survey found that among campaign donors, those making $125,000 or more gave an average of $1,500, compared to an average of $107 among those making less than $15,000.[37] Moreover, critics claim, interest groups that represent wealthy Americans and business or corporate interests are more powerful than groups representing, for example, the poor or working class. In the 2011–12 election cycle, business PACs contributed about $2.7 billion to congressional and presidential candidates, while labor PACs contributed just $177 million.[38]

Fourth, and perhaps most important, critics argue that the current system does not do enough to combat corruption, or at least the appearance of corruption. Critics note that candidates and political parties still find ways to raise large amounts of money that violate the spirit of campaign finance law. For example, candidates and their parties sometimes establish "joint fund-raising committees," as did both McCain and Obama in 2008. A donor can write a single check to this committee; this donation is then distributed to the candidate, national party committees, and perhaps state parties. Such donations cannot exceed contribution limits, but nevertheless, critics argue, the overall impact of a single large check gives wealthy donors added clout. Furthermore, committees are established to fund the presidential nominating conventions, which can raise unlimited sums from corporate and union general treasuries and PACs. This is because of an FEC loophole defin-

---

[37] Sidney Verba, Kay Lehman Schlozman, and Henry E. Brady. 1995. *Voice and Equality: Civic Voluntarism in American Politics.* Cambridge, MA: Harvard University Press, p. 365.

[38] OpenSecrets. "Business-Labor-Ideology Split in PAC & Individual Donations to Candidates, Parties, Super PACs and Outside Spending Groups." www.opensecrets.org/bigpicture/blio.php (accessed 3/25/13).

ing convention funds as "motivated by a desire to promote the convention city and not by political considerations"—a proposition critics find highly dubious.[39]

Fundamentally, critics are concerned that the money that donors and organized interests give and spend can influence elected leaders. Stories about the possible influence of money are common. During the debate over health care reform in 2009, a *Washington Post* story noted that Max Baucus (D-Mo.), chair of the Senate Finance Committee, who was a key figure in drawing up health care legislation, was also a "leading recipient of Senate campaign contributions from the hospitals, insurers, and other medical interest groups hoping to shape the legislation to their advantage."[40] Another story implicated Senator Christopher Dodd (D-Conn.), who had received numerous contributions from hedge funds even as the Senate Banking Committee, which Dodd chaired, was considering legislation that would regulate those funds.[41] In the minds of critics, campaign contributions may lead to policies favored by donors, rather than policies that would serve other important goals and perhaps even the general good of the country.

A proposed solution to many of these potential problems with campaign finance rules is public financing, and especially a clean elections system like that in Maine. Clean elections systems can help equalize resources among candidates by providing equal amounts of public funding to all candidates and by forbidding any other fund-raising by the recipients of public funding. With equal amounts of funding, the campaign might then be more competitive, improving the quality of information provided to voters and giving them a more meaningful choice. In addition, with almost all campaign financing coming from the government, there is little to no chance that wealthy donors or interest groups will have a disproportionate or corrupting influence. Advocates of clean elections have proposed a similar system for federal elections, the Fair Elections Now Act, which could, in the words of one of its proponents, make "elected officials beholden to the people they're supposed to represent instead of the wealthy special interests."[42]

---

[39] *Federal Register* 68, 153 (8/8/2003): 47401–02.

[40] Dan Eggen. 2009. "Industry Cash Flowed to Drafters of Reform." *Washington Post*, July 21.

[41] Manu Raju. 2010. "Hedge Fund Managers Invest on Hill." *Politico*, April 13.

[42] Public Campaign. "Bipartisan Fair Elections Now Act Reaches Majority of Majority in US House." www.publicampaign.org/pressroom/2010/02/04/bipartisan-fair-elections-now -act-reaches-majority-of-majority-in-us-house (accessed 4/9/11).

Complicating the Case for Reform

How well do the arguments for campaign finance reform withstand empirical scrutiny? And are there good arguments in support of the system as it stands? Answers to these questions suggest that the American system of campaign finance, however imperfect, may have its merits.

Arguments for reform include two primary claims about the current system: simply stated, money buys elections and money buys legislators' votes. But can we verify that these statements are true? The first claim is difficult to assess. Consider that incumbents tend to raise much more than challengers. Is this disparity in fund-raising the actual reason that incumbents win? Or do incumbents raise so much because they are already anticipated to win, and donors often prefer to give to the likely winner? And how do we separate the effects of incumbents' fund-raising advantage from the other advantages they have as incumbents, including their work on behalf of constituents and consequent visibility? These sorts of advantages may help explain why incumbents were re-elected at such high rates even *before* they were so dominant in fund-raising. For example, in the early 1980s, House incumbents were typically spending about 1.5 times as much as challengers; in the 2000s, they typically spent about 2.5 or 3 times as much. But incumbents' re-election rates in the early 1980s were above 90 percent, slightly higher than in the 2000s, even though their fund-raising advantage increased in the 2000s. Moreover, challenger fund-raising appears more important than incumbent fund-raising: the money that challengers spend is more strongly associated with additional votes than is the money that incumbents spend.[43] Thus, the high re-election rate of incumbents is not necessarily due *only* to their fund-raising advantage.

This may explain why more stringent campaign finance rules do not necessarily transform elections, making them more competitive and incumbents more vulnerable. For example, some research has compared states with different levels of limits on individual donations.[44] Although lower limits are associated with smaller victory margins for incumbents—and therefore with more competitive elections—they do not produce more actual defeats for incumbents. The evidence on the effects of clean elections is similarly equivocal. Public financing programs appear to reduce the

---

[43] Gary Jacobson. 2009. *The Politics of Congressional Elections*, 7th ed. New York: Pearson Longman, pp. 47–49.

[44] Thomas Stratmann and Francisco J. Aparicio-Castillo. 2006. "Competition Policy for Elections: Do Campaign Contribution Limits Matter?" *Public Choice* 127, 1: 177–206.

amount of time that candidates spend fund-raising but do not necessarily make elections more competitive.[45]

The claim that money buys legislators' votes also needs examination. There is relatively little evidence that it actually occurs. First, because of contribution limits, the amount that any donor or interest group can give is small, relative to the large amount of money that many candidates routinely raise and spend. Candidates who raises millions of dollars are not likely to "sell" their votes to a PAC for a measly $5,000.

Second, many donations to campaigns are strategic: the donors do not want to waste their money on someone who will never support their agenda. Instead, they give to members who are already supportive, perhaps because these members simply have beliefs about policies that are similar to the donors' or because members are responding to their constituents, who also agree with donors. Consider this hypothetical example. The National Farmers Union PAC gives an incumbent congressman $5,000 for his re-election campaign. The congressman represents a rural district in Iowa whose economy revolves around growing corn. After the election, he votes to give additional government subsidies to corn farmers. Did he vote this way because he simply believes that government subsidies are necessary, because many of his constituents are farmers and others who benefit from subsidies, or because he got that PAC contribution?

None of this is to say that campaign donations are ineffectual. Some research suggests that donations are more likely to buy the involvement of an elected official on an issue, if not his vote. Donations appear to motivate representatives to be more active in promoting the issue on congressional committees, for example. However, this is true only for representatives who already share the donors' positions.[46] Donors may also get more "access" to an elected official—that is, a greater opportunity to advocate for their views in front of a representative or her staff. Of course, this does not imply that the representative will always agree with these views. Ultimately, campaign

---

[45] Peter L. Francia and Paul S. Herrnson. 2003. "The Impact of Public Finance Laws on Fundraising in State Legislative Elections." *American Politics Research* 31, 5: 520–39; Kenneth R. Mayer, Timothy Werner, and Amanda Williams. 2006. "Do Public Funding Programs Enhance Electoral Competition?" in *The Marketplace of Democracy: Electoral Competition and American Politics*, eds. Michael P. McDonald and John Samples. Washington, DC: Brookings Institution Press, pp. 245–67.

[46] Richard L. Hall and Frank W. Wayman. 1990. "Buying Time: Moneyed Interests and the Mobilization of Bias in Congressional Committees." *American Political Science Review* 84, 3: 797–820.

donations may not be quite as powerful an influence as reformers claim and media coverage often suggests.

The American system of campaign finance can also be defended on philosophical grounds. Two of the features that reformers routinely target—private donations and unlimited spending by candidates—could in fact be considered valuable. By allowing private donations to candidates, the American system creates an opportunity for citizens and interest groups to have a voice and help to elect candidates who they believe can best represent them. By allowing unlimited spending, the American system allows for more campaign activity, including advertising that communicates information about the candidates, activities that mobilize citizens to vote, and so on. This point was made in the *Buckley v. Valeo* decision: "A restriction on the amount of money a person or group can spend on political communication during a campaign necessarily reduces the quantity of expression by restricting the number of issues discussed, the depth of their exploration, and the size of the audience reached." Given that Americans still do not always know much about the candidates or vote in large numbers, it could be counterproductive to limit campaign spending.

Leaving aside arguments about the merits of the current campaign finance system, there is one further challenge that critics of the system face: there is often little incentive for incumbent leaders to reform the system. Despite the public's complaints about money in elections, polls reveal that opinions about dramatic reforms, such as public financing, depend on how the poll question is worded. For example, a 2010 poll found that two-thirds of respondents supported public financing when described this way:

> Under this plan, candidates for Congress could run for office without raising large campaign contributions. Instead they would collect a large number of small contributions from their home state in order to qualify for a limited amount of public funding for their campaign. They would be prohibited from taking any contributions over 100 dollars or any contributions from lobbyists. Contributions of 100 dollars or less would be matched with public funds on a four to one basis, up to a strict limit.[47]

However, a 2007 Gallup poll found that the public actually preferred that presidential candidates *not* accept public financing.[48] Over half of respondents

---

[47] Common Cause. "Bipartisan Poll on Support for Public Financing." www.commoncause .org/site/pp.asp?c=dkLNK1MQIwG&b=4773901 (accessed 4-9-11).

[48] Lydia Saad. 2007. "Americans Prefer Presidential Candidates to Forgo Public Funding." *Gallup*, April 27. www.gallup.com/poll/27394/Americans-Prefer-Presidential-Candidates -Forgo-Public-Funding.aspx (accessed 4/9/11).

(56 percent) believed that candidates should "opt not to take public financing and spend whatever money they can raise on their own" rather than to "agree to take public financing and accept spending limits." The public's reluctance to embrace public financing wholeheartedly reflects their ambivalence about using government money—in other words, their taxes—to fund campaigns.

It is actually not clear that the public pays much attention to how candidates finance their campaigns. In an October 2008 Gallup poll, about 70 percent of voters either did not know whether Barack Obama and John McCain had accepted public financing or were mistaken in their view.[49] Finally, the public typically considers campaign finance reform far less important than the economy, foreign affairs and war, health care, education, and a host of other issues. Indeed, the legislation that became BCRA languished for years until a major scandal involving the energy company Enron—which had developed a close relationship with many elected politicians even as it was covering up financial problems that would eventually lead to bankruptcy—prompted action.

Without a significant push from the public, incumbent leaders are often reluctant to embrace reform. This is entirely rational: they were elected under the status quo. Changing the rules introduces uncertainty into their bids for re-election. Incumbent leaders are especially nervous about public financing because they often believe it will help their opponents to be more competitive—and, of course, this is precisely the outcome desired by some proponents of public financing. The point is not who is wrong or right. The point is that the implications of campaign finance rules for elected leaders often mean that their best strategy is not to change the rules.

Conclusion

Debates about the efficacy of the current system of campaign finance laws in the United States reinforce the important connection among rules, reality, strategy, and citizens. The American system is unusual among democracies in that candidates and other actors have been given a wide degree of latitude with respect to what they can say, when they can say it, and how

---

[49] Jeffry M. Jones. 2008. "Campaign Financing Appears to Be Non-Issue for Voters." *Gallup*, October 30. www.gallup.com/poll/111652/Campaign-Financing-Appears-NonIssue-Voters .aspx (accessed 4/6/11).

they pay for it. Recent changes in campaign finance law have increased the amount of money in federal election campaigns, mostly by allowing interest groups to solicit and spend funds more freely. Some observers have gone so far as to suggest that trying to keep money out of politics is like trying to keep ants out of a kitchen: plugging one hole will only lead the ants to find another as long as there is any sugar around. Nevertheless, proponents of campaign finance reform seek to plug as many holes as possible, even as others defend the current system and do not mourn the failures of regulation. This again highlights the fact that campaign finance rules reflect a fundamental philosophical trade-off between free speech, on the one hand, and the potentially corrupting influence of money, on the other.

KEY TERMS

public funding (p. 82)

Tillman Act (p. 87)

political action committee (PAC) (p. 87)

Federal Election Campaign Act (FECA) (p. 89)

Federal Election Commission (FEC) (p. 89)

Bipartisan Campaign Reform Act (BCRA) (p. 89)

soft money (p. 91)

hard money (p. 91)

express advocacy (p. 92)

magic words (p. 92)

issue advocacy (p. 92)

independent expenditure committees (p. 93)

super PACs (p. 93)

527 organization (p. 93)

501(c) organizations (p. 97)

Buckley v. Valeo (p. 98)

clean elections systems (p. 100)

Citizens United v. Federal Election Commission (p. 102)

FOR DISCUSSION

1. According to Supreme Court decisions about campaign finance, why are contributions to candidates limited while spending by candidate is unlimited?

2. Why are the costs and benefits to a candidate of funding their campaign via: (a) money raised from private donors; (b) public funding; and (c) their own money?

3. How did BCRA and the *Citizens United* decision affect the ways in which political parties and interest groups can raise and spend money in elections?

4. What are reasons for and against the argument that money corrupts politicians?

 Visit StudySpace for quizzes and other review material.
wwnorton.com/studyspace

CHAPTER 5

Modern Campaign Strategies

In the summer of 1988, Vice President George H. W. Bush trailed the Democratic nominee, Michael Dukakis, by 16 points in the polls. Prior to the Republican Party's August convention, Bush's campaign team convened to discuss the latest polling results. Bob Teeter, Bush's pollster, gave a lengthy description of the mood of the country, including the public's issue priorities and positions, but stalled and stammered when he came to public perceptions of Bush's personal characteristics. He tried, as best he could, to suggest that the vice president was not perceived as being "very forceful." Bush blanched at this, pointing out his service in World War II, his stint as director of the CIA, and his time as ambassador to China. Teeter tried to explain that the public had a more general impression, one rooted in a "gut reaction." This reaction had to be corrected if Bush were to escape from the shadow of President Reagan and win the White House. Bush pushed Teeter on the specifics behind the numbers; Teeter hemmed and hawed, unsure how to explain the problem without offending the vice president. Finally, James A. Baker III, a Bush confidant, intervened: "What Bob is telling you, George, is that the people think you're a pussy, and we need to turn you into a prick."[1]

This example demonstrates in coarse but effective terms that the basis of a good campaign strategy is, first, to recognize the reality of the campaign, or the broader context in which the campaign is being run. The next step is to set an appropriate goal that, if achieved, will win the election. The beauty of the Baker quote is its simplicity: George H. W. Bush's main problem in 1988, the reason he was lagging behind Democratic challenger Michael Dukakis, was that Americans did not think Bush was strong enough to lead the country. The campaign (and its candidate) needed to recognize this and take bold steps to change perceptions of Bush. They did this by having Bush aggressively contrast his positions on crime and defense with Dukakis's. Both the style and substance of Bush's speeches

---

[1] Story related to Daron Shaw by someone present at the August 1988 meeting.

and advertisements sought to portray him as tough — tough on criminals, tough on enemies of the United States, and tough on his Democratic opponent. In the end, Bush swayed a sufficient number of independents — 64 percent of whom supported him — to win the White House.[2] His "tough guy" strategy may not have won him the race, but it is difficult to see how he would have won had his campaign not dealt with what many analysts called "the wimp factor."

The goal of this chapter is to describe and consider the role of strategy (and strategists) in American political campaigns. We begin by defining strategy and discussing how a modern campaign develops a strategy. Next, we outline the important strategic decisions of a campaign, examining both professional practice and academic research. Among other things, we argue that campaigns are selective with respect to what they say and who they say it to. Some voters are critical to victory and they receive most of the campaign's attention. The skill with which a campaign identifies and convinces these voters can be important for the outcome of the election. We then examine what a campaign looks like, how it is organized, and the role of political consultants. Finally, we discuss the normative implications of the rise of more professionalized, strategic campaigns.

Core of the Analysis

- A campaign must develop a strategy in order to compete effectively in a competitive district or state.
- Campaigns try to mobilize supporters and persuade undecided voters.
- Campaign strategy involves decisions about whether to run, which issues to emphasize, what positions to take on issues, whether to attack the opposition, and how to allocate resources to different constituencies and media.
- These strategic decisions depend strongly on the broader rules and realities that candidates confront.
- Campaign organizations have general features in common but vary considerably depending on the size and scope of the campaign.
- Modern political campaigns rely on professionals to devise and execute their strategies, and to organize their campaigns.

---

[2] This figure is based on results from the 1988 American National Election Study, www .electionstudies.org/nesguide/2ndtable/t9a_1_2.htm (accessed 12/10/10).

How Are Campaign Strategies Constructed?

Assuming a candidate has decided to run—a decision we will consider in greater detail later in this chapter—there are many tasks the campaign must address immediately. The campaign needs a physical space for a headquarters, so that people have a place to work. The candidate has to announce his or her candidacy. There are people who must be contacted, including past candidates and party leaders, whose expertise, advice, and endorsement are all potentially valuable. The campaign needs to identify the main issues the candidate intends to run on and prepare position papers. Finally, the campaign must purchase some of the staples of the modern campaign: computers, computer servers, an Internet connection, cell phones, and materials for brochures, bumper stickers, buttons, and pamphlets.

But perhaps more than anything else, a campaign needs to quickly develop a **campaign strategy**. Put simply, a strategy is a proposed pathway to victory. It is a plan for how to win, and it is driven by an understanding of who will vote for the candidate and why they will do so. The political scientist Joel Bradshaw posits four key propositions for developing a successful campaign strategy.[3] First, in any election the electorate can be divided into three groups: the candidate's base, the opponent's base, and the undecided. Second, past election results and survey research make it possible to determine which people fall into each of these three groups. Third, it is neither possible nor necessary to get the support of all people everywhere to win the election. Research should allow a campaign to determine how best to mobilize the candidate's base and persuade the undecideds. Both mobilization and persuasion are central to a campaign's efforts. Fourth, and last, once a campaign has identified how to win, it can act to create the circumstances to bring about this victory. In order to succeed, campaigns should direct campaign resources—money, time, and message—to key groups of potential voters and nowhere else. Resource allocation is therefore defined by strategy.

Vote Targets

Implicit in these propositions is the need to develop specific **vote targets** (or vote goals). These targets are based on estimates of what the upcoming election will look like: how many total votes the campaign believes will be cast in the election, how many it will need to win, how many votes its candidate can expect no matter what, and how many **persuadable** (or **swing**) **votes** are out there.

---

[3] Joel Bradshaw. 2004. "Campaign Strategy," in *Campaigns and Elections American Style*, 2nd ed., eds. James A. Thurber and Candice J. Nelson. Boulder, CO: Westview Press.

TABLE 5.1 Turnout in Ohio Gubernatorial Elections, 2002–10

Year	Registered Voters	Total Votes	Turnout Rate
2002	7,113,826	3,356,285	47%
2006	7,860,052	4,185,597	53%
2010	8,037,806	3,956,045	49%
Average	**7,670,561**	**3,832,642**	**50%**

Source: Ohio Secretary of State, Elections and Ballot Issues.

These estimates are derived from examining data from recent comparable elections. Let us say that our candidate is running for governor in a general election in Ohio. The simplest way to develop an estimate for the total votes to be cast in the upcoming election is to look across the most recent gubernatorial elections (see Table 5.1).

Notice that we are not looking at turnout in presidential years, which is invariably higher than in midterm elections; we only want to look at data from comparable elections. Notice also that the Ohio turnout rate varies a bit from year to year, from a high of about 53 percent in 2006 to a low of about 49 percent in 2010. The number of registered voters, however, appears to increase every year. It increased by 746,226 from 2002 to 2006, and by 177,754 from 2006 to 2010. For the 2014 election, it is reasonable to assume that (1) turnout will be about 50 percent of registered voters, and (2) the number of registered voters will be greater than 8,037,806. In a real election campaign, we would be able to access updated registration numbers from the Ohio secretary of state. For illustrative purposes, though, let us assume that registration will increase by approximately 200,000 for our election. That gives us 8,237,806 registered voters. If we assume that 50 percent of those who are registered vote in the governor's race, the total number of votes cast will be about 4,118,903.

So how many votes do we need to win? This depends, of course, on the number of candidates in the race. If it is simply a contest between major party candidates—Republican versus Democrat—our candidate will need slightly more than 50 percent of the vote. If there are minor party or independent candidates, a candidate could conceivably win with less than 50 percent (a plurality, but not a majority). But let us assume that we have a two-party election on our hands. A bare majority (50.1 percent) of our expected electorate

TABLE 5.2 Votes Won in Ohio Governor Elections, 2002–10

Year	Republican Candidate	Democrat Candidate	Other Candidates	Republican Candidate's Percentage
2002	1,865,007	1,236,924	126,977	58%
2006	1,474,331	2,435,505	113,019	37%
2010	1,889,186	1,812,059	156,224	49%

Source: Ohio Secretary of State, Elections and Ballot Issues.

would be 2,063,570. Most campaigns round up when estimating a vote target because they want to avoid a situation where they meet their vote target but lose the election because of unexpectedly high turnout. So let us be very cautious and say our target is 2.2 million votes.

Next, our campaign should have an expectation about what our candidate's base vote is. This is usually based on the candidate's party affiliation. In other words, how many votes would a "bad" candidate from the party get in an election in which conditions favored the other side? Again, we turn to past results to estimate this (Table 5.2).

Consider things from the perspective of the Republican candidate. The election results vary a great deal—from a Republican high of almost 58 percent in 2002 to a low of just under 37 percent in 2006. In many ways, 2006 was a low-water mark for the Republican Party, both in Ohio and across the nation. Republican president George W. Bush was deeply unpopular, a controversial war was dragging on in Iraq, and the economy was beginning to show signs of recession. Moreover, in Ohio, the Republican gubernatorial candidate, Ken Blackwell, was widely regarded as having run an especially inept campaign. Thus, we can take the 2006 result as an estimate of the Republican base vote, the minimum that a Republican candidate can expect to win. If we use the figure of 37 percent of the expected turnout, our estimate of the Republican base vote is 1,523,994.

To generate an estimate of the persuadable vote, we need an upper estimate of what a candidate from our party can achieve. In other words, how many votes would a "good" Republican candidate get in an election in which conditions favored the Republican Party? The 2002 election provides just such an example. The public rallied behind President Bush and the Republicans after the terrorist attacks of 9/11 and when the economy seemed to be slowly emerging from the recession of 2000–01. Furthermore, the Republican gubernatorial candidate Robert Taft was a popular figure from a legendary Ohio political family. Let us therefore take his 58 percent result as an estimate of the high end for a Republican candidate. The difference between these extremes is 58 minus 37 percent, or 21 percent. So our estimate of the persuadable vote for our upcoming Ohio governor's race is 21 percent of the total expected vote of 4.1 million, or approximately 865,000 voters.

This last estimate is critical. To recap, we assume that approximately 4.1 million voters will cast ballots in the Ohio governor's election in 2014. We have a vote target of 2.2 million, and we estimate that our base vote is slightly over 1.5 million voters. The swing vote in the state is 865,000. To get from our base (1.5 million) to our target (2.2 million), we need to win 700,000 of the 865,000 swing votes (81 percent).

We can also generate vote targets for each county in the state based on previous election results; we might use the three most recent elections to calculate the average contribution of each county to the total statewide party vote (Table 5.3). For example, take Cuyahoga County, where the city of Cleveland is located. It contributed, on average, 7.6 percent of the total Republican vote in Ohio in the past three elections. For the 2014 election, we would multiply this number by the total statewide vote target (2.2 million) to generate a target for Cuyahoga of 167,204 Republican votes. This can be done for every county and even the precincts within a county.

TABLE 5.3 Election Results and Vote Targets for Selected Ohio Counties

County	2010 Kasich Votes	2006 Blackwell Votes	2002 Taft Votes	Average Contribution to Republican Vote Total	Vote Target for 2014 Election (based on a statewide target of 2.2 million)
Cuyahoga	148,611	107,258	142,874	7.6%	167,204
Franklin	169,487	122,601	156,712	8.6%	188,395
Hamilton	143,222	141,374	160,223	8.6%	188,918
Montgomery	89,218	76,189	95,891	5.0%	110,235
Statewide	1,889,186	1,474,331	1,865,007		2,200,000

Source: Ohio Secretary of State, Elections and Ballot Issues.

Profiling Vote Targets

How can the campaign hope to win over the swing voters it needs to meet its target? First and foremost, the campaign must identify who these voters are. Campaigns typically use surveys and, to a lesser degree, focus groups to do this. Initially, the campaign will conduct surveys to ascertain what sorts of people are persuadable. Almost all campaign surveys are **probability samples**, in which some number of individuals from a certain population are randomly selected and asked a set of questions. The key to a probability sample is that every individual in the population of interest has a known probability of being selected. Because selection is random, a small number of completed interviews (usually between 400 and 1,000) reveal the general opinions held throughout the population, with a known and relatively small (or at least acceptable) margin of error. In much the same way a doctor can make inferences about your health based on a small sample of your blood, we can make inferences about public opinion based on a small sample of randomly chosen citizens.

Thinking back to our governor's race, a survey (or poll) can thus be used to ask registered voters in Ohio whom they intend to vote for in the upcoming election. For those people with a preference, we can also ask how strongly they prefer their candidate. A survey allows us not only to identify how many people are currently undecided or might be moved from their current prefer-ence, but also to see if persuadable voters are more common among certain groups, such as women, young people, or Latinos. In addition, we can exam-ine the issue preferences of persuadable voters to develop a plan for winning them over.

Once surveys have been analyzed, many campaigns conduct in-depth interviews with small groups of persuadable voters to gather additional data and test specific issue positions. These are called **focus groups.** They have been a part of political campaigns since the mid-1980s, when campaign con-sultants noticed that businesses were using them to enhance their under-standing of client preferences. They range in size between eight and twenty participants, and are led by a "facilitator" whose job is to pose questions and encourage full participation from all members. Focus groups differ from polls in that participants are not selected randomly. In fact, they are intentionally recruited based on certain characteristics that the campaign associates with persuadable voters (for example, gender, age, or ethnicity). Because of this, focus group participants do not necessarily represent what the larger popula-tion thinks; they are simply suggestive of how certain subgroups think about politics and the election. And while focus groups do not provide statistically generalizable information, they provide a depth of information that cam-paigns often find valuable.

Together, polls and focus groups give a campaign a strong sense of what sorts of voters they need to win over and the kinds of appeals that will most effectively accomplish this. This knowledge can be used to craft stump speeches, position papers and press releases, and television and radio advertisements.

The second step to identifying swing voters involves rating the persuadability of all registered voters in the district. This step involves two major tasks. Both tasks represent large and expensive undertakings, and thus they are typically done only in presidential, gubernatorial, U.S. Senate, and hotly contested U.S. House races. Smaller campaigns, as we discuss in Chapter 10, may rely on cheaper and less sophisticated strategies.

The first task is to acquire a list of registered voters and augment it with demographic information on each voter. As we discussed in Chapter 3, the major political parties have compiled extensive databases on voters, including names, addresses, phone numbers, previous voting history, demographic attributes such as gender or race, and financial and consumer data such as home values.

Then, the campaign uses information from the poll about who is persuadable to determine how open each voter on the list is to appeals from its candidate. In other words, the campaign builds a statistical model of persuadability based on the results of the poll, and then uses this to predict the persuadability of every individual in the voter file. The campaign can then isolate specific voters for mailings, phone calls, or in-person visits, all based on a combination of data from the poll and the voter list. This process, called **microtargeting**, was developed in the 2000 and 2002 elections to allow individual-level targeting. Microtargeting avoids the need to make **voter identification** (or **voter ID**) **calls,** in which every voter on the voter list is called and asked her preferences for the upcoming race.

It is difficult to microtarget based on a standard campaign poll. A poll of 500 people, for example, will not have a sufficient number of people in certain groups—such as college students—to make reliable inferences about what these groups think. Nor will a standard poll ask enough questions about a respondent's background to take advantage of the information available in voter databases. Thus, microtargeting typically requires a very large poll—say, of 6,000 or more respondents—with additional questions about the respondents' backgrounds and habits. Microtargeting is expensive, but it's much less expensive than a round of statewide voter ID calls.

The Context of Voter Targeting

Targeting voters effectively not only requires polling data and an accurate voter list but also an understanding of the reality associated with the particular election. Perhaps the most important aspect of the reality is whether the candidate is an incumbent. For the incumbent, the election is to some degree a referendum on how things have gone on her watch. Citizens will associate prevailing conditions—the state of the economy, crime rates, traffic flow, and so on—with the incumbent candidate and will reward or punish her accordingly. In this context, it is more difficult to persuade voters; people have seen the incumbent in action and have formed opinions. Conversely, if the candidate is a challenger running against an incumbent, he will try to convince people that the incumbent has done a poor job and that it is time for a change. In addition, the challenger will be less familiar to constituents in the district. People prefer someone they know, and they are more likely to recognize the name of the incumbent than that of the challenger. In sum, when an incumbent is running for re-election, most of the campaign is about defining her record. Targeting is thus constrained by real-life conditions.

If there is no incumbent, the central question remains who will do a better job, but people do not have recent and relevant experience to guide their assessments. Perhaps more to the point, in an **open-seat** race it is much easier to craft a strategy to persuade people to support your candidate. Other factors can come to the fore.

Another important reality is the partisan makeup of the district. As we discussed in Chapter 2, the characteristics of a candidate's constituency affect nearly every dimension of campaign strategy. If 60 percent of voters in the district are Democratic, 20 percent are Republican, and 20 percent describe themselves as independent, the Democratic candidate will likely emphasize traditionally partisan appeals (and will usually win). The Republican candidate will need to win over some independents and Democrats, and is therefore likely to emphasize candidate-related appeals. This was the case in the 2010 U.S. Senate race in Massachusetts between Martha Coakley, a Democrat, and Scott Brown, a Republican, in which Brown pulled off a 52–47 percent upset victory in a heavily Democratic state. He focused on voter anger with the status quo and convinced some Democrats that the race was about something besides traditional party labels.

But consider another district in which 30 percent of voters are Republican, 30 percent are Democratic, and 40 percent describe themselves as independent. Here the campaign will likely target the broad swath of independents. This was the case in the Nevada U.S. Senate race in 2010, where the incumbent Democrat, Harry Reid, defeated the Republican challenger, Sharron Angle. Angle's ties to the Tea Party movement and her unorthodox views on several issues helped Reid paint her as an extremist. He won 57 percent of independents en route to a surprisingly easy win.

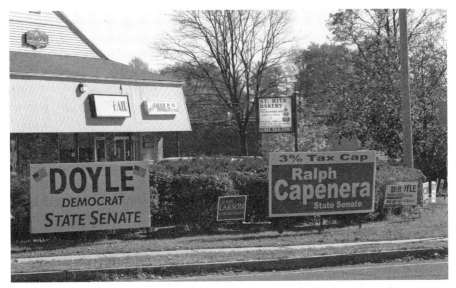

When campaign strategists target voters, they look closely at the partisan make-up of the district. Based on this information, the campaign's strategy can emphasize mobilizing voters from the candidate's party or winning over independent voters (or even some voters from the opposing party).

Although both state and national factors matter, they are not all-powerful. For example, Brown (a Republican) won in arguably the most Democratic of states. Reid (a Democrat) won in a year when Republicans swept the House and almost took the Senate. The dominance of the Democratic Party in Massachusetts and the sour national mood in 2010 (both of which contribute to what we refer to as the political "reality" of a given election) shaped their respective campaign strategies, but both campaigns were able to target and mobilize electoral majorities.

Strategic Campaign Decisions

Thus far we have emphasized the nature of strategy but have said little about how it influences the specific decisions that face every political campaign. We now examine a range of strategic decisions that face most campaigns, paying particular mind to the similarities and differences between campaign professionals and political scientists in how they think about these decisions.

The Decision to Run

We are so used to thinking about who wins and loses elections that sometimes we forget an important prior question: who decides to run for office in the first place? Elections are significantly shaped by who chooses to run and who sits things out. For example, in 1992, New York governor Mario Cuomo's decision not to run for president opened the door to Arkansas governor Bill Clinton. In 1996, General Colin Powell's decision not to run all but assured Kansas senator Bob Dole of the nomination. In 2004, former vice president Al Gore decided not to run, enhancing the prospects for Massachusetts senator John Kerry. In 2008, Vice President Dick Cheney and former Virginia governor George Allen never considered running for president, helping to make Arizona senator John McCain a front-runner. The effect of these decisions—while most obvious at the presidential level—is felt in races at all levels.

Political consultants and political scientists have similar views about what drives the decision to run. When thinking about whether to run for office, there are several important factors for a candidate and her advisers to consider. One is *motivation*. Does the candidate want to run for office, or is she being dragged reluctantly into the fray? While we tend to think of politicians as uniformly ambitious, many are ambivalent about moving up the political ladder. For example, an incumbent might prefer his current position to running for higher office and potentially losing. If local and statewide offices are prestigious and attractive, fewer talented politicians will want to seek higher office.[4] A concrete example of ambivalence comes from the 2008 presidential campaign. After the election was over, the campaign manager for Representative Ron Paul, a candidate for the Republican nomination, said of Paul, "We couldn't get him for six months to say that he wanted to be president."[5] For candidates who do want to run, it is also important to understand the reasons that they want to run. Their motivations—duty to country, particular policy goals, and so on—will help inform strategic campaign decisions.

In gauging motivation, it is also important to know how the candidate's family feels about her candidacy. For example, does she have a spouse who is willing to assist and endure the campaign? Does she have children? Is she willing to move the family around and use them in the campaign? Maybe more to the point, is the candidate willing to endure the potentially embarrassing scrutiny of her immediate and extended family? And does she have secrets that she would like to keep from her family? A concern about separation from his children was one thing that made Barack Obama hesitate

---

[4] Cherie Maestas, Sarah A. Fulton, L. Sandy Maisel, and Walter J. Stone. 2006. "When to Risk It? Institutions, Ambitions, and the Decision to Run for the U.S. House." *American Political Science Review* 100: 195–208.

[5] Institute of Politics. 2009. *Campaign for President: The Managers Look at 2008.* New York: Rowman & Littlefield, p. 22.

before declaring his candidacy in 2008. One of his advisers, David Plouffe, told an audience after the campaign, "He's got young kids and he's very close to them. That was really the biggest hurdle—could he reconcile his desire to see his family a lot?"[6]

A second factor to consider is *resources*. Perhaps the most important question here is whether the candidate can raise money. As we discussed in Chapter 4, the American system of campaign finance puts the onus of fund-raising on the candidate, and little can be accomplished without money on hand. Besides money, other resources that affect a candidate's decision to run include credentials (has the potential candidate held an office that gives her relevant experience?) and time (can she take time off work and away from her family to campaign effectively?).

A third factor is whether the candidate can assemble a campaign organization. Does she have an experienced, enthusiastic staff? Is there adequate outside help available, or have the best pollsters, consultants, media people, and field organizers already committed to other campaigns? Modern-day campaign organizations often look like small armies. It is ideal to put an organization in place at the beginning of the campaign.

A final factor for a candidate and advisers to consider in deciding whether to run is the *opportunity* (or lack thereof) presented in the election. Opportunities derive from the realities that candidates face at a particular time and place. Opportunities are crucial because they often determine *when* a candidate will run, as opposed to whether she has a general inclination to run. Smart candidates will wait until the odds are in their favor. The probability of winning is especially affected by the realities of the election. What is the makeup of the electorate? For example, would the candidate be willing to run when the electorate is primarily composed of members of the opposite party? And what is the nature of the competition? Will the candidate face a competitive primary challenger? Will she face a competitive general election opponent? What are the resources that the opponents have? What about conditions in the country? How is the economy doing? How popular is the incumbent president? All of these things may influence whether the candidate feels she can win.

The role of opportunity suggests that candidates can be thought of as "strategic politicians."[7] In some ways, potential candidates are rational actors looking to maximize the chances that they will win. Given the costs of

---

[6] Institute of Politics, 2009, p. 29.

[7] Gary C. Jacobson and Samuel Kernell. 1983. *Strategy and Choice in Congressional Elections.* New Haven: Yale University Press.

running, and the potential damage to their reputation if they run and lose, they are unlikely to run unless they believe there is a significant chance they will win. Thus, strategic politicians rarely challenge dominant incumbents, rarely run in a district where they are outnumbered by partisans from the other side, and rarely run if the prevailing national mood is against their party.[8] Conversely, they look for races where the incumbent is retiring or weak. They tend to run in districts where most voters share their party affiliation. They tend to run if there is a national tide favoring their party. This mentality creates something of a self-fulfilling prophecy: strategic politicians rarely run unless they calculate favorable odds, so incumbents almost never face tough competition unless other factors are decidedly against them. To be sure, not every candidate will appear rational. There are plenty of quixotic campaigns being waged every election year. But there are still strong incentives for politicians to think strategically about the decision to run.

Political science research on the decision to run suggests that three of these factors—motivation, resources, and opportunity—matter simultaneously. A good example comes from the research of Jennifer Lawless and Richard Fox on why so few women hold elective office, relative to their share of the population. This research has shown that, although women candidates are as likely as male candidates to win elections, they are less likely than men to run in the first place. In part, this is a question of motivation. Women report less enthusiasm for the rigors of campaigning, such as fund-raising. They also seem to perceive themselves as lacking in resources. One of these is their credentials: women are less likely than men to see themselves as qualified. Another resource is time: even women who are employed full time in high-status professions, such as law or business, report spending more time on household tasks and child care than do men in similar professions. Finally, they see fewer opportunities. Relative to men, they are more likely to believe that elections in their community are competitive, that raising money will be difficult, and that female candidates are less likely to win.[9]

---

[8] Candidates will occasionally run for office even though their prospects are not good. Sometimes they run because the upside of victory is enough to offset the downside of a loss. Long-shot presidential candidates fall into this category. At other times, candidates run in order to lay the groundwork for a later run for office. For example, up-and-coming Texas Republican Ted Cruz (the former solicitor general) challenged the much-better-known and well-financed Lieutenant Governor David Dewhurst for the 2012 GOP Senate nomination, possibly calculating that even a losing effort could enhance his status with the public and fund-raisers. (Cruz won the primary and general elections.)

[9] Jennifer Lawless and Richard Fox. 2005. *It Takes a Candidate: Why Women Don't Run for Office*. New York: Cambridge University Press.

Issue Priorities

Perhaps the most obvious strategic question of a campaign involves issues. Which issues should a candidate emphasize? Candidates select issues for their campaign agenda with care and then seek to emphasize only those issues—"staying on message," as the saying goes. Choosing issue priorities is a critical strategic decision because candidates want to control the campaign agenda wherever possible. Some issues will work to a candidate's advantage, and some will not. A candidate who keeps the focus on issues where the public favors her policy positions may win over persuadable voters and perhaps win the election. For example, in the 2008 presidential election Barack Obama wanted to focus attention on the economy, health care, and the Bush administration's handling of Iraq, while John McCain wanted to focus on national security, taxes, and limiting government. In some ways, the main fight in the campaign was more about the agenda than specific proposals. Once most Americans decided the election was a referendum on the state of the economy, Obama (arguably) had won.

Campaign consultants also believe strongly in the importance of agenda control. Many of them assume that citizens do not care much about politics and only pay attention to the "loudest" moments of the campaign. Thus, while citizens' perceptions are malleable, candidates only have a couple of shots at telling them what the election is about. The result is that campaigns focus on one or two issues, **framing** (or presenting) them in simple, easy-to-understand terms. Each side attempts to define what matters.

Why might candidates choose some issues and not others? Here, the reality that candidates confront is crucial. Events outside of their control put certain issues on the agenda, leading the public to prioritize those issues and leaving candidates little choice but to address them. In the 2004 presidential election, John Kerry and George W. Bush both felt compelled to talk about terrorism because of the terrorist attacks of September 11, 2001, and the ongoing war in Iraq. In the 2012 presidential election, both Obama and Mitt Romney talked a great deal about the economy. The issue was nettlesome for both sides, as Obama had been unable to turn the economy around in his first term, while many still blamed Romney's Republican Party for the collapse of 2008. Still, when certain issues become national priorities, as the economy did in 2012, it is common to see opposing candidates have similar agendas.

Candidates also base their agendas on the traditional strengths of their parties. In Chapter 1, we noted that the reputation a political party has developed for attention to a particular issue gives that party greater credibility on the issue. This example of a reality of campaigns and elections is known as **issue ownership**, a term that suggests that parties come to "own" issues because of their reputations.[10] Observers would typically say that the Republican Party owns the issues of national security, taxes, and crime, while the Democratic Party owns health care, education, and entitlement programs like Social Security and Medicare.

If candidates emphasized only the issues their party owns, then we would expect to see them talking past each other, rather than engaging one another on the issues. In reality, although candidates sometimes put greater emphasis on their party's "owned" issues, they often talk about all sorts of other issues, even those "belonging to" the other party.[11] In part, this is because national events demand it. Also, strategic candidates may be able to frame any issue in a way that is favorable to them. In the 1996 presidential election, Democrat Bill Clinton discussed the issue of crime, which had been traditionally seen as an area where the Republican Party had an advantage, by emphasizing prevention strategies, such as community policing, rather than punishment strategies, such as longer prison sentences.[12]

Campaign agendas are also influenced by the candidate's own personal experiences and reputation. Regardless of the reputation of their party, candidates often develop areas of policy interest, expertise, and accomplishments. They can talk credibly about these issues by highlighting their own achievements. For example, in the 2000 presidential election, George W. Bush emphasized education a great deal, even though this was supposedly an issue owned by the Democratic Party. As governor of Texas, he had worked to improve primary and secondary education, and he believed that the state's progress gave him the credibility he needed to "trespass" on the Democrats' territory. Although personal experience can matter, candidates do discuss many issues about which they have limited expertise or experience. This again suggests that candidates are confident that they can frame issues in favorable ways, no matter what the reality is.

Issue Positions

While formulating their agendas, candidates also have to determine what positions they should take on these issues. In doing so, they face a choice: Should they simply take a position that is popular with citizens, or should they seek to persuade citizens to adopt their own point of view?

---

[10] John R. Petrocik. 1996. "Issue Ownership in Presidential Elections, with a 1980 Case Study." *American Journal of Political Science* 40: 825–50.

[11] John Sides. 2006. "The Origins of Campaign Agendas." *British Journal of Political Science* 36, 3: 407–36.

[12] David B. Holian. 2004. "He's Stealing My Issues! Clinton's Crime Rhetoric and the Dynamics of Issue Ownership." *Journal of Politics* 26: 95–124.

FIGURE 5.1 The Median Voter Theorem

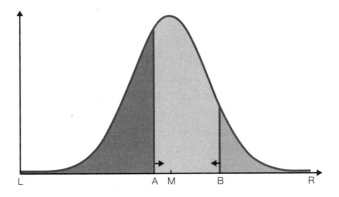

The logic of taking popular positions can be explained using the **median voter theorem**.[13] This theorem assumes that voters can be arrayed on a spectrum that captures the range of positions on a particular issue—from, say, liberal to conservative. Candidates seek to position themselves on that spectrum nearest to the hypothetical voter who would provide the winning vote for them: the median voter. The median voter is the person who falls in the exact middle of the spectrum. That is, half of all voters are more liberal than this hypothetical person and half are more conservative. The candidate who wins the median voter, as well as all of those voters who are on the same side as the candidate, wins the election.

A diagram may help to illustrate. The bell-shaped curve in Figure 5.1 represents how many voters are positioned at each point along this spectrum, arrayed from left ("L") to right ("R"). The median voter is labeled "M." The two candidates are labeled "A" and "B." Currently, Candidate A appeals to more voters than Candidate B because he is closer to the median voter M. Both candidates could improve their support by adopting policy positions that move them closer to M.

The median voter theorem may seem too abstract to guide campaign strategy. After all, campaigns want to appeal to real voters, not some hypothetical median voter. However, the basic logic of the median voter theorem is quite evident in how campaign professionals and political commentators think about campaigns. For example, we often hear about candidates who are "moving to the center," with the presumption that this enables them to

---

[13] Anthony Downs. 1957. *An Economic Theory of Democracy*. New York: Harper & Row; Harold Hotelling. 1929. "Stability in Competition." *Economic Journal* 39, 153: 41–57.

appeal to more "moderate" or "independent" or "swing" voters whose support would allow them to win the election.

There are several reasons that the prediction of the median voter theorem might not hold true. For one, candidates are constrained in the positions they take. If moving toward the median voter means contradicting some previous position, then the candidate may damage his credibility and risk earning a label like "flip-flopper"—as with John Kerry in 2004 and Mitt Romney in 2012.

Candidates also have different constituencies to appeal to, with views that often differ from those of the hypothetical median voter. Candidates must raise money by appealing to donors, recruit volunteers by appealing to activists, and earn endorsements by appealing to interest groups. Donors, activists, and interest groups tend to have very strong opinions about political issues—opinions that are often more ideologically extreme than those of the average citizen. Taking moderate positions on issues may have more costs than benefits if it alienates ideologically driven supporters.

The challenge of appealing to multiple constituencies with different opinions may lead candidates to avoid specific positions on issues. In Chapter 3, we noted that American campaigns have often centered on biography and personality, offering only vague platitudes about political issues. There may be advantages for candidates in this, even though it seems counter to the conventional wisdom that candidates must take clear stands on the issues. Keeping their positions vague allows candidates to say things that are unobjectionable and popular—"I want to save Social Security" or "Our children need a good education." Various constituencies may interpret such statements as endorsing their particular positions, even when candidates have not done so explicitly. Candidates who take vague positions also provide less for the media and opposing candidates to pick apart. Studies of campaigns find that ambiguity is common and that, consequently, citizens often do not know candidates' positions on specific issues.[14]

This lack of knowledge among citizens points to one final problem with the median voter theorem: it assumes that citizens know where they stand on issues, know where the candidates stand, and vote accordingly. But as we noted earlier, there is reason to suppose that the average citizen is not that attentive to the campaign or to politics generally. Certainly many campaign professionals believe this, and much political science research supports this view. In Chapter 12, we discuss the assumption of the median voter theorem, as well as the strategies by which voters choose candidates, in more detail.

---

[14] Benjamin Page. 1978. *Choices and Echoes in Presidential Campaigns.* Chicago: University of Chicago Press.

If the average citizen does not assess the candidates based on their issue positions, then candidates may be empowered to pursue another strategy: attempting to persuade voters to support their positions on issues. Whether candidates can do so speaks to a more general question: the ability of campaigns to affect what citizens think. Just as candidates attempt to frame the election around particular issues, they would like to persuade citizens to adopt their positions on those issues. In Chapter 12, we discuss at greater length how successfully candidates can do this. As we will see, campaign consultants and political scientists come to somewhat different conclusions on this question, with political scientists more skeptical than campaign consultants about how much candidates can change public opinion.

Whether to Attack

Few things attract more attention during campaigns than attacks, which may come from candidates, parties, interest groups, and others. Despite the apparent proliferation of attacks, whether to campaign negatively—or "go negative"—is a complex decision that is largely contingent upon the reality of the race.

Negative campaigning can be defined simply as any criticism leveled by supporters of one candidate against the opposing candidate.[15] By contrast, **positive campaigning** (sometimes called "advocacy") focuses only on the background, record, and views of the sponsoring candidate. Of course, campaigns are not limited to one or the other. A campaign message or advertisement may mix positive and negative information. Such advertisements, sometimes called **contrast advertisements**, focus on the differences—in qualifications, record, or issue positions—of the main candidates in the race.

Campaigns make decisions about other specific aspects of a negative message. One aspect is a campaign's content: Should the negative ads criticize a candidate for her stand on issues that concern voters, or for her personal qualities? Another aspect is civility: Should a negative campaign be critical but respectful, or is it useful to be ugly or mean-spirited? However, in this discussion, we simply focus on the general question of whether to campaign negatively, and not on specific questions about how to do so.

According to some political scientists and many campaign practitioners, the main factor affecting whether to attack is the political reality surrounding the race: in particular, which candidate is the front-runner and which the underdog. The candidate who is ahead in the polls is less likely to attack than the candidate who is behind. This finding emerges in both academic research

---

[15] John G. Geer. 2006. *In Defense of Negativity: Attack Ads in Presidential Campaigns.* Chicago: University of Chicago Press, p. 23.

and in a survey of campaign consultants.[16] For this reason, incumbents are less likely to attack than their opposition. Only if support for the opposing candidate appears to be increasing would an incumbent seek to define him via negative campaigning. For example, an incumbent with a lot of political baggage who is facing a well-financed, impressive challenger may wish to go negative before the challenger begins campaigning in earnest. This happened in the 2010 Senate race in Nevada, when the incumbent, Harry Reid, aired early **attack ads** against the challenger, Sharron Angle. Little-known challengers, or any candidates lagging in the race, may feel they need to attack. Many challengers are not well known in their districts. Yet challengers run little risk of further increasing the incumbent's name recognition advantage by airing negative ads because incumbents are already well known in their districts. Moreover, attacking the incumbent raises doubts about his fitness for office and can open the door for a challenger. Attacks on the incumbent are also more likely than positive campaign messages to draw news media coverage.[17]

Although it seems like common sense to advise front-runners to stay positive and underdogs to go negative, large-scale studies of campaign messages and advertisements in American presidential elections suggest that front-runners and underdogs do not always follow this advice.[18] Sometimes incumbents run campaigns that are more negative than the challengers'. Indeed, it is not uncommon for candidates well ahead in the polls to pound away on the underdog. In the 1964 election, Democrat Lyndon Johnson had a commanding lead throughout the campaign, but still relentlessly attacked the Republican candidate, Barry Goldwater.

There's another potential issue with negative campaigning: it may not actually win votes. As we will see in Chapters 11 and 12, it is far from certain that negative advertising affects whether citizens vote or for whom they vote. Ultimately, there is enough uncertainty with regard to who should go negative and to what extent negative campaigning affects voters to produce a wide range of professional opinion on the matter.

Where to Campaign

Whether a candidate is running for president or for city council, the decision about where to deploy precious campaign resources is always hotly debated. Should the presidential candidate go to Florida or to Ohio for that last-minute

---

[16] Stergios Skaperdas and Bernard Grofman. 1995. "Modeling Negative Campaigning." *American Political Science Review* 89: 49–61; John Theilman and Allen Wilhite. 1998. "Campaign Tactics and the Decision to Attack." *Journal of Politics* 60, 4: 1050–62.

[17] Travis N. Ridout and Glen R. Smith. 2008. "Free Advertising: How the Media Amplify Campaign Messages." *Political Research Quarterly* 61, 4: 598–608.

[18] Geer, *In Defense of Negativity*; Emmett H. Buell, Jr., and Lee Sigelman. 2009. *Attack Politics: Negativity in Presidential Campaigns since 1960*, 2nd ed. Lawrence: University of Kansas Press.

campaign stop? Should the city council candidate have greeted voters entering the polls in Precinct 1 or to Precinct 4? The assumption shared by consultants and scholars is that a campaign's resources must be allocated strategically to achieve maximum effect.

After George W. Bush's re-election in 2004, campaign consultants began to refer to his model of campaigning as the **Bush model**, in contrast to the **Clinton model** of former president Bill Clinton.[19] The Bush model focuses on mobilizing partisans. In the 2004 presidential election, Bush's campaign worked exceptionally hard to identify and reach out to Bush supporters in places like the Florida panhandle and southern Ohio. These people, the Bush team assumed, would probably vote for Bush if they could be persuaded to turn out. Much of the campaign was therefore targeted at supportive areas where turnout and enthusiasm lagged.

By contrast, the Clinton model focuses on persuading independent and weakly partisan voters. Prior to the 1996 presidential election, Clinton's team developed a series of issue positions that were tailored to the sensibilities of these voters. These were not necessarily the "big" issues of the day, but rather a series of minor but symbolically important concerns, such as school uniforms to combat gang activities and additional federal funding for municipal police. These issues and positions were then communicated in an extensive television advertising campaign during the summer of 1995 that targeted top media markets with large numbers of independent voters.

There are, of course, combinations of the Bush and Clinton models. Most campaigns seek to mobilize partisans *and* persuade independents. To do so, they rely on detailed plans for allocating resources. As discussed earlier, most major campaigns use polling and voter identification data to estimate the number of persuadable voters in their state or county. They can then price out the cost of a visit or television ad in that state or county, and calculate the price per persuadable voter. A campaign is thus able to rank-order all states or counties (or precincts) by cost-effectiveness, and can allocate dollars based on this ranking. Other factors may induce a campaign to visit a certain county or advertise in a certain market, but professional campaigns tend to adhere closely to their analytical rankings. Political science research confirms this.[20] For example, research on presidential campaigns from 1992 through 2008 shows that television advertising expenditures were mostly based on price-per-persuadable-voter estimates.[21] Campaigns below the

---

[19] Mark Halperin and John F. Harris. 2008. *The Way to Win*. New York: Random House.

[20] Daron R. Shaw. 2006. *The Race to 270*. Chicago: University of Chicago Press.

[21] Taofang Huang and Daron Shaw. 2009. "Beyond the Battlegrounds: Electoral College Strategies in the 2008 Election." *Journal of Political Marketing* 8, 4: 272–91.

presidential level are not as exacting in their deployment of resources. This is partly because the consulting talent, available data, and allocation options decrease with more localized elections, making it more difficult to develop and execute a rigorous plan for resource allocation.

How to Campaign

Should the campaign use its funds to run television advertisements on the broadcast networks? Or should it purchase cable television advertisements instead? Would radio advertisements would be better? Or maybe Internet advertisements? What about billboards, lawn signs, bumper stickers, and buttons? And how much time and effort should be spent on the ground game—face-to-face campaigning by the candidate, staff, and volunteers? These are nuts-and-bolts decisions that a campaign strategist must make. In some respects, they are questions of tactics as opposed to strategy. Tactics are the means by which strategic goals are accomplished and thus they are often driven by strategic calculations.

Tactics are most affected by available resources. Candidates would prefer to draw on as many tactics as possible—saturating every form of mass media with advertisements, for example—but often they cannot afford to do so. If candidates have enough money to run advertisements on broadcast television, which is the most expensive medium and also likely to reach the largest audience, then they will. If they do not, then the question becomes whether other mass media, such as cable television or radio, are affordable. Campaigns with even fewer resources often rely more on the ground game, which consists of personal campaigning by the candidate and outreach by volunteers, both door-to-door and over the phone. Well-funded campaigns will combine a ground game with the "air war" of advertising on radio and television.

In the past decade, there has been something of a renaissance of interest in the ground game. Both political consultants and political scientists believe that personal contact with potential voters is effective, especially if the contact is from familiar and credible sources of information, such as friends and neighbors—that old-fashioned door knocks and other forms of personal outreach are often more effective than direct mail or phone banks. Political science studies have confirmed this: personalized contact is much more effective than mail or telephone calls in mobilizing citizens to vote, although phone calls made by professional telemarketers can be effective, especially compared to phone calls with a pre-recorded voice.[22]

---

[22] Donald P. Green and Alan S. Gerber. 2004. *Get Out The Vote!* Washington, DC: Brookings Institution Press.

How Candidates (Try to) Use New Media

In Chapter 3, we saw how changes in technology affected fund-raising and volunteer-recruitment efforts. New forms of media, including those aimed at audiences on the Internet, are becoming increasingly prominent in other aspects of campaigns as well. Candidates, political parties, and interest groups create Web sites, blog about the campaign, and communicate with supporters via Facebook and Twitter.

Campaigns also often try to produce or push content that "goes viral," meaning it is redistributed continuously online and becomes fodder for the news. In the second presidential debate in 2012, for example, President Barack Obama countered Mitt Romney's comment that the U.S. "Navy is smaller now than at any time since 1917" with a zinger that won the night. "You mentioned the Navy, for example, and that we have fewer ships than we did in 1916," Obama told Romney. "Well, Governor, we also have fewer horses and bayonets, because the nature of our military's changed." The "horses and bayonets" comment delighted the Twittersphere: The hashtag #horsesandbayonets became the number one trend on Twitter in the United States and third in the world. At one point, the phrase was mentioned on Twitter nearly 60,000 times in one minute, according to data from Tospy, a social Web analytics tool. The Obama campaign capitalized on the traffic, buying the search term "Bayonets" on Twitter. Within minutes of Obama's comment, a "Horses and Bayonets" Tumblr featuring GIFs and images went live, and a Horses and Bayonets Facebook page already has more than 3,000 likes.

New media are valuable to candidates because these media empower citizens to produce their own content, giving them a sense of ownership in the campaign. In 2008, the recording artist will.i.am produced an online song and video called "Yes We Can," using footage from Obama's New Hampshire primary-night speech. The video was played millions of times on YouTube, won an Emmy award, and was eventually used by the campaign.

At the same time, this empowerment of citizens to produce their own content limits the control candidates have over their campaign message. In 2008, an employee of a Web site development firm working for the Obama campaign produced a Web video attacking Hillary Clinton that was uploaded to YouTube. The video borrowed from a 1984 Apple Computer ad that portrayed Microsoft as an authoritarian menace. The Obama campaign denied involvement and the employee was forced to resign. In another incident, Barack Obama offered free Web sites and blogs to his supporters at my.barackobama.com. Some users who objected to Obama's positions on civil liberties issues used these Web sites to blast Obama. Because the criticisms were coming from Obama supporters, the traditional media gave them more credence.

Candidates also must understand other limits of new media. They are unlikely to reach many undecided voters, as visitors to candidate Web sites are overwhelmingly committed supporters. Moreover, using new media to mobilize supporters is not always successful. Research has shown that sending e-mails to supporters does not necessarily make them more likely to register or vote.[1] In sum, new media give candidates a new array of tools but certainly no magic bullets. (We take a closer look at new media in campaigns and elections in Chapter 7.)

---

[1] David W. Nickerson. 2007. "Does Email Boost Turnout?" *Quarterly Journal of Political Science* 2, 4: 369–79.

In recent elections, both parties have invested significant resources in developing a field organization that can carry out personalized mobilizations. Union organizations arguably started this move in the 1998 and 2000 campaigns. Republican Party organizations, spooked by the Democrats' get-out-the-vote machine that built on the efforts of the unions, countered with their own volunteer efforts in 2002 and 2004. In 2008 and 2012, the Obama campaign created an extensive field organization of trained volunteers. In fact, the more modern, online forms of social networking—candidate Web sites, Facebook, and Twitter—are being used to drive the sorts of in-person outreach that, after the advent of television, had seemed like a thing of the past. For example, Steve Hildebrand, the deputy national campaign director for Obama's 2008 campaign, said, "We didn't make the assumption that people signing up on our Web site meant that they were going to help the candidate or even vote for him. From the beginning, we had an initiative to take our online force offline."[23]

Thus, offline forms of personal contact will likely continue to be significant, alongside online organizing and, in the case of advertising, on-air messages. For the moment, however, television advertising continues to be the linchpin of contemporary campaigns, especially in statewide and federal races.

Organizing for Strategic Success

The various strategic decisions we have discussed do not get made by themselves. When a candidate decides to run for office, she needs to identify knowledgeable people to help her design a strategy and then set up an organization so that important questions are decided and plans are implemented. But the fact that campaigns face common dilemmas in determining and implementing a strategy does not mean than there is one common solution; in fact, there is no such thing as a "typical" campaign. Campaigns vary in their resources: some have huge budgets and target millions of citizens, and some have tiny budgets and target hundreds or only dozens. Naturally, they will have diverse organizations as well. Moreover, although many campaign organizations include similar positions of authority—with strategists who (no surprise) are in charge of developing strategy and a campaign manager who is in charge of organizing the campaign and implementing the strategic plan—these positions do not always have the same job description or the same place in the organization's hierarchy. Campaign managers are not necessarily at the top

---

[23] Quoted in Tim Dickinson. 2008. "The Machinery of Hope." *Rolling Stone*, March 20. www .rollingstone.com/news/coverstory/19106326 (accessed 12/10/2010).

of the organization. A chief strategist is usually, but not always, a centrally important position. Political directors are typically in charge of organizing the field staff, but some engage in overall messaging strategy as well. Personal relationships can drive the structure of the organization, with positions created to accommodate specific people that the candidate wants for specific purposes.

It is instructive to examine briefly the campaign organizations of Mitt Romney and Barack Obama in the 2012 presidential race. Although presidential campaigns offer a "deluxe" example of what a campaign can be, smaller campaigns try to do many of the same things, if on a much smaller scale in terms of people and resources. The presidential campaign of the Republican nominee Mitt Romney evolved throughout the year. Initially, Romney's campaign team (Figure 5.2) moved from state to state as the GOP's primary season unfolded. After clinching the nomination, the organization in Boston was solidified and fleshed out below the top positions; additional senior advisers were added, with fundraising, paid media, and polling becoming focal points. Intent on avoiding the "who's in charge?" problems that plagued the McCain campaign throughout much of 2008, lines of authority for the Romney team

FIGURE 5.2 Mitt Romney's Presidential Campaign

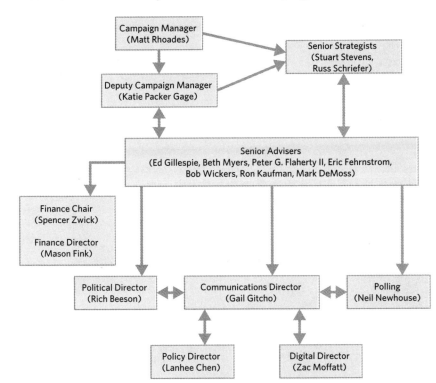

were clearly established, with Stuart Stevens serving as the point person for strategic decisions and Matt Rhoades serving as the final word on organization and staffing.

Barack Obama's 2012 presidential campaign, like his 2008 campaign, is best represented as a sort of loop (or circle), in which information flowed in a particular pattern but which also allowed different players to be involved in the decision-making process. Obama had numerous people serving in key positions, and it was not always clear who outranked whom (Figure 5.3). Nevertheless, David Axelrod, senior strategist, had the final say on most important decisions, while Jim Messina, the campaign manager, and David Plouffe, who was able to act as something of an overlord for the organizational apparatus, were usually deferred to on matters involving voter outreach, volunteers, and targeting. The Obama campaign thus maintained the traditional distinction between a campaign strategist and a campaign manager noted above: campaign strategists are usually in charge of developing a plan and honing the candidate's message, while campaign managers are usually in charge of running the day-to-day operations of the campaign.

FIGURE 5.3 Barack Obama's Presidential Campaign

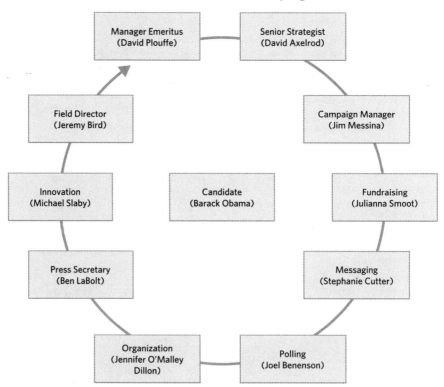

Who Are Campaign Strategists?

As described in Chapter 3, the modern American campaign is candidate-centered and dominated by television. This means that candidates recruit and develop their own advisers. The importance of television for communicating messages made people with expertise in public opinion and television advertising exceptionally valuable for candidates. As a consequence, a class of professional campaign consultants emerged in the 1950s; these professionals have become the main purveyors of strategic advice in American elections.

The Backgrounds of Campaign Strategists

Although the development of professional campaign consultants is relatively new, there have always been strategists in American campaigns. Alexander Hamilton may have been the most famous political consultant of the early days of the new republic, as he constantly schemed and plotted how to win elections for those who shared his federalist views. James Madison was only slightly less aggressive as Thomas Jefferson's top political strategist, although Jefferson himself was also an active strategist. Indeed, we could put together quite a catalog of campaign strategists from before the modern campaign era.

In today's campaigns, how does someone become a campaign consultant or strategist? First, there are those who become proficient at a specific campaign endeavor, and parlay this into a broader role crafting and overseeing strategy. For example, in the 1960s and 1970s, people with a background in public relations or consumer advertising were much sought after by campaigns, as candidates attempted to develop personal loyalty among constituents through persuasive self-promotion. Public relations and advertising professionals naturally favored using market research to drive messaging, and using mass media (especially television) to deliver these messages. Roger Ailes, who worked for Richard Nixon, Ronald Reagan, and George H. W. Bush, and is now president of Fox News, is a good example.

People with a background in journalism or speechwriting have also become successful strategists. Some have moved up by serving as the liaison between the candidates and the news media, while others have served as speechwriters before taking on the broader role of strategist. Democrats Bill Moyers (who served Lyndon Johnson) and Bob Shrum (who worked for eight Democratic presidential candidates, including Edward Kennedy and John Kerry) are prime examples.

Pollsters, who are trained in the art and science of ascertaining what the public is thinking, have also become campaign strategists. Doug Schoen, Bill Clinton's pollster, later served as Hillary Clinton's presidential campaign strategist. Bob Teeter, a legendary Republican pollster, served as George H. W. Bush's presidential campaign strategist and manager in 1992.

More recently, people who are good at direct mail or telemarketing campaigns have used this success as a way of becoming general strategists. Both of these activities require a strong sense of which voters the candidate should address and what messages move them. Republican strategist Karl Rove dominated direct mail campaigning in Texas before taking up much broader responsibilities for George W. Bush.

Finally, the emergence of campaign management schools has provided another route by which aspiring strategists can hone their craft. As yet, there are few examples of campaign school graduates becoming superstars, but the ranks of congressional and even presidential campaigns are now populated with people who cut their teeth at these academies.

A different path to becoming a campaign strategist consists of developing relationships with particular candidates and marshaling them through their political careers. These individuals may have only a few clients throughout their careers, but they play a major role for those clients. James A. Baker III built his career in law but entered politics at the urging of his friend George H. W. Bush. He served in the Ford, Reagan, and Bush administrations, but only in a handful of campaigns, the most prominent of which involved Bush. Baker's particular value to Bush was as someone who had his best interests at heart, someone who could tell him the unvarnished truth, and someone who knew his strengths and weaknesses inside out. Only Baker could have given Bush the salty advice described at the beginning of this chapter.

Regardless of their path into the business, professional campaign strategists have attained much greater visibility in recent decades and are even referred to as gurus. Their lionization can be traced to a classic work of campaign journalism, Theodore White's *The Making of the President*.[24] White's narrative of the 1960 campaign details the machinations of Robert Kennedy and other advisers to John F. Kennedy, noting their disciplined targeting of states and voting groups and aggressive voter registration strategy, among other things. White also discusses the opposing side, in particular Richard Nixon's disastrous pledge to campaign in all fifty states, and the challenge of attacking the elusive and charismatic Kennedy. The implication was clear—JFK's victory was, at least in part, due to the cool, methodical, professional campaign strategy developed by his team. The elevation of the strategist had begun, and soon many would become well known: Hamilton Jordan (for Jimmy Carter), Ed Rollins (for Ronald Reagan), James Baker and Lee Atwater (for George H. W. Bush), James

---

[24] Theodore S. White. 1964. *The Making of the President, 1960*. New York: Atheneum.

The "superstar" strategists of recent years have included David Axelrod, left, and Karl Rove, right. Axelrod is credited with helping Obama win in 2008 and now serves in the Obama administration, while Rove is known for devising George W. Bush's strategy in 2000 and 2004 and also went on to work in White House.

Carville and Dick Morris (for Bill Clinton in 1992 and 1996, respectively), Karl Rove (for George W. Bush), and David Axelrod (for Barack Obama in 2008).

Despite the visibility of superstar strategists, we know very little about their actual impact on contemporary elections. Commentaries like *The Selling of the President* have criticized the mass marketing techniques so often employed in contemporary campaigns, on the advice of consultants.[25] But little has been written on how much campaign consultants actually help candidates win. What evidence exists suggests that hiring consultants is no panacea.[26] In part, this may reflect how much both campaign strategy and election outcomes are constrained by the rules governing elections and the reality that candidates face. Political scientists are therefore less likely than campaign professionals to attribute the success of candidates to the strategic genius of their advisers. This skepticism is at the heart of the more general disagreement between campaign consultants and political scientists with respect to whether campaigns "matter."

Conclusion

In the run-up to the 2004 election, the Democratic presidential nominee, John Kerry, spent much of August dealing with allegations—aired mostly on talk radio, Internet blogs, and cable television—that he had inflated his Vietnam War service record. The source of these charges, a group calling itself Swift Boat Veterans for Truth, had taken advantage of a lull in the campaign season to grab the headlines and gain some attention. The Kerry campaign refused

---

[25] Joe McGinniss. 1969. *The Selling of the President*. New York: Simon & Schuster.

[26] Stephen Medvic. 2001. *Political Consultants in U.S. Congressional Elections*. Columbus: Ohio State University Press.

to engage the story for several days and then finally offered a halfhearted response, prompting further questions. Over the month of August, meanwhile, Kerry's three-point lead in the national polls disappeared, and in early September President George W. Bush came out of the Republican convention with a five-point lead he never relinquished. It is unclear whether Kerry's slide was caused by the Swiftboaters. It is also unclear whether a stronger, more forceful response would have helped him. But these questionable strategic and tactical choices by the Kerry campaign are the stuff of political legend.

In this chapter we have delineated what a campaign strategy is, discussed several key strategic decisions that campaigns make, and considered the perspectives of both campaign consultants and political scientists. We have also discussed how campaigns organize to make strategic decisions, and examined who campaign strategists are. The central notion is straightforward: campaign strategists want to win elections, and everything they do can be understood as a rational, if sometimes imperfect, effort to achieve this goal. Practitioners and academics tend to agree on many of the factors that candidates can and should consider when deciding if they should seek higher office, emphasize a particular issue, run an attack ad, or focus resources on a particular constituency. The central question, however, is how much these strategic decisions matter—a topic we will return to in subsequent chapters.

How should we view campaign strategy in light of the philosophical ideals spelled out in Chapter 1? We will explore this topic at greater length in

In 2008, a group called Swift Boat Veterans for Truth ran ads questioning presidential candidate John Kerry's record as a war hero in Vietnam. Was Kerry's hesitation in responding to these ads a fatal strategic mistake?

Chapter 13, but we can highlight one issue here. Intrinsic to campaign strategy is this notion: some citizens are more valuable than others. That is, campaigns routinely identify subsets of citizens to target—such as swing voters or voters in a certain geographic area—and ignore many others. This approach may run counter to several ideals. The laserlike focus of campaigns on partisan supporters or swing voters or any other groups may violate the ideal of political equality. Of course, we are most concerned that citizens are equal in the eyes of the law, not in the eyes of campaign consultants. Nevertheless, this decision involves a trade-off of values. Similarly, targeted voters inevitably receive much more information about the campaign than do other voters, challenging the ideal of deliberation. The information that voters receive clearly differs depending on whether they are the targets of a campaign's strategy. That campaign strategy may fail to live up to these ideals reflects this simple fact: campaign strategy is fundamentally about winning elections, not about upholding civic standards.

KEY TERMS

campaign strategy (p. 122)

vote targets (p. 122)

persuadable/swing votes (p. 122)

probability sample (p. 126)

focus groups (p. 126)

microtargeting (p. 127)

voter identification/voter ID calls (p. 127)

open seat (p. 128)

framing (p. 133)

issue ownership (p. 134)

median voter theorem (p. 135)

negative campaigning (p. 137)

positive campaigning (p. 137)

contrast advertisements (p. 137)

attack ads (p. 138)

Bush model (p. 139)

Clinton model (p. 139)

FOR DISCUSSION

1. Do campaigns attempt to convince all voters to support their candidate? Why or why not?

2. What factors influence whether or not a candidate chooses to run for an office?

3. Why are challengers more likely than incumbents to run negative advertisements?

4. How has the rise of public opinion polling influenced campaigns?

 Visit StudySpace for quizzes and other review material.
wwnorton.com/studyspace

CHAPTER 6

Political Parties and Interest Groups

In 2006, Congressman Joe Schwarz of Michigan's 7th District was challenged in the Republican primary by Tim Walberg, a former state representative. Interest groups and party organizations spent more than $1 million on the race. President Bush, Senator John McCain, and the National Republican Congressional Committee (NRCC) supported Schwarz. The anti-tax group Club for Growth and Right to Life of Michigan supported the more conservative Walberg. Walberg beat Schwarz in the primary and prevailed in the general election. But two years later, he lost the congressional seat to Mark Schauer, a Democratic state senator. In fact, Schwarz, embittered by the continued intervention of interest groups, crossed party lines to endorse Schauer. Explaining his endorsement, Schwarz said: "I object to political dabblers who stand for nothing other than to create havoc and dabble in a congressional race where they truly have no interest. . . . The Club for Growth is in and I can't as a matter of principle stay out of it any longer."[1]

In 2010, while Schwarz considered an independent run for Michigan governor, Walberg sought to challenge Schauer in the congressional race. But the NRCC recruited Brian Rooney, the brother of a Florida congressman, to run against Walberg in the Republican primary. Most observers saw the primary as pitting ideological consistency against electability: Walberg was conservative but, given his 2008 loss, perhaps not electable. Walberg claimed the two goals were not in conflict: "My own loss came as a result of just a very bad election year. It was not because of my record."[2] The 2010 results seemed to prove him correct. In a better year for conservatives, Walberg won the Republican primary; in a better year for Republicans, he also won the general election and returned to Congress.

---

[1] Ken Thomas. 2008. "Former Rep. Endorses Schauer." *Associated Press*, September 3. www
.wilx.com/news/headlines/29959174.html (accessed 7/1/10).

[2] Gautham Nagesh. 2010. "GOP Primary in Michigan's 7th District Starting to Heat Up."
The Daily Caller, March 10. http://dailycaller.com/2010/03/10/gop-primary-in-michigans
-7th-district-starting-to-heat-up (accessed 7/1/10).

Why did conservative interest groups campaign against a Republican congressman in 2006, jeopardizing the party's chance of holding the seat? Why did the former congressman disavow his party's candidate in the following election? To be sure, this infighting is unusual; most of the time, party leaders, the party's candidates, and interest groups affiliated with that party are on the same side. The strategies of political parties and interest groups, however, can diverge from those of candidates. In this Michigan district, there were disagreements about the relative importance of ideology and electability and about which candidates would advance each goal.

Party organizations and interest groups often run their own campaigns, attempting to structure voting decisions and raise policy issues in order to influence election outcomes or claim credit for them. The involvement of parties and interest groups in campaigns can be long-term or short-term. Some groups are created for a single election. For example, as mentioned in Chapter 5, the Swift Boat Veterans for Truth aired campaign commercials in 2004 questioning John Kerry's military service. After the election, they merged with another group and then disbanded. By contrast, the liberal group MoveOn.org, which was originally created to respond to efforts to impeach President Clinton in 1998, has survived much longer. In 2004, it ran the first television ads to answer the Swiftboaters' charges, before the Kerry campaign had even responded. Party organizations and interest groups sometimes start their electoral efforts long before the beginning of any particular campaign. For instance, the Republican-affiliated organization GOPAC recruits and trains candidates to run for state and local offices. Under the leadership of Newt Gingrich, it was credited with helping to build the farm team of candidates that enabled the 1994 Republican takeover of Congress.

Parties and interest groups have diverse roles in campaigns — recruiting candidates, running advertisements, and mobilizing voters. Parties and interest groups also have a permanent place in American politics, helping to structure

Core of the Analysis

- Political parties and interest groups strategically intervene in elections by recruiting candidates, airing advertisements, and mobilizing voters.
- Political parties and interest groups have somewhat distinct motives from those of the candidates that they support.
- Political parties and interest groups have not lost much influence, despite attempts by some reformers to weaken them.
- Political parties and interest groups fall short of achieving some democratic values, but it is unlikely that democracy could function without them.

the competition between candidates in elections. They act as intermediaries between the public and officeholders. For example, there are citizens and candidates who think of themselves as environmentalists, and parties and interest groups help bring these individuals together. For most candidates and many voters, decisions about whom to support in any one election follow from more basic political decisions: selecting a party and deciding which interests to support.

In this chapter, we will address several questions about the role of political parties and interest groups in campaigns. What are political parties and interest groups and why do we have them? Why do we have so few parties and so many interest groups? How do parties and interest groups behave in campaigns? Is their influence rising or declining? In what circumstances is their influence most evident?

We will also consider broader questions about how parties and interest groups fit into American politics. How do parties and groups strategize about campaigns? How do electoral rules and broader political and economic realities influence their strategies? Each of these questions raises key philosophical concerns about parties and interest groups: Do they serve or undermine democratic values in campaigns? Even if Americans are dissatisfied with parties and interest groups, do viable alternatives exist? Are parties and interest groups just dabblers that "create havoc" in elections, as Schwarz complained, or are they important avenues for free speech that help guide public opinion? To address these questions about parties and interest groups, we first have to understand their behavior.

Political Parties

Political parties are groups of people with the shared interest of electing public officials under a common label. The two major political parties in the United States, the Democrats and the Republicans, share this goal; they compete to win elections. Each party has policy goals, of course, but it is their electoral goals that unite parties and distinguish them from other kinds of groups.

American political parties are nevertheless amorphous groups, including everyone from elected officials to fund-raisers to individual voters. It can be difficult to answer seemingly straightforward questions about political parties. For example, who is in charge of the Democratic and Republican parties? The president is usually the most prominent spokesperson for his party; during presidential campaigns, the presidential nominees generally have this role. Barack Obama became the leader of the Democratic Party in 2008 as the party's nominee for president, although he held no formal position within the party organization. When a party loses a presidential election, it often creates a leadership vacuum that is not filled until four years later. Thus, it was difficult to determine who was in charge of the Republican Party following the 2008 election. The closest to an official head, Republican National Committee (RNC) Chairman Reince Priebus, was elected in 2011 as a largely unknown candidate running on the promise that he would be different from Michael Steele, the previous chairman, who was dogged by controversy. (In the most notorious episode, Steele had to explain a $2,000 RNC expenditure at a bondage-themed West Hollywood topless nightclub in 2010.) Yet Priebus does not run any government departments, vote in Congress, or appear on voter ballots. Senate Minority Leader Mitch McConnell and House Speaker John Boehner are the governing heads of the Republican Party. Yet reporters have often looked to former vice presidential candidate Sarah Palin or talk show host Rush Limbaugh to represent the views of the Republican Party. In 2010, former RNC chairman Ed Gillespie and political operative Karl Rove even created several organizations that competed with the RNC by raising money for Republican Party candidates. The Republican Party also has separate chairs for its House and Senate campaign committees and state parties. If the RNC chair is not in charge, who is?

It is equally unclear who the members of parties are. If your friend says that she is a Republican, this does not necessarily mean that she holds any official title in the party or is even officially registered with the party. In many states, individuals do not need to register with a political party in order to vote in that party's primary; in some states, there is no official party registration at all.

Who Speaks for the Republican Party? a. House Speaker John Boehner and Senate minority leader Mitch McConnell; b. Republican National Committee Chairman Reince Priebus; c. Conservative radio talk show host Rush Limbaugh; d. 2008 Republican vice presidential candidate Sarah Palin; or someone else?

Perhaps we should consider anyone who thinks of himself or herself as a Democrat or Republican to be a member of the party. Yet political scientists have found that even people who view themselves as unaffiliated with either party often vote consistently for one party's candidates. The same is true of elected officials who call themselves independent. As of 2012, two U.S. senators, Bernie Sanders of Vermont and Angus King of Maine, were listed as Independents, but both work with the Democratic leadership.

To make sense of political parties, the political scientist V. O. Key suggested three manifestations of political parties: the **party-in-the-electorate**, the

TABLE 6.1 Three Aspects of the Major American Parties		
Aspect of Party	**Democrats**	**Republicans**
Party-in-the-electorate	• Democratic registrants • People who identify themselves as Democrats • Democratic primary voters • Democratic general election voters	• Republican registrants • People who identify themselves as Republicans • Republican primary voters • Republican general election voters
Party-as-organization	• Democratic National Committee • Democratic Senate Campaign Committee • Democratic Congressional Campaign Committee • State and local party committees	• Republican National Committee • Republican National Senate Committee • Republican National Campaign Committee • State and local party committees
Party-in-government	• President (Barack Obama) • Senate Majority Leader (Harry Reid) • House Minority Leader (Nancy Pelosi)	• Senate Minority Leader (Mitch McConnell) • Speaker of the House (John Boehner)

party-as-organization, and the **party-in-government**.[3] The party-in-the-electorate includes all citizens who identify with the party. This is where your friend who claims to be a Republican would fit. The party-as-organization comprises the institutions that administer party affairs, including the official bodies that raise funds and create the rules for the party. This is where Priebus and the RNC fit. The party-in-government consists of the elected leaders and appointed government officials who shape party policy goals. This is where Obama, McConnell, Boehner, and other members of Congress fit. Each of these manifestations of the party is somewhat independent of the others. Partisans in the electorate do not decide how party leaders operate. Reince Priebus speaks for the party organization, but he cannot tell Republican senators how to vote. In studying campaigns and elections, we pay most attention to the party-as-organization, which assists the candidates, and the party-in-the-electorate, which votes for them.

Why Do We Have Parties?

Parties have the potential to help make democratic government work. Parties can facilitate democracy in several ways. First, they aggregate and articulate

---

[3] V.O. Key, Jr. 1952. *Politics, Parties and Pressure Groups*, 3rd ed. New York: Crowell.

interests. Every citizen and politician has his or her own interests and ideas, but democracy requires that they work with others in order to achieve these goals. Parties help individuals to decide which of their principles and goals are most important and to find people that agree with them. Second, parties organize coalitions. If every ethnic, religious, and economic group nominated its own candidates, it would be difficult for any group to obtain a majority of the vote. Parties enable groups to unite under broader umbrellas. Third, parties coordinate elections and mobilize voters. Without them, candidates would have to convince voters individually that they share their views; and they would have to mobilize their own constituencies. Party labels make it is easier for voters to form opinions about the candidates. Fourth, parties coordinate the legislative process. While this role is not as important for elections, it does allow voters to learn how their vote will likely translate into public policy. Finally, parties facilitate collective political action. Both electing candidates and governing require individuals to work together, and parties provide a crucial means by which people join together in pursuit of shared goals.

Just because parties have the potential to serve the interests of democracy, however, does not mean this is the reason they were created. Most of the Founders feared parties, even as they later participated in them. As he left office, George Washington warned of "the baneful effects of the spirit of party." Nevertheless, political parties quickly developed and took on increasingly important roles in American government. Political parties serve the needs of politicians.[4] Politicians with shared interests and policy goals want durable legislative majorities in order to pass legislation. They also want a reputation or "brand" that voters recognize and can use when voting. They need an infrastructure that helps persuade and mobilize voters during elections. Parties serve all of these functions. Political parties also developed to promote the policy goals of various interest groups.[5] Interest groups often affiliate with political parties in order to advance their policy goals. By working through a party, interest groups seek to influence which candidates the party nominates and which candidate ultimately wins each election. The alternative to a political party—negotiating with individual candidates and legislators to support a group's agenda—is simply far more costly. Individual candidates could easily play one group off the other, essentially supporting whichever group would provide them the most benefit.

---

[4] John Aldrich. 1995. *Why Parties?* Chicago: University of Chicago Press.

[5] Marty Cohen, David Karol, Hans Noel, and John Zaller. 2008. *The Party Decides: Presidential Nominations Before and After Reform.* Chicago: University of Chicago Press.

What About Third Parties?

The United States has had two major parties for most of its history. Since 1864, the Republicans and Democrats have dominated competition for national office. It is rare for any candidate not affiliated with either major party to get elected to federal office. At the presidential level, the most successful third-party or independent candidates have won at best a handful of states and thus come up woefully short in the Electoral College. This was true for such candidates as Theodore Roosevelt, who ran as the Progressive Party nominee in 1912; Strom Thurmond, who ran as the States' Rights Democratic Party (or Dixiecrat) nominee in 1948; and George Wallace, who ran as the American Independent Party's nominee in 1968. Roosevelt won only seven states. Thurmond and Wallace did not win any states outside the Deep South. More recently, an independent candidate, Ross Perot, won 19 percent of the popular vote but no electoral votes in 1992. Consumer advocate Ralph Nader received only 2.7 percent of the popular vote as the Green Party candidate in 2000 and less than 1 percent as an independent candidate in 2004.

The primary difficulties third parties have in U.S. elections are posed by the rules of the electoral system. As discussed in Chapter 2, the use of single-member districts and plurality elections favors congressional candidates from the two major parties. Plurality voting within the Electoral College—whereby the candidate who wins the most votes in each state wins all of that state's electoral votes—hurts the chances of national third parties or independent candidates at the presidential level. There are other legal hurdles for third parties, including requirements for getting on the ballot (see Chapter 2). With the playing field tilted so strongly against them, third parties routinely find it difficult to attract media coverage, raise money, recruit experienced candidates, or earn a seat in candidate debates. Moreover, the major parties frequently adapt to a third-party threat, thereby neutralizing it. At the state and local levels, the Democratic and Republican parties often conform to the local political terrain. This makes it hard for a third party to develop a regional base of support. For example, the fact that local and state candidates in the South can and will conform to the South's conservative political culture makes it difficult for a new and strongly conservative party to take root in that region.

Despite these difficulties, third parties and independent candidates are sometimes successful. Some do get elected to office. For example, the Green Party and the Libertarian Party have elected more than 200 officeholders between them, mostly in local elections. Third parties and independent candidates can also influence the issues discussed in campaigns. Both the Democrats and the Republicans, felt compelled to respond to Ross Perot's

BOX 6.1

What Is the Tea Party?

In 2009, thousands of activists organized protests and attended congressional town hall meetings to oppose Obama's policy agenda, including health care reform legislation. In the 2010 and 2012 elections, they supported several candidates and were credited with changing election outcomes. They called themselves the "Tea Party movement," emphasizing their link to the values of the American founders by evoking the Boston Tea Party.

Is the Tea Party a viable alternative to the two major parties? Many Tea Party activists consider themselves independents. They opposed the Republican Party's preferred candidate in several elections, including the 2010 Delaware primary where incumbent Republican congressman Mike Castle was defeated by the Tea Party favorite Christine O'Donnell (pictured here). Some were previously active in third parties like the Libertarian Party, the Constitution Party, and the American Independent Party. They supported the Conservative Party candidate in New York's 23rd congressional district in 2010.

But in other respects, the Tea Party movement substantially overlaps with the Republican Party. Attendees at Tea Party events in 2009 were more likely to consider themselves Republicans than Democrats. Republican respondents to public opinion polls are consistently more supportive of their activities. Former and current Republican Party activists and consultants helped organize their protests and campaigns. Republican officeholders and candidates spoke at their events. Most Tea Party activists want to support Republican candidates, rather than organize a third party. Their overall goal is not to

replace the Republican Party but to move it in a conservative direction.

If not a separate party, is the Tea Party movement an interest group? On the one hand, Washington interest groups like FreedomWorks and Americans for Tax Reform provided logistical support for their initial protests and their town hall meeting attendance strategy. Tea Party activists have also created several nonprofit organizations and PACs to fund candidates and intervene in elections. They also engage in lobbying. On the other hand, Tea Party activists have not coalesced around any one organized leadership. And they employ tactics that are more typical of social movements than of organized interest groups. The first Tea Party events were protests, and Tea Party activists describe themselves as learning from the civil rights movement and liberal activists who advocated similar tactics. In sum, the Tea Party movement remains something of a hybrid, featuring attributes of a political party, an interest group, and a social movement, but remaining largely aligned with or even part of the broader Republican Party.

concerns about the federal budget deficit in 1992. But this small amount of policy influence also makes third parties short-lived. One or both of the two major parties can adopt their issues and lure their supporters away.

What Role Do Parties Play in Campaigns?

Political parties play central roles in contemporary campaigns, with the party-in-the-electorate, the party-as-organization, and the party-in-government all having some impact on the electoral process. The vast majority of Americans identify with or lean toward either the Democratic or the Republican Party and vote loyally for candidates from their preferred party. This makes the partisan complexion of a district or state a central feature of the reality that candidates confront. In Chapter 5, we discussed how candidates and campaign consultants carefully count partisans of both camps as well as independent or undecided voters when planning their campaign strategy. The party-in-the-electorate is important in another way: it forms the volunteer base of each party. Party volunteers knock on doors, make phone calls, and talk to others in support of their party's candidates. In local elections for city council, school board, or county commission, volunteer networks and party activists are often the only visible party involvement.

The Role of the Party Organization The party-as-organization plays a central role in political campaigns. Party organizations such as the national committees, state committees, and legislative campaign committees recruit candidates and raise money for them. Recruiting candidates is harder than it might seem. In 2012, more than 32 members of the House of Representatives and 2,400 state legislative candidates faced no opposition candidate from the other party. Parties try to recruit quality candidates who are well known to the electorate and have relevant experience for the office they seek. Candidates who have previously held elected office are much more likely to win future elections, so they are often the first people party organizations try to draft. Parties also work to minimize retirements within their ranks, because incumbents are more likely to win elections than newcomers.

Traditionally, the party organization also selected the party's nominees for general elections. As discussed in Chapter 3, before 1972, unpledged party delegates selected presidential nominees at the national conventions. That changed with reforms to the presidential primary system that emphasized primaries and caucuses. Primary elections became more important in nominations for lower-level offices as well, although party nominees for some statewide or local offices are still selected at party conventions or by party leaders. In many states, party organizations can also replace candidates who are no longer able to run, or select nominees for special elections. For example, after incumbent Senator Paul Wellstone was killed in a plane crash in October 2002, the Minnesota state party quickly put former vice president Walter Mondale on the ballot as a replacement. And even where party organizations no longer officially nominate their own candidates, party officials can influence primary results with their money or endorsements. They often discourage primary challengers, leaving only one candidate. Especially when party leaders unite behind one front-runner, their preferred candidate usually wins the primary election.

The other main task of party organizations is to raise money for their candidates. As discussed in Chapter 4, parties are quite successful at raising money, despite the ban on soft money contributions. They contribute some of this money directly to individual campaigns. They spend other money to produce and broadcast television advertisements. The party organization sometimes pays campaign consultants, pollsters, and other vendors of campaign goods and services. Party money is also used to build local party organizations and pay for get-out-the-vote drives.

Party organizations tend to concentrate their resources on races that are closely contested and most likely to tip the balance of power in legislatures. They want their resources to maximize the number of their representatives who get elected by helping candidates who can win. This means that many candidates with minimal resources and little chance of winning do not get help from the parties. The way a party distributes its resources also sends important signals to other actors. Politicians who have leadership PACs will often donate to many of the same candidates that the parties invest in. Interest groups affiliated with the parties also follow their lead. Party organizations sometimes make their priorities explicit by distributing lists of targeted districts or winnable elections to guide other actors.

Of course, parties are not necessarily unified when developing a campaign strategy. In Chapter 4, we noted the conflict between Howard Dean and Rahm Emanuel over whether the Democratic Party should devote resources to all of the states or only to competitive races. Another traditional conflict within party organizations is the trade-off between ideological purity and electability. Parties want elected officials who support their party's agenda. Yet sometimes candidates who are more ideologically moderate and less consistently partisan are more likely to win elections, especially in swing districts where voters are evenly divided along partisan lines. Races without incumbents are more likely to cause open party dissension along these lines. In a 2009 special election in New York's 23rd congressional district, the local

Choosing a Gubernatorial Primary Candidate

Entering the 2010 Michigan gubernatorial campaign, the Republican Party was confident. State public opinion had moved against the Democrats, including Governor Jennifer Granholm who was retiring. The most popular potential Democratic candidate, the lieutenant governor, decided not to run. The expected Republican victory brought several quality candidates into the primary field. Early primary polls showed the race divided between Mike Cox, the popular attorney general from the Detroit area, and Congressman Pete Hoekstra, from the more conservative western part of the state.

Republican leaders and interest groups tried to unify behind a candidate. Cox received endorsements from Right to Life of Michigan PAC and the Michigan Chamber of Commerce along with the previous Republican candidate for governor. Yet western Michigan voters still supported Hoekstra.

Rick Snyder, a businessman with no ties to state party or interest group leaders, began with almost no public support but took advantage of the dissension. At the state's largest party gathering, the Mackinac Republican Leadership Conference, Snyder unexpectedly won the straw poll. Newspapers explained the victory by reporting that Snyder had paid for many college Republicans to enjoy the splendid conference weekend on Mackinac Island, which they used for partying of the traditional variety.

By using his own wealth, Snyder was also able to advertise directly to voters rather than court the state's interest groups. His folksy advertising campaign, begun with a television ad during the Super Bowl, christened him as "one tough nerd," a successful outsider who would shake up the state's politics.

The state's party establishment and interest groups, meanwhile, did not take him seriously. Republican leaders continued to decide between Hoekstra and Cox because they were seen as more ideologically conservative and loyal to the party than Snyder. Shadowy groups designed to avoid recognition also waged a two-way battle on the airwaves. A group calling itself the Michigan Taxpayers Alert ran ads in support of Cox, attacking Hoekstra for supposed support of tax increases. Another group calling itself the Foundation for a Secure and Prosperous America ran misleading ads on behalf of Hoekstra, attacking Cox for alleged ties to the disgraced Detroit mayor Kwame Kilpatrick. While Cox and Hoekstra responded to attacks from one another, Snyder ran only positive ads and remained largely unscathed.

Snyder benefited not only from lack of consensus among Republican leaders but also from state election law. Because Michigan does not ask voters to register by party, independents and Democrats can decide to vote in the Republican primary. In 2010, nearly twice as many people voted in the Republican primary as the Democratic primary, including many who do not identify as Republicans. Snyder, seen as the most moderate candidate, received many of their crossover votes and won the primary.

Republican leaders ended up with a nominee with few ties to the party. Pro-life interest groups helped bring about a victory by the candidate who supported their cause the least. Snyder took advantage of the opening as conservatives failed to rally behind one alternative. In November, Snyder was elected governor in a landslide.

Republican Party nominated State Assemblywoman Dierdre Scozzafava. But the Conservative Party of New York nominated Doug Hoffman. Conservative interest groups and some Republicans, such as Sarah Palin, split with the local party and endorsed Hoffman. Scozzafava eventually withdrew from the race and endorsed Bill Owens, the Democrat. Owens then won the seat. It is rare that intraparty feuding reaches that level, but such cases show how decentralized parties sometimes fail to reach consensus.

The Role of Party-in-Government The party-in-government also influences campaigns and election outcomes. For better or worse, candidates with a party label are tied to the party's elected leaders. With Barack Obama as president, other Democratic politicians are seen as favoring his agenda, and Republican politicians are seen as opposing it. If Obama's approval rating is low, it may hurt all Democratic candidates. If the Democratic leadership in Congress advances a legislative program, it will also reflect on Democratic candidates. Many Democratic candidates in 2012, for example, had to defend health care reform, the stimulus package, and other controversial legislation associated with their party's actions in government. The same dynamics play out in state races, where candidates are seen as favoring or opposing their current governor's agenda. In legislative races at the state and national level, candidates are also affected by the current balance of power between the parties. The party with a majority in the legislature gets to set the agenda, typically earns more donations from access-oriented contributors, and can time legislation to maximize its impact on elections.

Candidates associated with the political party in power, especially incumbents, are judged on the basis of almost anything that occurs during their party's reign. Even adverse weather conditions like the dust storms of the 1930s, or events that have nothing to do with public policy, such as the 1916 shark attacks that inspired the movie *Jaws*, have been shown to move the mood of the electorate against the incumbent party.[6]

Legislators also must work through their party to pass bills that benefit their districts, such as legislation to support local road projects. Bringing federal money or other benefits to their districts can help increase an incumbent's popularity and prospects for re-election. Legislative party leaders know of this power; they often decide which of their incumbents to favor

---

[6] Christopher H. Achen and Larry M. Bartels. 2004. "Blind Retrospection: Electoral Responses to Drought, Flu, and Shark Attacks." Estudio/Working Paper 2004/199. www.march.es/ceacs/publicaciones/working/archivos/2004_199.pdf (accessed 7/22/10).

with local goods or legislative achievements based on the importance of their district in the next election.

Rules, Reality, and Party Strategies

Like candidates, political parties are strategic actors that have to make decisions within the context of both the reality on the ground and the rules set by government. The major rules that affect the parties are the election laws (Chapter 2) and the campaign finance laws (Chapter 4). The most relevant election laws for parties involve primary elections. There are long-running legal disputes about the extent to which parties can control their own nomination processes, which typically means control over primary elections. Some states mandate open primaries, where independents can vote in either party's election, but many party organizations prefer closed primaries, where only party members can vote. Parties have also attempted to set their own dates for primary elections and administer the voting, but most states demand that party rules conform to state laws and procedures. This often means that the two parties have to hold their elections on the same day.

The State of California has implemented a series of reforms intended to weaken the influence of party organizations in primary elections. In 1996 voters enacted a "blanket primary": all of the candidates from both parties were listed on the ballot, allowing voters to vote in the Democratic primary for one office and in the Republican primary for another (see Chapter 2). The Supreme Court struck down this law in 2000, finding that it violated a political party's First Amendment freedom of association. In 2010 California voters passed another initiative that created a system similar to Louisiana's: candidates from all parties run together in the first round of voting, and the two candidates with the most votes advance to the general election. This means that two Democrats (or two Republicans) might be the only candidates on the final ballot. Under this system, party organizations that convince fewer of their candidates to run for each office have an advantage.

Campaign finance rules affect how parties can raise and spend money. As discussed in Chapter 4, before the Bipartisan Campaign Reform Act of 2002 political parties could accept unlimited contributions—or "soft money"—to spend on party-building activities and issue advertising. BCRA made soft money contributions illegal. Donors reacted by creating the so-called "527" organizations to channel the money that they previously directed to parties. BCRA's ban on soft money has not yet been overturned, despite several rulings weakening its restrictions on independent groups and corporations.

Federal campaign finance law does benefit political parties in one sense: unlike other organizations, such as 527s, parties are allowed to coordinate their campaign expenditures with the candidates they support. These **coordinated expenditures** allow parties to cooperate with candidates in developing messages and communicating them to voters. Of course, party organizations also make independent expenditures that are not coordinated with candidates. A party can thus intervene in a federal election by donating money to the candidate, donating money to state party organizations, coordinating expenditures with the candidate, and running its own advertisements.

Parties are not only affected by rules but are also constrained by the same reality that candidates face. For example, the **party identification** of voters is relatively stable (see Chapter 12); parties cannot easily convince citizens to change their identification and "join" another party. Similarly, parties cannot easily change how the public perceives them and their leaders. "Issue ownership," discussed in Chapter 5, means that the public trusts one party more than another to deal with certain problems. For example, voters have traditionally trusted Democrats more than Republicans to handle education, while Republicans have typically been trusted to handle national security issues.

Parties are also constrained by the prevailing economy and the balance of power in government. Many citizens come to disapprove of the party that presides over an economic recession and support the party that presides over an economic boom. Parties will often find it harder to recruit quality candidates and prevent incumbents from retiring when economic conditions are unfavorable.

A party's ability to win seats in an election can depend on the current partisan balance. The party that controls the majority of seats may find that there are few remaining seats that they can win because they've already won so many of the competitive seats. Meanwhile, the minority could conceivably win back the marginal seats. In 2010, one of the reasons the Republicans were able to win 63 more seats in the House of Representatives than they previously held was that they had lost so many seats in competitive districts in the 2006 and 2008 elections.

Parties find themselves constrained in part by the decisions of other actors, including candidates and interest groups. At times, these actors may work at cross-purposes with the party they support. Candidates who are fearful of losing independent voters may renounce aspects of their party's accomplishments and agenda. Interest groups that are otherwise allied with the party may even work against that party's incumbents. For example, liberal interest groups and bloggers supported Ned Lamont's 2006 campaign against the incumbent Democrat, Senator Joseph Lieberman, because they felt that Lieberman was too conservative. Lamont won the primary but then lost the general election to Lieberman, who ran as an independent. Again, these kinds of disputes are rare. Parties and their allies among interest groups, consultants, and candidates typically strive to develop similar agendas and to target a similar set of competitive races.

Are Political Parties in Decline?

Although some observers have claimed that political parties are in decline, political scientists are skeptical of these claims. Political parties are certainly not in decline in government. Research shows that political parties in government have become more, not less, unified in the last 40 years and thus are able to exert better control of the legislative process when they are in the majority.[7]

Most arguments for party decline emphasize the apparent disregard for parties within the electorate—substantial percentages of the public identify as "independent," profess to dislike the major parties and their leaders, and favor a system with competitive third parties or independent candidacies. But too much should not be read into these sentiments. As we noted earlier, most citizens who claim to be "independent" still lean toward one of the major parties and tend to vote for that party.[8] These voters are really "closet partisans." Moreover, party identification is actually becoming *more* important in congressional, presidential, and state elections. This does not mean that the majority of citizens are familiar with the platforms of the political parties or have political opinions that are always closely aligned with their preferred party. These things are true of only the most well-informed citizens. Party identification, however, is a useful shortcut for reaching candidate judgments with or without detailed information.[9]

Perhaps the best evidence for party decline comes from the decreasing role of party organizations in elections. In Chapter 3, we discussed how a certain kind of strong party organization known as a "party machine" gradually declined after the nineteenth century because of reforms such as the secret ballot. The rise of candidate-centered elections in the latter half of the twentieth century created a relationship whereby parties are in service

---

[7] Nolan McCarty, Keith T. Poole, and Howard Rosenthal. 2006. *Polarized America: The Dance of Ideology and Unequal Riches*. Cambridge, MA: MIT Press.

[8] Bruce E. Keith, David B. Magleby, Candice J. Nelson, Elizabeth Orr, Mark C. Westlye, and Raymond E. Wolfinger. 1992. *The Myth of the Independent Voter*. Berkeley: University of California Press.

[9] Wendy M. Rahn. 1993. "The Role of Partisan Stereotypes in Information Processing about Political Candidates." *American Journal of Political Science* 37, 2: 472–96.

to candidates rather than in control. There is indeed some evidence that candidates position themselves independent of parties and create their own constituencies, fund-raising operations, and volunteer networks—although parties still provide important resources that help with fund-raising, polling, get-out-the-vote operations, and other aspects of a campaign.

As we have seen, today's party organizations also have less control over selecting nominees to run in the general election than they did several decades ago. In presidential elections, the national party conventions used to select the presidential nominees largely independent of the voters. State parties once performed similar roles. With the rise of direct primaries for presidential and legislative elections, party organization leaders no longer have complete control over who becomes a party nominee.

However, parties may have regained significant influence over presidential nominations.[10] They do this during the "invisible primary"—the period of time before the actual presidential primaries begin, when party leaders can observer and interact with potential candidates and each other. The goal of this process is to develop a consensus around a particular candidate so as to avoid a protracted and divisive primary process. One way in which party leaders signal their support for a candidate is via an endorsement. These endorsements strongly correlate with which candidate wins the nomination, even after taking into account the candidates' support in polls, the amount of money they raise, and the amount of media coverage they receive.

This attempt by decentralized parties to reach consensus is not always successful, as the 2008 primaries suggest: neither Barack Obama nor John McCain won the support of enough party leaders to make the primary election results a foregone conclusion. Instead, both parties, and particularly the Democratic Party, experienced a lengthy and intensely competitive primary season. But in many other presidential election years, the nominee with the most support from party leaders quickly emerges as the winner.

Debates over the rise and decline of parties often return to the definitional controversies that began this chapter. Who constitutes the party? If it is anyone who endorses candidates, then the party includes elected officials, party officials, affiliated interest groups, celebrities, and others with access to money or organization. If it is anyone who gives money, it includes PACs, business leaders, professionals, activists, and constituents that want something from government. The more narrowly the party organization is defined, the more it becomes clear that this organization does not resemble a centralized

---

[10] Cohen et al., *The Party Decides*.

machine, and the more evidence there is for its decline. By contrast, the more broadly parties are defined, the more influence—via money, endorsements, and so on—they appear to have.

Interest Groups

An **interest group** is a collection of people acting on the shared goal of influencing public policy. Although parties also have policy goals, interest groups differ from parties in key respects. Most important, interest groups do not run their own candidates for office. Further, interest groups typically seek more specific policy goals than do parties. Interest groups are not necessarily aligned or affiliated with any one party. Some groups assist or attempt to influence members of both parties. This is true even in campaigns, where certain groups will support members of both parties. Finally, some interest groups do not participate in elections at all, focusing instead on lobbying policy makers after they are elected. But because election results influence policy outcomes, many interest groups do participate in campaigns and can be important actors in elections.

There are several major types of interest groups. The largest sector of groups in Washington, D.C., represents businesses. More than 3,000 individual corporations or trade associations have a political office in or near Washington.[11] These include large groups such as the National Association of Manufacturers and the American Farm Bureau Federation that, through affiliates, regularly give money to campaigns and participate directly in them. Yet most corporations do not have political action committees, make campaign contributions, or air their own campaign advertisements. A second sector of interest groups represents occupations and includes professional associations like the American Medical Association and the American Bar Association. The largest of these groups participate in elections, but most professional associations represent occupations with relatively few members and do not participate in campaigns. A third sector of interest groups, labor unions, regularly participates in campaigns. Most labor unions—for example, the American Federation of State, County and Municipal Employees (AFSCME) and the Service Employees International Union (SEIU)—usually support Democratic candidates. A smaller number of unions, such as the Teamsters Union, sometimes endorse candidates from both parties. A final sector includes the hundreds of groups that seek

---

[11] Washington Representatives. www.lobbyists.info (accessed 5/20/11).

to represent social groups or ideological perspectives, rather than the economic interests pursued by corporations, professional associations, and unions. Groups that represent a social group include the National Association for the Advancement of Colored People (NAACP), which works on behalf of African Americans. Some groups represent a general ideological orientation, such as the American Conservative Union. These groups usually refer to themselves as public interest groups. Other groups advocate for a single issue—in the case of the National Rifle Association (NRA), the rights of gun owners. Public interest and single-issue groups are more likely

---

BOX 6.2

How the National Rifle Association Enforces Support for Gun Rights

The National Rifle Association's political influence is legendary. Its reputation was sealed in 1994, when many incumbents that the group opposed, including House Speaker Tom Foley, lost, thereby shifting control of Congress to the Republicans. Several of these members, including Foley, had defected from supporting gun rights on only one significant occasion—by supporting the assault weapons ban in a crime bill—but that was enough to earn the NRA's retaliation. According to many observers, including former president Bill Clinton, the NRA's intervention cost these members their seats in Congress. "The gun lobby claimed to have defeated nineteen of the twenty-four members on its hit list," Clinton reported in his autobiography, "They did at least that much damage and could rightly claim to have made [Newt] Gingrich the House Speaker."[1]

Political scientists are more cautious about attributing influence to interest groups. Many other factors contributed to the Republican Party's victories in 1994, and there is little evidence that the NRA's television ads or the votes of gun

rights supporters were the deciding factors. For the NRA's purposes, however, it may not matter. Their reputation benefited regardless, enabling them to exert more influence on members of both parties. The NRA's CEO, Wayne LaPierre, regularly presides over large showcase rallies that highlight its goals in influencing government. Interest groups that intervene in elections can gain in two ways: actual influence on election outcomes, and an enhanced reputation for influence; the NRA has proven adept at both.

---

[1] Bill Clinton. 2005. *My Life: The Presidential Years*. New York: Vintage Books, p. 215.

to participate in elections than economic groups, but they are less numerous and have fewer resources.[12] The 2012 campaign also witnessed a large increase in groups created only to advertise in one campaign.

Why Does the U.S. Have So Many Interest Groups?

The United States has a large and growing number of interest groups. The increase has been particularly dramatic since the 1960s. What has caused this trend? A basic reason is the expansion of government. As governments at all levels in the United States, but particularly the federal government, have taken on more responsibilities, they now regulate more entities and provide resources to more people. This creates an incentive for such entities and people to organize so as to receive more favorable regulations and additional resources.

A second reason for interest group expansion is improved strategies for organizational maintenance. A key innovation was direct mail fund-raising, by which an organization could regularly solicit contributions from an expanding list of like-minded Americans. Today, organizations maintain e-mail lists and Web sites to further facilitate fund-raising appeals.

A third reason is that prominent social movements have served as models for other groups to mobilize. After the success of the African American civil rights movement, for example, other minority groups mobilized—a trend furthered by the increasing ethnic and religious diversity of the United States. Successful mobilization by one side can also stimulate mobilization by the other. A conservative group called the American Action Network was recently founded to respond to the liberal Center for American Progress, which was originally founded to counter conservative think tanks like the Heritage Foundation. The Heritage Foundation was itself founded to counter the liberal Brookings Institution. This pattern of response and counter-response is common.

A fourth factor in the proliferation of interest groups is the nature of the rules concerning these groups, specifically the federal tax and campaign finance laws that encourage organizations to create separate affiliated groups for distinct purposes. As noted in Chapter 4, many interest groups are registered with the Internal Revenue Service (IRS) as 501(c) nonprofit corporations or as 527 groups. Interest groups also create political action committees (PACs) to accept contributions and donate them directly to political candidates. Some organizations have a combination of affiliates of different types. For example, EMILY's List, a supporter of female Democratic candidates, is a

---

[12] Jack Walker. 1991. *Mobilizing Interest Groups in America: Patrons, Professions, and Social Movements*. Ann Arbor: University of Michigan Press.

PAC with affiliated 527s. Progress for America is a conservative 501(c)4 organization with a 527 affiliate. The Center for American Progress is a 501(c)3 with a 501(c)4 affiliate. The NRA is a 501(c)4 with a PAC. State and local laws differ in how these organizations are treated and whether they can participate in state and local elections. As a result, organizations with state or local affiliates can have even more complicated structures.

Campaign finance rules drive the formation of new groups in another way as well. Because the laws require that the sponsors of advertisements be disclosed in the advertisements themselves, some groups create new organizations with names designed to appeal to the electorate. In a 2010 California ballot initiative campaign dealing with auto insurance, the side funded by insurance companies called itself "Californians for Fair Auto Insurance Rates" and created the "California Senior Advocates League" to promote its cause. In 2010, the Alabama Education Association, a liberal teachers association, even funded the "True Republican PAC." This PAC disingenuously ran advertisements critical of the teaching of evolution to weaken conservative support for the incumbent GOP candidate in the Republican primary. Campaign finance laws, in other words, encourage the same groups of people to create multiple organizations for legal and public relations purposes.

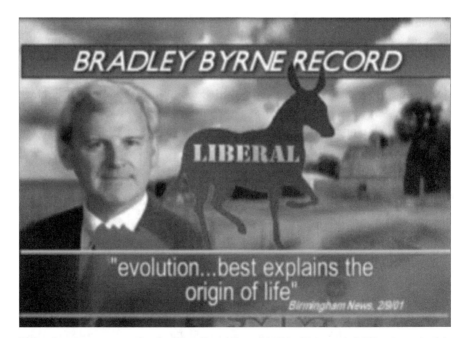

This advertisement, run by the "True Republican PAC" in Alabama's 2010 gubernatorial election, attacked a candidate for his belief in evolution. However, reports later surfaced that tied the PAC to the state teachers' association and indicated that the goal of the ad was to weaken conservative support for Republicans.

An increase in campaign activity by interest groups has accompanied the general increase in the number of groups. More interest groups have meant more interest group campaigning. Yet not all upward trends followed the same trajectory. The largest increase in PACs occurred in the late 1970s and early 1980s. Soft money contributions by interest groups spiked in the late 1990s. Expenditures by 527s were concentrated in the 2004 election cycle. Independent expenditures have increased most dramatically since 2006. In 2012, independent expenditures in federal elections eclipsed total PAC contributions for the first time, tripling the totals from the previous campaign. These trends in soft money and independent expenditures were caused more by changes in campaign finance laws than by changes in the number of groups trying to influence campaigns. As Figure 6.1 illustrates, the numbers of lobbyists and PACs have risen only slightly in the past decade.

How Are Interest Groups Involved in Campaigns?

Although the majority of interest groups do not get involved in campaigns, many groups contribute money and endorse candidates. Organizations with members commonly communicate with and attempt to mobilize their members

FIGURE 6.1 Number of Registered Political Action Committees and Lobbyists, 1998–2012

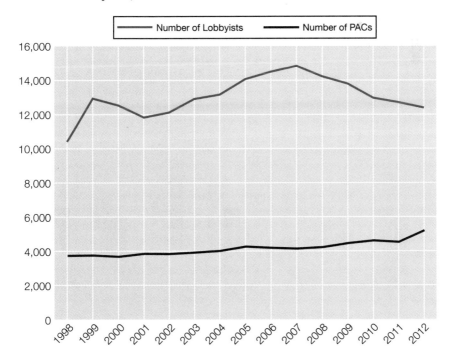

Source: Lobbyist data are from the Center for Responsive Politics, based on data from the Senate Office of Public Records. The PAC data are from the Federal Election Commission.

to volunteer and turn out to vote. A small number of interest groups engage in their own advertising, including an increasing number that are founded exclusively for this purpose.

Because of donor disclosure requirements, campaign contributions are the type of interest group electioneering that is easiest to track. Interest groups often donate money to candidates and parties through their affiliated PACs. Total PAC contributions have been increasing since the 1990s—see Figure 4.4 in Chapter 4—even as the number of PACs has held relatively steady. Most PACs are associated with professional associations, unions, or corporations. Corporate executives also make individual contributions to candidates. The Center for Responsive Politics tracks total giving by industries over time, combining PAC giving with donations from individuals associated with a company. In 2012, according to their data, total giving by entities affiliated with business accounted for more than 60 percent of large federal campaign contributions; labor unions contributed 5.4 percent, and ideological interest groups contributed 10.5 percent. Ideological and single-issue PACs are becoming more numerous, but their contributions still account for a small portion of total PAC giving. Within the corporate sector, the financial industry donates more money than any other corporate sector, with companies in law, energy, health, and communications also accounting for a large portion of contributions (see Figure 6.2). Corporate sectors differ not only in how much

FIGURE 6.2 **Total Political Contributions by Industry Sector**

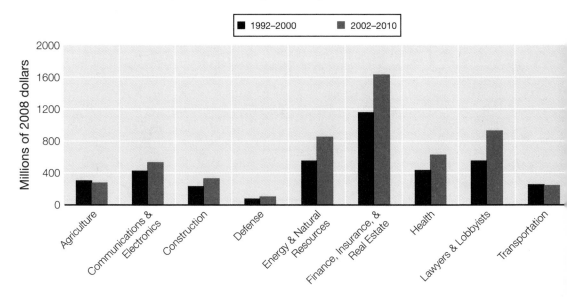

Source: Data from opensecrets.org. Includes individual contributions, PAC contributions, and soft money.

they donate but in who receives their donations. The building materials and oil and gas industries consistently favor Republicans, while the entertainment and publishing industries consistently favor Democrats. Unions are bigger supporters of Democratic candidates than any industry sector. Although PACs are clearly important donors, their contributions must be put in context: as we discussed in Chapter 4, PACs donate less money to American political campaigns than individuals, although many of these individuals are employees of corporations with political interests.

Interest groups can also participate in elections by running their own advertising campaigns as independent expenditures. According to the Center for Responsive Politics, the interest groups most involved in independent expenditure campaigns in 2008 were the SEIU, the NRA, and the American Federation of State, County, and Municipal Employees (AFSCME). In 2012, Super PACs dominated outside campaign intervention, spending more than $631 million. The top super PACs were called American Crossroads, Restore Our Future, and Priorities USA Action. New 501(c) organizations officially claiming to advance social welfare, rather than focus on politics, were nonetheless also funneling money toward campaign advertising. Traditional interest groups like the U.S. Chamber of Commerce, the SEIU, and the NRA also continued to spend at high levels. In total, conservative non-party committees spent well over twice as much as their liberal adversaries. Together, these interest groups allocated over four times as much as political parties to independent spending.

Campaign advertisements aired by parties and interest groups are much more likely to be negative than those aired by candidates. Interest groups are less concerned than candidates or parties with protecting their reputation and are willing to risk any backlash from negative advertising. Interest group ads are less obviously tied to the candidate that they are supporting, although voters may not necessarily distinguish interest group ads from candidate ads. Interest group advertisements are also more likely to focus on policy issues than candidate advertisements. Candidates are more concerned with sharing their biographies, whereas interest groups often want make the issues that concern them more central to the campaign.

Contributions and independent expenditures may be the easiest way to measure interest group involvement in campaigns, but they are not the only ways in which interest groups try to influence elections. Interest groups also use newer forms of media to get their campaign messages out and support specific candidates. Many groups have large e-mail lists and groups of online supporters on social networking sites like Facebook and Twitter. Many groups mobilize their members to support causes or candidates via donations or other forms of activism. At times, online activists and blogs, such as the liberal

Daily Kos, become interest groups in themselves, raising money and endorsing candidates.

Interest groups also sometimes pursue independent efforts to mobilize and persuade voters. Unions have long engaged in grassroots mobilization of their members. In 2004, 527s on the Democratic side, such as America Coming Together, also worked to mobilize voters. Many interest groups produce voter guides or endorse slates of candidates. The Christian Coalition handed out millions of voter guides outside churches in 1994, making it clear that they believed Republican candidates were pro-life and pro-family whereas Democratic candidates were not. In local races, groups often place door-hangers throughout a district, listing all of the candidates that they are supporting.

Interest groups that undertake these campaign activities often claim to speak for broader constituencies, such as all voters from a particular ethnic or religious group. Organizations and leaders that represent a particular group can help to reinforce the allegiance of group members in the voting public to a party or set of candidates.. Arguably, the loyalty of African American voters to the Democratic Party arises in part because most black leaders are allied with the party.[13] Republican candidates also sometimes attend NAACP conventions, if only to avoid appearing to ignore African Americans. Candidates may also sign on to a group's policy agenda, such as Americans for Tax Reform's "Taxpayer Protection Pledge," which entails a promise not to raise taxes. Candidates signing the pledge expect not only to gain the support of individuals affiliated with the interest group, but also to signal to all voters opposed to taxes that they share their views. Gaining the support of interest groups is particularly likely to translate into votes if group members perceive a common fate, believe that one of the major political parties best represents their interests, and tend to vote together consistently. The efforts of interest groups and their leaders may be especially important in local elections, where voters may know more about their neighborhood association, union, or business association than they know about many of the candidates. In these elections, there will often be a direct negotiation between candidates and local group leaders over which candidates will receive the votes of group members.

However, candidates cannot be certain that earning the endorsement of groups or their leaders will lead group members to vote for them. For example, early in the 2008 campaign for the Democratic presidential nomination, Hillary Clinton scooped up endorsements from African American legislators and interest groups, but ultimately this did not translate into enough sup-

---

[13] Paul Frymer. 1999. *Uneasy Alliances: Race and Party Competition in America*. Princeton, NJ: Princeton University Press.

port from black voters. One of Clinton's strategists, Mark Penn, expected only 70 percent of African Americans to support Obama in the 2008 primaries, but in some states, 90 percent did. This miscalculation was enough to cost Clinton her chance of winning a majority of the delegates to the Democratic convention. More generally, interest groups sometimes exaggerate their ability to "deliver" votes for a candidate. The views of group leaders are often more consistently ideological or strongly partisan than views of group members. Members may be more divided than leaders in their loyalties to parties or candidates. Ultimately, although candidates typically seek the support of sympathetic interest groups, the number of voters any group can deliver is uncertain.

Rules, Reality, and Interest Group Strategies

Interest groups, like parties, are strategic actors that have to make decisions in the context of the rules set by government and the reality on the ground. The main rules that impact interest groups are campaign finance laws. As we have seen, these laws set limits on how much any group can donate, and encourage groups to establish multiple subsidiaries—501(c) organizations, 527 organizations, PACs—in order to stay within the law. Groups are also prohibited from coordinating their advertising or mobilization efforts with candidates. Candidates cannot use the resources of interest groups, even office space or printed materials, without counting those resources as in-kind contributions, subject to disclosure and contribution limits. Furthermore, tax law limits the activities of many interest groups if they are organized as tax-exempt nonprofit organizations. Depending on their tax status, interest groups may be prohibited from publicly endorsing candidates or engaging in campaign activity.

Interest group strategies are also constrained by certain realities that they may not be able to change during any particular campaign. Some interest groups represent more popular issue positions than others. Some represent issues that are already of great concern to voters, but others need to stimulate interest in their issue areas. Some groups find it easier to raise money and thus have more resources to use in elections than others. Candidates may inevitably cater to the wealthiest groups and those most able to deliver large numbers of votes.

Interest group strategies also depend on how their agenda and issue positions correspond to those of incumbent politicians.[14] Groups whose agendas are well served by incumbent politicians will typically support them, regardless of party, and will seek to maintain their access to these politicians and thus ensure that government policy continues to match their preferences.

---

[14] Michael M. Franz. 2008. *Choices and Changes: Interest Groups in the Electoral Process.* Philadelphia: Temple University Press.

Evidence of this strategy can be seen among interest groups that give to members of both parties. For example, the defense and aerospace industry—which has earned many billions of dollars in government contracts—routinely gives considerable sums to both parties. In 2012, the top donor within the industry, Northrop Grumman, gave 42 percent of its donations to Democrats and 57 percent to Republicans. By contrast, interest groups whose views are not well represented among incumbents—typically ideological and single-issue groups—will seek to replace these incumbents, often with representatives who are more liberal or conservative than the average legislator. The actions of the Club for Growth discussed at the beginning of the chapter exemplify this strategy, as the group often seeks to replace Republican incumbents with more conservative alternatives.

Substantial interest group resources—particularly in the form of independent expenditures—are often targeted at a few competitive races. This can complicate life for the candidates in these races. Interest groups often emphasize a message different from that of the candidate they support—a message that may center on their narrow agendas rather than the concerns of the average voter. Their message may also be more controversial, such as the Willie Horton advertisement discussed in Chapter 4—one broadcast by an interest group that was ultimately disavowed by the candidate, George H. W. Bush, it was meant to support.

Evaluating Political Parties and Interest Groups

Political parties and interest groups play important roles in elections but they are also frequently scrutinized and criticized. The major parties tend to have low approval ratings. Interest groups are often labeled "special interests" by politicians and even citizens—and thus presumed to be opposed to the broader public interest. To evaluate whether parties and interest groups are helpful or harmful for democracy, we can ask several key questions.

First, do parties and interest groups help voters make informed choices, or do they manipulate voters? On the one hand, information from parties and interest groups can help voters select the candidate whose views are most consistent with their own. In fact, some voters use party affiliation and interest group endorsements to decide which candidates they should support. On the other hand, some interest group advertising is notoriously misleading, and interest groups cannot be held as accountable as candidates for their deceptions. Moreover, voters may have different priorities than parties or groups, so the information provided by parties and groups is not as helpful. For example, some voters focus on the characteristics of individual candidates, while parties and interest groups care more about candidates' views on issues.

Second, do parties and interest groups contribute to free choice? Here too the picture is mixed. The two major political parties provide for competitive elections in many places and especially at the national level. They are roughly equal in their resources, the quality of their candidates, and the support they command from voters. Clearly this is better than the one-party systems in some authoritarian regimes. At the same time, the Democratic and Republican parties certainly do nothing to alter the American system's bias against third parties and independent candidates who might represent other preferences among the public; indeed, the major parties often find new ways to try to exclude the competition. Interest groups serve the goal of free choice by representing a diversity of perspectives, which helps to ensure that Americans from a variety of backgrounds have a voice. However, they are likely to represent constituencies that are wealthier and have more to gain from government policy, which tends to heighten inequalities in political influence.

Third, do parties and interest groups contribute to deliberation? In one sense, they do. Competition between the major parties and among various interest groups provides a great deal of information to citizens and also helps to clarify similarities and differences in what candidates, parties, and groups believe. The independent role of interest groups can be especially important, as they often raise issues that candidates are less likely to discuss. But in other ways, parties and interest groups do not contribute to healthy deliberation. Much like candidates, parties and groups intend to persuade voters, not promote conversation. Moreover, if parties and groups largely focus on communicating and mobilizing their own supporters, there is little that would encourage communication among those with a diversity of opinions.

The normative goal that parties and interest groups most strongly advance is free speech. Both parties and interest groups empower individuals and organizations other than the candidates. They highlight the concerns of voters and may advocate views other than those that the candidates themselves articulate. Even if we are dissatisfied with the current role of parties and interest groups, we should ask whether there is a viable alternative to them. Because most major democracies feature parties, it is hard to know what elections would look like without them. It is true that many local elections are nonpartisan (see Chapter 10), but this does not necessarily stop parties from forming, if only informally. Even without official parties, candidates tend to develop stable alliances. One could argue that this is good, in that identifiable "teams" of candidates are easier for voters to evaluate than a mass of Lone Rangers. Some reformers say that there actually should be more parties rather than fewer. They believe that a multi-party system would provide voters more diverse options and better represent the range of views in the public. However, as we noted in Chapter 2, multiparty systems also make it more difficult for elected leaders to coordinate after elections in order to pass legislation.

Would we be better off without interest groups? There have been numerous attempts to limit interest group involvement in American campaigns, most prominently via campaign finance law. However, courts have invalidated some of these laws, arguing that interest groups deserve free speech protection because they advocate for the concerns of their supporters. Even if the courts had not ruled in this way, it seems unlikely that interest groups could be weakened. There will always be incentives for advocates of a cause to band together and seek to influence parties and candidates. In fact, this may benefit democracy, inasmuch as most citizens have some political views that they believe politicians should take account of. Interest groups merely help citizens accomplish this. Hillary Clinton was roundly booed in 2007 when she told an audience of liberal bloggers that "lobbyists, whether you like it or not, represent real Americans," citing associations of nurses and teachers.[15] But sometimes, that is true.

Conclusion

In 2014, voters will again go to the polls to select a member of the House of Representatives. For the political parties, each race will be one among many that will help decide majority control of Congress. The parties will decide what resources to invest by comparing each race with others that might tip the balance. Conservative interest groups like the Club for Growth will attempt to enforce ideological consistency without costing their party seats in Congress. Parties and interest groups will join candidates in trying to woo voters. Their efforts may influence the choices voters make.

In the abstract, most citizens disdain parties. But despite persistent claims of decline, America's two major political parties are here to stay. As groups of citizens, officeholders, and organizations, parties guide voters, they train and organize candidates, and they govern. Similarly, citizens are no more kind to "special interests." Nevertheless, interest groups continue to donate to candi-

---

[15] Kim Chipman. 2007. "Clinton Draws Fire from Obama, Edwards over Lobbyists." Bloomberg, August 5. www.bloomberg.com/apps/news?pid=newsarchive&sid=aNCxpEpsbL9g &refer=politics (accessed 5/20/11).

dates, air advertisements, and mobilize their followers. Attempts to regulate their influence typically succeed only in redirecting it. Whatever burdens parties and interest groups create for democracies, it is difficult to imagine that democracy could work without them.

KEY TERMS

political parties (p. 153)

party-in-the-electorate (p. 154)

party-as-organization (p. 155)

party-in-government (p. 155)

coordinated expenditures (p. 164)

party identification (p. 164)

interest group (p. 167)

FOR DISCUSSION

1. Would American elections improve if party organizations and interest groups were more involved in selecting party nominees and informing voters about the differences between candidates or would it be better to leave campaigning to the candidates? How would elections change with more or less party and group involvement?

2. If you were working for an interest group, how would you suggest attempting to influence elections in your state? Would you provide money to their campaign, work to mobilize your own membership, or seek to influence voters directly through an advertising campaign? What are the advantages and disadvantages of each approach?

3. Should political parties seek to maximize the seats that they control in Congress, running less loyal and less ideologically-consistent candidates in the districts where they have fewer identifiers, or only support those candidates that adhere to the party's platform? Why?

4. What are the most significant changes in the role of political parties and interest groups in American elections since the 1960s? Has either set of institutions gained or lost influence?

 Visit StudySpace for quizzes and other review material.
wwnorton.com/studyspace

CHAPTER 7

Media

In March 2008, with Hillary Clinton trailing Barack Obama in their battle for the Democratic presidential nomination, the American news media became obsessed with five-year-old remarks by Obama's retired pastor Jeremiah Wright. The commotion began not with attacks by Clinton or statements by Obama, but with the March 13 airing by ABC News of videotaped excerpts from sermons by Wright. In one sermon, Wright said, "The government gives [African-Americans] the drugs, builds bigger prisons, passes a three-strike law and then wants us to sing 'God Bless America.' No, no, no. Not God Bless America. God damn America — that's in the Bible — for killing innocent people." In another sermon, given after the September 11, 2001, terrorist attacks, Wright said: "Now we are indignant, because the stuff we have done overseas is now brought back into our front yards. America's chickens are coming home to roost."[1]

As other news organizations began to pursue the story, talk radio hosts and bloggers repeated the details. Fox News commentator Sean Hannity said, "I will not let up on this issue," and referred to Wright in 45 different episodes of his television program.[2] Millions of viewers also watched the Wright videos on YouTube. Obama, Clinton, and Republican nominee John McCain could not avoid the story. Obama initially distanced himself from Wright, but on March 18 he delivered a speech called "A More Perfect Union," which discussed race relations in the United States and attempted to place Wright's views in historical context. John McCain publicly defended Obama, even as he condemned Wright's remarks. The Clinton campaign, however, subtly criticized Obama. "You choose what church you want to attend," Clinton told a newspaper editorial board; "[Wright] would

---

[1] Brian Ross and Rehab el-Buri. 2008. "Obama's Pastor: God Damn America, U.S. to Blame for 9/11." *ABC News*, March 13. http://abcnews.go.com/Blotter/DemocraticDebate/story?id=4443788&page=1 (accessed 9/22/10).

[2] Media Matters. 2009. "Hannity Just Can't 'Get Over' His Rev. Wright Obsession," July 31. http://mediamatters.org/research/200907310032 (accessed 9/22/10).

not have been my pastor," she said at a press conference.[3] After Wright defended himself in speeches and media appearances, Obama terminated his church membership. Still, his association with Wright continued to figure in news coverage. The videos of Wright's sermons were also used in television ads by four different Republican interest groups, although never by the McCain campaign.

The saga of Jeremiah Wright highlights several important features of the news media and their role in contemporary American campaigns. First, the media's interest in Wright illustrates their news values, the criteria by which they judge stories to be newsworthy. Media organizations believe that stories with conflict and emotion appeal to their audience.

Second, the media's coverage of this story diverged sharply from what the implicated candidate, Barack Obama, wanted to discuss. Although candidates attempt to shape media coverage to benefit themselves, media outlets often pursue a different agenda. This is because the incentives of reporters are not the same as those of candidates. Reporters view their job as sharing useful information and analyzing factors that may affect elections or government, rather than passing along unfiltered campaign messages. By contrast, candidates repeat their campaign messages again and again, frustrating reporters who want new information. These conflicting agendas create tension between the candidates and news media.

Third, candidates often feel forced to respond to media coverage, no matter how much they may want to repeat their preferred message. Candidates believe

Core of the Analysis

- The news media typically seek to be objective but also to generate stories that will interest their audience.
- Candidates seek to persuade the public by influencing news content.
- The agendas of candidates and the news media often diverge, creating conflict between them.
- Media coverage can affect citizens, but its impact is often limited because citizens' attitudes are difficult to change.
- The news media do not always live up to democratic ideals, but citizens share some of the responsibility for the shortcomings in media coverage of campaigns.

---

[3] Mike Wereschagin, David Brown, and Salena Zito. 2008. "Clinton: Wright 'Would Not Have Been My Pastor.'" *Pittsburgh Tribune-Review*, March 25. www.pittsburghlive.com/x/pittsburghtrib/news/breaking/s_558930.html (accessed 9/22/10).

that the news media are an important source of information for the public and thus a platform that they must use to deliver their message. So rather than ignore the media, candidates attempt to reshape media coverage. Barack Obama's speech about race relations is one example, and largely a successful one, based on the positive response at the time.

Fourth, the Wright episode suggests an irony: despite the media's extensive coverage of the story, it is unclear that this episode had much effect on the public. Obama's poll numbers scarcely moved when the Wright story broke and when Wright reemerged to defend himself a month later. This apparent lack of impact reflects two key facts: many citizens do not pay close attention to politics in the news, and it is often difficult to change the minds of those who do.

Fifth, the Wright episode raises important questions about the news media's role in campaigns and whether it is conducive to democratic values. One might easily criticize the media's focus on this story as excessive and irrelevant. Are there more important issues than what Obama's pastor said five years before the campaign? A similar question can be asked about stories from the news media's coverage of the 2012 campaign, such as the uproar over Mitt Romney's secretly recorded remarks at a campaign fundraiser. Ultimately, do the news media uphold or undermine the ideals we have for campaigns and elections?

In this chapter, we begin by discussing the different types of news media outlets and comparing the size of their audiences. In particular, we distinguish "traditional" news media from "new media." We leave the discussion of candidate advertising, sometimes called paid media, to other chapters (especially Chapter 5). Here we are concerned with news coverage. We then describe how both rules and reality structure the campaign coverage that the news media produce. We emphasize how the economics of the news business shape the content of the news. We next consider how the news media and candidates interact, noting the necessity of this relationship for both but also the tensions within this relationship. Having described the nature of news coverage, we then evaluate how much it actually affects public opinion. The central point here

Barack Obama with Jeremiah Wright.

is that the media's impact is constrained by the public's interest in the news and willingness to believe what they read, see, or hear. Finally, we examine how well the news media help campaigns meet the standards introduced in Chapter 1. This question is crucial because most people rely on the news media for information about political candidates. Certainly few people have the chance to meet the candidates or interact with them, except perhaps in small local races. This makes it all the more important that the news media provide the information that the public needs.

Who Are the News Media?

Most people find out information about political campaigns from the mass media. We can think of the mass media as including all types of communication designed to reach large audiences. This definition includes music, movies, and entertainment, but news coverage is the mass media content most likely to influence elections. The mass media can be separated into two groups. The **traditional media**, which are sometimes referred to as the "mainstream media," include newspapers, news magazines, and radio and television news. These have historically been central to American politics. The **new media** category includes outlets designed to reach Internet audiences, such as blogs, as well as other outlets whose content and style differ from the traditional media. Not everything that appears online, however, should be considered new media. Most newspapers and television stations publish a lot of content online and the most popular news Web sites are traditional media outlets.

Historically, the daily newspaper was the primary source of news for most Americans. Newspaper stories allow regular and in-depth coverage of candidates, issues, and campaign events. Although newspapers are still a popular source of information, especially for older Americans, the audience for the printed product has been shrinking. In 2011, on average 44.4 million copies of newspapers were distributed every day, compared to a peak of 63.3 million in 1984.[4] However, newspaper Web sites are among the most popular online news sources. Even if newspapers no longer dominate campaign news coverage, they are still a source of information for citizens, politicians, and journalists and often shape the coverage of other media outlets. Newspapers are also the main source of coverage for many smaller-scale campaigns. A nice illustration of this point comes from a study of Pittsburgh during a 1992 newspaper strike. Without access to a newspaper, Pittsburgh residents did find other sources of information on that year's presidential and Senate elections, but they lacked information on House races.[5]

Network television news also reaches a large audience, although its audience is likewise declining. In 2011, the nightly news on ABC, CBS, and NBC together averaged 22.5 million viewers per day, down from more than 50 million in 1980. Morning news shows, such as NBC's *Today* and ABC's *Good Morning America*, averaged a total of 13.1 million daily viewers. Local

---

[4] Newspaper Association of America. "Total Paid Circulation." naa.org/TrendsandNumbers/Total-Paid-Circulation.aspx (accessed 2/3/11).

[5] Jeffery Mondak. 1995. *Nothing to Read: Newspapers and Elections in a Social Experiment*. Ann Arbor: University of Michigan Press.

television news is more popular, with almost 23 million viewers in its earlier time slot (between 5 and 7:30 P.M.) and more than 25 million viewers in its later time slot (10 P.M. to 12 A.M.).[6] Network news coverage favors stories with better visuals and less depth than newspapers. For example, in 2004, the average **sound bite** from presidential candidates broadcast on television news was only 7.8 seconds long.[7] Public television, which offers more coverage and longer sound bites, is the exception.

Cable news viewership is smaller but has more than doubled since 2000. The average prime-time audience reached 3.3 million in 2011, with daytime viewership exceeding 2 million. Fox News Channel dominates CNN, CNN Headline News (now HLN), and MSNBC in each time period throughout the day, in part because many Fox News viewers watch repeatedly. However, CNN often has more total viewers than Fox News in a given month because it draws additional viewers when there is breaking news.[8] On cable news channels, top stories are repeated throughout the day, with content similar to network news shows. In the evenings, cable news channels are dominated by punditry, with Fox News offering mostly conservative commentators and MSNBC offering mostly liberals.

Radio news also serves a niche audience. The United States has more than 1,500 commercial news or talk radio stations and 268 National Public Radio (NPR) member stations. NPR's news shows have an audience of 26.8 million listeners per week, while a total of 53 million listeners per week tune in to commercial news and talk radio.[9] In 2011, the top talk radio hosts were all conservatives: Rush Limbaugh with 15 million listeners, Sean Hannity with 14 million listeners, and Michael Savage with 9 million listeners.[10] Commercial radio news features content similar to cable television, especially in its commentary and its regular updates of news headlines. NPR, by contrast, is known for in-depth coverage and longer interviews.

---

[6] These figures are based on Nielsen ratings for ABC, NBC, CBS, and Fox affiliates. All viewership numbers are available from the Pew Project for Excellence in Journalism. "The State of the News Media 2012." www.stateofthemedia.org/2012/ (accessed 3/26/13).

[7] Stephen J. Farnsworth and S. Robert Lichter. 2006. *The Nightly News Nightmare: Television Coverage of U.S. Presidential Elections: 1988–2004*. Lanham, MD: Rowman & Littlefield.

[8] Pew Project for Excellence in Journalism. "The State of the News Media 2010." www .stateofthemedia.org/2010/ (accessed 9/22/10).

[9] These figures are based on Arbitron ratings. Listenership numbers are available from the Pew Project for Excellence in Journalism. "The State of the News Media 2012."

[10] These figures are from *Talkers Magazine*'s list of "Top Talk Personalities." The full list, with listenership numbers, is available from the Pew Project for Excellence in Journalism. "The State of the News Media 2012."

Beyond official news outlets, some entertainment programming also offers political content. Late night talk show hosts such as David Letterman, for example, made more than 3,000 jokes about political candidates and issues during the 2000 presidential campaign, with Bill Clinton and George W. Bush the most frequent targets.[11] Political satirists Jon Stewart and Stephen Colbert, who are each watched by approximately 1.5 million viewers each night on Comedy Central, devoted more coverage to the 2004 presidential election than the nightly network newscasts.[12]

These aggregate statistics in the audience for media are also apparent in surveys that ask individuals where they get their news. Figure 7.1 shows the changes over time in news consumption from television, newspapers, radio, and the Internet. Newspaper readership and radio listenership declined throughout the 1990s and 2000s, while television news viewership declined and then stabilized—in part because the decline in the audience for network news was offset by the increase in the audience for cable news. At the same time, the number of people receiving news online is increasing rapidly. This is particularly true among young people. Although those under 30 are only half

FIGURE 7.1 Where People Get Their News

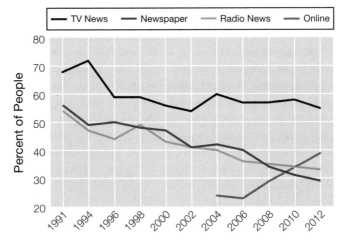

Source: Pew Research Center for the People and the Press. 2012. "In Changing News Landscape, Even Television is Vulnerable." www.people-press.org/2012/09/27/in-changing-news-landscape-even-television-is-vulnerable/ (accessed 3/26/13).

---

[11] David Niven. 2003. "The Political Content of Late Night Comedy." *International Journal of Press/Politics* 8, 3: 118–33.

[12] Julia R. Fox, Glory Koloen, and Volkan Sahin. 2007. "No Joke: A Comparison of Substance in *The Daily Show* with Jon Stewart and Broadcast Network Television Coverage of the 2004 Presidential Election Campaign." *Journal of Broadcasting & Electronic Media* 51, 2: 213–27.

as likely as those over 60 to report that they generally follow the news, the median age of the online news consumer is 20 years younger than the general population. But this does not mean that online news consumers are ignoring newspapers or television: the 20 most popular news Web sites include those of seven print newspapers and five television stations.[13]

Similar trends are evident in consumption of news about campaigns. Figure 7.2 shows where citizens got information on the 2000, 2004, 2008, and 2012 presidential campaigns. In 2000, network television dominated as a source

FIGURE 7.2 **Where People Learn About the Presidential Campaign**

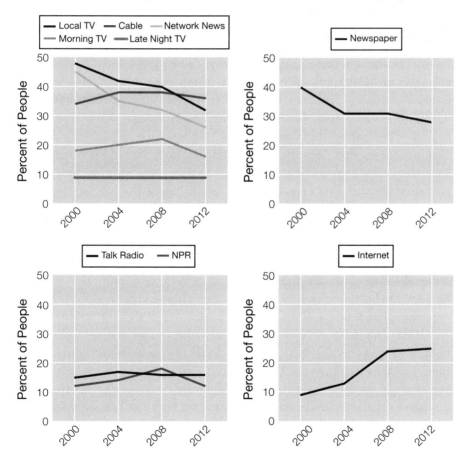

Source: Pew Research Center for the People and the Press. 2012. "Cable Leads the Pack as Campaign News Source." www.people-press.org/2012/02/07/cable-leads-the-pack-as-campaign-news-source/ (accessed 3/26/13).

---

[13] See Alexa Internet, Inc. "Top Sites by Category—News." www.alexa.com/topsites/category/Top/News (accessed 9/22/10).

of campaign information, but its advantage has been declining. Cable television has become a more prominent source, but the Internet's increasing appeal is most obvious. In 2000, 9 percent said they received presidential campaign information from the Internet, compared to 25 percent in 2012.

These trends in media consumption demonstrate how both the media and their audience have changed in recent years. They also hint at some of the challenges that the news media face today, particularly declining audiences for some types of media and narrower audiences for each source. The need to attract an audience is crucial and, as we will see, profoundly affects how the media cover campaigns.

Government's Limited Oversight of the News Media

Like other actors in campaigns, such as candidates, parties, and interest groups, the news media are influenced by rules. In this case, rules involve constitutional doctrine and government policies that affect—or, more important, do not affect—the content of media coverage. The First Amendment's guarantee of a free press means that there are relatively few rules that constrain media coverage. Given that Supreme Court interpretations of the First Amendment have allowed the media to publish stories about classified government programs, where the stakes are obviously much higher than in political campaigns, the media can largely report on political campaigns as they see fit.

The restrictions that do exist pertain mainly to broadcast radio—radio that uses the AM/FM spectrum—and broadcast television, which includes the major networks (ABC, NBC, CBS, and Fox) and their affiliates but not cable television networks. The Federal Communication Commission regulates broadcast radio and television because there is limited space on the broadcast spectrum. Think of the FM radio dial, which has space only between 87.5 and 108.0 megahertz. In order to prevent radio and television stations from fighting over space, the FCC licenses specific frequencies to particular stations. In exchange, however, these stations must abide by a few restrictions. For example, programming that the FCC considers "indecent" because of its sexually explicit content cannot be aired except between 10 P.M. and 6 A.M. in order to mitigate the possibility that children will be exposed to it. However, these restrictions do not apply to other kinds of media, such as print publications, cable television, satellite radio, and the Internet. This is why, for example, sexual content is more common, and much more explicit, in these media.

The FCC rule that is most relevant to political campaigns is the **right to equal time**. Stations with FCC licenses are required to provide "equal time" to all candidates for office. In other words, they cannot simply devote attention to a favored candidate and ignore the others. This means that if a station sells time to a candidate who wants to air television advertisements on that station, it must make the same opportunity available to all candidates for that office. However, there are important loopholes that allow unequal time. The FCC has declared that certain events are exempt from this rule, including news interviews and on-the-spot news events, like a presidential press conference. The incumbent president, whether or not he is running for re-election, gets news coverage simply for doing things that presidents do — giving press conferences, traveling to foreign countries, and so on. These activities are exempt from the equal time rule; thus, news outlets do not have to balance their coverage of a presidential press conference with, say, a speech by the opposing presidential candidate. The FCC also exempts presidential debates from the equal time rule. The organizers of the debates can thus exclude third-party candidates without running afoul of the rule. This creates an advantage for candidates of the two parties.

One interesting application of the right to equal time occurred in the 2008 presidential primary. One of the Republican candidates, former Tennessee senator Fred Thompson was also an actor who regularly appeared on the television show *Law and Order*. Episodes of *Law and Order* were regularly shown on NBC and cable television networks such as TNT. Even before Thompson's candidacy was official, NBC declared that it would stop showing episodes that featured Thompson. TNT did continue to show *Law and Order* reruns because as a cable network it is not subject to the equal time restriction.[14] Another example involves the former Denver Bronco offensive lineman Dan Neil, who decided to run for the Texas state legislature in 2010. Neil was co-hosting a local sports talk show in Austin, Texas, from 6 to 9 A.M. every weekday morning. His opponent's campaign formally requested that the station either remove Neil from the airwaves or give their candidate three hours of free air time every weekday. Although Neil's show was apolitical — mostly focusing on the University of Texas's football program — the station asked that Neil take a "vacation" until after the election.

Note, however, that the right to equal time does not require media outlets to broadcast coverage of campaigns or political news generally. In some situations, television news outlets have not carried presidential speeches or presidential debates. During the 2000 presidential election, for example, Fox and NBC did not broadcast the first debate between Al Gore and George W. Bush. Instead, NBC aired a World Series baseball game and Fox aired an episode of a science fiction program called *Dark Angel*.

---

[14] *Seattle Times*. 2007. "TNT Won't Pull Reruns Starring Thompson," September 1. http://seattletimes.nwsource.com/html/nationworld/2003863480_campdig01.html (accessed 5/23/11)

BOX 7.1

Political Blogs

The growth of new media has spawned a good deal of commentary about their transformative impact and the "impending death" of traditional media. But these claims are often exaggerations. In reality, traditional and new forms of media are often inseparable and actually depend on each other. The case of blogs is a useful illustration.

Blogs have been touted as a form of "citizen media" in which individuals can become reporters and commentators. But the universe of blogs, or the blogosphere, is not dominated by casual citizens but by traditional media organizations. Relatively few blogs generate large audiences, and many of those that do are hosted by large news outlets, such as the *Washington Post* or the *New York Times*. By adding blogs to their sites, traditional media outlets have imitated the behavior of new media outlets and blurred the boundaries between new and old media.

Some commentators hoped that blogs would become alternative sources of news, challenging the hegemony of the big newspapers and television networks. This has happened from time to time, particularly when blogs pushed a story first, leading traditional media to report on it. During the 2004 presidential campaign, Dan Rather of CBS News questioned the U.S. National Guard service record of George W. Bush, holding up memos that supposedly came from Bush's superiors at the time of his service. Conservative blogs questioned the authenticity of those memos, arguing that their typeface was not available on typewriters available to the military at the time. CBS News eventually retracted the report and asked Rather to leave the show.[1]

Such cases are the exception, however. Blogs rely on the mainstream media for news collection, in part because few bloggers have the resources to gather and report news. In fact, most political blog posts are links to articles in the traditional media, with limited commentary.[2]

Moreover, a blog needs traditional news media to generate an audience for its content. To gain traction for their stories, bloggers need them to be picked up by television and newspapers. In general, the influence of blogs is tied not to their readership among the public but to their influence on reporters from traditional media outlets.[3]

Blogs and bloggers make a unique contribution not so much as news reporters but as commentators and activists. Many of the most prominent political blogs are ideological or partisan in nature. So far liberals have been far more prominent than conservatives in the blogosphere, although ideological extremists are more prominent than moderates in both liberal and conservative blogs.[4]

Political bloggers tend to self-segregate, with both liberal and conservative bloggers linking and responding mainly to bloggers with similar views.[5] Their audiences are also self-segregated, with people reading blogs they agree with. Few people read both conservative and liberal blogs.[6] Thus, blogs are more effective at reinforcing people's existing political beliefs and perhaps spurring them to act on them than they are at changing anyone's mind.

---

[1] Associated Press. 2005. "CBS Ousts Four for Roles in Bush Guard Story," January 10. www.msnbc.msn.com/id/6807825/ (accessed 9/29/10).

[2] Laura McKenna and Antoinette Pole. 2008. "What Do Bloggers Do: An Average Day on an Average Political Blog." *Public Choice* 134, 1, 2: 97–108

[3] Henry Farrell and Daniel W. Drezner. 2008. "The Power and Politics of Blogs." *Public Choice* 134, 1, 2: 15–30.

[4] Matthew Hindman. 2005. "The Real Lessons of Howard Dean: Reflections on the First Digital Campaign." *Perspectives on Politics* 3: 121–28.

[5] Eszter Hargittai, Jason Gallo, and Matthew Kane. 2008. "Cross-Ideological Discussions among Conservative and Liberal Bloggers." *Public Choice* 134, 1, 2: 67–86.

[6] Eric Lawrence, John Sides, and Henry Farrell. 2010. "Self-Segregation Or Deliberation? Blog Readership, Participation, and Polarization in American Politics." *Perspectives on Politics* 8, 1: 141.

The Need for Profits and the Norm of Objectivity

The minimal requirements that the government places on news media out-lets mean that these outlets can largely cover—or not cover—politics and campaigns as they see fit. News outlets are thus free to base decisions about coverage on other factors. Because of this, coverage of campaigns is power-fully shaped by the prevailing reality or context in which the media operate. Obviously, news outlets have practical constraints of time, space, personnel, and other resources. They cannot cover every potentially newsworthy event and must make choices. In addition, their choices are guided by two aspects of reality: the profit motive and the norm of objectivity.

The Profit Motive

The economics of the news business demand that the news be profitable, first and foremost. The need to turn a profit is not new in the news busi-ness, but it has grown more imperative with time. Many news outlets today are owned by large corporations that do not have a personal investment in the news product, as a family that owns a newspaper might have had (and families owned most of the country's major newspapers until recently). Cor-porations are not content to lose money maintaining a news operation simply for the satisfaction of creating a quality news product. Thus, news outlets are expected to generate revenue and keep costs down.

This is a significant challenge. Many of the most prestigious news outlets— including major newspapers and television networks—are losing audience share and thus losing advertising dollars. Newspapers in particular are suffer-ing, as their classified advertising revenue has declined sharply, due in part to the advent of Web sites like Craigslist. Online audiences for newspapers are grow-ing but, as yet, newspapers have not figured out a way to make as much money from their online content as they did from their print editions (Figure 7.3). At the same time, covering politics, including political campaigns, is not cheap. The length of many American campaigns means that news outlets must com-mit significant resources if they want to provide continuous coverage.

Faced with these challenges, news outlets can either cut costs or raise addi-tional revenue. The cost-cutting measures undertaken by some news organi-zations are well known. Newspapers and television news organizations have eliminated reporting positions and other staff, and newspapers have cut back on the size of their print editions.[15] Some newspapers, such as Denver's *Rocky*

---

[15] See *Wall Street Journal*. 2009. "Pressure on the Presses." http://online.wsj.com/public/resources/documents/NEWSPAPERS0903.html (accessed 5/23/11).

FIGURE 7.3 Newspaper Advertising Revenue

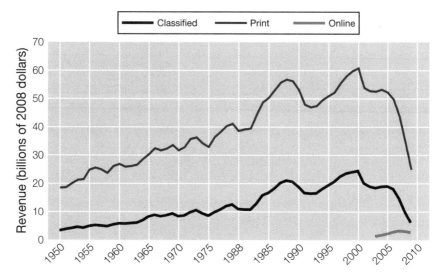

Source: Newspaper Association of America.

Mountain News, have closed outright. News outlets have also changed the kinds of news they gather firsthand. Many have closed foreign and domestic news bureaus, reducing the number of reporters who are based in places outside of the outlet's hometown. They are also reconsidering whether to expend resources to get relatively "expensive" stories—for example, whether to send reporters with the president on his travels.[16]

These sorts of cuts can affect coverage of campaigns. Most obviously, news outlets may simply devote less time to covering campaigns. This is not as true for presidential campaigns, which continue to command vast resources, as for many state and especially local campaigns, which we discuss further in Chapter 10. Reporters may simply not be assigned to cover those campaigns. News organizations also look for more cost-effective ways to cover campaigns. One strategy is to employ part-time reporters who carry handheld video cameras and follow the candidates around, waiting for something to happen. This is much cheaper than employing a full-time reporter and a camera crew. In 2007, one ABC reporter taped Mitt Romney getting a (perfectly chaste) hug from several enthusiastic Hooters waitresses—a clip that was played and replayed for a day or two.

---

[16] Brian Stelter. 2010. "When the President Travels, It's Cheaper for Reporters to Stay Home." *New York Times*, May 23. www.nytimes.com/2010/05/24/business/media/24press.html (accessed 5/23/11).

The second strategy for economic success is raising revenue. Some news outlets, such as the *New York Times*, have decided to raise revenue by charging for access to their news online; the cost is likely to be a declining audience. Most outlets, however, have sought to increase the size of their audience. News media often appeal to the public with stories that are laden with emotion, have stimulating visual images, or are simply sensationalistic. This is nothing new, of course. As we discussed in Chapter 3, newspapers in the nineteenth century began covering scandals, sports, crime, politics, and other stories in an often lurid way. But the continued rise of **infotainment**—a combination of informational and entertainment programming—is evident today. For example, the nightly news broadcasts have increased their coverage of celebrities, athletes, and famous criminals but not their coverage of business leaders and political figures. They have decreased the fraction of important congressional votes that they cover.[17] It is easy to criticize the news media for this, but news consumers may also bear some responsibility. Certainly these sorts of decisions often reflect careful monitoring of what the audience actually reads, watches, or hears.

The news media also seek to build an audience by establishing new outlets. The development of cable television and the Internet facilitate this. Cable television technology means that news outlets do not have to scramble for scarce broadcast licenses from the FCC. Internet technology means that content can be produced with lower distribution costs. In the case of newspapers, online editions save the cost of newsprint, printing presses, and employees to deliver the paper to people's homes. These technologies are particularly tempting to new media outlets, which see in these technologies—and in the declining audiences for traditional media—an opportunity to lure media consumers.

The Norm of Objectivity

Economic pressures are not the only influence on the contemporary news media. Most reporters, editors, and other news professionals subscribe to a set of norms that inform how they do their jobs. The most important of these norms is objectivity. Objectivity is actually a relatively recent feature of the news media. In Chapter 3, we described how the American print media were largely partisan until well into the twentieth century. Newspapers used to be directly allied with political parties and factions, who in turn helped to fund their costs of production and printing.

---

[17] James T. Hamilton. 2004. *All the News That's Fit to Sell*. Princeton, NJ: Princeton University Press.

The decline of the partisan press came about partly because newspapers became financially profitable and partly because journalism became more professionalized. Professionalism meant that journalists began to perceive themselves as autonomous actors who were not beholden to any political actor. They wanted to decide what to cover and how to cover it, and were not satisfied to transcribe the speeches of politicians verbatim. Journalists sought to report on events firsthand by seeking out information and interviewing sources.

With changes in professional practice came changes in the content of news. Journalists began to see it as their job to report on events fairly and accurately, with appropriate attention to all sides of controversial issues. The norm of objectivity became codified in the guidelines of news organizations. For example, the code of the American Society of Newspaper Editors, which was founded in 1922, included a principle of "impartiality": "News reports should be free from opinion or bias of any kind." This principle was taught to aspiring journalists in newly founded journalism schools; the first, at Columbia University, was founded by Joseph Pulitzer in 1902. Technology also helped enable the spread of more objective journalism. The development of the telegraph in the 1830s led to the creation of **wire services** like the Associated Press. Wire services—named for the wires used to send messages via telegraph—produce content that is shared among news outlets. Thus, stories could be disseminated quickly to many outlets. A similar pattern evolved in radio and television news, where local stations chose to affiliate with national networks and use their news products.

An autonomous and impartial press also began scrutinizing the government and politicians more closely. Often this meant looking for evidence of scandal and malfeasance. Events such as the Vietnam War and the Watergate scandal weakened trust in political leaders and fueled the rise of investigative reporting. Some things that journalists knew about but did not report on—such as the extramarital affairs of Presidents Franklin Roosevelt and John F. Kennedy—became fair game for later generations of journalists.

This talk of objectivity might seem dated to today's media consumers. After all, with the proliferation of cable news talk shows and blogs, is objective journalism not a thing of the past? The short answer is "no." There is a larger audience for traditional news outlets, which generally strive to be ideologically neutral, than for outlets with an ideological or partisan agenda.

Nevertheless, these ideological and partisan outlets are clearly flourishing, as the growth in the audience for Fox News, MSNBC, the Huffington Post, and others suggests. One reason has to do with economic incentives, which can take precedence over the norm of objectivity. With news outlets seeking to appeal to an audience, it is natural that some may choose an ideological approach. This strategy will not earn them the loyalty of the majority of news consumers, some of whom are on the opposite side ideologically and others of whom prefer impartial news. But it can earn them a niche audience that is sizable enough to produce subscription and advertising revenues. Furthermore, advances in technology make niche broadcasting—sometimes called **narrow-casting**—financially viable. Many niche media products, such as Web sites, can be produced relatively cheaply.

In sum, the rules and reality that affect the news media present something of a paradox. On the one hand, the government does relatively little to regulate the media, which gives them considerable discretion to write and publish what they wish. On the other hand, the news media face significant constraints of time and resources, even with the Internet providing essentially infinite space for news. Indeed, those resources have been shrinking for many outlets. The news media must therefore continue to find ways to cut costs or increase revenue by catering to consumers. This has lead to an increasingly diverse media landscape, with most outlets continuing to observe the traditional norm of objectivity but other outlets pursuing a partisan or ideological agenda for a smaller but loyal audience. These constraints affect how the news media covers campaigns.

What Gets Covered, and How?

A top priority for most campaigns is to get the news media to cover their candidate and her message. This is often easier said than done. Campaigns vie with other candidates, other races, and the events of the day for the media's attention. Getting the media to communicate the campaign's message is partly a matter of skill and partly a matter of conditions, luck, and what we have been calling "reality."

Which Races Get Covered?

In deciding which campaigns to cover, the media face constraints related to all of the factors we have discussed. They must allocate their limited resources while stimulating interest among their audience. In general, the media are more likely to cover a campaign when the race is competitive. Races where one candidate cruises to easy victory rarely generate stories that the media consider newsworthy. The front-runner can campaign conservatively, never risking an event where she might slip up and say something controversial.

The challenger, if there is one, lacks the resources to promote his candidacy or draw unfavorable attention to the front-runner. If new polls are conducted and released, they show little change. In sum, nothing dramatic happens.

The media is also more likely to cover a campaign when the office at stake has more authority. The national news media cover the presidential campaigns extensively, as well as a few campaigns for governor and senator. They rarely cover campaigns for state legislature or local offices, or even the House of Representatives. To the extent that they cover House races, the national news media focus on the broader competition between Democrats and Republicans for majority control, rather than the particular candidates or issues in each race. Local media, especially newspapers, cover more state and local elections, but they also report on the presidential campaign and the battle for control of Congress.

When the media do cover a campaign other than the presidential campaign or a particularly competitive race, it is often because it has some feature that appeals to the audience. For example, the media are drawn to celebrity candidates, like former California governor Arnold Schwarzenegger. They are drawn to scandals, particularly if sex or money—or, even better, money for sex—is involved. The scandal that befell Jack Ryan, Barack Obama's Senate opponent in 2004 (discussed in Chapter 1), is one example. Another involved Representative Mark Foley (R-Fla.), who during the 2006 campaign was alleged to have exchanged suggestive e-mails and text messages with several teenage boys who served as House pages.

Which Aspects of Campaigns Get Covered?

When news media do cover election campaigns, what do they cover? Although newspapers typically run general profiles of the candidates and the campaign, the vast majority of news is driven by events. What kinds of events do the media judge to be particularly newsworthy? We speak of their criteria for newsworthiness as **news values**. These include, among others, novelty, personality, and conflict.

The first and most important news value is *novelty*. The term "news" does contain the word "new," after all. Typically, this means that the news follows what happened recently—that is, since the last edition, newscast, or update to the blog or Web page. Candidates and their advisers know this, of course, so they organize a continuous stream of new events to gain the media's attention. Consider the events that take place before the actual campaign begins. Potential candidates coyly suggest that they might enter the race in order to generate speculation in the media. When a politician formally announces her candidacy, it is treated as news, even when it is a foregone conclusion that she

Covering a Potential Celebrity Candidate

Real estate mogul and reality television star Donald Trump spoke to the Conservative Political Action Conference, a traditional venue for potential Republican presidential candidates, on February 10, 2011. Media outlets began including him in lists of potential candidates and assessing his support in public opinion polls. In a March 17 interview on *Good Morning America*, Trump criticized potential rival candidates and questioned whether Barack Obama was born in the United States. Reporters regularly corrected Trump's claims, but Trump refused to drop the issue and claimed to have hired investigators to research Obama's birth certificate in Hawaii. He took advantage of nearly every invitation to be interviewed on television, hurling accusations at his potential opponents. He spoke at a Tea Party event, calling Obama the worst president in history. By April, several polls showed Trump leading the Republican field of potential presidential candidates.

The media had to decide whether to take Trump's candidacy seriously and whether to repeat and analyze his allegations. After all, he had voter support and was making newsworthy statements. In 2000, Trump had explored a third-party candidacy for president, but he advocated liberal policy positions such as support for national health care and a large wealth tax. Strangely for a Republican candidate, he had recently donated to Democratic candidates and rarely voted in primary elections. Some reporters suggested that his proto-campaign was an elaborate publicity stunt designed to increase ratings for *The Celebrity Apprentice*, his television program. Reports even suggested that he would announce his candidacy on the season finale.

Reporters expected that interviews with Trump would generate high ratings. To justify their coverage as news, they only needed to cite his support in the polls and argue that the media should correct his misstatements. Yet many were clearly skeptical of his candidacy. These mixed feelings produced a series of narratives on the news itself, on the issue of whether Trump should be taken seriously. Thus, reporters could claim to be evaluating their own behavior and questioning Trump, all the while substantially improving his visibility and repeating his claims.

Meanwhile, other candidates had to decide how to respond to Trump's sudden rise. Trump chided Mitt Romney as a "small business guy," literally arguing that his bigger bank account was a credential for his candidacy. That Trump could outpoll other candidates did not look good for them — but the other candidates did not know whether he was running and did not expect him to be a serious competitor. The biggest concern was that Trump was accounting for most of the spring 2011 television coverage of the presidential campaign, taking the place of Sarah Palin as media spectacle. Obama eventually decided to respond to Trump's allegations, releasing his long-form birth certificate on April 27, 2011.

Even when reporters suspect that a potential candidate is engaged in a publicity stunt, they rarely turn away. If politicians produce material that appeals to news values, they can take advantage of the enhanced coverage. This puts their competitors in a quandary: should they attempt to make crazier statements to generate attention or toil at traditional campaign forums away from the spotlight?

will be running. Politicians sometimes even hold multiple "announcements" in different media markets, as well as issuing press releases and online videos.

The media also value *personality*. Newsworthy stories often involve compelling people, and news audiences are presumed to be engaged by the "characters" in the campaign—whether they are good or bad. During the campaign, the news media will repeatedly dwell on the biographies of candidates in an attempt to understand what they are "really like." There are stories about where the candidates grew up, whether they were popular in high school, and so on. During the 2004 presidential campaign, a *New York Times* reporter wrote a profile of John Kerry, focusing on his experiences in high school and the views of his former classmates. The reporter argued that "the personal qualities that propel him—and daunt him—are the same ones that buoyed and bedeviled him when he was 16."[18]

The media also attempt to characterize a candidate's personality. Journalists play amateur psychologist, looking for evidence of candidates' personality traits in their words and deeds.[19] Al Gore was repeatedly characterized as stiff and awkward and, in a different vein, dishonest. George W. Bush was characterized as dumb and resentful of his more successful father and older brother. Barack Obama was portrayed as intellectual and emotionally unflappable. John McCain was described as angry. Here is one example, from a *Washington Post* story published during the 2008 presidential campaign:

> Some depict McCain . . . as an erratic hothead incapable of staying cool in the face of what he views as either disloyalty to him or irrational opposition to his ideas. Others praise a firebrand who is resolute against the forces of greed and gutlessness.[20]

In 2012, Mitt Romney was regularly characterized as wealthy and out of touch. Reporters were quick to pounce after Romney challenged a primary opponent to a $10,000 bet during a televised debate. According to pundits, the bet showed that he had no idea what money meant to ordinary Americans. Late in the campaign, portions of a secretly recorded fund-raising video surfaced in which Romney said that 47 percent of Americans "are dependent on government." This only reinforced his elitist image in the media narrative of the campaign.

---

[18] Todd Purdum. 2004. "Prep School Peers Found Kerry Talented, Ambitious, and Apart." *New York Times*, May 16.

[19] Kathleen Hall Jamieson and Paul Waldman. 2003. *The Press Effect*. New York: Oxford University Press.

[20] Michael Leahy. 2008. "McCain: A Question of Temperament." *Washington Post*, April 20.

All of these characterizations may have some truth to them, and clearly reporters do try to document these characterizations with information from sources. But regardless of their accuracy, stories about personality are endlessly fascinating to the news media.

Another news value in campaign coverage is *conflict*. It is easier to generate newsworthy stories when the candidates, their surrogates, the parties, interest groups, and other campaign actors are at each other's throats. (Fortunately, all of these actors often comply.) The media's emphasis on negativity is evident in how it portrays campaign advertisements: negative ads, and especially ones with outlandish claims, are discussed to a far greater extent than positive ads—even when positive ads are actually more numerous.[21] Candidates can sometimes get the media to cover negative ads simply by releasing them on the Internet, without ever paying to air them on television. In 2008, an Obama Web video criticized McCain for his inability to use computers; it never ran, but it prompted several news stories. The same was true of a McCain ad criticizing Obama for allegedly supporting "comprehensive sex education" for kindergartners.

The media cover candidate debates or other joint appearances with a similar hope for conflict. When the candidates do not disagree, the event is less newsworthy, perhaps frustratingly so from the media's perspective. In February 2008, a debate between Hillary Clinton and Barack Obama was billed as "fight night" on CNN. CNN commentator Jack Cafferty previewed the debate by saying: "Remember last week, the heated debate in South Carolina? Tonight could make that seem like a garden party." But Clinton and Obama, fearful that the South Carolina debate was too rancorous, came out and played nice, much to the media's disappointment. A *New York Times* reporter who was behind the scenes with CNN staff observed their exasperation.[22] One CNN producer complained that the debate was "like a press conference" rather than the no-holds-barred brawl they apparently wanted to see. Rarely does one see reporters and producers reveal news values so explicitly.

A fourth news value is *skepticism*. Today's professional journalists are trained to be dubious about the claims that politicians make, and perhaps for good reason. Thus, what candidates say is rarely taken at face value. At a minimum, the norm of objectivity requires news outlets to engage in "he said,

---

[21] Travis N. Ridout and Glen R. Smith. 2008. "Free Advertising: How the Media Amplify Campaign Messages." *Political Research Quarterly* 61, 4: 598–608.

[22] Brian Stelter. 2008. "Even As the Candidates Make Nice, the TV Crew Hopes for a Fight." *New York Times*, February 4.

she said" journalism, pairing claims by one candidate with responses by the opponent. Reporters sometimes engage in fact-checking, evaluating candidates' claims in advertisements and elsewhere for their accuracy. Some news outlets have even created fact-checking Web pages, like the *St. Petersburg Times'* PolitiFact.com, which regularly monitors the statements of politicians and ranks them on a scale from "true" to "pants on fire."

Perhaps the preeminent focus of campaign coverage, however, is *strategy*. This kind of campaign coverage is sometimes known as **horse race journalism**. Horse race campaign coverage focuses on which candidate is ahead or behind, who is gaining or losing ground, and what the candidates are trying to do to win (in other words, their strategies), much the way the announcer at a horse race describes which horse is winning, surging, or faltering. One study of network television news found that more than 70 percent of coverage focused just on the horse race.[23] A study of print, broadcast, and Internet news outlets during September and October 2008 found that 53 percent of coverage of the presidential campaign was about the horse race, while only 20 percent dealt with policy issues.[24] In the 2012 campaign, horse race coverage declined to 38 percent of coverage and policy coverage increased slightly to 22 percent. It is easy to see why horse race coverage is so appealing. For one, there are many ways to determine who is ahead or behind: fund-raising, endorsements, polls, the size of rallies, and so on. These indicators can be frequently updated, as candidates release fund-raising numbers or as media outlets field new polls, creating fresh grist for a story. Similarly, candidate debates are scored in terms of who "won" or "lost." Stories about undecided voters also generate horse race coverage, as these voters can be canvassed again and again to see if they have moved toward a candidate. Television networks sometimes convene small groups of undecided voters to watch presidential debates and then interview them after the debate.

Within the context of horse race coverage, the media's discussion of strategy allows them to engage in what is sometimes called **interpretive journalism**. Reporters do not simply report on what the candidates do and say. They provide further analysis and interpretation. That is, they attempt to tell their audience why the candidates are doing what they are doing and thereby

---

[23] Farnsworth and Lichter, *The Nightly News Nightmare.*

[24] Project for Excellence in Journalism. 2008. "Winning the Media Campaign: How the Press Reported the 2008 Presidential General Election," October 22. www.journalism.org/sites/journalism.org/files/WINNING%20THE%20MEDIA%20CAMPAIGN%20FINAL.pdf (accessed 5/23/11); Project for Excellence in Journalism. 2012. "Winning the Media Campaign 2012," November 2. www.journalism.org/analysis_report/winning_media_campaign_2012 (accessed 3/26/13).

reveal the candidates' underlying strategy. This type of coverage grows out of how journalists see their obligations as professionals. Their job is not to narrate events but to provide context. Reporters draw on their perceived expertise to read between the lines and to help their audience understand what is "really going on."

Is Campaign Coverage Biased?

Thus far, we have focused on how news values shape campaign coverage. But the most frequent public criticism of campaign coverage is that it is ideologically biased. One version of this complaint singles out specific news outlets as biased. Some of these complaints may have merit, as newspaper coverage tends to favor incumbent candidates that the newspaper supports on its editorial page.[25] But it is difficult to know whether this kind of bias simply reflects the preferences of that newspaper's audience. Any bias may be coming from the "demand side," which is based on what the audience wants, rather than the "supply side," which is based on what the news media provides. The same could be said of cable news outlets. Some of the programming decisions on the more conservative Fox News and the more liberal MSNBC may be driven by the partisan biases of each network's audience.

The more important complaint about bias does not single out specific news outlets but targets all news outlets. Supporters of each candidate complain that "the media" as a whole favor a different candidate. President George H. W. Bush's 1992 campaign made this claim, producing bumper stickers that said "Annoy the Media: Re-Elect Bush!" Some people even assert that this bias is chronic and that the media favor the Republican or Democratic party in election after election. Of course, it is easy to find examples of news coverage that seem more favorable to one candidate or the other. Yet it has been difficult to prove that candidate coverage is consistently biased toward one party or ideology. Despite persistent claims of many conservatives, news coverage is not consistently more favorable toward liberal or Democratic candidates. Although journalists tend to be more liberal than the general public, studies examining the actual content of that coverage have found little evidence of consistent bias in either direction.[26] This is likely because the norm of impartiality

---

[25] Kim Fridkin Kahn and Patrick J. Kenney. 2002. "The Slant of the News: How Editorial Endorsements Influence Campaign Coverage and Citizens' Views of Candidates." *American Political Science Review* 96: 381–94.

[26] David H. Weaver, Randal A. Beam, Bonnie J. Brownlee, Paul S. Voakes, G. Cleveland Wilhoit. 2006. *The American Journalist in the 21st Century: U.S. News People at the Dawn of a New Millennium*. New York: Routledge; D. D'Alessio and M. Allen. 2006. "Media Bias in Presidential Elections: A Meta-Analysis." *Journal of Communication* 50, 4: 133–56.

is so strongly ingrained in journalists. Instead, most partisan bias is in the minds of citizens, rather than in the news. Even when members of the two parties are watching the same coverage, Democrats believe that media coverage is more favorable toward the Republican candidate and vice versa.[27]

This is not to say that the media are not biased in other ways. Most important, news coverage tends to be more favorable to candidates who are ahead in the polls. Reporters write stories about how the losing campaign is "in disarray" and "floundering," while extolling the strategic prowess of the winning campaign. This bias was evident during the 2008 presidential campaign.[28] News coverage of Barack Obama in September and October of that year was slightly more positive than negative: 36 percent of stories were positive and 29 percent were negative, with the rest being neutral. By contrast, 57 percent of stories about John McCain were negative and only 14 percent were positive. Why is this not just evidence of pro-Obama bias? One reason is that coverage of Obama varied from week to week. In the week immediately after the Republican convention, when McCain took the lead in national polls, coverage of Obama was more negative than positive—just as we would expect if the media were less favorable to the "losing" campaign. Further evidence is that stories about polling and strategy were much more positive than negative toward Obama. In other words, horse race coverage was more favorable to the candidate winning the horse race. The moral of the story is that whatever their personal political preferences, reporters have other biases that more strongly affect their campaign coverage.

How Do Candidates and the News Media Interact?

Modern campaign strategy seeks to influence news media coverage and to use the news media to reach potential voters. Political consultants consider media outlets to be another place to deliver their candidate's message. They speak about "earned media" or "free media," meaning news coverage given to the candidates, as distinct from their "paid media," or advertising. There are many ways in which candidates seek to transmit messages via the news media. They interact directly with the media in interviews, meetings with newspaper editorial boards, and press conferences. They hold public events and give speeches, and invite reporters to attend. They issue press releases, report polling data,

---

[27] William P. Eveland and Dhavan Shah. 2003. "The Impact of Individual and Interpersonal Factors on Perceived News Media Bias." *Political Psychology* 24, 1: 101–17.

[28] Project for Excellence in Journalism, "Winning the Media Campaign."

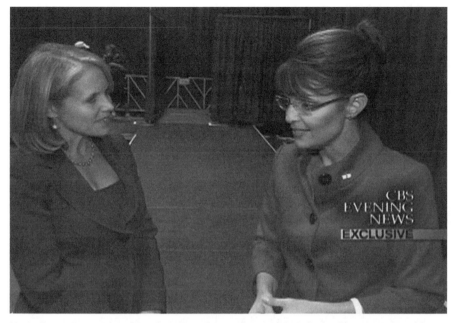

Katie Couric interviewed Sarah Palin in September 2008. Palin had been criticized for avoiding reporters before the interviews. Once they aired, she was criticized for being unprepared.

publish policy position papers, and announce endorsements. They also leak stories to selected reporters. Nearly everything a candidate does is designed to be picked up in the next day's newspaper, the night's television broadcast, the next hour's update to a Web site, or the next minute's tweet.

Candidates want every interaction with the news media to be on their terms. They seek to control when and where the interaction takes place, whom they interact with, and what they talk about. Thus, candidates often prefer to avoid the unexpected. For example, candidates cannot anticipate every question that will be asked at a press conference or television interview, and unexpected questions are more likely to trip them up and lead to some misstatement or gaffe. In 2008, Sarah Palin, the Republican vice presidential nominee, had a disastrous interview with CBS News anchor Katie Couric. Palin seemed unable to answer simple questions—such as which newspapers she read—and generally appeared hesitant and apprehensive. As a result, candidates sometimes eschew interviews or press conferences, limiting their interactions with reporters and confining their public appearances to rallies and speeches. Moreover, campaigns often take further steps to ensure that rallies and speeches lead to good media coverage—for example, by screening the attendees to guarantee that only cheering supporters, and not jeering opponents, are in the audience.

Candidates also plan their advertising around its anticipated media exposure. Many ads are shown much more by news shows, at no cost to candidates, than as a result of air time that candidates purchase. President Lyndon Johnson's 1964 "Daisy" ad, which featured a little girl counting flower petals before seamlessly shifting to a countdown for the detonation of a nuclear weapon, aired only once but brought significant media coverage and controversy because of the implication that Johnson's opponent, Barry Goldwater, would lead the country into nuclear war. The original ads purchased by the Swift Boat Veterans for Truth in 2004 (see Chapters 5 and 6) were aired sparingly but became fodder for newscasts. After the initial flurry of coverage, the group was able to raise enough money to run the ads more widely.

On the one hand, the media strategies of campaigns help the media do their job. The media want to tell their audience how day-to-day events might affect election outcomes, and campaigns strive to provide something eventful every day. The media are also looking for a good story, preferably one with drama and conflict. The candidates are often only too happy to argue with or leak scandalous tidbits of information about each other.

On the other hand, there are fundamental conflicts between the agendas of candidates and the news media. Candidates may schedule new events every day, but the content of those events is often repetitive. Because candidates want to present a consistent message, they repeat the same speech over and over. The audience at the speech will not have heard it; in fact, the candidate will have just flown into their town an hour before. But the reporters who traveled with the candidate on that plane have been to dozens of towns and heard the speech dozens of times. The day-to-day routine of a campaign does not always satisfy the media's desire for fresh new story lines every day.

Moreover, when candidates attempt to turn every public appearance into a rally, this rarely supplies the sort of drama and conflict that the media want. If everybody is cheering for the candidate, nobody is arguing. The national party conventions are a good example. The media have long complained that live coverage of the conventions is simply not newsworthy. In 1996, ABC News anchor Ted Koppel actually left the Republican convention midway through the proceedings, declaring, "This convention is more of an infomercial than a news event. Nothing surprising has happened; nothing surprising is anticipated."[29] From the perspective of the party, this is what is supposed

---

[29] *Nightline*. 1996, August 13. Transcript.

to happen. The media are expected to report that conflict is limited and the party has a consistent message.

But perhaps the most fundamental conflict between reporters and campaign organizations is that reporters do not have to deliver the candidate's message and often do not want to. This is what a professionalized press does: it makes its own decisions about what is important, rather than simply repeating what the candidate thinks is important. For example, although candidates spend most of their speeches talking, even if vaguely, about their policy agendas and goals, the media often talk about the horse race, especially when polls suggest that the race is becoming more competitive.[30] Even when journalists and commentators focus on what the candidates are talking about, they typically subject the candidates' messages to their own analysis. They comment on a candidate's statement or compare it to previous statements or opposition views. Often, the story the reporter writes is not the same one that the candidate hoped she would write.

Reporters are influenced by factors other than the candidates' messages. Newsworthy events such as the financial crisis of 2008 drive the news media's agenda and force candidates to respond accordingly. Reporters also stereotype the candidates; they cover what they think they should see, rather than what the candidates are actually saying. Female candidates, for example, have great difficulty enticing the media to cover their positions on issues considered "masculine," like national security and crime, but have no trouble generating coverage of their positions on "feminine" issues such as health care and education.[31]

Frequently, reporters follow the story lines developed by other reporters or commentators. This is the phenomenon of **pack journalism**. Reporters who cover campaigns tend to travel together, talk to each other, and read each others' stories. Because they fear missing an important story, they tend to converge on similar ideas and themes. Inside-the-Beltway publications like Mark Halperin's blog, and Politico's "Playbook" provide daily digests of what reporters are thinking and talking about and are read widely within the media. Needless to say, candidates are not convinced that these insiders get the story right: "If Politico and Halperin say we're winning, we're losing," Obama's campaign major David Plouffe said repeatedly during the 2008 campaign.[32]

---

[30] Danny Hayes. 2009. "The Dynamics of Agenda Convergence and the Paradox of Competitiveness in Presidential Campaigns." *Political Research Quarterly* 63, 3: 594–611.

[31] Kim Fridkin Kahn. 1994. "The Distorted Mirror: Press Coverage of Women Candidates for Statewide Office." *Journal of Politics* 56, 1: 154–73.

[32] Mark Leibovich. 2008. "Between Obama and the Press." *New York Times Magazine*, December 17. www.nytimes.com/2008/12/21/magazine/21Gibbs-t.html (accessed 9/24/10).

As a result of these differences, the relationship between candidates and the media is a lot like a marriage: sometimes cozy and sometimes combative. In *Journeys with George*, a documentary about George W. Bush's 2000 presidential campaign, Bush is depicted playing games with the reporters covering him. He gives them nicknames, spends time in their section of the plane, and attempts to make friends with many of them. He even kisses the cheek of the movie's producer, who happens to be the daughter of Representative Nancy Pelosi (D-Calif.). But Bush's relations with the news media were sometimes more frosty. At one campaign event, he was overheard telling Vice President Dick Cheney, "There's Adam Clymer—major league asshole—from the *New York Times*."[33] This contradictory behavior reflects the tension in the relationship between candidates and the news media. They need to stay on good terms with one another but they have differing goals and incentives.

The Effects of Media Coverage on Citizens

Campaigns seek to influence media coverage because they believe it will influence what the public thinks about the candidates and thus the election's outcome. But the effects of media coverage are often not that dramatic. The media cannot easily move public opinion.

It is particularly difficult for information presented by the media to *persuade* people to change their opinions. For example, as news coverage of a candidate became more favorable, one might expect the public's view of that candidate to become more favorable as well. This is not so common for two reasons. First, many people do not follow politics very closely. They are unlikely to read, see, or hear much about a political campaign, and thus their opinions about the candidates, if they have any opinions, will not change. Second, among those who do follow politics, relatively few people are undecided about political candidates, especially at higher levels of office, such as the presidency. Instead, these people tend to interpret information from the news media in ways that support the choice they have already made.[34]

Because of this, a much more common effect of media coverage is to strengthen or *reinforce* people's preexisting views. Supporters of two different

---

[33] Jake Tapper. 2000. "A 'Major League Asshole.'" Salon.com, September 4. www.salon.com/news/politics/feature/2000/09/04/cuss_word (accessed 9/24/10).

[34] David O. Sears and Richard Kosterman. 1994. "Political Persuasion," *Persuasion: Psychological Insights and Perspectives*, eds. Sharon Shavitt and Timothy C. Brock. Boston: Allyn & Bacon, pp. 251–78.

candidates who see a news report on the campaign will each see yet more reasons to support their favored candidate and oppose the other candidate. Even a news report that is highly unfavorable to a particular candidate is unlikely to change the opinions of that candidate's supporters. People have an impressive ability to ignore, rationalize, or argue against information that is contrary to their views.[35] They find reasons to dispute such a report or dismiss its importance. This is one reason the Jeremiah Wright incident had so little effect on people's opinions of Barack Obama.

If the media are less effective at persuasion—or changing what people think—they are more effective at changing what people think about. One way in which the media does this is **agenda setting**. The idea is simple: the more the media report on something, the more the public regards it as important. If the media talk a lot about health care, citizens are more likely to cite health care as an issue of concern. In one of the earliest studies of agenda setting, researchers measured the amount of attention to various issues in newspapers in Chapel Hill, North Carolina, during the 1968 presidential campaign.[36] At the end of the campaign, they conducted a survey of Chapel Hill residents. The issues emphasized in the newspapers were those that the public considered important. Subsequent studies that use experimental manipulations of media coverage have demonstrated the same finding: people who are randomly assigned to view newscasts with several stories about an issue will believe that issue to be more important than people who watch newscasts with no stories about it.[37] These findings provide candidates even more reason to try to shape the election's agenda, as we discussed in Chapter 5.

Related to agenda setting is a process called **priming**. The media influence or "prime" the criteria citizens use to make judgments by the degree of emphasis issues receive, even if the media are not explicitly telling the public to make judgments in this manner. In fact, priming occurs even when media reports do not mention the candidates in the context of discussing an issue. The more reporters discuss an ongoing war, the more the public will judge the president for his performance on the war, even if reporters do not explicitly credit or blame the president for the war.

---

[35] Michael F. Meffert, Sungeun Chung, Amber Joiner, Leah Waks, and Jennifer Garst. 2006. "The Effects of Negativity and Motivated Information Processing During a Political Campaign." *Journal of Communication* 56, 1: 27–35.

[36] Maxwell E. McCombs and Donald L. Shaw. 1972. "The Agenda-Setting Function of Mass Media." *Public Opinion Quarterly* 36, 2: 176–87.

[37] Shanto Iyengar and Donald R. Kinder. 1987. *News That Matters*. Chicago: Chicago University Press.

An example of priming during a political campaign involved Senator Gary Hart (D-Colo.), who ran in the 1988 presidential primary. Hart, who was married, was caught having an affair with a young woman named Donna Rice. Reporters actually discovered a picture of Rice sitting on Hart's lap aboard a yacht named, appropriately enough, *Monkey Business*. Because of this scandal, people's own moral values became stronger predictors of their attitudes toward Hart as the campaign progressed, with those who were morally conservative being less favorable to Hart. In other words, news media coverage of Hart's affair "primed" moral values, making them an important factor in the public's judgments of Hart.[38]

Finally, the news media affect citizens by *informing*. The news coverage of campaigns can help citizens learn relevant facts about the candidates, including candidate biographies and issue positions (even if issues are generally not the main focus of campaign coverage). As campaigns attract more media coverage, citizens are more likely to recognize and recall the names of the candidates

Mark Kirk (R-Il) won election to the U.S. Senate in 2010, after serving in the House of Representatives. As a commander in the U.S. Naval Reserve, Kirk emphasized his military credentials. News coverage criticized his miscrediting and embellishing of an award won by his military unit.

---

[38] Laura Stoker. 1993. "Judging Presidential Character: The Demise of Gary Hart." *Political Behavior* 15, 2: 193–223.

and to identify the issues that the candidates are discussing.[39] Although it can be difficult to separate the informing effect of the media from that of other information sources, such as campaign advertising, media coverage plays an important role.

None of these effects are mutually exclusive. The information conveyed in the news media could simultaneously educate people about a candidate's position on an issue (informing), make them feel that issue is an important problem (agenda setting), and lead them to draw on that issue when deciding whom to vote for (priming). Candidates' attempts to influence news media coverage, if they are successful, might also have multiple effects simultaneously.

There are, however, inherent limits to how much the media influence opinions. We have already noted that many people do not pay attention to political news or already have well-defined viewpoints that are unlikely to change. Contemporary changes in the media landscape are making it even more difficult for news media coverage to influence public opinion about politics. Since the rise of cable television and the Internet, Americans who do not want to watch news have been able to choose from an increasing array of other programming, such as sports, cooking shows, and movies. With more channels, most people can avoid the news. The result is an increasingly divided electorate, where some people pay attention to news, learn about politics, and participate in political activities while the rest of the population largely tunes out.[40] Giving people more media choices has led to a citizenry that may be less susceptible to any political messages in the news media.

Evaluating the News Media's Role in Campaigns

How well do the news media uphold the standards of free choice, equality, and deliberation by which we might judge political campaigns? In some ways, the media meet the standard of free choice, which highlights the needs of citizens to learn about the candidates in order to cast an informed vote. Coverage of campaigns can help citizens learn who the candidates are and what they stand for. But often the coverage is not designed with education in mind. Many campaigns receive little attention from the news media. For

---

[39] Kim Fridkin Kahn, and Patrick J. Kenney. 1999. *The Spectacle of U.S. Senate Campaigns.* Princeton, NJ: Princeton University Press.

[40] Markus Prior. 2007. *Post-Broadcast Democracy: How Media Choice Increases Inequality in Political Involvement and Polarizes Elections.* New York: Cambridge University Press.

those that do get attention, media coverage often emphasizes what is new, dramatic, or scandalous. This is not due to any partisan or ideological biases. Unlike the candidates themselves, the news media—or at least those outlets that strive for objectivity—are not seeking to manipulate citizens into voting for particular candidates. Instead, they are simply seeking to build and maintain an audience. If juicy revelations surrounding a candidate's divorce emerge, then the media will feature these revelations in order to attract an audience—regardless of whether this is the most important information for citizens to learn.

We can also ask whether news media contribute to equality. A central question here is whether news media coverage helps to address information inequality, whereby those citizens who are habitually attentive to politics learn a great deal but those who are inattentive to politics learn very little. There is always the potential for information in the news media to reach a wide and diverse audience. But this happens rarely—usually when a big story breaks and receives nonstop coverage in multiple outlets. More often, the many channels and Web sites available to consumers encourage segmentation, with political junkies getting their fill of campaign news, and most other people watching entertainment and sports programming. Of course, this is not the fault of the news media. It is a consequence of innovation in the broader media environment.

A third standard is deliberation. In a large democracy, deliberation must be mediated: Americans cannot all talk to one another or to the candidates face-to-face. Thus, it is up to the media to convey information that clarifies the views of each side. In some ways, this happens. The media's interest in conflict means that they will often report on the differences among the candidates. At times they play referee, intervening as if moderating a debate, investigating the claims that candidates make, and helping citizens understand what the candidates are saying, and whether it is truthful. Watchdog Web sites like PolitiFact.com are one means by which to do this. Of course, the news media's ability to serve as a watchdog depends in part on the economic prospects for the news business. Cuts in newsroom budgets tend to limit investigative journalism and lead outlets to rely on less experienced journalists.

If we conceive of deliberation as involving face-to-face conversation among citizens, there is less evidence that media facilitate this. New forms of media, such as blogs, have the potential to allow millions to communicate and respond to one another's views. Yet so far blog audiences are largely self-segregated, with partisans speaking only to one another, and disinterested citizens opting out of the conversation.

Scholars and commentators raise other ethical concerns about media coverage. Some argue that the media are too adversarial and thus too quick to criticize candidates or seize on any hint of scandal, no matter how minor.[41] Some fear that negative media coverage of campaigns may have made people more cynical about politics generally.[42] But there is a delicate balance here. In a democracy, we also need the news media to hold candidates accountable, and certainly many media outlets see this as one of their roles. So is critical coverage of candidates necessary? Does it go too far? There is no easy answer to these questions. Often it is in the eye of the beholder where accountability ends and cynicism begins.

Furthermore, blaming the media gets us only so far. Consider a study conducted during the 2000 presidential campaign.[43] Participants in the study were sent a CD containing a variety of information about the candidates, Al Gore and George W. Bush, which was culled from various news reports. There were stories about the candidates and their biographies, their views on issues, strategy and the horse race, and a few other topics. Participants could read whatever they wanted on this CD, and their decisions were tracked by researchers. What did people gravitate to? Stories about candidates and strategy—precisely the kinds of topics that the news media are so often criticized for emphasizing. In fact, people who pay a lot of attention to politics, and are thus likely to be regular readers of the news, are more likely to read these kinds of stories. Thus, the news media's focus on campaign strategy and the horse race may simply give consumers the information they want. This is what we would expect when news organizations need to maintain and build an audience in order to sell advertising. Of course, we should not simply shift our blame from the news media to news consumers. The point is that it is not always easy to tell how much blame each deserves.

Conclusion

The frenzy surrounding the broadcast of Jeremiah Wright's sermons during the 2008 election illustrates several key facts about how the news media cover campaigns. The attention to Wright reflected, first and foremost, the

[41] Thomas E. Patterson. 1993. *Out of Order*. New York: Knopf.

[42] Joseph N. Cappella and Kathleen Hall Jamieson. 1996. "News Frames, Political Cynicism, and Media Cynicism." *Annals of the American Academy of Political and Social Science* 546: 71–84.

[43] Shanto Iyengar, Helmut Norpoth, and Kyu S. Hahn. 2004. "Consumer Demand for Election News: The Horse Race Sells." *Journal of Politics* 66, 1: 157–75.

news values of journalists. The story was new. It involved drama and controversy. It had inflammatory rhetoric and good visuals. This is why it featured so heavily in news coverage.

The story's salience demonstrates how the news media's agenda may diverge from the candidate's agenda. Certainly Barack Obama did not want to talk about his pastor's old sermons. But he was forced to engage nonetheless. Candidates cannot avoid interacting with the media because it is an important way in which they speak to the public. Thus, Obama did not react by simply criticizing the media. Instead, he sought to play the media's game and give them something new to report on—something more favorable to him. His speech on race relations was an attempt to seize control of the agenda and change the subject.

The Wright episode also shows us how difficult it is for the news media to affect public opinion. When the videos of Wright's sermons first appeared, the campaign had been under way for months. Those paying attention to politics had already formed opinions of the two Democratic front-runners, Obama and Hillary Clinton. After the first few weeks of the Democratic primaries, few events affected the candidates' poll numbers—even events that featured a line like "God damn America." News coverage of political campaigns often implies that campaign events have a powerful impact on the public. In essence, the news media seem to believe in their own power. In reality, their effect on the attitudes of Americans is much more limited.

At their best, the news media can uphold the ideals we would like political campaigns to embody. Journalists can convey the messages from candidates while also serving as watchdogs. News coverage can contrast the views of the parties, correct untruths, and direct attention to important issues and to the candidates' strengths and weaknesses. At the same time, the coverage also focuses on sideshows and horse race trivia, while ignoring the bigger picture—a fact that must be blamed not only on the news media themselves but on citizens who consume news. Campaigns show us the best and worst of the contemporary news media.

KEY TERMS

traditional media (p. 184)

new media (p. 184)

sound bite (p. 185)

right to equal time (p. 188)

blogs (p. 190)

infotainment (p. 193)

wire services (p. 194)

narrow-casting (p. 195)

news values (p. 196)   pack journalism (p. 205)
horse race journalism (p. 200)   agenda setting (p. 207)
interpretive journalism (p. 200)   priming (p. 207)

FOR DISCUSSION

1. Who is more responsible for the weaknesses of campaign coverage in the American news media: reporters or consumers? Do citizens get the news they ask for?

2. If you were starting a blog about campaigns in your state, what would you cover? Would you repeat candidate messages or independently analyze the strengths and weaknesses of each side? How would you generate an audience? Would the need to build your audience change the types of stories that you covered?

3. How should the media have covered the saga of Jeremiah Wright's sermons? Could they have ignored it? Was it a legitimate campaign issue?

4. What changes will new media bring to campaigns over the next few election cycles? Will bloggers ever replace newspaper and television reporters as important actors in campaigns? How will the candidates change their behavior in response to the rise of new media?

 Visit StudySpace for quizzes and other review material.
wwnorton.com/studyspace

CHAPTER 8

Presidential Campaigns

In late August of 2000, the Bush campaign team watched on television as the Democratic nominee, Al Gore, and his running mate, Joe Lieberman, boarded a boat in Wisconsin for a quick trip down the Mississippi River. The general reaction was mild contempt. "What are they doing? Another boat trip? Been there, done that," someone said, pointing out that George H. W. Bush and his vice-presidential nominee, Dan Quayle, had taken a riverboat trip in 1988 before the Republican convention. Bush's senior strategist, Karl Rove, was not so dismissive: "Somebody get me an atlas!" he shouted. After examining the Democrats' planned route, Rove quickly realized that Gore and Lieberman would be visiting places that were inaccessible to Bush. Bush's airplane was too big to land in any Iowa airfield east of Des Moines. The only alternative for reaching the areas of southwest Wisconsin and eastern Iowa along the Mississippi was for Bush to fly to Des Moines or Milwaukee and do a two- to three-day bus tour. Rove opted not to do this, using direct mail, paid phone calls, and prominent Republican officials to reach out to potential voters in the places that Gore and Lieberman visited by boat. On Election Day, Gore won Iowa and Wisconsin by a combined total of 11,000 votes. Exit polls and election returns showed that Gore did especially well in the parts of these states along the Mississippi River.

It is far from clear, however, that Gore's riverboat trip won him these two states. In fact, it is far from clear that this trip was even the best use of the candidate's time and energy. One might argue, for instance, that this time would have been better spent in Florida, which Gore lost by a mere 537 votes, thus losing the election. Still, the decision to make the trip illustrates the strategic considerations that animate modern presidential campaigns. And in close elections these strategic decisions might be critical.

The phrase *"might* be critical" reflects the skepticism among political scientists about the extent to which presidential campaigns affect election outcomes.

This is not to say presidential campaigns do not matter. They do reinforce citizens' underlying partisan loyalties and raise the salience of fundamental factors such as the state of the economy. But campaigns do not necessarily decide who wins; broader political and economic realities may be more significant. Campaign consultants, by contrast, are much more confident that presidential campaigns affect public opinion and therefore the outcome of the election. Consultants tend to believe that campaign strategy is often decisive in who wins.

In this chapter we explain how political scientists and campaign strategists understand the role of presidential campaigns in the electoral process, and seek to reconcile their somewhat different views. We argue that campaigns act strategically to maximize the chances that they will win the White House. In developing strategies, presidential campaigns are influenced by two institutional arrangements. First, there is the series of statewide nominating contests—primaries and caucuses—during the first five months of a presidential election year. Second, there is the Electoral College, in which electors cast the deciding ballots for president. The electors are determined largely by winner-take-all statewide popular vote outcomes. Both arrangements demonstrate how electoral rules affect campaign strategy. Maximizing the prospects for victory also means acknowledging the political reality of a given presidential election cycle. Candidates are likely to pursue different strategies depending upon whether the economy is strong or weak, whether the country is at war or peace, and which party presently holds the White House.

Core of the Analysis

- Presidential candidates have two goals: to secure their party's nomination and then to win a majority of Electoral College votes.

- Electoral rules structure the presidential nominations process, and as candidates campaign for their party's nomination, they encounter a variety of election formats in different states.

- Nominating conventions provide critical boosts to the presidential candidates, while events that occur later in the campaign tend to have a smaller impact.

- The Electoral College structures the general election campaign, and candidates target particular states in order to win the necessary electoral votes.

- Political reality—especially the state of the economy—has an enormous influence on presidential elections.

In September 2000, Al Gore and his wife, Tipper, took a boat trip down the Mississippi River to campaign in the battleground states of Wisconsin and Iowa. This trip may have increased support for the Democratic ticket in rural areas of these states.

We first examine a presidential campaign's basic goals. We then turn to the three major stages of presidential elections — the nomination contest, the national convention, and the general election — taking care to consider the important rules and broader realities that affect strategy at each stage. We also discuss the effects that conventions and debates typically have on public opinion. We conclude by considering how well modern presidential campaigns serve American democracy.

Goals of Presidential Campaigns

Two goals have to be met to win the White House. The first goal is to amass a sufficient number of **delegates** to secure a party's nomination at the national convention. Most delegates (roughly 75 percent) are selected in statewide primary elections, caucuses, and conventions. Of these methods, primary elections are the most common.

The second goal is to win enough states in the general election to garner at least 270—a majority—of the 538 available Electoral College votes; this determines who wins the presidency. Note that the goal is *not* to win a majority of the popular vote; this is usually necessary to claim enough states to win 270 electoral votes, but not always. In fact, there have been presidents who lost the popular vote but still won the election: John Quincy Adams (1824), Rutherford B. Hayes (1876), and George W. Bush (2000). There is even some evidence that John F. Kennedy lost the popular vote in 1960.[1]

The problem is that these two goals can be somewhat incompatible. To win the nomination a candidate must win the votes of a plurality of partisans. But partisans, whether Republican or Democrat, tend to be more ideological than the average voter in the general election. This gives candidates the incentive to move away from the political center in order to cater to ideologues and win the nomination, and then back toward the center to win the election. (More will be said about this spatial theory of voting in Chapter 13.) One could certainly argue that this is what happened to the campaigns of Bob Dole (1996), John Kerry (2004), John McCain (2008), and Mitt Romney (2012), all of whom shifted their positions on certain issues between the primary and general elections. Some recent candidates can also seek to avoid the inconsistency of following strident partisan appeals during presidential primaries with more inclusive, moderate policy appeals. George W. Bush (2000) and Hillary Clinton (2008) were careful not to embrace primary strategies that were inconsistent with their longer-term plans for the general election. But this strategy is risky too: appealing to more centrist general election voters can alienate hard-core partisans who play a major role in primaries and caucuses.

---

[1] Brian J. Gaines. 2001. "Popular Myths about Popular Vote–Electoral College Splits." *PS: Political Science and Politics* 74.

Winning the Nomination

Before the convention and the general election campaign, presidential candidates have several important tasks to accomplish. We focus on two of the most important: contesting the party's primaries and caucuses, and selecting a vice-presidential candidate to be the running mate.

Primaries and Caucuses

In Chapters 3 and 6 we discussed how the political parties no longer directly control the nominating process. As a consequence, individual candidates must campaign state by state, in primary elections and party caucuses. These elections determine who the state party will send to represent the state at the national party nominating convention. These representatives are called delegates. To win the nomination at the convention, a candidate has to accumulate delegates by winning an array of statewide elections, each with distinct rules, over a period of several months. This makes four different kinds of rules important: how states structure these elections, how delegates are allocated to candidates, how delegates are selected to attend the national convention, and the order in which states hold their elections.

States typically employ either caucuses or primary elections to determine delegates. **Caucuses** are relatively closed affairs in which registered partisans attend meetings at election precinct locations and vote to select delegates to the county or state party conventions. Typically, these delegates are "pledged" to support a particular presidential candidate at the next level. The actual delegates to the national convention are then selected at the state convention. To be successful in a caucus state, a candidate must have a committed group of followers and an organization that can deliver these followers to the caucus locations. The first contest of the presidential nominations process is the Iowa caucuses.

More commonly, states use some form of **primary election** to determine delegates to the national convention. The form of the primary election affects the kinds of voters who can participate. As we discussed in Chapter 2, primaries can be closed, open, or semi-closed. In closed primaries, only registered partisans can vote. That is, only registered Democrats can vote in the Democratic primary, and only registered Republicans can vote in the Republican primary. In open primaries, voters can choose the primary in which they will vote, regardless of their party, but they may only vote in one party's primary.[2] In semi-closed primaries, both unaffiliated voters and those regis-

---

[2] In fact, most open primary states do not have registration by party.

tered as members of a party can vote in that party's primary; so, for example, registered Republicans and independents may vote in the Republican primary. Candidates will thus face more or less ideological electorates depending on the type of primary. For example, a socially conservative candidate who appeals to the Republican base would stand a better chance in a closed primary state than in an open primary state in which independents and Democrats are allowed to vote. The first primary of the presidential election year, in New Hampshire, is a semi-closed primary.

Most states allocate delegates in proportion to the percentage of the vote won by a candidate in the primary or caucuses. Under this system, a candidate with 40 percent of the vote in a state's primary gets 40 percent of the delegates from that state. The Democratic Party mandates a proportionality rule for its nomination process. In the Republican nomination process, some states have used a winner-take-all rule, allocating all delegates from the state to the winning candidate regardless of the vote margin. However, the winner-take-all rule may soon be phased out and replaced with a proportional rule.

To select the individual delegates, some states (such as New York) use a direct vote, others (such as California) allow the candidates to select as many delegates as they are entitled to based on the primary or caucus results, and still others (such as Texas) allow delegates to pledge themselves to candidates and then stand for election at the state convention. These differing arrangements affect what a campaign must do to maximize the number of delegates it can obtain. For example, in Texas, delegates are allocated in proportion to the vote a candidate gets statewide and by the proportion won in each of the state's congressional districts. Delegates to county conventions are then selected in precinct caucuses; delegates to the state convention are selected at the county conventions; and delegates to the national convention are selected at the state convention. This multistage process (known as the "Texas two-step") means that candidates need committed supporters in as many parts of the state as possible. In 2008 the Obama campaign was able to maximize delegate totals in several states through a mastery of complex caucus and convention selection processes.

In addition to the delegates selected through the competitive processes of these statewide nomination contests, roughly one-quarter of delegates to the national nominating conventions achieve that status because they are office-holders or occupy certain positions within the party. These are referred to as "at-large" delegates (or "superdelegates") and are not pledged to support any particular candidate based on a statewide vote. They are free agents who must be persuaded, one by one, by the candidate and campaign. Hillary Clinton's

2008 campaign worked long and hard to convince the at-large delegates to ignore Obama's edge in pledged delegates and to vote for her at the convention. In the end, however, at-large delegates sided with Obama, who had won more total votes in all the primaries and thus more pledged delegates.

The primaries and consequent delegate selection occur in a sequence, with some states' primaries or caucuses held as early as January and others as late as June (Table 8.1). The early contests—especially the Iowa caucuses and the New Hampshire and South Carolina primaries—can have an effect on the process that is disproportionate to the actual number of delegates from those states. This is because their results are seen by both the news media and citizens as conveying important information about the **viability** of the candidates, or their chances for winning the nomination.[3] Because the political parties no longer dictate the nominee, the news media and citizens seek ways to simplify the choice, especially when many candidates are running for a party's nomination. The early races thus serve to winnow (that is, narrow) the field. Some candidates drop out because their performance in Iowa, New Hampshire, or South Carolina indicates they have no chance of winning the nomination. In 2008, ten Democrats and eleven Republicans sought their parties' nominations; one week after the South Carolina primary on January 19, only eight remained in the running: Barack Obama, Hillary Clinton, and John Edwards on the Democratic side, and John McCain, Rudy Giuliani, Mitt Romney, Mike Huckabee, and Ron Paul on the Republican side. In 2012, eleven Republicans were on the ballot in at least three presidential primaries, but by January 19, 2012, five had dropped out (Michele Bachmann, Herman Cain, Rick Perry, John Huntsman, and Gary Johnson); two others were never a factor (Fred Karger and Buddy Roemer).

The importance of early contests gives state legislatures the incentive to move their primaries and caucuses earlier in the calendar so that they will exert greater influence on the nominating process. This is known as **front-loading**. The national party organizations, aware that a system in which all states hold early primaries might help a charismatic but still relatively unknown and flawed candidate win the nomination, have discouraged front-loading in order to provide additional time for citizens to learn about the candidates. The Republican National Committee, for example, adopted a "preferred" calendar for 2012, with no primaries or caucuses scheduled before February 1 and some penalties for states that jumped to the front of the calendar. But the

---

[3] John Aldrich. 1980. *Before the Convention*. Chicago: University of Chicago Press; Larry Bartels. 1988. *The Dynamics of Presidential Primaries*. Princeton, NJ: Princeton University Press.

TABLE 8.1 2012 Republican Presidential Primary Calendar

Date	State	Contest	Rules
Saturday, January 7	Wyoming	Caucus	Closed
Monday, January 16	Iowa	Caucus	Closed
Tuesday, January 24	New Hampshire	Primary	Semi-closed
Saturday, January 28	South Carolina	Primary	Open
Tuesday, January 31	Florida	Primary	Closed
Tuesday, February 7	Alabama	Primary	Open
	Connecticut	Primary	Closed
	Delaware	Primary	Closed
	Georgia	Primary	Semi-closed
	Minnesota	Caucus	Open
	Missouri	Primary	Closed
	New Jersey	Primary	Semi-closed
	New York	Primary	Closed
	North Dakota	Caucus	Closed
Tues.–Sat., February 7–11	Alaska	Caucus	Closed
Saturday, February 11	Louisiana	Primary	Closed
Tuesday, February 18	Nevada	Caucus	Closed
Tuesday, February 21	Hawaii	Caucus	Closed
	Wisconsin	Primary	Open
Tuesday, February 28	Arizona	Primary	Closed
	Michigan	Primary	Open
Tuesday, March 6	Massachusetts	Primary	Semi-closed
	Ohio	Primary	Semi-closed
	Oklahoma	Primary	Closed
	Rhode Island	Primary	Semi-closed
	Tennessee	Primary	Open
	Texas	Primary	Open
	Vermont	Primary	Open
	Virginia	Primary	Open
Tuesday, March 13	Mississippi	Primary	Open
Tuesday, March 20	Colorado	Caucus	Closed
	Illinois	Primary	Open

(continued)

TABLE 8.1 (continued)

Date	State	Contest	Rules
Tuesday, April 3	Kansas	Caucus	Closed
	Maryland	Primary	Closed
	Washington, D.C.	Primary	Closed
Tuesday, April 24	Pennsylvania	Primary	Closed
Saturday, May 5	Maine	Caucus	Closed
Tuesday, May 8	Indiana	Primary	Open
	North Carolina	Primary	Semi-closed
	West Virginia	Primary	Semi-closed
Tuesday, May 15	Idaho	Primary	Closed
	Nebraska	Primary	Semi-closed
	Oregon	Primary	Closed
Tuesday, May 22	Arkansas	Primary	Open
	Kentucky	Primary	Closed
	Washington	Caucus	Closed
Tuesday, June 5	California	Primary	Closed
	Montana	Primary	Open
	New Mexico	Primary	Closed
	South Dakota	Primary	Closed

Source: Data are from Josh Putnam's "Frontloading HQ" Web site: http://frontloading.blogspot.com/2010/12/2012-presidential-primary-calendar.html (accessed 8/22/11).

calendar demonstrates that the RNC's preferences were not realized, as state legislatures remain the ultimate authorities for election dates.

Taken together, these features of the presidential nominating process have important implications for campaign strategy. Candidates face a demanding task. They must develop a campaign organization that can compete in a rapid-fire sequence of contests with different eligible voters and different rules: the precinct caucuses in Iowa, the semi-closed primary election in New Hampshire a week later, the open primary election in South Carolina two or three weeks after that, and then the numerous primaries (including New York, Georgia, Missouri, and New Jersey) that mark "Super Tuesday." It is a significant test and one that requires money, attention from news media, and the support of at least some within the party organization.

Thus, the first strategic decision we discussed in Chapter 5—whether to run in the first place—entails a calculation about whether the candidate can muster the needed resources. Candidates must ask themselves whether they can raise the money necessary to assemble campaign organizations across the many states holding nominating contests. If they cannot, then they must answer a different question: whether they have enough appeal to convince voters in one of the early states to support them and thereby make them a player in subsequent contests. Some of these candidates craft an appeal based on their unique positions on issues. For example, in 2008 Ohio congressman Dennis Kucinich presented himself as more liberal than the other Democratic contenders. In the 2008 and 2012 Republican primaries, Texas congressman Ron Paul presented himself as the only truly libertarian candidate, one distrustful of government intervention both in the economy and in people's personal lives.

For candidates that do run, subsequent decisions will depend on how prominent they are. **Front-runners**—candidates with a lot of money and who are well known by the electorate—must decide how much time and money to spend in the early states, since some of them are small and thus have fewer delegates than the large states whose primaries fall on Super Tuesday and later in the calendar. Hillary Clinton's national campaign in 2008 emphasized the early contests in Iowa and New Hampshire, which was a controversial strategy. She could have ignored Iowa, for example, and perhaps minimized the significance of an upset victory by Barack Obama or John Edwards, who both campaigned and organized tirelessly there. But ignoring Iowa would have raised questions about her front-runner status: Was she afraid of losing? How dominant was she really? The 2008 primary race was made even more complicated by the fact that two major states—Michigan and Florida—had moved their primaries up to January even though the national parties threatened not to seat either state's delegates at the national conventions. How were candidates to respond to this situation? Clinton chose not to campaign in those states but left her name on the ballot. Obama honored the ruling of the national party by staying out of Florida and Michigan, and not working to have his name placed on the ballot on those states—a decision made easier by the fact that Clinton was favored to win both states.

Lesser-known candidates face a different strategic challenge: Which of the early contests are the most promising targets for pulling off an upset and thereby generating important publicity for the campaign? Surpassing low expectations and thereby triggering favorable media coverage generates momentum. Candidates with momentum can build on early victories to win later primaries and ultimately the nomination. Candidates who benefited from momentum include Jimmy Carter in 1976, George H. W. Bush in 1980, Gary Hart in 1984, Pat Buchanan in 1992, John McCain in 2000, Howard

Dean in 2004, and Rick Santorum in 2012. Not all of these candidates won the nomination, however, illustrating that early victories are not always enough.

In 2012, several Republican candidates sought to generate momentum by winning early caucuses or primaries on favorable terrain. Rick Santorum targeted Iowa (skipping New Hampshire), while John Huntsman targeted New Hampshire (skipping Iowa), and Newt Gingrich targeted South Carolina (largely bypassing New Hampshire). By way of contrast, in 2008 Barack Obama's circumstances were somewhat different. He was clearly an underdog relative to Clinton, but he was also very well financed. He was thus able to pursue something of a hybrid strategy. He was more selective than Clinton in allocating resources to states, but he did not narrow his focus to a few early states. Obama began to build organizations in several states—especially those with caucuses, where organization often matters more than money. He also fought vigorously in the early contests. Indeed, his early victories in Iowa and then South Carolina were arguably essential to generate the money and support necessary to mount efforts in the later contests and ultimately to win the nomination.

Given the importance of fund-raising, primary contenders must also decide whether to accept public funds. As we discussed in Chapter 4, the Federal Election Campaign Act (FECA) provides public money for presidential candidates who meet fairly attainable thresholds—$5,000 in contributions of $250 or less across at least 20 states. But the money comes with conditions: the recipient must abide by state-by-state as well as overall spending limits. In 2012, the overall limits were about $45.6 million. Ever since Steve Forbes targeted Bob Dole with millions of dollars in negative ads in the 1996 New Hampshire Republican primary, some candidates have been reticent to accept public funds. George W. Bush in 2000; Bush, John Kerry, and Howard Dean in 2004; Barack Obama, Hillary Clinton, John McCain, Mitt Romney, Mike Huckabee, and Rudy Giuliani in 2008; and Barack Obama, Mitt Romney, Rick Santorum, Newt Gingrich, Ron Paul, Rick Perry, Herman Cain, Michele Bachmann, and John Huntsman in 2012 all declined public funds and continued fund-raising throughout the primary season. This made these candidates' nomination contests far more expensive than their predecessors'.

The National Conventions

For all intents and purposes, the nominating contest is over when one candidate has earned a sufficient number of delegates to claim a majority at the convention. Oftentimes, this threshold is determined by the news media, or even the candidates themselves, who update their "delegate counts" after every contest. The result, of course, is not official until the **roll-call vote** at the convention. Still, there is pressure on the other candidates to drop out and rally behind the winner after the result begins to look clear.

Choosing a Running Mate

After the nominations are clinched, the presidential campaign enters the preconvention phase. The 2008 Democratic contest was unusual because it lasted so long; typically, the delegate contest is decided by the end of March and the nominee has until mid- or late summer to prepare for the convention. An important part of this phase is the selection of the vice-presidential nominee, a decision that will drive media coverage before and during the convention. There are at least five strategic options for the vice-presidential pick. The first is to select someone whose knowledge and expertise compensate for the shortcomings of the presidential candidate. In 2008, Barack Obama, a first-term senator from Illinois with almost no foreign policy experience, selected Joe Biden, a six-term senator who served as chairman of the Foreign Relations Committee. In 2000, Texas governor George W. Bush also sought to bolster the foreign policy credentials of his presidential campaign by selecting former defense secretary Dick Cheney.[4]

A second option is to choose someone who can help the candidate carry a state or region. For example, John F. Kennedy's selection of Texas senator Lyndon Johnson in 1960 helped win the state for the Democrats and bolster their standing with conservative white party members. More generally, presidential nominees often select running mates from large states, like Texas, where there are more electoral votes in play.

A third option is to select someone from a political or demographic group whose support the candidate needs. In 2012, Mitt Romney was viewed unenthusiastically by conservatives due to his support of health care reform in Massachusetts and his formerly pro-choice position on abortion. To win over conservatives, he selected Wisconsin representative Paul Ryan, who was the architect of the House Republicans' aggressive deficit reduction plan.

A fourth option is to select someone to heal intraparty wounds. In 1980, Ronald Reagan reached out to his chief rival from the primaries, George H. W. Bush. In 1976, Gerald Ford almost asked Reagan to be his running mate even

---

[4] Lee Sigelman and Paul J. Wahlbeck. 1997. "The 'Veepstakes': Strategic Choice in Presidential Running Mate Selection." *American Political Science Review* 91, 4: 855–64.

though the two had had a bruising struggle for the nomination. In 2008, many Democrats urged Obama to ask Hillary Clinton to join the ticket despite their nomination fight. In the end, however, both Ford and Obama saw more downside than upside to this strategy.

Finally, a fifth option would be to select someone who reinforces the image of the candidate. Although it may seem counterintuitive, the vice-presidential selection need not always be about shoring up weaknesses. In 1992, Bill Clinton asked Tennessee senator Al Gore to be his running mate. Both were young, white, and southern. But Clinton's campaign strategists saw the virtue of reinforcing their candidate's image as a new, fresh face.

Presidential candidates must also decide when to announce their choice of a running mate. Announcing several weeks before the convention maximizes the time that both the presidential and vice-presidential nominees are on the trail and ensures that there will be two media "hits" (the announcement plus the convention). In contrast, announcing the pick right before the convention helps to maximize the impact of the convention. In recent years, major-party candidates have typically opted for the second strategy. In 2008 both Obama and McCain, for example, named their running mates within the week before their nominating conventions.

Conventions as Showcase Events

The Republican and Democratic national conventions mark the formal transition from the nominating process to the general election campaign, even though the general election is always the ultimate goal as the nominating contest unfolds. Like the nominating process, today's conventions are quite different than they were through the 1960s. Before 1972, the political parties exercised a great deal of control over the nomination, and the conventions were deliberative bodies where party officials and state delegates bargained and cut deals to arrive at a consensus choice for the nomination. Today, conventions are essentially four-day public relations spectacles, during which the nominees present themselves to the American electorate.

The candidate's travel to the convention is itself also a part of the convention process. Candidates publicly preview the message of their nomination acceptance speech, as well as the entire fall campaign. In 2008, John McCain spent the days before the Republican convention talking about reforming Washington, and seeking to reassert his image as someone who would challenge entrenched interests. Candidates also reveal the constituencies and states that they believe are critical to victory. George H. W. Bush campaigned from a Mississippi riverboat in the days leading up to the 1988 Republican convention in New Orleans, visiting Missouri, Arkansas, and Louisiana.

National conventions used to be the setting in which the party's presidential nominee was selected. Today, the nominee is almost always determined in advance of the convention, through primary elections and caucuses.

Al Gore visited a series of battleground states in the Rocky Mountains just before the 2000 Democratic convention in Los Angeles.

Despite the attention the campaigns and the news media give to these appearances, their impact is minimal. Both the timing and the location of the conventions have greater potential influence. Unfortunately for the candidates, the parties choose the location well in advance of the actual campaign, after a selective bidding process. Parties also set the timing in advance. Traditionally, the party that is not in power holds its convention first, and sometimes there is a significant gap between the two conventions. For example, in 1992, seven weeks separated the conventions—the Democrats held theirs in mid-July and the Republicans held theirs in late August. More recently, both parties have attempted to hold their conventions as late as possible, after the summer Olympics but before Labor Day.

Campaign strategists have three goals at the convention: tell voters what the past four years have been about, identify how the current candidates are different, and offer a vision for the country. Most conventions thus begin with a narrative of what has happened over the past four years. Speakers at the convention of the party out of power (the "out-party") talk about what has gone wrong and why there is a need for change. Speakers at the convention of the incumbent party talk about what has been successfully accomplished and how it occurred. These contrasting narratives are usually conveyed by well-known politicians on Monday and Tuesday nights of the convention week. Then conventions tend to focus on the contrasts between the candidates, with convention speakers describing the choice before the nation: What are the stakes and options the party faces? What would the party's candidate do, and how does that differ from the opposing candidate? This is usually accomplished in the Wednesday speech of the vice-presidential nominee. Last, the party and its candidate have to offer a vision for the future. Where is the country headed, and how it will get there? This is the goal of the presidential nominee's speech on Thursday night.

Convention Effects

Do conventions actually affect what the public thinks of the two candidates? Yes, they do. Each party's nominee garners additional support from the public after the convention. This is commonly referred to as the **convention bump** (or **convention bounce**). More precisely, the convention bump is defined as the candidate's share of the two-party vote in trial-heat polls conducted 1–7 days after the convention minus his share of the two-party vote in polls conducted 1–7 days before the convention. The average convention bump is about six points, as measured by polling data from Gallup (see Table 8.2). As we will see, this effect is much larger than that of other presidential campaign events, such as the debates. Political scientists believe that it is larger for two main reasons. First, conventions occur relatively early in the general election campaign, when there are a larger number of citizens who are undecided or only weakly committed to a candidate. There is thus a greater potential for persuasion. Later in the campaign, with fewer undecided voters, events serve mainly to strengthen preexisting opinions about the candidates—the phenomenon of reinforcement that we discussed in Chapter 7. Second, conventions produce news stories that tend to be favorable to the candidate being nominated. This is what the hoopla of conventions is designed to do. This effect is amplified by the fact that the opposing candidate is likely to campaign less vigorously during this period, knowing that it is not easy to compete with the speeches and images of the other party's convention.

Of course, not all conventions give candidates the same size bump. Bill Clinton's 1992 convention stands out as the most effective since 1964, although it was due mostly to an unusual occurrence: on the last day of the Democratic convention, Ross Perot, who had run as an independent candidate, dropped out of the race, thus leaving his supporters, about one-third of likely voters, looking for a new candidate to support. More often, the size of the convention bump depends on how well the candidate is doing given prevailing political realities, such as the state of the economy and approval of

TABLE 8.2 Convention Bumps, 1964–2012

Year	Candidate	Democratic Convention City	Bump	Candidate	Republican Convention City	Bump
2012	Obama	Charlotte	+3	Romney	Tampa	−1
2008	Obama	Denver	+4	McCain	St. Paul	+6
2004	Kerry	Boston	−1	G. W. Bush	New York City	+2
2000	Gore	Los Angeles	+8	G. W. Bush	Philadelphia	+8
1996	Clinton	Chicago	+5	Dole	San Diego	+3
1992	Clinton	New York City	+16	G. H. W. Bush	Houston	+5
1988	Dukakis	Atlanta	+7	G. H. W. Bush	New Orleans	+6
1984	Mondale	San Francisco	+9	Reagan	Dallas	+4
1980	Carter	New York City	+10	Reagan	Detroit	+8
1976	Carter	New York City	+9	Ford	Kansas City	+5
1972	McGovern	Miami Beach	0	Nixon	Miami Beach	+7
1968	Humphrey	Chicago	+2	Nixon	Miami Beach	+5
1964	Johnson	Atlantic City	+3	Goldwater	San Francisco	+5

Source: www.gallup.com/poll/109702/conventions-typically-result-fivepoint-bounce.aspx (accessed 5/5/11). 2012 estimates calculated by authors using Gallup Poll figures (see www.gallup.com/video/109906/obama-sees-convention-bounce.aspx (accessed 5/5/11).

the incumbent president.[5] Candidates who are favored by these realities but are for other reasons underperforming in the polls will tend to get a larger bump—in part because convention messages often include messages about the economy and the incumbent president.

The General Election

After the convention balloons have popped and the confetti has been swept up, the presidential candidates and their running mates hit the campaign trail, followed by a gaggle of reporters. At the same time, the campaigns blanket the

---

[5] Thomas Holbrook. 1996. *Do Campaigns Matter?* Beverly Hills, CA: Sage Publications.

airwaves with radio and television advertisements. But the states and media markets where the candidates travel and broadcast advertisements are not chosen at random. Moreover, candidates assiduously court some citizens more than others. Understanding contemporary presidential campaigning requires an understanding of the rules and reality that govern it. The resulting system, though often criticized, has positive as well as negative implications for democratic values.

The Electoral College

The strategic context of the general election is dominated by the institutional reality of the Electoral College. According to Article 2 of the Constitution, each state has a number of electoral votes equal to its total number of representatives to the U.S. Congress — that is, its members in the House plus its two senators. The passage of the Twenty-third Amendment gave the District of Columbia three electoral votes. In sum there are 538 electors (based on 435 House members plus 100 senators plus three electors from DC).[6] As noted earlier, the strategic goal is thus to win some combination of states whose electoral votes total at least 270.

The Constitution originally called for the candidate winning the second-most electoral votes to be the vice president. This situation became untenable with the emergence of political parties. In the 1800 election, the Republican-Democrats and the Federalists ran two candidates each in an effort to win the presidency and vice presidency. The simultaneous election of these different positions meant that the parties had to ensure that their "top" candidate would win a majority while their second candidate would get the next most votes. But the victorious Republican-Democrats miscalculated, and Aaron Burr, their second choice, wound up with the same number of votes as their first choice and presumptive presidential candidate, Thomas Jefferson. To add insult to injury, the defeated Federalists considered throwing their support behind Burr in a potential House vote, although key Federalists, including Alexander Hamilton, ultimately sided with Jefferson, making him president. The Twelfth Amendment was soon passed (in 1804) to "fix" the system. The

---

[6] Most states use a winner-take-all rule in assigning Electoral College votes to candidates: the candidate with the most votes in the state gets all of the state's electoral votes. This is a matter of state law, however, and Maine and Nebraska allocate two votes based on the statewide vote and then allow votes in the congressional districts to determine the remaining electors. In 2004, Colorado voters considered a ballot proposition that would have awarded presidential electors based on district-by-district results; this complicated things for the presidential campaigns, as this Election Day vote could have significantly affected the simultaneous awarding of electors. Ultimately, voters rejected the plan and Bush won all eight of Colorado's electoral votes.

Electoral College has often been the subject of controversy. One criticism involves the method for determining electoral votes. The formula—the total number of representatives plus the total number of senators—was derived to secure the support of small states in the fight over the ratification of the Constitution; it creates a bias in favor of those smaller states. For example, Wyoming has one elector for every 165,000 residents, while California has one for every 617,000. However, some argue that the Electoral College actually benefits large states because carrying a large state by a tiny margin creates an Electoral College windfall due to the winner-take-all rule. For example, Bill Clinton won 70 percent of the electoral vote despite only getting 49 percent of the popular vote in 1996.

Concern about the representation of states has led to various attempts for reform. For instance, a group called National Popular Vote has called for state legislatures to commit their state's electoral votes to the candidate who receives the most popular votes nationwide. These bills would take effect only when enough states passed them to represent a majority of electoral votes; that is, sufficient votes to elect a president. As of 2013, eight states (plus DC) have passed such bills into law and another four have bills pending in the current legislative session. The laws would in effect create a system under which the president wins by a plurality of the popular vote. Support for this proposal is buttressed by public opinion polls, which indicate that Americans would prefer to have the president elected via a simple national vote, and by controversies like the one after the 2000 presidential election, when some questioned the legitimacy of George W. Bush's victory, given that Al Gore won more popular votes. The reform is also designed to circumvent the difficulties in actually amending the Constitution to replace the Electoral College with another system. However, at this point in time, it seems unlikely to pass in enough states to affect presidential elections in the near future.

Recent Trends in Electoral College Outcomes The Electoral College's role makes it important for presidential candidates to understand the partisan complexion of individual states. Some states tend to produce close presidential elections, while others are predictably Republican or Democratic. Furthermore, some states are more likely to actually swing from one party to the other in different presidential elections. Table 8.3 shows how states might be categorized based on the 2000, 2004, 2008, and 2012 elections, with states that voted the same way every time ("base states") distinguished from those that produced mixed results ("battleground states"; see also Figure 8.1). The Democrats start off with a near majority in the Electoral College because

TABLE 8.3 Classification of States Based on Presidential Votes, 2000–2012

Base Democratic States (18 states + DC, 242 electoral votes)*	Battleground States (10 states, 116 electoral votes)	Base Republican States (22 states, 180 electoral votes)
California (55)	Colorado (9)	Alabama (9)
Connecticut (7)	Florida (29)	Alaska (3)
Delaware (3)	Indiana (11)	Arizona (11)
District of Columbia (3)	Iowa (6)	Arkansas (6)
Hawaii (4)	Nevada (6)	Georgia (16)
Illinois (20)	New Hampshire (4)	Idaho (4)
Maine (4)	New Mexico (5)	Kansas (6)
Maryland (10)	North Carolina (15)	Kentucky (8)
Massachusetts (11)	Ohio (18)	Louisiana (8)
Michigan (16)	Virginia (13)	Mississippi (6)
Minnesota (10)		Missouri (10)
New Jersey (14)		Montana (4)
New York (29)		Nebraska (5)
Oregon (7)		North Dakota (3)
Pennsylvania (20)		Oklahoma (7)
Rhode Island (4)		South Carolina (9)
Vermont (3)		South Dakota (3)
Washington (12)		Tennessee (11)
Wisconsin (10)		Texas (38)
		Utah (5)
		West Virginia (5)
		Wyoming (3)

*Note: 2012 electoral votes in parentheses.

FIGURE 8.1 The Results of the 2000–2012 Presidential Elections

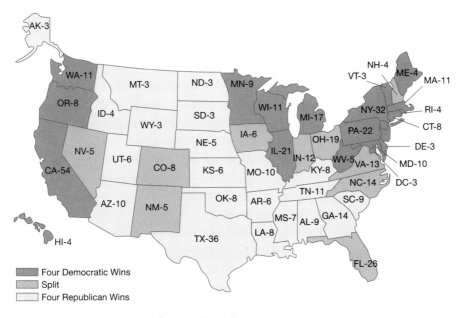

Note: 2012 electoral votes presented after state abbreviation.
Source: Rhodes Cook, Alice V. McGillivray, and Richard M. Scammon. 2010. "America Votes 28: Election Returns by State, 2007–2008." Washington, DC: CQPress.

they dominate large states such as California, New York, Pennsylvania, New Jersey, and Illinois, which together have 138 electoral votes. In these elections, Democrats have dominated the northeastern, upper midwest, and Pacific coast states. Republican candidates have dominated in the southern and mountain west states, creating what analysts call the **Republican L**.

The outcomes of recent elections have thus hinged upon the results in a handful of states. As shown in Table 8.3 and Figure 8.1, forty states (and DC) voted for the same party in the 2000, 2004, 2008, and 2012 presidential elections, while ten states did not: Colorado, Florida, Indiana, Iowa, Nevada, New Hampshire, New Mexico, North Carolina, Ohio, and Virginia. These states combined for 116 electoral votes in 2012, and when they have favored a single candidate, as they did Obama in 2008, they provide that candidate with a comfortable margin of victory. Other states, such as Michigan, Missouri, Oregon, Pennsylvania, Washington, and Wisconsin, are sometimes considered **battleground (or swing) states** by campaign experts even though they have consistently (but narrowly) favored one party or the other. Although knowledgeable people may differ with respect to which states are battleground states, the main point is that battleground states are targeted in presidential campaigns.

TABLE 8.4 Electoral Vote Changes Based on the 2010 Census

Safe Democratic States	Battleground States	Safe Republican States
Illinois (–1)	Florida (+2)	Arizona (+1)
Massachusetts (–1)	Iowa (–1)	Georgia (+1)
Michigan (–1)	Nevada (+1)	Louisiana (–1)
New Jersey (–1)	Ohio (–2)	Missouri (–1)
New York (–2)		South Carolina (+1)
Pennsylvania (–1)		Texas (+4)
Washington (+1)		Utah (+1)
Overall: –6	Overall: no change	Overall: +6

The decennial U.S. census can change the playing field. As mandated by the Constitution, House seats, and therefore electoral votes, are reapportioned according to changes in state populations. Based on the 2010 census, states that were safely Democratic in 2008 lost six seats and those that were safely Republican gained six seats (Table 8.4). This will not help Democratic candidates in the next decade and beyond, but it might not hurt them very much either. In 2008, for example, Barack Obama would have won by a healthy margin even if that election had been conducted with the new allocation of electoral votes.

Strategic Impact of the Electoral College We have emphasized the effects of rules on campaign strategy, and the presidential election is an obvious example. In particular, the Electoral College affects how and where candidates campaign. Presidential campaigns begin with a list of targeted states that are necessary for them to get 270 electoral votes. Whether (and how much) to campaign depends not only on how competitive the state is and whether it is critical to achieving 270 votes, but also upon the relative cost of campaigning in that state compared to other target states. Thus, candidates concentrate their television ads and in-person visits on the most cost-effective states and media markets on their list.[7]

---

[7] Daron Shaw. 2006. *The Race to 270*. Chicago: University of Chicago Press.

In 2012, both the Obama and the Romney campaigns focused on television advertising and visits to states the campaigns determined to be critical to the election outcome. Obama spent 56 percent of his total advertising budget, an estimated $225 million, on ads in ten media markets that his campaign deemed crucial. Romney spent approximately 53 percent of his total television advertising budget, an estimated $263 million, on his top ten markets (Table 8.5). Their visits were also concentrated on battleground states, with the top five most-visited states receiving 66 percent of all presidential visits (Table 8.6). Furthermore, visits to non-battleground states were typically to hold fund-raising events.

In 2012, the presidential candidates were roughly equal with respect to resources. In 2008, however, Obama was much better financed than McCain. Indeed, the data show that while Obama and McCain made roughly equivalent numbers of campaign visits overall, Obama and the Democratic Party

TABLE 8.5 Romney and Obama TV Ad Spending: The Top Ten Media Markets

Romney and Republican Groups		Obama and Democratic Groups	
Washington, DC	$41 million	Washington, DC	$34 million
Denver, CO	$29 million	Denver, CO	$30 million
Cleveland, OH	$28 million	Cleveland, OH	$27 million
Tampa, FL	$27 million	Orlando, FL	$22 million
Charlotte, NC	$27 million	Tampa, FL	$21 million
Las Vegas, NV	$25 million	Las Vegas, NV	$21 million
Orlando, FL	$23 million	Charlotte, NC	$17 million
Miami, FL	$21 million	Miami, FL	$16 million
Columbus, OH	$16 million	Columbus, OH	$15 million
Cincinnati, OH	$14 million	Boston, MA	$12 million
Boston, MA	$12 million	Cincinnati, OH	$10 million
TOTAL	**$263 million**	**TOTAL**	**$225 million**

Source: Data are from the *Washington Post*, as provided by Kantar Media/CMAG. Updated on 11/14/12 and inclusive of all TV ad buys from 5/11–11/5/12.

TABLE 8.6 Romney/Ryan and Obama/Biden Appearances: The Top Ten States

Romney/Ryan		Obama/Biden	
Ohio	69	Ohio	55
Florida	46	Florida	44
Virginia	42	Virginia	30
Iowa	26	Iowa	29
Colorado	25	New York	21
California	21	District of Columbia	20
New York	18	California	18
Pennsylvania	16	New Hampshire	18
Nevada	15	Colorado	17
Wisconsin	14	Wisconsin	17
New Hampshire	13	Nevada	15
TOTAL	**305**	**TOTAL**	**284**

Source: *Washington Post.* Candidate appearances include all events, including fund-raisers, 5/29–11/6/12.

vastly outspent McCain and the Republicans on television advertising. This disadvantage made it imperative for McCain to deploy his resources as strategically as possible. Conversely, this advantage allowed Obama to advertise in places normally considered out of reach for Democratic candidates, such as Virginia, Indiana, and North Carolina—states that he ultimately carried.

Although all presidential campaigns target battleground states, they differ in how ambitious their targeting is. Some campaigns, such as George H. W. Bush's 1988 campaign, play "offense" by targeting a number of states that usually vote for the other party. Other campaigns, such as Bill Clinton's in 1996, play "defense" by looking to solidify states that voted for them last time or that look "safe" in the current election. Still other campaigns, such as Al Gore's in 2000, concentrate on a very small number of highly competitive battleground states in an attempt to create a narrow Electoral College majority—a tactic referred to as "threading the needle." Finally, campaigns can employ a "mixed" strategy—emphasizing defensive campaigning at one

Putting Together an Electoral College Plan

In the 2008 presidential election, Barack Obama won 52.9 percent of the national popular vote to John McCain's 45.6 percent. More important, Obama won 365 electoral votes to McCain's 173. Obama's electoral coalition included Democratic strongholds, such as California, New York, and Massachusetts, as well as traditionally Republican states, such as Indiana and North Carolina. These results — and the issues and attitudes that drove them — will fascinate political scientists for years. But for campaign professionals, the results of the 2008 election (and, to a lesser degree, those of 2004) become the baseline for drawing up the 2012 battleplan.

In devising their plan for the 2012 election, the starting point for Obama's team was that the 2010 census had changed the map. For the 2012 election, 18 states saw a change in their electoral votes because of the decennial census. Obama's 2008 coalition was worth 6 fewer points in 2012—359 electoral votes—because of these adjustments. Compared to Bush's re-election campaign, Obama was also defending more turf. This was because Obama's victory in 2008 was much larger than Bush's in 2000. In all, there were six states decided by fewer than five percentage points in 2008: Florida, Indiana, Missouri, Montana, North Carolina, and Ohio. Obama carried four of the six, losing only in Missouri and Montana. Factoring all of this into its plans, Obama's 2012 campaign used Kerry's 2004 coalition as its starting point and identified five potential paths to 270 electoral votes. First, there was the "West Path." If Obama won Colorado (9 electoral votes), New Mexico (5) and Nevada (6), and added them to Kerry's 246 electoral votes, he would have 266. Add in the 6 electoral votes from Iowa, and he'd

have 272. The second path for Obama was the "Florida Path," which meant winning the Sunshine State and its 29 electoral votes. That total added to Kerry's 246 electoral votes would equal 275. The third path was the "South Path," which involved adding North Carolina (15 electoral votes) and Virginia (13) to Kerry's total to reach 274. The fourth path was the "Midwest Path," which involved adding Ohio (18 electoral votes) and Iowa (6) to Kerry's total to get to 270 on the nose. Finally, there was the "expansion path," which had the president losing critical states but still winning the election by bringing others into the fold. Under this scenario, the re-election campaign wouldn't hold on to Kerry's wins in Pennsylvania and New Hampshire, losing their 20 and 4 electoral votes, respectively. He would also fail to win Ohio and Florida. But by re-winning Colorado, Nevada, New Mexico, and adding Arizona (11 electoral votes), a more likely proposition than in 2008 when John McCain (R-AZ) was running, Obama would get to 272.

Beyond these basics, Obama's campaign monitored other states to see if they might deviate significantly from their 2008 vote. Perhaps the economy had been particularly bad in an otherwise "blue" state. Or perhaps a local issue had adversely affected the president's standing. On the flipside, the president may have had an opportunity to pick up a state or two because of favorable issues or shifts in the underlying demographics of the state. Texas, for example, has been reliably Republican since 1980, but its growing Hispanic population could tilt it more toward the Democrats in coming years. All of these factors were weighed and balanced, with the results driving candidate attention and millions of dollars in political advertising.

stage of the campaign, and then offensive campaigning at another stage. George W. Bush's campaign organization did this in 2000, casting a very broad net early and then narrowing it considerably when data showed progress in some states but not in others.[8]

Electoral College strategies are not set in stone, however. Campaigns may adjust these strategies during the campaign itself. By the month before the general election, the campaigns should have enough polling information to abandon some states, add others, or simply narrow the battlefield to those states that are absolutely essential to victory. In 2008, the Obama campaign added Indiana and North Carolina to their list of targets based on late September polling that showed Obama was ahead in those traditionally Republican states. In 2000, George W. Bush decided to make a concerted effort to win Tennessee (the home state of his opponent, Al Gore) and West Virginia (which had not voted for a Republican presidential candidate since 1964) after early October polls revealed competitive contests.

The targeting strategies of presidential candidates mean that most recent presidential elections have been decided by voters in a handful of states. Is this fair? Might it be that certain states—Ohio, Florida, and Nevada, for example—receive disproportionate public policy commitments and advertising revenue, resources that distort a supposedly representative system? Advocates of Electoral College reform certainly think so. In any case, criticism of the candidates or their campaigns for this reality is misplaced: they are simply responding to the rules of the current system.

Political and Economic Realities

Presidential campaigns are substantially constrained not only by the rules of the elections but also by political reality. In any given election a campaign is dealt a set of cards. How the campaign plays the cards is important, but the luck of the draw has a major impact on who wins the hand. Three factors in a presidential election are particular important: incumbency, war, and the economy. Of these, the economy is usually considered paramount.

Incumbent presidents have natural advantages. They have the advantage of experience, having run a previous presidential campaign. They have the trappings of the office of presidency, including the pomp and circumstance and an enhanced ability to make news, communicate with the public, and shape the national agenda. They also have an easier road to the party's nomination, with typically no opposition or only token opposition. It is no surprise, then, that two-thirds of incumbent presidents who seek re-election win. Typically,

---

[8] Shaw, *The Race to 270.*

they begin the campaign with a larger lead than nonincumbent candidates and hold on to a larger portion of this lead during the campaign.[9]

Ongoing wars matter in both positive and negative ways. An incumbent president up for re-election at the outset of a war will likely benefit from the public's tendency to rally behind the president in times of crisis. But it has been rare for an election to occur just as a conflict is getting under way. At the same time, it is often thought that presidents will seek to create such a crisis right before the election—sometimes referred to as an "October Surprise." This, too, is rare, in fact. Historically, wars have more often had a negative impact on the incumbent president's re-election bid. The number of American military personnel killed in action during war tends to sour voters on the mission, producing more negative evaluations of the president's job performance, and reducing his support at the polls.[10] This was particularly consequential for the Democratic Party in both 1952 and 1968, when Presidents Truman and Johnson were presiding over the wars in Korea and Vietnam, respectively.

The economy is the most powerful influence on presidential elections. The candidate of the incumbent party, and especially an incumbent president, is much more likely to win if the economy is growing strongly. In recent presidential elections, there is a powerful relationship between the incumbent party's share of the vote and economic indicators like the growth in average disposable income in the year before the election. The upward sloping line of Figure 8.2 captures the trend: as economic growth increases, so does the incumbent party's share of the vote. Jimmy Carter, who ran for re-election when incomes were shrinking, won only 45 percent of the two-party vote. But his successor, Ronald Reagan, was re-elected easily, thanks to the booming economy of 1984.

The powerful impact of the economy creates strategic imperatives for the candidates. Candidates who benefit politically from the state of the economy tend to make it the central issue of their campaign. Thus, an incumbent president or incumbent party candidate will emphasize the economy during periods of economic growth. Conversely, the opposition party will emphasize the economy during an economic downturn. Candidates who are not favored by the economy need to change the subject by emphasizing some other issue or issues.[11]

---

[9] James E. Campbell. 2000. *The American Campaign: U.S. Presidential Campaigns and the National Vote.* College Station: Texas A&M University Press.

[10] Douglas A. Hibbs, Jr. 2000. "Bread and Peace Voting in U.S. Presidential Elections." *Public Choice* 104: 149–80.

[11] Lynn Vavreck. 2009. *The Message Matters: The Economy and Presidential Campaigns.* Princeton, NJ: Princeton University Press.

FIGURE 8.2 Election Year Income Growth

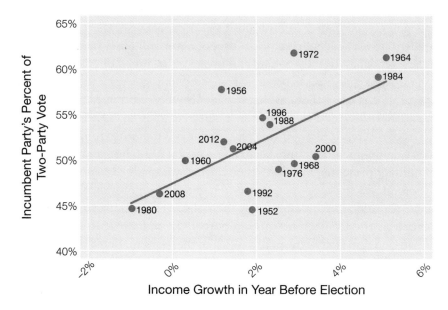

Income Growth in Year Before Election

The Fall Campaign

As the campaign gets under way after the conventions, candidates must make a series of strategic decisions within the context of Electoral College math and broader realities. We discuss several important parts of that process: message development, the timing of campaign activity, the candidate debates, and mobilizing supporters to vote.

Message Development As presidential candidates shift from the primary campaign to the general election campaign, they often refine their message, particularly to address contrasts with their opponent. As we discussed in Chapter 5, campaign messages are designed to appeal to undecided voters or mobilize sympathetic partisans. Typically, campaigns rely on polls and focus groups to discern which issues are salient to the public, which issue positions are most popular, and how issues can be framed to improve the campaign's chances for success. Candidates have their own ideas about political issues, of course, but no serious presidential campaign makes a move without surveying public opinion. Campaigns do not always follow the results of their polls, but they need to know how the public will likely react to the campaign's message.

As candidates decide what issues to emphasize, they are thinking not only about the broader political realities but about any other factor that might advantage or disadvantage them. One factor is the political reputation of their party. In 1988, George H. W. Bush's campaign manager, Lee Atwater, decided that his candidate would do best if the election were about crime, taxes, and national defense. He was confident that Americans would trust his candidate to handle these issues more effectively than the Democratic candidate, Massachusetts governor Michael Dukakis. A second factor is the particular positions of "swing voters." As we discussed in Chapter 5, campaigns have an incentive to locate themselves close to the so-called median voter, so that candidates will maximize their appeal to the public. This strategy makes sense because many Americans hold fairly centrist positions on political issues.

But calculations about issue agendas and positions are fraught with difficulties. What if a candidate would prefer to ignore an issue that is a top priority of the party's base? What if a candidate's position appeals to a slim majority of voters overall but is unpopular with the base? And what if the popular position contradicts the candidate's previous position? Candidates naturally want to avoid contradicting themselves. In 2004, for example, Democrat John Kerry attempted to explain how in 2003 he had supported a bill allocating $87 billion for the troops fighting the Iraq War, but then ended up opposing the funding bill that ultimately was passed. He famously said, "I actually did vote for the $87 billion before I voted against it." This quote was later used by the Bush campaign to portray Kerry as a flip-flopper.

Presidential campaigns can sometimes finesse the challenges of message development by delivering different messages via different media. In television ads and public speeches, candidates focus on broadly salient issues and popular positions. In direct mail, phone calls, and e-mails, candidates focus on issues and positions popular with their party's base. This is because they can use **narrow-casting**, targeting a smaller audience using these media, and without the visibility that mass media entail. In 2008, for example, John McCain used direct mail to Republican households to emphasize his pro-life position on abortion, even as he made no mention of this issue in his television advertising. Similarly, Obama never mentioned race in his television or radio advertising; telephone calls to black households, though, focused on his being the first black major-party candidate.

When asked about his opponent's claim that he "had a plan" to defeat him, the former heavyweight boxing champion Mike Tyson said, "Everyone has a plan until they get hit in the mouth." This statement applies to every presidential campaign ever run. Despite all of the planning that goes into developing a message, life intervenes. Campaigns are particularly sensitive to the harsh judgments of the electorate, and they have up-to-the-minute feedback loops in the form of polls from all of their battleground states. By mid- to late September, they have enough information about public opinion to know whether they need to change course or not.

Front-runners have less need to make adjustments, unless their lead is shrinking. The trailing candidate, however, may decide to do something different. The most common major strategic adjustment is often to "go negative." In 1988, George H. W. Bush was trailing by double digits when his campaign made a strategic decision to attack Michael Dukakis's record as governor of Massachusetts. This was deemed easier and more effective than rebuilding Bush's image. After all, Bush had been in the public eye for over two decades, while Dukakis was a newcomer and had received little scrutiny during the Democratic primaries. In August, Bush strongly criticized Dukakis's record on crime and the environment. By early September, Bush strongly had pulled ahead and the entire dynamic of the election had changed.

Timing Although the Electoral College dominates decision making about where campaign activity occurs, when that activity occurs is a separate question. Some campaigns prefer to husband their resources and end the campaign with a massive advertising blitz, presumably when more citizens are paying attention. In 2008, John McCain's campaign spent much of its resources in the final ten days. The campaign strategists assumed that citizens are more affected by the last thing they see or hear, and that the best strategy was to match Obama's ad expenditures in the battleground states during the closing days. Other campaigns like to spend more of their resources earlier, hoping to define the race at the opening of the campaign. Still others expend resources during such high-profile events as the conventions and debates. For example, George W. Bush increased his television advertising during the 2000 presidential debates, while Al Gore significantly decreased his advertising on those days. Bush wanted to reinforce the themes he articulated during the debates, whereas Gore believed the debates and their attendant news coverage rendered additional campaigning superfluous.

There is no conclusive evidence that any particular timing strategy is best. The relatively large size of convention bumps are consistent with the notion that it is easier to influence the public's preferences early in the campaign when more people have yet to develop strong opinions of the candidates. In the 2004 and 2008 presidential elections, polling showed that citizens made up their minds about the candidates quite early in the campaign season, and much earlier than they had in 2000. However, other evidence suggests that many citizens do not pay attention to the campaign until late in the process and that the effects of a television advertisement or candidate visit usually dissipate after only a few days.[12]

---

[12] Alan Gerber, James Gimpel, Donald Green, and Daron Shaw. 2011. "The Influence of Television and Radio Advertising on Candidate Evaluations: Results from a Large Scale Randomized Experiment." *American Political Science Review* 105, 1: 135–150. Daron Shaw and James Gimpel, forthcoming. "What If We Randomized the Governor's Schedule?" *Political Communication.*

Candidate Debates Every fall campaign has its share of important events. But televised candidate debates stand out as the only potentially significant events that a campaign knows are coming. These are the most watched events of the campaign, and underdog candidates often look to them with the hope that they will reshape a race.

The Commission on Presidential Debates is a bipartisan commission established in 1987 to ensure that debates are a part of every presidential campaign. The commission sponsors the debates, varying their geographic location and format in an effort to engage as much of the public and to provide as much information as possible. After the major-party candidates accept their nominations, the commission produces a debate schedule and the campaigns are obliged to either accept or decline their recommendations. If they decline—or even suggest direct negotiations between the campaigns, as George H. W. Bush did in 1992 and George W. Bush did in 2000—they must explain their reasoning to the news media and the public. Any campaign that does not immediately accept the commission's recommendations will surely face the accusation that their candidate is dodging the debates, and so the standard in recent years has been to accept.

During the debates, campaigns have several goals. The first and most obvious goal is to "do no harm"—that is, avoid the sort of gaffe that drives subsequent news media coverage and undermines the campaign's effort to control messaging. To minimize the chances of a major mistake, presidential candidates prepare well in advance, usually for an hour or two each week during the summer and early fall and then all day for three to four days before the debate itself. Campaigns run mock debates for the candidate, using stand-ins for the opposition and staging the aggressive questioning that sometimes occurs. These efforts are videotaped and then critiqued on the basis of style and substance. Campaign staff make sure the candidates absorb voluminous briefing books on issues; candidates are then quizzed and asked to redress substantive weaknesses.

During the debate, candidates essentially seek to implement a miniature version of their overall campaign strategy. They emphasize issues and appeals that benefit them, avoiding issues on which their opponent has the advantage. Viewers may not tune in to the debate for very long and may not be paying much attention, so candidates want to broadcast the strongest case for their candidacy. This is why candidates often seem to be answering questions besides the ones that were actually asked. When challenged, candidates tend to respond to every charge made by the opposition. They do this because it has been shown that viewers may assume that any charge, no matter how outrageous, is true if not contradicted.

In the presidential debates of 1960, Richard Nixon's performance was poorly received by television viewers. Those listening on radio were more impressed.

Candidates also address their answers to the television audience and not to the other candidate or the audience in the hall (unless the debate is held in a town hall format, with actual citizens asking questions). The reaction of those in the auditorium is much less important than the reaction of those watching on television, and especially the news media. Media coverage of the debates is actually more important for influencing public opinion than the debates themselves.[13] For example, immediately after the first debate of the 2000 presidential campaign, Al Gore was judged to have scored a slight victory over George W. Bush, but subsequent media coverage of several questionable claims he made during the debate, as well as mocking coverage of his colorful makeup, turned opinion around. One week after the debate, Bush was judged to have been the winner. The lesson here reinforces the main goal of debates (do no harm) but also emphasizes the need for the campaign to defend its candidate's performance in order to shape news media interpretations.

Despite all the preparation and strategizing that goes into debates, and despite the public's opinions about who did or did not win a particular debate, there are rarely large changes in public support for the candidates after a debate. Simply put, most debates have little impact on the polls and on the election's outcome. Because debates occur relatively late in the campaign, most people have made up their minds. People then view debates through partisan lenses: the vast majority of partisans believe that their candidate won. In a CNN poll conducted after the first 2008 presidential debate, 85 percent of Democrats thought Obama had won and 64 percent of Republicans thought McCain had won. Moreover, whereas during each convention one party dominates the news, debates consist of opposing messages from both parties. In a sense, these messages tend to cancel each other out, making it difficult for either party's candidate to get much of a boost in the polls from the debate.

Mobilizing Citizens   At the end of the campaign, the candidate's staff works furiously to reach out to supporters and encourage them to vote. Complicating

---

[13] Richard Johnston, Kathleen Hall Jamieson, and Michael Hagen. 2004. *The 2000 Presidential Election and the Foundations of Party Politics.* New York: Oxford University Press.

this effort is the rise of **convenience voting**, a term that includes a variety of ways in which citizens can vote without actually going to their polls on Election Day (Figure 8.3). Methods of convenience voting include early voting, voting by mail, and voting by absentee ballot. In 2012, close to thirty percent of Americans cast their presidential votes before Election Day. Presidential campaigns must therefore ensure that supporters get absentee ballot applications or information about early voting locations well in advance of the relevant deadlines.

Campaigns have to time their outreach appropriately. In 2012, 50 percent of Florida voters voted early, so it would have been foolish to launch an extensive get-out-the-vote operation in late October. Campaigns must also monitor early voting records from the states to see which of their targets have failed to vote (these individuals receive additional outreach) and which have voted (these individuals may be asked to contribute to or volunteer for the campaign).

As Election Day draws near, candidates visit the most critical locales and groups. In 2008, Barack Obama added last-minute stops in Indiana, a reliably Republican state that nonetheless looked to be leaning toward Obama (he ended up carrying the state by a single point). In an effort to drive more (and more favorable) coverage, they sometimes try gimmicks to get the news media's attention. In 2000, for example, Al Gore vowed to campaign without

FIGURE 8.3 Convenience Voting across the States, 1992–2012

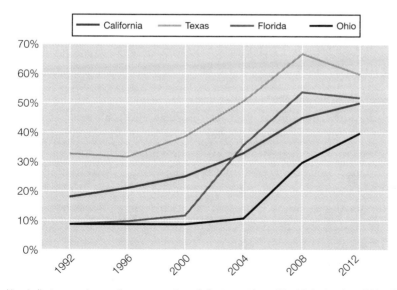

Note: Lines indicate convenience voting as a percentage of all votes cast in presidential elections from 1992 to 2012.
Source: The underlying data were compiled by the Associated Press and provided to members of the National Election Pool (NEP) for the 2012 elections.

sleep for the final 72 hours of the campaign. His midnight and early morning events produced large crowds and extensive media coverage.

Gore's personal efforts and the perceived success of the Democratic Party's last-minute organizational outreach prompted a comparable effort by the Republicans in 2002 and 2004. This "72-hour plan" featured extensive door-to-door campaigning and phone calls in the three days before the election. It was credited with mobilizing the Republican base in key areas. Naturally, Democrats responded in kind. In 2008 and 2012, Obama and the Democrats flooded neighborhoods with volunteer workers and also utilized e-mail lists and social networking Web sites to greatly extend the range and scope of their outreach.

On Election Day, citizens have to be contacted (via phone and e-mail) and mobilized to vote (using buses, cars, walks, etc.). As the day wears on, reports from precincts allow campaign staff to know where they are "light" (getting fewer targeted votes) and "heavy" (getting all or most targeted votes). Campaign attention can be refocused accordingly. Lawyers are also employed to file motions to keep the polls open in places where candidates expect to win and where there might be "irregularities," such as too few ballots or long lines. This has become a standard tactic in recent elections, especially among Democrats, who want to ensure that lower-income and minority precincts are properly equipped. Of course, the 2000 presidential election showed that the election may not end on Election Day. In 2004, 2008, and 2012, Democratic and Republican campaigns allocated money not only for election night parties for staff and supporters but also for media operations to influence news media reportage of close contests as well as for legal teams in case of recounts.

Conclusion

American presidential elections illustrate a crucial feature of elections everywhere: they depend a great deal on the rules and realities that candidates confront. For presidential candidates, the rules of the nomination process and the Electoral College strongly affect strategies—the decision to run, the states to target, and so on. Candidates are also constrained by the realities of whether an incumbent is running, whether the country is at war or at peace, and whether the economy is prospering or struggling. As a result, candidates will often find it difficult to persuade the public. Political scientists and campaign professionals have different perspectives on how much these factors constrain campaign effects: academics emphasize the limits to what electioneering can accomplish, while practitioners emphasize the small effects that a good campaign can produce—effects that could decide a close election.

Do American presidential elections meet democratic ideals? Both the nominations and the general election processes frequently elicit criticisms. For one, some claim that the nominating process produces unrepresentative candidates. Specifically, the complaint is that the sequence of primaries and caucuses allows small and ideologically extreme groups to exercise disproportionate influence by electing their favored candidates in states such as Iowa or New Hampshire. A cursory examination of the historical record casts doubt on this claim. Republicans John McCain, Robert Dole, George H. W. Bush, and Mitt Romney and Democrats Bill Clinton, Al Gore, John Kerry, and Barack Obama hardly seem out of the mainstream. One could argue that Ronald Reagan was more conservative than the average Republican or that Michael Dukakis was more liberal than the average Democrat, but their records as governors offer many examples of pragmatism. Moreover, this is consistent with political science research demonstrating that while presidential primary electorates tend to be older and slightly more ideological than the party electorate as a whole, they are not necessarily ideologically extreme.[14]

A second complaint is that the national conventions are just public relations events. There is no deliberation about the candidates and little meaningful debate about the parties' platforms. This complaint is undoubtedly justified. It is less clear, however, that conventions themselves are simply fluff. Conventions help to unify parties after divisive primaries. They also allow the candidates to present themselves and their campaigns to a wide swath of citizens. The nominees' speeches are often rich in information about their policy agendas and goals.[15] After the conventions, citizens typically express more interest in the campaign.[16] The television networks may claim that the conventions are staged, but it may not be a bad thing to allow the parties to speak directly to the American people once every four years.

A third complaint is similar to the second: debates are uninspired and scripted. This may be true at times, but debates still have positive consequences. After the debates, citizens tend to be more interested in the campaign, feel more favorably about the candidates, and be more knowledgeable

---

[14] John G. Geer. 1988. "Assessing the Representativeness of Electorates in Presidential Primaries." *Journal of Politics* 32, 4: 929–45.

[15] Marion Just, Tami Buhr, and Ann Crigler. 2000. "Shifting the Balance: Journalist versus Candidate Communication in the 1996 Presidential Campaign," in *Campaign Reform: Insights and Evidence*, eds. Larry M. Bartels and Lynn Vavreck. Ann Arbor: University of Michigan Press.

[16] For data from the 2000 campaign, see Richard Johnston, Michael G. Hagen, and Kathleen Hall Jamieson. 2004. *The 2000 Presidential Election and the Foundations of Party Politics*. New York: Cambridge University Press.

about the candidates in some ways.[17] However, the knowledge they've gained is not always about the candidates' positions on issues. Thus, it is quite possible that debates could be reformed to become more informative or empowering. Citizens seem especially impressed by the town hall debate format, suggesting that more direct citizen involvement in the debates would be desirable. There are also those who would like to see more debates, spread out over the entirety of the campaign.

A final set of complaints concerns the Electoral College. Perhaps the most prominent of these is that the Electoral College is not as democratic as a direct popular vote and can produce a winner who did not win the popular vote. Other complaints center on the perceived built-in biases of the Electoral College—most notably, that it favors smaller states and leads candidates to focus on battleground states and ignore others. In particular, critics fear that this focus on battleground states leads citizens in other states to be less motivated to vote on Election Day.

Defenders of the Electoral College respond that discrepancies between the Electoral College and popular vote are rare. They also note that battleground states are actually quite representative of the country as a whole.[18] Moreover, although citizens in battleground states, and particularly those with lower incomes, can be mobilized by campaign activity, citizens outside battleground states are not turned off.[19]

Would a new presidential election system have comparable or even greater drawbacks? A direct national vote may not stop candidates from campaigning selectively. For instance, Democrats would be tempted to spend a lot of time in major urban areas such as New York, Chicago, and Los Angeles, mobilizing reliably Democratic constituents. Republicans, meanwhile, would have incentives to concentrate in suburban areas around cities such as Dallas, Atlanta, and Phoenix. For candidates to campaign nationally, they might also have to work harder and spend more money than they currently do. This would make presidential campaigns even more arduous and expensive than

---

[17] Larry Bartels. 2000. "Campaign Quality: Standards for Evaluation, Benchmarks for Reform," in *Campaign Reform: Insights and Evidence*, eds. Larry M. Bartels and Lynn Vavreck. Ann Arbor: University of Michigan Press; Thomas Holbrook. 1999. "Political Learning from Presidential Debates." *Political Behavior* 21,1: 67–89.

[18] Darshan J. Goux and David A. Hopkins. 2008. "The Empirical Implications of Electoral College Reform." *American Politic Research* 36: 857–79.

[19] James G. Gimpel, Karen M. Kaufmann, and Shanna Pearson-Merkowitz. 2007. "Battleground States versus Blackout States: The Behavioral Implications of Modern Presidential Campaigns." *Journal of Politics* 69,3: 786–97; Keena Lipsitz. 2009. "The Consequences of Battleground and 'Spectator' State Residency for Political Participation." *Political Behavior* 31: 187–209.

they currently are—and the challenges and costs of campaigns are already criticized as discouraging potential candidates from running and allowing too much money into politics.

Of course, it is entirely possible that the presidential-election system could be improved. But alternatives entail trade-offs among competing values, with any improvements creating new and even unforeseen problems. This is not an excuse for inaction; rather, it is a reminder that the words "perfection" and "democracy" rarely appear in the same sentence.

KEY TERMS

delegates (p. 217)

caucuses (p. 218)

primary election (p. 218)

viability (p. 220)

front-loading (p. 220)

front-runner (p. 223)

roll-call vote (p. 225)

convention bump/convention bounce (p. 228)

Republican L (p. 233)

battleground/swing states (p. 233)

narrow-casting (p. 241)

convenience voting (p. 245)

FOR DISCUSSION

1. Why do states want to move their primary dates up in the election calendar? What is this process called? What is the effect of this process on campaigning?

2. How are the national party conventions different today compared to conventions in the 1950s?

3. How does the Electoral College affect the strategies of presidential campaigns?

4. Why might a presidential candidate want to campaign relatively early in the fall? Why might she want to campaign relatively late?

Visit StudySpace for quizzes and other review material.
wwnorton.com/studyspace

CHAPTER 9

Congressional Campaigns

In the summer of 2007, North Carolina Democrats were scrambling to find a candidate willing to challenge Republican senator Elizabeth Dole. Dole's re-election in 2008 seemed inevitable; she was a two-time cabinet secretary, a former presidential candidate, former president of the American Red Cross, and most important, the incumbent. She also had an impressive campaign war chest. All of the obvious Democratic choices, including the current governor and his predecessor, declined to challenge Dole. When she was first approached by Democratic Party officials, Kay Hagan, a North Carolina state senator, also refused, but she later reconsidered and entered the race. After Hagan won the Democratic nomination in June 2008, the Democratic Senatorial Campaign Committee (DSCC) decided that Dole was more vulnerable than previously thought and began to pour money into the state. By this time, Dole's weaknesses were glaring. Although she was born in North Carolina, she left the state after college and did not return until 2001 to run for the Senate seat. This left her open to the charge that she was out of touch with North Carolinians. Dole could also be linked to the unpopular President George W. Bush, who had encouraged her to run in 2002. The DSCC drove these messages home in a barrage of ads. Hagan was also helped by Barack Obama's well-organized campaign operation in North Carolina, which mobilized record numbers of young people and African Americans, most of whom voted Democratic.

Dole sealed her fate in the final weeks of the campaign by airing an attack ad that claimed Hagan had accepted money from "a leader of the Godless Americans PAC." The ad ended with a picture of Hagan and a voice-over of a woman — who viewers could reasonably (and incorrectly) assume was Hagan — saying, "There is no God." If Dole's opponent had been anyone but Hagan, the attack might have struck a mortal blow. Hagan had in fact attended a Democratic Party fundraiser whose co-hosts included two individuals who were associated with a group called the Godless Americans PAC. But Hagan was also a former Sunday school teacher and an active member of her Presbyterian church. As a result, major newspapers in North Carolina described Dole's attack as "indecent" and "worse than dishonest."[1] Hagan responded to Dole's attack with her own ads, including one accusing Dole of "bearing false witness against a fellow Christian." On Election Day, Hagan won the seat with 53 percent of the vote, defeating an incumbent senator who just a year earlier had been considered invincible.

Kay Hagan's election to the Senate in 2008 illustrates the hard reality of congressional elections: not only are their outcomes often driven by factors beyond candidates' control, such as the state of the economy and how voters feel about the president, but even a seemingly invincible candidate can lose under certain circumstances. It also shows how candidates can make strategic mistakes. In this case, Dole may have been able to eke out a narrow victory had she not aired the "Godless" advertisement.

The Hagan-Dole race also reflects the fact that national party committees have their own strategies. The DSCC, along with the National Republican Senatorial Committee (NRSC), the Democratic Congressional Campaign Committee (DCCC), and the National Republican Congressional Committee (NRCC), draw up lists of races to target each election cycle. When they decide to support a candidate, campaign finance law allows them to spend as much as they want on the election as long as they do not coordinate their activities with the candidates. A national party committee sometimes spends more on a race than does the party's candidate.

Core of the Analysis

- The rules governing congressional elections and campaign finance directly shape the strategies of House and Senate candidates.
- The political fortunes of congressional candidates often hinge on factors beyond their control, such as the popularity of the president and the state of the economy.
- Potential congressional candidates are ambitious and are strategic about when they run.
- Voters typically know little about congressional candidates and especially about challengers.
- Incumbents have substantial advantages over challengers in congressional races.

---

[1] "Dole's Desperate Turn to Big Lie Advertising." *Charlotte Observer,* October 30, 2008; "Dole's Attack on Hagan's Faith Drives Heated Campaign Lower." *Greensboro News and Record,* October 30, 2008.

When Democrat Kay Hagan (above) ran for the U.S. Senate in North Carolina in 2008, she initially seemed to have little chance of winning. However, strategic mistakes by her opponent, incumbent senator Elizabeth Dole, and the broader political and economic realities in 2008 helped Hagan win the seat.

Hagan's victory also illustrates how House and Senate candidates can "piggyback" on the efforts of a presidential candidate. Hagan benefited from Barack Obama's organizational efforts and his appeal among African American voters in North Carolina. All of these factors created a "perfect storm" that helped bring down a Senate incumbent. As we will learn in this chapter, incumbents have an enormous advantage in congressional elections, so Dole's defeat was anything but expected.

In this chapter we explore the nature and effects of congressional campaigns. As with presidential campaigns, we find that the impact of congressional campaigns depends on the particular rules governing the elections. Constitutional provisions and campaign finance law are especially important. We also find that incumbents have a substantial advantage over challengers in most congressional races. Consequently, challengers typically need fortuitous circumstances and a strong campaign to beat incumbents. Recent elections illustrate this point: in 2006, 2008, and 2010, an unusually large number of incumbents were defeated, owing to voter frustration with the war in Iraq and the state of the economy. These conditions made it easier for the minority party to recruit and fund challenger candidates.

Rules, Reality, and Who Runs for Congress

If you decide to run for Congress, few legal obstacles stand in your way. As we discussed in Chapter 2, the constitutional requirements entail only a minimum age, U.S. citizenship for a period of years, and residency in the state that you want to represent. If you satisfy these requirements and can meet state requirements for having your name appear on the ballot, such as paying a filing fee or collecting a certain number of signatures, you can run for Congress. Because the bar for running is so low, one might assume that people from all walks of life can and do run for office. If this were the case, we would expect Congress to be representative of the electorate in terms of demographic characteristics, such as age, income, race, and gender. Yet, as we shall see, those who seek to run and those who eventually win share certain characteristics that make them unrepresentative of the broader electorate.

Most individuals who run for office are ambitious and strategic. Politicians are rarely content to hold one job for long and are always looking for opportunities to advance. Congressional candidates have usually held a lower political office that has provided them with experience and connections that are helpful to their campaign. Serious candidates are also strategic, which means they will enter a race only when their prospects of winning are good. If a candidate runs and loses, then the connections and resources that one has may dry up. Thus, individuals who are ambitious and strategic run for office only when they believe the odds of winning are good.

The person with the best odds of winning an election is the **incumbent**, or the person who already occupies the office. Figure 9.1 shows the percentage of House and Senate incumbents seeking re-election who then won. From 1946 to 2012, the average percent of House incumbents running who were re-elected was 92 percent, while the average for Senate incumbents was 80 percent. Even in bad years for incumbents, they are much more likely to be re-elected than defeated. For example, 2010 was one of the worst years for House incumbents, but even so, 86 percent of the House incumbents who ran still won re-election.

Because the odds of their winning are so high, only extraordinary circumstances such as poor health will keep incumbents from running for re-election. Incumbents may also step down because of scandal. Sixty-six members of the House decided to retire after the 1992 House banking scandal, in which many representatives had written checks from their House bank accounts without the funds to cover those checks.

FIGURE 9.1 Percentage of House and Senate Incumbents Seeking Re-election Who Won, 1946–2012

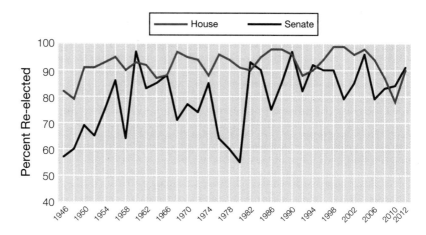

Source: Gary Jacobson. 2009. *The Politics of Congressional Elections.* New York: Longman, pp. 28–29. Additional data for 2008-2012 collected by the authors.

House incumbents may also decide to retire when their districts change after redistricting and they face the prospect of courting a new or mostly new constituency. As we discussed in Chapter 2, districts are usually drawn in a manner that protects incumbents of both parties, but anti-incumbent redistricting can occur if a party that has been out of power for a while gains control of the redistricting process. In Chapter 2, we described an unusual mid-decade redistricting undertaken by Texas Republicans in 2003. Their plan targeted ten Democratic incumbents, most of whom faced the prospect of competing in the 2004 election in substantially changed districts.[2] Although many of these incumbents decided to run in their new districts and lost, one incumbent—Congressman Jim Turner, a Democrat who had served Texas's 2nd District for six years—saw the writing on the wall. Republican state legislators had moved most of Turner's district into the 8th District, leaving him in the solidly conservative 6th District, which was represented by a ten-term Republican incumbent, Joe Barton. As a result, Turner decided to retire rather than run for re-election in 2004.

House and Senate incumbents may also retire if they feel that the country is experiencing a wave of anti-incumbent sentiment or a wave of sentiment

---

[2] Steve Bickerstaff. 2007. *Lines in the Sand: Congressional Redistricting in Texas and the Downfall of Tom DeLay.* Austin: University of Texas Press.

that favors the opposing party. For example, in the 2010 midterm election many Democratic incumbents found their once safe seats to be suddenly competitive and decided to retire rather than face tough re-election campaigns. Congressman Bart Gordon, a Democrat from Tennessee, was one such incumbent. Although the voters in his district usually voted for Republican presidential candidates, they liked Gordon and re-elected him 12 times. But many voters were angry at Gordon for supporting the agenda of President Obama and the Democratic leadership, especially on issues like health care and the environment. When polls began showing that he was in jeopardy of losing his seat and the Republican Party began aggressively recruiting candidates to run in his district, Gordon stepped down.

When incumbents decide to retire, their decision creates an **open seat**, or a contest between non-incumbents. Open seats are significant because they attract quality challengers who recognize that their chances of winning are higher with the incumbent out of the picture. A **quality challenger** is a candidate with the experience and backing necessary to run a competitive campaign. In contrast, **political amateurs** are candidates who have no political experience and are unlikely to win an election. Quality challengers are highly strategic candidates, basing their decision to run on whether the incumbent is running, or is vulnerable because of a scandal or a national political tide. Quality challengers also assess the incumbent's ability to attract votes and money. For example, if an incumbent has been winning by smaller margins or is struggling to raise money, potential challengers may assume that the incumbent is vulnerable.

Challengers have to consider whether they will be supported by their own party. The clearest indication of the party's support is whether the party has recruited a person to run. The "**Hill committees**"—the NRSC, DSCC, NRCC, and DCCC—encourage prospective candidates throughout the country to run for office. Much like scouts in sports, the parties are always looking for community leaders who might make successful candidates for office. These individuals are courted by party leaders and sent to workshops to learn how to run campaigns. They may also be provided with lists of potential contributors. Without such support, an ambitious and strategic individual might make the rational calculation that it is better to keep her current job than to run for Congress.

Because winning a congressional election requires resources and connections, certain types of individuals are more likely to run than others. On average, those who choose to run are more educated and wealthier than most Americans. They are also overwhelmingly white and, as we discussed in Chapter 5, male. Quality challengers tend to work in business, the law,

Political Amateurs and the 2010 Midterm Elections

The 2010 midterm election will be remembered for the "shellacking" Democrats received by the Republicans. The GOP picked up six seats in the Senate and a stunning 63 in the House, giving them control of that body. The election will also be remembered for its colorful cast of candidates, including a range of "witches, wing-nuts and wackos,"[1] many of whom were political amateurs—candidates without any prior political experience. Americans were angry with Washington in 2010 due to the economic recession and high unemployment. At such times, political amateurs can exploit their outsider status to make a run for Congress.

Among the most colorful amateurs of 2010 was Christine O'Donnell, a Tea Party–backed candidate who defeated the longest-serving congressman in Delaware history, Representative Mike Castle, in the primary. O'Donnell came under attack for allegedly using campaign funds to pay a portion of her rent. Her campaign took another hit when Bill Maher released footage from a 1999 *Politically Incorrect* show in which she admitted to having "dabbled" in witchcraft. Her response, a television advertisement that began "I'm not a witch," was spoofed on *Saturday Night Live* and became a Songify This sensation with more that 3 million hits.[2]

Odd political amateurs ran on the Democratic side as well. Alvin Greene, who challenged Senator Jim DeMint of South Carolina, attracted the most media attention of any 2010 campaign, according to a Pew Research Center study, because he appeared to win the primary without running a campaign and was charged with felony obscenity charges the day after his primary election. Greene's proposal to create jobs by hiring people to make Alvin Greene action figures also raised eyebrows.

Most political amateurs do not engage in such bizarre antics, but any election that promises to be a landslide for one party will attract candidates who know that their chances of winning—although in many cases still meager—are higher than they would be under normal circumstances. Some of these candidates are bound to be peculiar.

Elections that promise to be landslides also attract politically experienced challengers. These more experienced candidates tend to run in the most competitive races, however, while political amateurs run more often in uncompetitive ones. For example, in 2010, 93 percent of the Republican candidates who ran in safe Democratic districts were political amateurs, while 80 percent of the Democrats that ran in safe Republican districts were amateurs.[3] Thus, in many safe congressional districts across the country, the only alternative to the candidate of the dominant party is often a political amateur.

---

[1] David Canon. 2010. "The Year of the Outsider: Political Amateurs in the US Congress." *The Forum* 8, 4: Article 6.

[2] www.youtube.com/watch?v=44mqiBrBOzl (accessed 5/13/11).

[3] Canon, "The Year of the Outsider," p. 9.

or politics, with large networks that can be tapped for campaign resources. Thus, members of Congress are unrepresentative of the nation in terms of their education, wealth, race, and gender because the people who run for office are unrepresentative of the nation.

Campaign Organization and Funding

Once candidates have decided to run for Congress, they need to put together a campaign staff. As we have discussed, campaigns in the United States are candidate-centered, which means that candidates, rather than parties, are almost entirely responsible for raising money and putting together a campaign organization. This is true even if a party has recruited the candidate. The party might provide the candidate with a list of political consultants who have worked with other party candidates, but the candidate still must choose consultants that she feels will best help her win. And many candidates are left entirely to their own devices. They have to piece together a campaign staff as best they can.

Congressional campaign organizations range widely from bare-bones operations that are run by unpaid volunteers to big "Cadillac" organizations that are run by paid professional consultants. Amateurs with no prior political experience, and thus fewer contacts and resources, are more likely to have the former, while incumbents often have the latter. A well-funded congressional campaign typically has a campaign manager, who oversees the day-to-day operations of the campaign and helps develop strategy; there may also be a separate campaign strategist, as well as staff to deal with press relations, issue and opposition research, fund-raising, accounting, and grassroots organizing. The best-funded candidates, who include many House and Senate incumbents, may also hire consultants to conduct polls, develop radio and television advertisements, create direct mail pieces, and operate phone banks. An example of a campaign at this end of the spectrum was Hillary Rodham Clinton's 2006 Senate re-election bid in New York, in which she spent nearly $41 million despite having only token opposition. In addition to the tens of thousands of dollars paid each month to consultants, her campaign spent $27,000 on valet parking, $160,000 on private jet travel, and almost $750,000—more than the cost of most House campaigns—on catering and entertainment.[3]

---

[3] Ann Kornblut and Jeff Zeleny. 2006. "Clinton Won Easily But Bankroll Shows the Toll." *New York Times*, November 21.

The size and shape of congressional campaign organizations depends almost entirely on how much money they can raise. In 2012, the average House incumbent raised $1.6 million, while the average House challenger raised $267,000; the average Senate incumbent raised $12 million, while the average Senate challenger raised $1.4 million.[4] Congressional candidates differ greatly in how much they raise and spend, however. For instance, in 2012, incumbent senators Tom Carper (D-Del.) and Sheldon Whitehouse (D-R.I.) easily won re-election after spending just $5 million.[5] In contrast, Linda McMahon, the Senate Republican candidate in Connecticut, lost her race despite spending $50 million.[6] Remarkably, McMahon spent the same amount on a failed 2010 Connecticut Senate race.

The funding sources for congressional candidates are different from those for presidential candidates. First, unlike presidential candidates, congressional candidates are not eligible for public financing. They have no option but to raise money from individuals and political action committees (PACs). Congressional candidates differ in this respect from even Barack Obama and Mitt Romney, the only two presidential candidates who have declined public funding for their campaigns. Figure 9.2 shows that House candidates in 2012 raised 58 percent of their funds from individual contributions and 36 percent of their funds from PACs. The comparable figures for Senate candidates were 71 percent and 13 percent, respectively. In contrast, Obama and Romney raised nearly all of their funds from individuals and virtually nothing from PACs. PACs are limited to a contribution of $5,000 per candidate for each election cycle, making total PAC contributions a drop in the bucket for a presidential campaign but a more significant amount for congressional candidates. Presidential candidates also tend to avoid self-financing, while congressional candidates more often donate to their own campaign.

Despite these differences, congressional candidates, like presidential candidates, raise the bulk of their funds from individuals. But these individual contributions do not necessarily come from the candidates' districts or states, especially in competitive races. For example, House candidates in 2004 received an average of two-thirds of their individual contribu-

---

[4] Center for Responsive Politics. "Incumbent Advantage." www.opensecrets.org/overview/incumbs.php (accessed 3/5/13).

[5] Center for Responsive Politics. "Who's Raised the Least." www.opensecrets.org/overview/btmraise.php?Display=A&Memb=S (accessed 3/15/13).

[6] Center for Responsive Politics. "Who's Raised the Most." www.opensecrets.org/overview/topraise.php (accessed 3/15/13).

FIGURE 9.2 Comparison of House, Senate, and Presidential Candidate Funding Sources in 2012

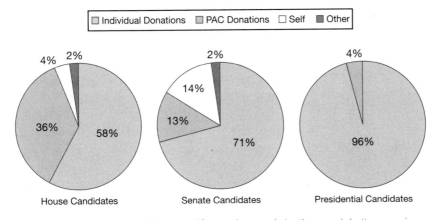

Note: Pie charts depict percentage of funds raised from each source during the general election campaign.
Source: Federal Election Commission.

tions from nonresidents.[7] Citizens who give to out-of-district (or out-of-state) candidates appear to be chiefly motivated by partisanship, seeking to increase their party's share of congressional seats.

Beyond individual and PAC contributions, it is becoming more common for House and Senate candidates to self-finance their campaigns and to rely on the help of outside groups, such as the super PACs and 501(c)(4)s discussed in Chapter 4. Whereas only 30 House and Senate candidates wrote themselves checks of $500,000 or more in 2004, 50 did so in 2012. As we discussed in Chapter 4, self-financed candidates do not always win, but they can give their opponents a run for their money. In 2012, outside groups unaffiliated with the parties spent $206 million on House races and $275 million on Senate races. This was approximately 19 percent of the amount that all House candidates spent on the election and 39 percent of the amount Senate candidates spent. Like candidates, outside groups are strategic, however, which means they target races where their money is likely to make a difference. For example, when control of the Senate was at stake in 2012,

[7] James G. Gimpel, Francis E. Lee, and Shanna Pearson-Merkowitz. 2008. "The Check Is in the Mail: Funding Flows in Congressional Elections." *American Journal of Political Science* 52, 2: 373–94.

outside groups focused their spending on the closest races, spending $37 million in Virginia, $31 million in Ohio, and $30 million in Wisconsin.[8]

The Primary

Like all candidates who run for a partisan office in the United States, congressional candidates must first compete for their party's nomination in a primary election. In the United States, it is not uncommon for congressional primaries to be uncontested. Such primaries usually feature a popular incumbent, whose seniority, power, and connections discourage would-be challengers. When incumbents do face primary challenges, they usually win for the same reasons. The one exception is when an incumbent faces another incumbent in a primary. This can occur in House elections when redistricting puts incumbents from previously neighboring districts in the same redrawn district.

Open-seat primaries occur when a party's incumbent has retired or when the party that is out of power chooses a candidate to challenge the incumbent in the general election. These are typically the most competitive primaries and the most likely to attract quality challengers. In such contests, the party normally remains neutral and lets the voters decide who the party should back in the general election. From time to time, however, the congressional campaign committees decide to back an open-seat-primary candidate who they believe has a good chance of beating a sitting incumbent. For example, in 2010 the DCCC decided to back State Representative Cedric Richmond, who was competing against three other Democrats for the party's nomination in Louisiana's 2nd District primary. This district, which includes most of New Orleans, usually votes Democratic; the incumbent, Republican Richard Cao, had won the seat only after the previous Democratic incumbent was beset by scandals. The DCCC believed Cao would lose if Richmond was the nominee, and they wanted to save Richmond from a bruising primary so that he would have sufficient standing and resources to run against Cao. With the DCCC's help, Richmond won easily and went on to reclaim the seat for the Democrats. This example is more the exception than the rule, however. Parties rarely get involved in congressional primaries because they have limited resources and prefer to save them for the general election.

---

[8] Center for Responsive Politics. "2012 Outside Spending, by Candidate." www.opensecrets .org/outsidespending/summ.php?disp=C (accessed 3/15/13).

Just like candidates in presidential primaries, candidates in House and Senate primaries must compete for votes from an electorate that is more ideological than the electorate in a general election. Thus, they must appeal to party stalwarts without jeopardizing their ability to attract the votes of moderates in the general election. One way to do this is to emphasize issues in the primary election that are ideological in nature — issues on which they can adopt positions that might be described as "modestly extreme," positions that appeal to ideological primary voters but are not as extreme as the views of some primary voters.[9] Then, in the general election, candidates move toward the center by emphasizing nonideological issues, such as personal character. They must be careful, however, not to change their agendas or positions too dramatically or else they might be criticized for "flip-flopping" or "waffling." This possibility encourages primary candidates to adopt only modestly extreme positions, since these positions will be easier to moderate in the general election, if necessary.

The 2010 election provided some good examples of candidates adopting more extreme positions to appeal to primary voters. Senator Arlen Specter, who had switched from the Republican Party to the Democratic Party in 2009, faced stiff competition in the Democratic primary because many voters were concerned about his Democratic credentials. In early 2010, when Specter announced his support of a controversial provision of the Obama healthcare proposal that would have created a government-run insurance plan, many suspected he was trying to cater to Democratic primary voters who tended to favor such a plan. The problem for Specter, however, was that he had opposed the public option as a Republican. Thus, it was easy for his opponent in the primary, Joe Sestak, to label Specter a flip-flopper.

The fate of some Tea Party–backed candidates, who tend to be very conservative, in recent elections illustrates the difficulty of shifting from a primary to a general election constituency. In 2012, a Senate candidate in Missouri, Todd Akin, brought down the ire of Democrats and even some Republican leaders when, shortly after defeating more moderate GOP candidates in the primary, he explained in an interview that he opposes allowing women who have become pregnant as the result of rape to have an abortion because such pregnancies are "really rare." They are rare, he

---

[9] Barry C. Burden. 2004. "Candidate Positioning in US Congressional Elections." *British Journal of Political Science* 34, 2: 211–27; Samuel Merrill III and Bernard Grofman. 1999. *A Unified Theory of Voting: Directional and Proximity Spatial Models.* New York: Cambridge University Press.

explained, because "if it's a legitimate rape, the female body has ways to try to shut that whole thing down."[10] Although Akin apologized for his comments and claimed he "misspoke," he forfeited his lead in the polls and ultimately lost to Democratic senator Claire McCaskill, who was one of the most vulnerable Democratic incumbents in 2012.

The General Election

Once candidates have secured their party's nomination, they must quickly turn their attention to the general-election campaign. Some candidates who were uncontested in the primary or did not have any serious challengers can even start their general-election campaign earlier if they have the resources to do so. Incumbents typically have these resources, so challengers face a particularly difficult path: while they are battling for the nomination, the incumbent has already started appealing to the general-election electorate.

Voters often know far less about House and Senate candidates than they do about candidates for president. According to a 2002 study, after an uncompetitive House election featuring an incumbent and a challenger, less than 15 percent of the people living in the district can remember the names of both candidates. After a competitive House election, approximately 40 percent of the electorate can remember the candidates' names. Citizens are typically more familiar with Senate candidates. Approximately one-third can remember their names after a noncompetitive election, while two-thirds can remember the names of both candidates after a competitive open-seat race.[11] These numbers suggest that many citizens vote for congressional candidates without knowing their names, let alone anything substantive about them. Congressional candidates and their political consultants are well aware of voters' lack of knowledge. Challengers, in particular, are acutely aware that people rarely vote for someone they do not know. Thus, many congressional candidates spend their entire campaign simply introducing themselves to voters. They do this by communicating with potential supporters and working to ensure that supporters turn out on Election Day.

---

[10] *The New York Times.* 2012, August 12. "Senate Candidate Provokes Ire With 'Legitimate Rape' Comment." www.nytimes.com/2012/08/20/us/politics/todd-akin-provokes-ire-with-legitimate-rape-comment.html (accessed 3/14/13).

[11] Paul S. Herrnson. 2004. *Congressional Elections: Campaigning at Home and in Washington.* Washington, DC: CQ Press, p. 190.

Developing a Campaign Message

As we discussed in Chapter 5, a key to winning an election is knowing the electorate. Candidates need to know who their supporters are and where they live. They also need to know who the persuadable voters are in their district or state and how to get their message to these voters.

The next step is to develop a message that appeals to the target audience, which requires understanding the issues that are important to the potential voters in the district or state. Candidates acquire this knowledge in several ways. Congressional candidates are often community leaders or have prior political experience that has given them knowledge of the jurisdictions in which they are running. They may be business leaders who know the state's economy, or state legislators who have passed bills designed to address problems in the state. Candidates also have extensive social and professional networks that can provide a sense of the issues affecting their communities. They also have help in developing their message from the organizations whose endorsements they seek. These groups not only help candidates contact their members but provide the candidate with information about their members' concerns. Finally, if candidates have enough money they can also hire a pollster to conduct surveys of the electorate. If the race is competitive, one of the congressional campaign committees or state party organizations may conduct polls and share them with their party's candidates.

Unlike presidential candidates, whose messages are focused almost exclusively on national politics, congressional candidates face the challenge of crafting a campaign message that addresses both local and national issues. The conventional wisdom is that local issues should predominate—a sentiment best captured by former Speaker of the House Thomas "Tip" O'Neill's famous assertion that "All politics is local." Yet, when local issues dominate a campaign, then both the Democratic and Republican candidates may end up taking very similar positions. For instance, candidates from a rural House district whose economy depends on farming may be united in their support of federal agricultural subsidies. When national issues dominate, candidates may have similar agendas—such as the need for jobs in a weak economy—but may take quite different positions. For example, to create jobs, Republican candidates may emphasize the need to cut business-related taxes to encourage them to hire workers, while Democrats often advocate government spending to stimulate job growth. The positions of individual congressional candidates will often be similar to the positions of their respective national parties. Studies of congressional elections show that national issues are more prevalent than local ones in campaign messages. As

In 2012, Republican Richard Mourdock lost his bid for an Indiana Senate seat against Democrat Joe Donnelly in part because he claimed a pregnancy occurring from rape was a "gift from God" and should not be terminated. Mourdock, a staunch conservative, had knocked off a popular centrist Republican, Senator Richard Lugar, in the primary due in large part to Tea Party support. The Indiana seat was crucial for the GOP to take control of the Senate.

a result, candidates often take different positions, in contrast to the median voter theorem discussed in Chapter 5.[12]

Communicating the Message

Once candidates have determined what they want to say to voters, they communicate that message in several ways. Like presidential candidates, congressional candidates rely on direct mail and on newspaper, radio, and television advertisements to communicate with voters, but the extent to which they rely on each of these is quite different. For example, a typical presidential campaign spends approximately 75 percent of its entire budget on television advertising, while the typical Senate campaign spends one-third of its budget and the average House campaign spends just 20 percent of its budget on television ads.[13] House candidates rely the least on television advertisements because they are expensive and House candidates typically have less money to spend per voter than Senate candidates. In fact, many noncompetitive House races feature no television advertising whatsoever.

---

[12] Stephen Ansolabehere, James M. Snyder, Jr., Charles Stewart III. 2001. "Candidate Positioning in U.S. Congressional Elections." *American Journal of Political Science* 45, 1: 136–59; Burden, "Candidate Positioning in US Congressional Elections."

[13] Herrnson, *Congressional Elections*, p. 85.

Another problem for House and Senate candidates is that television advertisements are purchased in predefined media markets. Large media markets often serve more than one congressional district, which means that a House candidate who purchases television advertisements may be paying for people in neighboring districts to see those ads. Media markets do not necessarily respect state borders either. If a state has a competitive Senate race, voters in neighboring states that share media markets with the competitive state may see advertisements in races in which they cannot vote. For example, New Jersey has no television media markets of its own. Its northern half lies in the New York City media market and its southern half in the Philadelphia media market. Thus, congressional candidates in New Jersey must purchase advertisements in one or both of these extremely expensive media markets if they want to get on television. It is not surprising that they often opt for other means of communicating with voters.

For all of these reasons, congressional candidates may rely less on television advertisements and more on other means of communicating with voters—including radio advertisements, billboards, newspaper advertisements, and yard signs. Congressional candidates, especially House candidates, can also rely much more than presidential candidates on communicating with citizens directly. Presidential candidates have no personal contact with most potential voters; the American electorate is simply too vast. Citizens

House challengers often have relatively little money to spend on advertising campaign events, so they may have to find creative ways to get their name and message out. In 2010, House candidate Jeff Barnett walked 80 miles across Virginia's 10th district as a way to generate publicity for his campaign.

"experience" presidential candidates only as talking heads on their television screens. In contrast, House candidates can have direct, unmediated contact with a much larger portion of their constituency. They attend parades, sporting events, or anywhere large numbers of potential voters congregate. This kind of direct contact is intended simply to increase name recognition and to make a favorable impression, not to convey substantive information about policy agendas or proposals. House challengers, who have less money to purchase advertisements, rely heavily on direct personal contacts to get their name out. It is not unheard of for House challengers to literally walk across their district to meet voters and generate publicity. For example, in 2010 a Democratic House candidate, Jeff Barnett, embarked on an 80-mile, six-day walking tour of Virginia's 10th congressional district as part of a bid to oust the Republican incumbent. Though such tactics might seem gimmicky, they are often one of the few means by which an underfunded challenger can generate name recognition. Although there are seven states which have only one representative, meaning that the state and congressional district have identical boundaries, Senate candidates usually have a much larger territory to cover than House candidates. As a result, it is often more practical for Senators to rely on television and radio than on personal contact with voters.

Congressional candidates also differ from presidential candidates in how much they depend on earned media. **Earned media** (or **free media**) is the publicity that candidates get by engaging in promotional activities. For example, candidates frequently hold press conferences or give speeches hoping that these events will be covered by the local media. Candidate appearances, such as Barnett's walking tour, have the same goal. Congressional candidates sometimes use gimmicks to attract news attention. In 2010, Van Irion, a Republican candidate from Tennessee's 3rd House district, always carried a pitchfork to symbolize his promise that he would clean up the "manure" in Washington. Irion also filed a lawsuit challenging the constitutionality of the health care reform legislation and personally traveled to Washington to give President Obama and congressional leaders a copy of the lawsuit. To be sure, presidential candidates also use gimmicks to generate free media, but the range of behavior that is considered appropriate or "presidential" limits both how much they can rely on them and how bizarre those gimmicks can be.

Mobilizing Voters

Congressional candidates use the same basic tactics that presidential candidates do to get their supporters to the polls on Election Day, including mailers, phone calls, and neighborhood canvassing. The main differences are the size and sophistication of their mobilization drives. Presidential candidates have vast resources at their disposal, including vans and shuttles to drive vot-ers to polling stations and computer databases that tell them exactly where their supporters live. This information is based on months of calling and knocking on doors. In presidential election years, congressional candidates benefit from the presidential campaigns' mobilization efforts because most voters who go to the polls to cast a ballot for the president usually cast a bal-lot for candidates in other races at the same time. In midterm election years, however, congressional candidates must turn out voters themselves, assisted by other organizations, including state and national party committees and interest groups. Despite those efforts, congressional campaigns rarely gener-ate the kind of interest among the electorate that presidential campaigns do. As a result, voter turnout in midterm elections is significantly lower than in presidential elections.

The Role of the Parties and the Hill Committees

As noted earlier, parties can play a significant role in congressional cam-paigns. The Hill committees are the party organizations that focus exclu-sively on electing party members to Congress. They accomplish this by targeting the handful of House and Senate races that are closely contested in each election cycle and ignoring the rest. Their first priority is to protect incumbents who are in jeopardy of losing their seats. Their second priority is to defend the seats of members of the party who are leaving office. When national political and economic conditions favor a party, that party may also target seats that have been controlled by the other party. In 2008, the Democrats saw a chance to capitalize on Barack Obama's popularity and the public's discontent with President George W. Bush. They adopted an aggressive congressional campaign strategy that ultimately yielded a gain of 21 seats in the House and eight seats in the Senate. In 2010, however, the weak economy and the declining popularity of President Obama embold-ened Republicans, who sought to reclaim not only those seats lost in 2008 but also seats that they had not pursued in decades. As a result the GOP picked up 63 seats and won control of the House in 2010.

The Hill committees do not rigidly adhere to campaign plans. In response to campaign events, they redirect resources to crucial races. They typically begin the election season with a list of 100–150 competitive House races and whittle that number down as the campaigns evolve and it becomes clear which ones will be the most fiercely contested. The committees can then make a direct contribution, coordinate expenditures with the candidate, or make an independent expenditure without a candidate's involvement. **Coor-dinated expenditures** involve collaboration between the committee and the candidate or a representative of the candidate. They are usually spent on services that are given to a candidate directly or performed by a political consultant on behalf of a candidate. The services might include the purchase of television and radio advertisements, direct mail, polling, or the organization of fund-raising events. Campaign finance law treats coordinated expenditures the same way it treats direct contributions to a candidate, which means they are subject to strict limits.

As a result, the Hill committees usually rely on **independent expenditures** to fund their campaign efforts. These expenditures are made without consulting or coordinating with a candidate. According to *Buckley v. Valeo*, the landmark campaign finance case discussed in Chapter 4, these expenditures cannot be limited in any way, allowing the committees to spend large sums of money on a race. For example, in 2012 both the DCCC and the NRCC targeted an open-seat contest in Arizona's 1st district. The NRCC spent $2.4 million to support its candidate, Jonathan Paton, while the DCCC spent $2.0 million to support its candidate, Ann Kirkpatrick. To put this amount of money in perspective, consider that Paton raised $1.5 million for his bid, while Kirkpatrick raised $2.3 million for hers. Thus, together the DCCC and the NRCC spent more than the candidates did in this race.

While the Hill committees tend to help candidates purchase campaign communications and provide technical expertise, state and local party committees more often help candidates with grassroots activities, such as voter registration and mobilization drives designed to get voters to the polls. In addition, they organize phone banks and neighborhood canvassing campaigns to knock on doors and provide voters with campaign literature.

The Incumbency Advantage

A defining feature of congressional elections that we have already alluded to is the enormous electoral advantage that incumbents enjoy over challengers. The **incumbency advantage** is defined as the vote share earned by an incumbent compared to what a non-incumbent would have earned if he or she had run.

The incumbency advantage can be attributed to several factors. For one thing, incumbents have greater political experience. They also have an easier time soliciting campaign donations than challengers do. Contributors like to back winners and are well aware that challengers lose most elections. Only challengers in competitive races or candidates in open-seat races can typically raise anything close to what incumbents raise. Similarly, parties and interest groups funnel resources to candidates who have a greater chance of winning. As a result, House incumbents typically raise about three times what their challengers do. Senate incumbents raise even more—approximately ten times as much as challengers. Quality challengers fare better than the average challenger, but they typically cannot match incumbents dollar for dollar.

Another important source of incumbents' advantage is their familiarity to voters. As of 2007, the average House member had served five terms, or 10 years, and the average senator had served two terms, or 12 years. Incumbents have thus had the chance to establish a relationship with the citizens they represent. Citizens see them in the news and around the district or state. Incumbents can also make use of certain perquisites of office to get publicity. For example, the **franking privilege**, which has existed since colonial times, allows members of Congress to send mail to constituents without postage. Although it cannot be used for campaigning purposes, to send holiday greetings, or to provide biographical information about representatives and their families, it can be used to send out newsletters and other informational mailings. Even so, the volume of franked mail increases in election years, suggesting that the mailings are being used for campaign purposes. In addition, members of Congress can employ staff for **casework**, which typically involves helping constituents deal with government bureaucracies. Whenever a staff member solves a constituent's problem, that constituent is likely to look upon the congressperson more favorably.

Contrast the situation of incumbents with that of challengers. Unless challengers are well known for other reasons, most citizens in their districts or states will know little about them and may not even be able to recognize their faces or names. And challengers have only limited resources to make themselves better known. Moreover, even if an incumbent is unpopular, many voters may still feel it is better to cast a ballot for the devil they know than the devil they do not know. The **personal vote**—that portion of an elected official's vote share that can be attributed to their relationship with constituents—accounts for as much as one half of the incumbency advantage.[14]

The size of the incumbency advantage is not, however, a constant. It has changed over time. One way to show this for the House is via a measure called "slurge." The term is a combination of "sophomore surge"—the average gain in vote share of candidates running for their second term—and "retirement slump"—the average loss in vote share that non-incumbents

---

[14] Stephen Ansolabehere, James M. Snyder, Jr., and Charles Stewart III. 2000. "Old Voters, New Voters, and the Personal Vote: Using Redistricting to Measure the Incumbency Advantage." *American Journal of Political Science* 44, 1:17-34.

FIGURE 9.3 The Incumbency Advantage in House Elections, 1946–2010

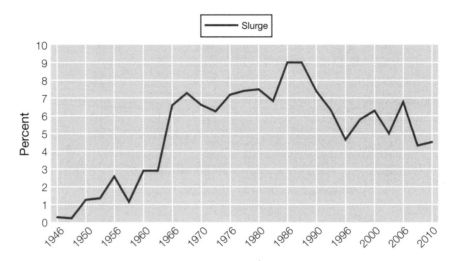

Source: Gary C. Jacobson. 2009. *The Politics of Congressional Elections*, 7th ed. New York: Longman, p. 32. Data for 2008 and 2010 provided by Gary Jacobson.

suffer compared to the vote share their predecessor received before retiring. Figure 9.3 shows that in the 1950s, the slurge hovered around one to two percentage points.[15] It climbed to 7 percentage points in the 1960s and 1970s and peaked at 9 points in the 1986 and 1988s. It then declined to 5 or 6 percentage points through the 1990s, maintaining the level through 2004. The large partisan tides of 2008 and 2010, which swept many incumbents out of office, reduced the incumbency advantage to just over 4 points.

It is difficult to calculate the slurge for the Senate because only one-third of senators are up for election in any election year. But other measures of the incumbency advantage for senators reveal a very similar pattern to the one in House elections. The incumbency advantage for Senate candidates hovered around two percent from the early 1900s (when a constitutional amendment was adopted for direct election of senators) until the 1950s, when it increased to approximately 3.5 percentage points. It increased further in the 1960s, to approximately 7 points, and again in the 1980s, to almost 10 points. It declined slightly thereafter but remains high.[16]

---

[15] Based on Figure 3-3 in Gary C. Jacobson. 2009. *The Politics of Congressional Elections*, 7th ed. New York: Pearson, p. 32.

[16] Ansolabehere and Snyder, "The Incumbency Advantage in U.S. Elections," table 4.

Why has the incumbency advantage generally increased over time? There are several explanations. For one, the increase in incumbency advantage in the 1960s has been linked to the growth in local television stations across the country.[17] At that time, local news broadcasts were widely watched, and, unlike today's broadcasts, they emphasized news stories about politics. Local television stations even relied on members of Congress to produce reports about their activities, which the stations then inserted into their local newscasts. In the 1970s, local television news began to focus less on political stories, and in the late 1970s audiences began watching local news broadcasts less often as their attention shifted to emerging cable television stations. Despite these changes, however, local news stations continued to cover incumbent activities and to do so in a largely positive manner, which has helped maintain the incumbency advantage.

Second, members of Congress have given themselves more official resources over the years, such as increased funds for franked mail, larger salaries for staff, and bigger travel budgets. These have allowed them to communicate more with their constituents and potentially increased their advantages over challengers.

Third, the Supreme Court decisions in the early 1960s that reformed the redistricting process may also have contributed to the incumbency advantage. These decisions require that virtually every district in the country change every 10 years through the processes of reapportionment and redistricting (which we discussed in Chapter 2). As a result, many candidates wait until the election following redistricting to determine whether they will run. Incumbents must decide how the new boundaries of their district affect their electoral prospects. Incumbents may decide to retire if their new districts are very different from their old districts, in which case the retirement slump is especially large. This is not only because the incumbent is retiring, but because the district has changed in a manner that disadvantages the incumbent's party.[18] Thus, the increase in the incumbency advantage for House members after the 1960s can be partly explained by changes in the reapportionment and redistricting process and their consequent influence on incumbent retirements.

Despite the many advantages incumbents have, they rarely act as if they are confident about winning. This creates a striking paradox in congressional

---

[17] Markus Prior. 2006. "The Incumbent in the Living Room: The Rise of Television and the Incumbency Advantage in U.S. House Elections." *Journal of Politics* 68, 3: 657–73.

[18] Gary W. Cox and Jonathan N. Katz. 2002. *Elbridge Gerry's Salamander: The Electoral Consequences of the Reapportionment Revolution*. Cambridge: Cambridge University Press.

elections: many incumbents are "running scared" despite overwhelming evidence that incumbents rarely lose.[19] Why? For one thing, incumbents do occasionally lose, as the case of Elizabeth Dole at the beginning of the chapter illustrates; for another, the cost of losing is high. When incumbents lose elections, they also lose their jobs and the political power and reputation that they have amassed. The loss might even mean the end of their political careers.

Incumbents are naturally vulnerable at two points in their career: immediately after they are elected, when they are still working to establish their reputation among their constituents, and later in their careers, when voters may begin to believe that they have become too enmeshed in Washington politics and have lost touch with their constituents. They are also at risk when caught up in a scandal or when political tides are working against their party. Incumbents can even lose in their own party's primary if they have run afoul of local party elites or powerful interest groups, who may line up behind an opposition candidate. (Think of the Michigan races described in the opening anecdote in Chapter 6.)

Thus, despite the high chance of victory, incumbents in campaigns often behave as if they are fighting for their political lives. This is one reason that they are constantly raising money for their next election bid: amassing a huge war chest helps scare off serious competitors. They want to avoid sending any signal that they may be vulnerable. Serious competitors know better than to compete with incumbents under most circumstances, so they bide their time until the district boundaries are redrawn or the incumbent decides to retire. As a result, most congressional elections pit incumbents against political novices, and, unsurprisingly, incumbents tend to win.

The Declining Competitiveness of Congressional Elections

In the late 1980s and early 1990s, competitive congressional elections started becoming rarer. A simple measure of competitiveness is the number of seats won or lost by the majority party in the House or Senate, or what

---

[19] Anthony King. 1997. *Running Scared: Why American Politicians Campaign Too Much and Govern Too Little*. New York: Free Press.

FIGURE 9.4 Net Partisan Turnover in House Elections, 1946–2012

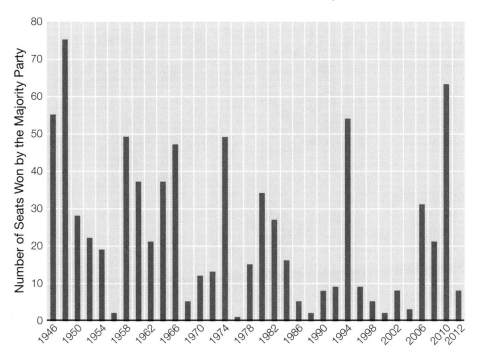

Source: Gary Jacobson. 2006. "Competition in U.S. Congressional Elections," in *The Marketplace of Democracy*, eds. Michael P. McDonald and John Samples. Washington, DC: Brookings Institution Press, p. 29. Data from 2006–12 added by the authors.

is also called the *net partisan turnover*. The more seats the majority party wins or loses, the more competitive the election is. Figure 9.4 shows that high-turnover elections have become less common in House elections. From 1946 to 1980, the average net partisan turnover in an election was 28 seats. From 1980 to 2012, it was 18 seats. In recent memory, two years stand out: 1994, when Democrats lost 54 seats, and 2010, when they lost 63. In both cases, Democrats lost control of the House. Again, such high turnover elections are far less common than they once were.

The decline in electoral competitiveness has several likely causes: the increased power of incumbency, increasing party loyalty, and redistricting. Electoral competitiveness has decreased only in House elections that feature an incumbent. It has not decreased in open-seat House races.[20] At the same

---

[20] Jacobson, *The Politics of Congressional Elections*, p. 30.

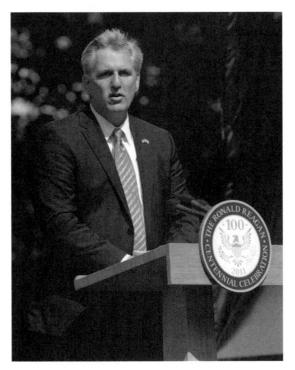

Because it can be difficult for challengers to defeat a well-known and well-funded incumbent, some incumbents run unopposed. For example, voters in California's 22nd district had only one choice (incumbent Kevin McCarthy, above) for U.S. House on the 2010 ballot.

time, Americans have become less willing to vote for political candidates from a different party.[21] To understand why this leads to declining competition, consider a district in which 60 percent of the voters are Democratic and 40 percent are Republican. If Democratic voters are willing to cross party lines, then a strong Republican candidate could make the election competitive. But if Democratic voters are unwilling to cross party lines, then this district would rarely have a competitive election.

---

[21] Joseph Bafumi and Robert Shapiro. 2009. "A New Partisan Voter." *Journal of Politics* 71: 1–24; Marc J. Hetherington. 2001. "Resurgent Mass Partisanship: The Role of Elite Polarization." *American Political Science Review* 95: 619–31; Larry M. Bartels. 2000. "Partisanship and Voting Behavior, 1952–1996." *American Journal of Political Science* 44: 35–50; Alan Abramowitz and Kyle Saunders. 1998. "Ideological Realignment in the U.S. Electorate." *Journal of Politics* 60: 634–52.

Redistricting may also account for declining competitiveness in House elections. Parties may have gotten better at using the redistricting process to draw district boundaries so that its members comfortably win elections. Increasingly sophisticated redistricting techniques involving computerized mapping programs are thought to help parties do this better. However, redistricting is a minor reason for the decline in electoral competitiveness in the House and cannot account for the decline in the competitiveness of Senate elections.

Declining competitiveness raises at least three concerns about the American electoral system. First, it can undermine democratic accountability. In a representative democracy, the main way to ensure that politicians are responsive to the views of citizens is to hold frequent elections; if the public is unhappy with a politician's actions, voters can replace the official. But if representatives know that their re-election is virtually guaranteed, they may be less responsive to citizens, relying more on their own views or on those of interest groups and lobbyists. Second, declining competitiveness can prevent the demographics of Congress from changing to reflect the electorate. This is a major problem for women and minorities, both groups of which are underrepresented in Congress. Finally, the demographics of a state or district can change considerably during an incumbent's tenure. If so, then the ideas and opinions of incumbents may be out of touch with those of their constituents. Without a competitive election, incumbents have little incentive to bring their views into line with this changing electorate.

At the same time, declining competition in congressional elections may not be a serious problem. One reason is that it is less important whether party control of a congressional district changes regularly than whether party control of Congress as a whole changes regularly. Despite the declining number of competitive districts, party control of Congress has changed frequently in the last three decades—and most recently in 2010. Naturally, critics of the current system have a response: that the framers of the Constitution did not want the legislature to represent parties—in fact, political parties did not exist in this country at that time—but to represent the diverse interests of the public. For example, the Constitution specifies that representatives are to be elected every two years so that they would be sensitive to the needs of their constituents. Thus, the rotation of power between the parties is irrelevant to critics, who believe that declining competitiveness undermines the theory of representation enshrined in the Constitution.

Another argument for why declining competitiveness may be of little concern is that even if incumbents almost always win the general election, they must fight for the party's nomination. Direct primaries were adopted precisely because they would introduce contested elections into jurisdictions that were dominated by a single party. Critics of this argument point out that most primaries are closed, meaning that only registered members of the party can vote in them and independent voters or opposite partisans have no say in who will represent them. Moreover, most primaries are not competitive; in fact, most House incumbents do not face any primary opposition.

Among the most important reforms that have been proposed to improve the competitiveness of congressional elections are term limits, public financing, and redistricting. The most obvious reform—one that is embraced by many citizens[22]—is term limits, which require incumbents to leave office after having served a certain number of terms. But as we discussed in Chapter 2, the Supreme Court has ruled that term limits are unconstitutional for federal officeholders, so term limits could be adopted only through a constitutional amendment.

Public financing for congressional candidates would entail providing all federal candidates with a minimum amount of money to help them get their campaigns off the ground. But as we noted in Chapter 4, it is not yet clear that such programs increase competitiveness. Moreover, it is not clear whether Congress or the public would ever support public funding. Critics of public financing have noted that it can create "false" competitiveness: some districts really are decidedly Republican or Democratic. Subsidizing candidates of the minority party in such districts seems unnecessary and perhaps even wasteful.

A third kind of reform involves redistricting. Proposed reforms include taking the redistricting process out of the hands of state legislatures and giving it to independent commissions. As we noted in Chapter 2, there is some evidence that independent commissions create more competitive districts. States can also adopt guidelines for drawing districts that promote competition, for example by requiring that competitive districts be created whenever possible. But it is unclear whether such guidelines are effective, and they can actually conflict with other priorities such as the imperative to create majority-minority districts under the Voting Rights Act. In 2000,

---

[22] Carol Weissert and Karen Halperin. 2007. "The Paradox of Term Limit Support: To Know Them Is Not to Love Them." *Political Research Quarterly* 60, 3: 516–530.

Arizonans adopted a proposition that established an Independent Redistricting Commission, as well as a list of criteria for redistricting that included competitiveness. The redistricting commission found, however, that once Native American and Hispanic (heavily Democratic communities) districts had been drawn to comply with the Voting Rights Act, few Democrats were left in the state to spread around in the interest of creating competitive districts.[23] As a result, the districts created by the new commission were no more competitive than the districts that had been drawn by the state legislature in the past.[24]

Conclusion

The Congressional scholar David Mayhew has described members of Congress as being "single-minded seekers of re-election."[25] Although this statement may be somewhat unfair to public servants who are motivated by other purposes, it is true that members of Congress want to be re-elected and spend a great deal of timed pursuing re-election, engaging in what has been described as a "permanent campaign." The two-year House election cycle means that House members are campaigning virtually all of the time, while senators have time to focus on governing before turning their attention to the next election. However, even those senators who are not up for election in a given cycle may campaign on behalf of other senators in their party who are running. Thus, elections are always central for members of Congress.

As a result of the permanent campaign, the lines between campaigning and governing have become blurred. Members of Congress have changed the rules and procedures of Congress to aid them in pursuing re-election. For instance, prior to the institution of electronic voting in 1973, many votes taken in the House and Senate were anonymous. Since then, it has become common to demand a recorded vote, which makes all votes public. This has

---

[23] Michael McDonald. 2006. "Redistricting and Competitive Districts," in *The Marketplace of Democracy*, eds. Michael P. McDonald and John Samples. Washington, DC: Brookings Institution Press, pp. 222–44; Michael McDonald. 2008. "Reforming Redistricting" in *Democracy in the States: Experiments in Elections Reform*, eds. Bruce Cain, Todd Donovan, and Caroline Tolbert. Washington, DC: Brookings Press, pp. 147–160.

[24] McDonald, "Reforming Redistricting," p. 150.

[25] David Mayhew. 2004. *Congress: The Electoral Connection*. New Haven, CT: Yale University Press, p. 17.

made the legislative process more transparent, while forcing members of Congress to think of every vote as a potential campaign issue.[26]

In addition, senators increasingly resort to the filibuster, so much so that it is now assumed that 60 votes are needed to pass a bill because it takes 60 votes to end a filibuster. Filibusters provide senators with a very visible way of signaling to interest groups—many of which have campaign PACs—that they are looking out for their concerns.[27] Although such procedures might serve electoral goals, they can undermine the collegiality of Congress and contribute to legislative gridlock.

Ultimately, focusing on electoral goals can make it difficult for party members to work together. At the same time, focusing on electoral goals is what keeps representatives "running scared" and in contact with their constituents—even if they are almost certain to win their next race. This is an important trade-off inherent in the "permanent campaign": it may improve the quality of representation even as it hurts the quality of governance.

KEY TERMS

incumbent (p. 253)	coordinated expenditures (p. 267)
open seat (p. 255)	independent expenditures (p. 268)
quality challenger (p. 255)	incumbency advantage (p. 268)
political amateur (p. 255)	franking privilege (p. 269)
Hill committees (p. 255)	casework (p. 269)
earned media/free media (p. 266)	personal vote (p. 269)

FOR DISCUSSION

1. What kinds of people make successful congressional candidates?

2. What roles do the parties play in congressional campaigns?

---

[26] David Brady and Morris Fiorina. 2000. "Congress in the Era of the Permanent Campaign," in *The Permanent Campaign and Its Future*, eds. Thomas Mann and Norman Ornstein. Washington, DC: American Enterprise Institute, p. 141.

[27] Sarah A. Binder and Steven S. Smith. 1997. *Politics or Principle? Filibustering in the United States Senate*. Washington, DC: Brookings Institution Press.

3. What are some of the causes and consequences of the incumbency advantage?

4. How does the goal of being re-elected affect the ability of members of Congress to govern?

 Visit StudySpace for quizzes and other review material.
wwnorton.com/studyspace

CHAPTER 10

State and Local Campaigns

On August 6, 2003, Arnold Schwarzenegger announced his candidacy for the governorship of California. The incumbent, Democrat Gray Davis, was subject to a recall election, wherein voters would determine first whether he would stay in or be recalled from office and then who would replace him if he were recalled. Schwarzenegger did not make his announcement at a rally or press conference, but on *The Tonight Show*, speaking to its host, Jay Leno. The ensuing campaign garnered no end of attention. One hundred and thirty-five candidates were on the ballot as alternatives to Davis, including Schwarzenegger, Lieutenant Governor Cruz Bustamante, State Senator Tom McClintock, and a host of colorful characters from outside politics: Gary Coleman, most famous for his role as a child actor on *Diff'rent Strokes*; Larry Flynt, the publisher of the pornographic magazine *Hustler*, whose campaign slogan was "Vote for a Smut-Peddler Who Cares"; and Mary Carey, an adult film actress whose movie credits included *Busty Beauties 3*. The California recall election had all of the trappings of a big, closely contested campaign. The candidates seeking to replace Davis raised over $37 million. There was national media attention, including 450 articles in the *New York Times* alone.[1] There were mini-scandals involving Schwarzenegger's alleged unseemly behavior toward women on some of his movie sets. In the end, 55 percent of voters chose to recall Davis, and Schwarzenegger was elected to replace him.

In August 2010, Greg David was mounting a campaign for another California political office: the city council of Mountain View. He pledged to spend no more than $1,000: $500 for a ballot statement and $500 for everything else. He said that he would make his campaign signs from recycled wood and leftover paint.[2] Across the country, in Wilkes-Barre, Pennsylvania, Terrence O'Connor ran for the

---

[1] A search for articles with the terms "California" and "recall election" turned up 450 articles in the *New York Times*.

[2] Daniel DeBolt. 2010. "Council Campaign on a Shoestring." *Mountain View Voice*, August 25. www.mv-voice.com/news/show_story.php?id=3272 (accessed 5/3/11).

state House of Representatives by doing little besides affixing large banners to his 1995 Ford Windstar minivan, donning a Revolutionary War–era costume that included a tri-cornered hat, and driving around the district to preach his message of lower taxes through a megaphone.[3] O'Connor's minivan might be called luxurious by some standards: Rory Allen, a candidate for the New York State Senate, often campaigned by driving a golf cart through the streets of the district.[4]

Our focus in this chapter is on state and local races — that is, elections other than those that occur at the federal level. State and local elections involve a wide array of offices, but an easy way to think about them is in terms of the three traditional branches of government. At the state and local levels, voters select members of the executive branch (such as governors, lieutenant governors, attorneys general, mayors), members of the legislature (state senates and houses, city councils), and often members of the judiciary (judges and justices). This entails a vast number of elections, simply because there are so many states and localities with governments — the 50 states, over 3,000 counties, over 19,000 cities or municipalities, and nearly 14,000 school districts.[5] In addition,

Core of the Analysis

- State and local political offices and election laws often differ from their federal counterparts, and these differences affect campaign strategies.

- National political realities shape both candidate strategy in and the outcomes of state and local races.

- State and local campaigns are increasingly adopting the techniques of national campaigns, and thereby becoming more expensive and professionalized.

- At the same time, many state and local campaigns attract scant media attention and require little fund-raising, thereby necessitating very different campaign strategies and tactics.

- Because state and local elections are largely invisible to most voters and to the media, small groups of activists may gain additional influence in these races.

---

[3] Andrew M. Seder. 2010. "Revolutionary Campaign Tactic." *Times Leader*, September 11. www.timesleader.com/news/Revolutionary_campaign_tactic_09-10-2010.html (accessed May 3, 2011).

[4] Brian Meyer. 2010. "Thompson Rolls Past Allen, Coppola." *Buffalo News*, September 15. www.buffalonews.com/city/politics/article190548.ece (accessed 5/3/11).

[5] John P. Pelissero. 2003. "The Political Environment of Cities in the Twenty-first Century," in *Cities, Politics, and Policy: A Comparative Analysis*, ed. John P. Pelissero. Washington, DC: CQ Press, p. 10.

In 2003, Arnold Schwarzenegger announced his candidacy for governor of California on *The Tonight Show*. His campaign generated massive media attention and millions of dollars in contributions.

many states and localities afford citizens an opportunity that does not exist at the federal level: the opportunity to vote on public policies, via ballot propositions, initiatives, and referenda.

The category "state and local" is very broad, as the contrast between the California recall election and the three examples of local campaigns reveals. Within this category are races that vary dramatically in their resources and thus the visibility of the campaigns themselves. Expensive statewide races, such as those for governor, are essentially analogous to U.S. Senate races. They have similar features to campaigns for federal office: professional consultants, pollsters, television and radio advertising, and so on. But many other races — in fact, most state and local races — have little if any of these features. Many such campaigns are run on a shoestring budget. Family and friends replace paid consultants. Lawn signs replace television advertisements. If one imagines a spectrum running from "campaigns in a golf cart" to "campaigns on *The Tonight Show*," most state and local races are closer to the golf cart end of the spectrum.

At the same time, in recent years state and local campaigns have become more professionalized. The average sum spent on many types of state and local races has increased over time, and some of them now resemble more expensive campaigns in various respects. Professional campaigns have also become increasingly common for offices and issues that previously did not feature prominent campaigns, such as elections to state courts and ballot initiatives and referenda. The strategic calculations for state and local candidates may therefore be changing gradually. At the least, serious state and local campaigns may come to rely less on megaphones and golf carts.

The shoestring nature of campaigns both reflects and perpetuates a simple fact about state and local elections: relative even to congressional elections, they are often profoundly uncompetitive. Incumbents frequently run without any challengers. Districts may be drawn so that only one party has a chance of winning. The news media's attention is usually elsewhere. Citizens turn out to vote in lower numbers and have little information to use in making a choice. Under these circumstances, highly organized parties, activists, and interest groups can influence the campaign and election outcomes in ways that may not coincide with the preferences of most citizens in the district. Thus, state and local races — the ones that most affect schools, homes, roads, and many other aspects of citizens' daily lives — are often the ones that live up to ideals of political campaigns the least.

We begin this chapter by discussing how local and state electoral rules affect these elections. We also consider how state and local elections depend on the prevailing political and economic winds — the "reality" that candidates must confront. How much do state and local officeholders find their fortunes bound up

Rory Allen ran for New York's State Senate by campaigning in a golf cart.

with broader trends — a weak economy, an unpopular party — that are beyond their control? We discuss the broader impact of rules and reality on the incumbency advantage — a feature of federal elections that is also important in state and local races and that strongly influences how competitive these races are.

We then describe how both rules and reality lead to differences among federal, state, and local campaign strategies, as well as the ways in which these strategies are becoming more similar, thanks to the creeping professionalization of state and local campaigns. We look at campaigns for state courts and ballot initiatives in particular. We also discuss how the uncompetitive features of state and local campaigns have historically advantaged, and continue to advantage, organized interests of various kinds, especially political parties. The concluding section considers the implications for democratic ideals.

Rules and Reality in Local Elections

Local elections typically operate under a very different set of rules than state and federal elections, and may also occur in a different context or "reality"—to use the term from the framework introduced in Chapter 1. Two important subjects of local electoral rules are nonpartisan ballots and at-large elections. The use of nonpartisan ballots reflects a particular philosophy of governance, historically associated with the Progressive movement at the turn of the last century. At that time, as we discussed in Chapter 6, many localities, especially large cities, were governed by party machines. Progressives thought that this created corruption, and they promoted reforms that stripped power from parties. One feature of these reforms was the institution of nonpartisan elections, in which candidates are listed on the ballot without any party affiliations. This curtailed the ways in which party machines could work to choose candidates and help them get elected to office—although, as we discuss later, this does not make parties irrelevant in contemporary city politics. It was also intended to promote the election of city officials who were more concerned with the practical challenges of policy making than with partisan politics. Today, over 75 percent of city council and mayoral elections are nonpartisan—differentiating them from the vast majority of state races and all federal races.

A second way local elections differ is in the types of constituencies that elected officeholders represent. Recall from Chapter 2 that districts for the U.S. House of Representatives elect a single representative; they are single-member districts. Many state legislatures also feature single-member districts. City council elections, by contrast, have different methods of representation. Less than 20 percent of cities use districts, sometimes called wards, exclusively—although district elections are more common in the largest metropolitan areas, such as Los Angeles. Just over 20 percent, use a mixed system, with some members elected from districts or wards, and other members elected at large—meaning that all voters in that city can vote for candidates for these seats. The majority of cities, however, use at-large elections exclusively; this is particularly true among small and medium-sized cities (that is, those with populations of less than 200,000).[6] Mayors, of course, are always elected in at-large elections.

Local elections also operate under somewhat different realities than state and federal elections. This is because local elections are often not held at

---

[6] Timothy B. Krebs and John P. Pelissero. 2003. "City Councils," in *Cities, Politics, and Policy: A Comparative Analysis*, ed. John P. Pelissero. Washington, DC: CQ Press, p. 172.

the same time as state and federal elections—another change instituted as part of the broader attempts to reform city governments. For example, more than half of city council elections are held at different times than state and national elections.[7] This helps to insulate local candidates from some of the events and issues that may may be prominent in elections for higher levels of office. Instead, local elections may center on issues unique to a community, with voters holding local officeholders accountable for their handling of the issues. Some natural disasters fall into this category. For example, in 2001, Tropical Storm Allison dumped as much as 37 inches of rain on Houston, Texas, causing massive flooding and 22 deaths. A survey conducted afterward found that nearly half of respondents gave credit or blame to the city or county governments for the handling of the flooding, while the state and federal governments were rarely mentioned. Those who blamed the city in particular were 10 points less likely to vote for the incumbent mayor who had presided over the response to the storm.[8] This illustrates how local issues may be especially important in local elections.

But if local elections are different from state and federal elections in these respects, they are quite similar in another: the advantages that accrue to incumbents. Indeed, with the nonpartisan ballot in place, voters are dependent on information other than party affiliation, especially their basic familiarity with the candidates. Small wonder, then, that incumbents typically do well in local elections. They are better positioned to have personal contact with voters. They are more likely to get endorsements from prominent leaders and media outlets. They are better able to raise money. Research on city council races has found that incumbents get a far larger share of the vote than non-incumbents and tend to win elections at rates only a little below those of incumbent members of Congress.[9] Despite the very different rules under which local elections are conducted, incumbency remains "the 800-pound gorilla."[10] As a consequence, many local elections—much like many congressional elections—are not very competitive.

---

[7] Krebs and Pelissero, "City Councils," p. 170.

[8] Kevin Arceneaux and Robert M. Stein. 2006. "Who Is Held Responsible When Disaster Strikes? The Attribution of Responsibility for a Natural Disaster in an Urban Election." *Journal of Urban Affairs* 28, 1: 43–53.

[9] Timothy B. Krebs. 1998. "The Determinants of Candidates' Vote Share and the Advantages of Incumbency in City Council Elections." *American Journal of Political Science* 42, 3: 921–35; Jessica Trounstine. 2011. "Evidence of a Local Incumbency Advantage." *Legislative Studies Quarterly* 36, 2: 255–280.

[10] Krebs and Pelissero, "City Councils," p. 178.

Rules and Reality in State Elections

The advantages that accrue to incumbent presidents, members of Congress, and even city council members are equally visible in state elections. In fact, state elections are on average less competitive than federal races. This is less true in statewide races, such as those for governor, than in races for state legislatures, where candidates run in smaller districts. Indeed, in state legislative elections, including both primary and general elections, substantial fractions of races are not even contested—meaning one candidate runs unopposed. There has been a striking decline in contested primaries for state legislative elections: from 1910 to 1938, 50 percent of primaries were contested, but from 1960 to 2000, only 25 percent were.[11] Large numbers of races are uncontested in the general election as well: in state legislative races in 2012, 38 percent of major-party candidates faced no major-party opposition.[12] By contrast, in the 2012 U.S. House general election, this was true of only 10 percent of seats. Naturally, this lack of competitiveness tends to advantage incumbents. In these same state legislative races, 21 percent of incumbents ran unopposed in both the primary and the general elections—albeit with significant variation among states (Figure 10.1).[13] It is especially rare for incumbents to face challengers who have raised as much money as they have, or even anything close to it. This is one reason that a few states have adopted "clean elections" laws (see Chapter 4): they wish to provide funding to lesser-known challengers.

The incumbency advantage in state legislative elections, as in congressional elections, depends on factors such as the partisan leaning of a state or district. In some state legislative districts, for example, one party is virtually guaranteed to win. But it also depends on the unique rules in each state that govern the powers of elected offices and the campaigns for those offices, and

---

[11] Stephen Ansolabehere, John Mark Hansen, Shigeo Hirano, and James M. Snyder, Jr. 2006. "The Decline of Competition in U.S. Primary Elections," in *The Marketplace of Democracy*, eds. Michael P. McDonald and John Samples. Washington, DC: Brookings Institution Press. Calculated from Table 4.1, p. 87.

[12] Ballotpedia. 2013. "2012 state legislative elections analyzed using a Competitiveness Index." http://ballotpedia.org/wiki/index.php/2012_state_legislative_elections_analyzed_using_a_Competitiveness_Index (accessed 3/28/13).

[13] Ballotpedia. 2013. "Incumbents with no primary or general election challengers in the 2012 state legislative elections." http://ballotpedia.org/wiki/index.php/Incumbents_with_no_primary_or_general_election_challengers_in_the_2012_state_legislative_elections (accessed 3/28/13).

FIGURE 10.1 Unopposed Incumbent Candidates in 2012 State Legislative Races

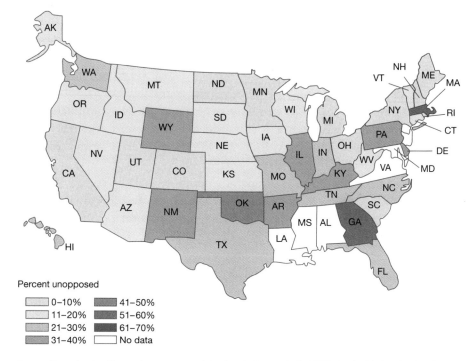

Percent unopposed

0–10%	41–50%
11–20%	51–60%
21–30%	61–70%
31–40%	No data

Source: "Incumbents with no primary or general election challengers in the 2012 state legislative elections." BallotPedia. http://ballotpedia.org/wiki/index.php/Incumbents_with_no_primary_or_general_election_challengers_in_the_2012_state_legislative_elections (accessed 3/29/13).

on the prevailing aspects of reality that may shape the decisions of candidates and the outcomes of elections. Both rules and reality affect the size of the advantage that incumbents possess.

Legislative Professionalism

One category of rules concerns the **professionalism** of the legislature. The U.S. Congress is perhaps the most salient model of a professional legislature: it is a full-time job that comes with a substantial salary and staff support. Being a legislator in the national legislature is essentially a profession, like being a doctor or lawyer. But this model is hardly universal. State legislatures are often far less professional. Depending on state law, they may meet for only a few months every other year, as in North Dakota and Montana. Legislators in some states receive only small salaries. In fact, New Mexico state legislators receive no salary, only reimbursement for expenses. State legislatures also vary widely in the number of staff employed to assist legislatures. California's professionalized state legislature has several thousand staff, but New Mexico's has less than 100.[14] Legislatures that are not as professionalized are sometimes called **citizen legislatures**.[15]

The professionalism of the legislature has a two-edged effect on the incumbency advantage. On the one hand, the more professionalized the legislature, the more its incumbents are likely to attract a challenger. This is not surprising: jobs in a professionalized legislature are particularly attractive. But at the same time, incumbents in professional legislatures are actually *less* vulnerable even though they more often face a challenger. They have more resources at their disposal. Like members of Congress, they can claim credit for significant legislative accomplishments and serve their constituents' needs via casework. They can use the perquisites of their office to raise more money than incumbents in citizen legislatures. This helps explain why incumbents in professionalized legislatures are re-elected at higher rates.[16]

Term Limits

Many state elections are affected by a rule that members of Congress never confront: term limits. As noted in Chapter 2, most states limit the number of terms a governor can serve, and a substantial minority limit the terms of state legislators as well. The most common limit for governor, following the restrictions on presidents, is two consecutive terms. Statewide offices therefore see more turnover than either the U.S. House or Senate, where incumbents can accrue a considerable advantage from their years of service, as we discussed in Chapter 9. Term limits can change the calculus of both aspiring and current officeholders. Aspiring officeholders know they will be able to run for an open seat on a regular basis. Current officeholders know that their tenure is short-lived and they may therefore be even more inclined to position themselves to run for higher levels of office once, or even before, their term has expired.

---

[14] These examples come from Keith E. Hamm and Gary F. Moncrief. 2004. "Legislative Politics in the States," in *Politics in the American States*, eds. Virginia Gray and Russell L. Hanson, 8th ed. Washington, DC: CQ Press.

[15] City councils also vary in their level of professionalization, although there have been fewer studies of how professionalization affects campaign strategies in local elections.

[16] John M. Carey, Richard G. Niemi, and Lynda W. Powell. 2000. "Incumbency and the Probability of Reelection in State Legislative Elections." *Journal of Politics* 66, 3: 671–700; Robert E. Hogan. 2004. "Challenger Emergence, Incumbent Success, and Electoral Accountability in State Legislative Elections." *Journal of Politics* 66, 4: 1283–1303.

The natural conclusion, then, would be that term limits make elections more competitive, by weakening the advantages of incumbents and increasing the number of open-seat races. However, the real story is more complicated. Term limits have been instrumental in reducing the number of incumbents running in elections, but this does not necessarily make elections as a whole more competitive.[17] Instead, what often happens is that when first-term officeholders run for re-election, they do so without a serious challenger. This is because serious challengers would rather wait until the incumbent leaves office at the end of the term limit than mount a long-shot challenge. Moreover, several factors often combine to make it difficult for more than one serious challenger to compete for a newly open seat. The district itself may be dominated by one party, due to its underlying demography or a prior gerrymander. Leaders in this dominant party may work to promote one favored candidate and thereby avoid a hotly contested primary. As a consequence, term limits do not consistently result in closer races.

Economic and Political Realities

Despite their power, incumbent state officeholders are not insulated from broader political and economic realities. They are certainly less insulated than local officeholders. Elections for state offices, like those for president or Congress, are strongly affected by fundamental factors such as the state of the economy. What is particularly striking about state elections is how they can be affected by conditions *outside* the state or locality. To be sure, we do not mean to suggest that individual states have no unique circumstances. One can often see clear differences between the dynamics of federal and state elections. For example, in the American South, the gradual shift from one-party rule by the Democratic Party to a strong tendency to support Republican candidates occurred much more quickly at the federal level than at the state level.[18] That said, the diverse characteristics of individual states do not make each governor's or state legislator's race independent from events in Washington or the country as a whole.

---

[17] Seth E. Masket and Jeffrey B. Lewis. 2007. "A Return to Normalcy? Revisiting the Effects of Term Limits on Competitiveness and Spending in California Assembly Elections." *State Politics and Policy Quarterly* 7, 1: 20-38; Scot Schraufnagel and Karen Halperin. 2006. "Term Limits, Electoral Competition, and Representational Diversity: The Case of Florida." *State Politics and Policy Quarterly* 6, 4: 448–62.

[18] Charles S. Bullock III. 2010. "Introduction: Southern Politics in the Twenty-first Century," in *The New Politics of the Old South*, eds. Charles S. Bullock III and Mark J. Rozell. Lanham, MD: Rowman & Littlefield, pp. 1–26.

Incumbent governors and their parties are judged not only on state economic performance but on national economic performance, even though there is almost nothing they can do to affect the national economy.[19] The effects of the national economy are stronger in citizen legislatures, as professionalized legislatures provide advantages to incumbents that make them less likely to be defeated when the economy is weak.[20]

Similarly, candidates for state and local offices are judged based on the performance of someone who may be thousands of miles away: the president. State and local candidates in the president's party will do better when the president is more popular. In fact, this is true regardless of whether a presidential election is occurring at the same time. Thus, just as the president's party loses seats in Congress when the economy is weak and the president unpopular, it loses seats in, and sometimes control of, state legislatures. The year 2010 was a case in point: just as the Democrats lost seats in Congress, they lost control of six governorships and nearly 700 state legislative seats (including the control of 21 different legislative chambers).[21]

Candidates for state and local office can also be helped by the presence of higher-profile candidates on the ballot, such as candidates for president. Rules governing the timing of federal, state, and local elections mean that, in some years, state and local elections may occur alongside more visible federal elections. However, in some states, gubernatorial elections never occur in the same year as presidential elections. In New Jersey and Virginia, gubernatorial elections are held "off-cycle"—that is, in years without prominent federal or statewide races (generally odd-numbered years)—so that they do not compete with any federal elections. The same is true of many local elections.

What happens when more-visible candidates are on the ballot? They may create a **coattails effect**: less-visible candidates will "ride the coattails" of a more visible popular candidate of the same party who is on the ballot, and thereby do better at the polls. The presence of presidential and senatorial

---

[19] John E. Chubb. 1988. "Institutions, the Economy, and the Dynamics of State Elections." *American Political Science Review* 82, 1: 133–54; D. M. Simon. 1989. "Presidents, Governors, and Electoral Accountability." *Journal of Politics* 51, 2: 286–304; D. M. Simon, C. W. Ostrom, Jr., and R. F. Marra. 1991. "The President, Referendum Voting, and Subnational Elections in the United States." *American Political Science Review* 85, 4: 1177–92.

[20] William D. Berry, Michael B. Berkman, and Stuart Schneiderman. 2000. "Legislative Professionalism and Incumbent Reelection: The Development of Institutional Boundaries." *American Political Science Review* 94, 4: 859–74.

[21] National Conference of State Legislatures. "Map of Post 2010 Election Partisan Composition of State Legislatures." www.ncsl.org/?tabid=21253 (accessed 5/3/11).

candidates on the ballot may help candidates for governor and state legislator. Similarly, the presence of gubernatorial candidates may help state legislative candidates. Coattails may matter more for challengers and open-seat candidates, who do not have the advantages of incumbency. Coattails also matter more in states where voters can cast a "straight-ticket" vote by pulling a single lever or punching a single button for all the Democrats or all the Republicans on the ballot. (Currently, 16 states allow straight-ticket voting, although that number has declined in recent years.[22]) Ultimately, all of these features of reality signal that the incumbent advantage is not inviolable, and in certain political or economic climates, incumbent state officeholders may become more vulnerable.

Campaign Strategies Big and Small

As the stories at the beginning of this chapter make clear, it is not easy to generalize about the strategies of state and local campaigns. At a minimum, of course, almost every candidate for any level of office wants the same thing: to win enough votes to win the election. But how candidates actually go about campaigning will depend on the office they are seeking.

As we have seen, some state and even local campaigns have all the features of many federal campaigns: large sums of money are raised and spent, consultants are hired, polls are taken, television advertisements are produced and aired, and volunteers are organized to canvass neighborhoods and get out the vote. A statewide campaign for governor, especially in a large state, is essentially a presidential campaign run on a somewhat smaller scale. In California's 2010 gubernatorial race, State Insurance Commissioner Steve Poizner spent over $20 million, almost all of it his own money, and lost in the Republican primary to Meg Whitman, who spent considerably more.[23] In fact, Whitman spent a total of $178 million in 2010 and still lost the general election; her opponent, Jerry Brown, spent a "paltry" $41 million.

But many state and local campaigns are not nearly so visible. Candidates raise little money. Their campaign organizations are composed of a few

---

[22] National Conference of State Legislatures. 2011. "Straight-Ticket Voting." www.ncsl.org/default.aspx?tabid=16597 (accessed 5/3/11).

[23] Follow the Money. "California 2010: Candidates, Current Election Totals." www.followthemoney.org/database/StateGlance/state_candidates.phtml?s=CA&y=2010&f=G (accessed 5/3/11).

friends and family, not a stable of well-compensated consultants. They take no polls and air no ads. One study of candidates for state legislatures in 1997–98 found that about 60 percent of both incumbents and challengers hired no professional political consultants.[24] This is particularly true for less professionalized political offices. For example, in Wyoming, which has a citizen legislature, the average candidate for the Wyoming State House spent only $5,000 in the 2008 election.[25] By contrast, Steve Poizner's gubernatorial primary campaign spent $5,200 on FedEx packages alone.[26] A political party official in New Mexico put it this way: "Many state House and Senate candidates don't even have fax machines, let alone political consultants."[27]

The news media pay little attention to these races, which reflects in part a more general trend away from covering state politics.[28] Even a California gubernatorial race may not get their attention. In 1998, California's race ended in an easy victory for the Democratic candidate, Gray Davis. The lopsided nature of this race did not stop either Davis or his opponent, Dan Lungren, from spending money, of course ($65 million in total).[29] But local television news took little notice: in the two months before Election Day, less than half of one percent of news coverage in California's five largest media markets was devoted to the gubernatorial race.[30]

How then do candidate strategies and tactics differ in less visible state and local races? A central difference is in how they communicate with voters. Television advertising, which can be expensive to produce and to air, is replaced with more cost-effective forms of communication, including radio

---

[24] Owen G. Abbe and Paul S. Herrnson. 2003. "Campaign Professionalism in State Legislative Elections." *State Politics and Policy Quarterly* 3, 3: 223–45.

[25] Hamm and Moncrief, "Legislative Politics in the States," p. 158; http://followthemoney .org.

[26] California Secretary of State. "Campaign Finance: Steve Poizner for Governor, 2010." http://cal-access.ss.ca.gov/Campaign/Committees/Detail.aspx?id=1311517&session=2009& view=expenditures (accessed 5/3/11).

[27] Quoted in Dennis Johnson. 2007. *No Place for Amateurs: How Political Consultants Are Reshaping American Democracy*, 2nd ed. New York: Routledge, p. 209.

[28] Jennifer Dorroh. 2009. "Statehouse Exodus." *American Journalism Review*, April/May. www.ajr.org/Article.asp?id=4721 (accessed 5/3/11).

[29] Follow the Money. "California 1998: Candidates, Current Election Totals." www .followthemoney.org/database/StateGlance/state_candidates.phtml?s=CA&y=1998&f=G (accessed 5/3/11).

[30] Martin Kaplan and Matthew L. Hale. 1999. "Where Was the Television News?" in *California Votes—The 1998 Governor's Race: An Inside Look at the Candidates and Their Campaigns by the People Who Managed Them*, ed. Gerald C. Lubenow. Berkeley, CA: Institute of Governmental Studies Press.

advertisements, mailings to voters, and printed advertisements like bill-boards and flyers.[31] Indeed, one prominent guide to local campaigns includes entire chapters on brochures and on lawn signs, including a discussion of the importance of buying weatherproof paper stock for the lawn signs.[32] State and local campaigns depend more on building a stable and active group of volunteers, who can stuff envelopes and canvass voters, although canvassing is increasingly central to campaigns at every level of office.

An excellent example of this kind of campaign was State Senator Mark Earley's 1998 campaign for the Republican nomination for attorney general of Virginia.[33] Earley faced three opponents, all of whom hired political con-sultants and aired television advertisements. Earley did not. He had been endorsed by a conservative Christian group, the Christian Coalition, and targeted his campaign at evangelical ministers (via a letter from his own pastor) and at religiously conservative voters (via 600,000 pieces of direct mail). He won both the primary and the general elections.

A second way in which state and local elections may differ from fed-eral elections is in the sorts of issues that candidates discuss. Many areas of federal policy and lawmaking are simply less relevant to state and local officeholders. Foreign policy is an obvious example. Conversely, gover-nors, state legislators, mayors, and city council members have more juris-diction over some policy areas than do federal officeholders. For example, although education and crime are discussed by federal candidates, much of the actual business of improving education and fighting crime goes on at the state and local levels, making these prominent campaign issues at these levels. Elections at all levels concern the economy, but some debates at local levels—for example, over zoning restrictions—do not occur at state and federal levels. Finally, the fact that state and local elections often occur in different years than federal elections gives state and local candidates an even greater ability to discuss issues that may not be on the president's or Congress's front burner.

We might also expect campaign strategies for state and local races to differ depending on the rules that govern them. A good example involves city council races, which may involve single-member district seats, at-large

---

[31] Robert E. Hogan. 1997. "Voter Contact Techniques in State Legislative Campaigns: The Prevalence of Mass Media Advertising." *Legislative Studies Quarterly* 22, 4: 551–71.

[32] Catherine Shaw. 2000. *The Campaign Manager: Running and Winning Local Elections,* 2nd ed. Boulder, CO: Westview Press.

[33] This example is from Johnson, *No Place for Amateurs,* p. 218.

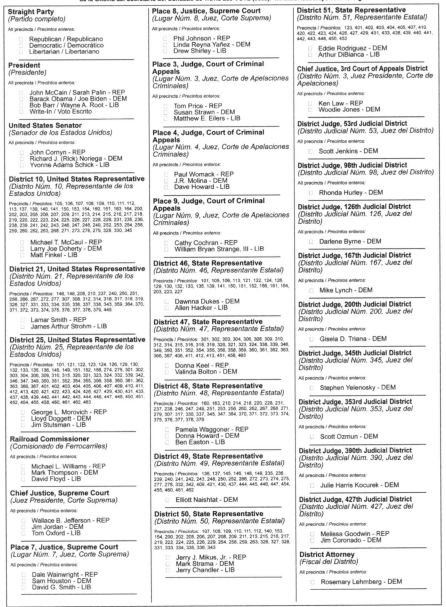

Travis County Clerk Elections Division

November 4, 2008 Joint General and Special Elections

División Electoral de la Secretaria del Condado de Travis

Elecciones Conjuntas Generales y Especiales de noviembre el 4 de 2008

If you do not know your election precinct, call **Voter Registration** at **854-9473**. For candidate information call the
Travis County Clerk's Election Division at 238-VOTE (8683). www.traviscountyelections.org.

*Si usted no sabe su precinto de elección, llame al Registrador de Votantes 854-9473. Para candidato información sobre la elección, llame la **División de Elecciones
de la Oficina del Secretario del Condado de Travis 238-VOTE (8683). www.traviscountyelections.org***

Straight Party
(Partido completo)

All precincts / *Precintos enteros:*

- ☐ Republican / Republicano
- ☐ Democratic / Democrático
- ☐ Libertarian / Libertariano

President
(Presidente)

All precincts / *Precintos enteros:*

- ☐ John McCain / Sarah Palin - REP
- ☐ Barack Obama / Joe Biden - DEM
- ☐ Bob Barr / Wayne A. Root - LIB
- ☐ Write-In / Voto Escrito

United States Senator
(Senador de los Estados Unidos)

All precincts / *Precintos enteros:*

- ☐ John Cornyn - REP
- ☐ Richard J. (Rick) Noriega - DEM
- ☐ Yvonne Adams Schick - LIB

District 10, United States Representative
(Distrito Núm. 10, Representante de los Estados Unidos)

Precincts / *Precintos:* 105, 106, 107, 108, 109, 110, 111, 112, 113, 137, 139, 140, 141, 150, 153, 154, 160, 161, 183, 164, 200, 202, 203, 205, 206, 207, 209, 211, 213, 214, 215, 216, 217, 218, 219, 220, 222, 223, 224, 225, 226, 227, 228, 229, 231, 235, 236, 238, 239, 241, 242, 243, 246, 247, 248, 249, 252, 253, 254, 258, 259, 280, 262, 263, 268, 271, 273, 278, 279, 328, 330, 345

- ☐ Michael T. McCaul - REP
- ☐ Larry Joe Doherty - DEM
- ☐ Matt Finkel - LIB

District 21, United States Representative
(Distrito Núm. 21, Representante de los Estados Unidos)

Precincts / *Precintos:* 146, 148, 208, 210, 237, 240, 250, 251, 256, 266, 267, 272, 277, 307, 308, 312, 314, 316, 317, 318, 319, 326, 327, 331, 333, 334, 335, 336, 337, 338, 343, 359, 364, 370, 371, 372, 373, 374, 375, 376, 377, 378, 379, 445

- ☐ Lamar Smith - REP
- ☐ James Arthur Strohm - LIB

District 25, United States Representative
(Distrito Núm. 25, Representante de los Estados Unidos)

Precincts / *Precintos:* 101, 121, 122, 123, 124, 126, 129, 130, 132, 133, 135, 136, 145, 149, 151, 152, 156, 274, 275, 301, 302, 303, 304, 306, 309, 310, 315, 320, 321, 323, 324, 332, 339, 342, 346, 347, 349, 350, 351, 352, 354, 355, 356, 358, 360, 361, 362, 363, 366, 367, 401, 402, 403, 404, 405, 406, 407, 409, 410, 411, 412, 413, 420, 421, 422, 423, 424, 426, 427, 429, 430, 431, 433, 437, 438, 439, 440, 441, 442, 443, 444, 446, 447, 448, 450, 451, 452, 454, 455, 458, 460, 461, 462, 463

- ☐ George L. Morovich - REP
- ☐ Lloyd Doggett - DEM
- ☐ Jim Stutsman - LIB

Railroad Commissioner
(Comisionado de Ferrocarriles)

All precincts / *Precintos enteros:*

- ☐ Michael L. Williams - REP
- ☐ Mark Thompson - DEM
- ☐ David Floyd - LIB

Chief Justice, Supreme Court
(Juez Presidente, Corte Suprema)

All precincts / *Precintos enteros:*

- ☐ Wallace B. Jefferson - REP
- ☐ Jim Jordan - DEM
- ☐ Tom Oxford - LIB

Place 7, Justice, Supreme Court
(Lugar Núm. 7, Juez, Corte Suprema)

All precincts / *Precintos enteros:*

- ☐ Dale Wainwright - REP
- ☐ Sam Houston - DEM
- ☐ David G. Smith - LIB

Place 8, Justice, Supreme Court
(Lugar Núm. 8, Juez, Corte Suprema)

All precincts / *Precintos enteros:*

- ☐ Phil Johnson - REP
- ☐ Linda Reyna Yañez - DEM
- ☐ Drew Shirley - LIB

Place 3, Judge, Court of Criminal Appeals
(Lugar Núm. 3, Juez, Corte de Apelaciones Criminales)

All precincts / *Precintos enteros:*

- ☐ Tom Price - REP
- ☐ Susan Strawn - DEM
- ☐ Matthew E. Eilers - LIB

Place 4, Judge, Court of Criminal Appeals
(Lugar Núm. 4, Juez, Corte de Apelaciones Criminales)

All precincts / *Precintos enteros:*

- ☐ Paul Womack - REP
- ☐ J.R. Molina - DEM
- ☐ Dave Howard - LIB

Place 9, Judge, Court of Criminal Appeals
(Lugar Núm. 9, Juez, Corte de Apelaciones Criminales)

All precincts / *Precintos enteros:*

- ☐ Cathy Cochran - REP
- ☐ William Bryan Strange, III - LIB

District 46, State Representative
(Distrito Núm. 46, Representante Estatal)

Precincts / *Precintos:* 101, 105, 106, 113, 121, 122, 124, 126, 129, 130, 132, 133, 135, 139, 141, 150, 151, 152, 156, 161, 164, 203, 223, 227

- ☐ Dawnna Dukes - DEM
- ☐ Allen Hacker - LIB

District 47, State Representative
(Distrito Núm. 47, Representante Estatal)

Precincts / *Precintos:* 301, 302, 303, 304, 306, 308, 309, 310, 312, 314, 315, 316, 318, 319, 320, 321, 323, 324, 338, 339, 346, 349, 350, 351, 352, 354, 355, 356, 358, 359, 360, 361, 362, 363, 366, 367, 406, 411, 412, 413, 451, 458, 463

- ☐ Donna Keel - REP
- ☐ Valinda Bolton - DEM

District 48, State Representative
(Distrito Núm. 48, Representante Estatal)

Precincts / *Precintos:* 160, 163, 210, 214, 218, 220, 228, 231, 237, 238, 246, 247, 249, 251, 253, 256, 260, 262, 267, 268, 271, 279, 307, 317, 330, 337, 345, 347, 364, 370, 371, 372, 373, 374, 375, 376, 377, 378, 379

- ☐ Pamela Waggoner - REP
- ☐ Donna Howard - DEM
- ☐ Ben Easton - LIB

District 49, State Representative
(Distrito Núm. 49, Representante Estatal)

Precincts / *Precintos:* 136, 137, 145, 146, 148, 149, 235, 236, 239, 240, 241, 242, 243, 248, 250, 252, 266, 272, 273, 274, 275, 277, 278, 332, 342, 409, 421, 430, 437, 444, 445, 446, 447, 454, 455, 460, 461, 462

- ☐ Elliott Naishtat - DEM

District 50, State Representative
(Distrito Núm. 50, Representante Estatal)

Precincts / *Precintos:* 107, 108, 109, 110, 111, 112, 140, 153, 154, 200, 202, 205, 206, 207, 208, 209, 211, 213, 215, 216, 217, 219, 222, 224, 225, 226, 229, 254, 258, 259, 263, 326, 327, 328, 331, 333, 334, 335, 336, 343

- ☐ Jerry J. Mikus, Jr. - REP
- ☐ Mark Strama - DEM
- ☐ Jerry Chandler - LIB

District 51, State Representative
(Distrito Núm. 51, Representante Estatal)

Precincts / *Precintos:* 123, 401, 402, 403, 404, 405, 407, 410, 420, 422, 423, 424, 426, 427, 429, 431, 433, 438, 439, 440, 441, 442, 443, 448, 450, 452

- ☐ Eddie Rodriguez - DEM
- ☐ Arthur DiBianca - LIB

Chief Justice, 3rd Court of Appeals District
(Distrito Núm. 3, Juez Presidente, Corte de Apelaciones)

All precincts / *Precintos enteros:*

- ☐ Ken Law - REP
- ☐ Woodie Jones - DEM

District Judge, 53rd Judicial District
(Distrito Judicial Núm. 53, Juez del Distrito)

All precincts / *Precintos enteros:*

- ☐ Scott Jenkins - DEM

District Judge, 98th Judicial District
(Distrito Judicial Núm. 98, Juez del Distrito)

All precincts / *Precintos enteros:*

- ☐ Rhonda Hurley - DEM

District Judge, 126th Judicial District
(Distrito Judicial Núm. 126, Juez del Distrito)

All precincts / *Precintos enteros:*

- ☐ Darlene Byrne - DEM

District Judge, 167th Judicial District
(Distrito Judicial Núm. 167, Juez del Distrito)

All precincts / *Precintos enteros:*

- ☐ Mike Lynch - DEM

District Judge, 200th Judicial District
(Distrito Judicial Núm. 200, Juez del Distrito)

All precincts / *Precintos enteros:*

- ☐ Gisela D. Triana - DEM

District Judge, 345th Judicial District
(Distrito Judicial Núm. 345, Juez del Distrito)

All precincts / *Precintos enteros:*

- ☐ Stephen Yelenosky - DEM

District Judge, 353rd Judicial District
(Distrito Judicial Núm. 353, Juez del Distrito)

All precincts / *Precintos enteros:*

- ☐ Scott Ozmun - DEM

District Judge, 390th Judicial District
(Distrito Judicial Núm. 390, Juez del Distrito)

All precincts / *Precintos enteros:*

- ☐ Julie Harris Kocurek - DEM

District Judge, 427th Judicial District
(Distrito Judicial Núm. 427, Juez del Distrito)

All precincts / *Precintos enteros:*

- ☐ Melissa Goodwin - REP
- ☐ Jim Coronado - DEM

District Attorney
(Fiscal del Distrito)

All precincts / *Precintos enteros:*

- ☐ Rosemary Lehmberg - DEM

Many state and local races are less visible to voters, who may know little about the candidates in down-ticket races (those below president and Congress). For example, voters in this Texas county were called on to elect numerous judges.

seats, or both. In cities with single-member districts, prevailing patterns of housing may mean that many districts are characterized by a large majority of one ethnic group. In turn, this means that candidates in any given district must appeal to voters from the dominant ethnic group. Washington, DC, is one example. It has eight members elected from wards and five members, including the chair, elected at large. City council wards tend to be majority white or black and elect white or black city council members, respectively. Candidates for at-large elections may not need to appeal to smaller ethnic groups, however: a winning coalition can be built from the dominant or majority ethnic group. One implication, then, is that candidates in at-large systems do less to appeal to ethnic groups who are minorities within the city, who then find it harder to gain representation on the city council. We return to this topic below.

Despite these differences in candidate strategy among federal, state, and local campaigns, all candidates at any level of office make similar kinds of strategic decisions about their message and the kinds of voters they will target. State and local candidates seek to articulate a message that defines and promotes their candidacy. They analyze past election results, precinct by precinct, and pore over registered voter lists to identify likely supporters who can then be targeted with campaign media and get-out-the-vote efforts. They work to contact those supporters and ensure their participation on Election Day. But in many state and local races, these efforts are difficult to see, aside from lawn signs and perhaps a volunteer with a clipboard knocking at your door.

The Push toward Professionalization

Even as state and local campaigns are, on average, less professionalized than federal campaigns, they have increasingly come to resemble federal campaigns—with more spending, television advertising, and use of consultants than in the past. For example, the average candidate for the California State Assembly spent $189,000 in 2000 and $248,000 in 2008.[34] State parties are also driving professionalization. They conduct polls and hire consultants to help formulate strategy that can then be implemented by the party's candidates. Many political consultants focus their practice within a given

---

[34] These figures are the amounts spent by the median candidate in 2008 dollars. The data are from http://followthemoney.org (accessed 5/3/11).

state and advertise their detailed knowledge of the local terrain. To some extent, the push toward professionalization is simply an arms race: once one side raises enough money to hire consultants and air television advertising, the other side will try to do likewise. The push to professionalization is perhaps most evident in two types of elections: for ballot initiatives and referenda and for state judicial offices.

Ballot Initiatives

Ballot initiatives and **referenda** are proposals placed on the ballot that allow citizens to change law and public policy. This mode of decision making is sometimes called "direct democracy" because such measures are voted on directly by citizens rather than by elected representatives. Twenty-eight states provide some means of direct democracy.[35] The number of initiatives or referenda varies by year, but in presidential and midterm elections from 1998 to 2008, there were an average of 193 nationwide.[36]

Although direct democracy does empower citizens in some respects, many ballot initiatives are hardly the results of grassroots organizing. Instead, interest groups and wealthy individuals work to place their proposals on the ballot and then spend money to promote them. A highly controversial ballot measure in a large state will ultimately cost supporters and opponents many millions of dollars. In 2008, the campaigns for and against California's Proposition 8, which sought to amend the state constitution to recognize marriages only between men and women, cost a total of $107 million. There is little that can be done to limit the amounts spent in ballot initiative campaigns. Supreme Court precedent forbids limits on donations to committees formed to support or oppose initiatives; it also forbids bans on corporate spending in ballot initiative campaigns. The logic is that initiatives, unlike candidates, cannot be corrupted by money, and thus there is no compelling interest that would allow restrictions on speech.[37]

With so much money involved, the tasks of getting measures on the ballot and promoting them now involve a wide array of campaign professionals. There are law firms who craft the wording of the initiative, and consulting firms who specialize in gathering the signatures needed to get the initiative

---

[35] Johnson, *No Place for Amateurs*, p. 196.

[36] Ballot Initiative Strategy Center. "The 2008 Initiative and Referenda Election Results." ballot.org/page/-/ballot.org/Research/2008%20Ballot%20Initiative%20%20Ref%20Election%20Preview%20-%20merged.pdf (accessed 5/3/11).

[37] Richard Hasen. 2005. "Rethinking the Unconstitutionality of Contribution and Expenditure Limits in Ballot Measure Campaigns." *Southern California Law Review* 78: 885–925.

The Potentially Public Act of Signing a Petition

To place an initiative on the ballot, the initiative's sponsors must typically collect thousands, if not hundreds of thousands, of signatures from registered voters. The sponsors will typically employ companies who specialize in gathering these signatures—one of the many ways in which ballot initiative campaigns have become more professionalized and therefore expensive.

The passage of Referendum 71 in Washington State in 2009 spawned a battle over a different issue: Should the names of the people who signed a petition to place this referendum on the ballot become public? Referendum 71 concerned a decision by the Washington legislature to extend domestic partner benefits to same-sex couples. It was placed on the ballot by opponents of domestic partner benefits and same-sex marriage, who hoped that Washington voters would essentially undo what the state legislature had done. Ultimately, 53 percent of voters supported the state legislature's decision, thus making domestic partner benefits part of state law.

During the campaign, some supporters of domestic partner benefits, and in particular a group called WhoSigned.org, requested the names of the 122,000 people who had signed petitions to place the referendum on the ballot. WhoSigned.org argued that Washington state law made these signatures a matter of public record, available to anyone upon request. The Washington secretary of state agreed.[1]

Meanwhile, opponents of domestic partner benefits argued against the release of the petitions. A spokesman for one group, Protect Marriage Washington, claimed that publicizing the names of the signatories would leave them vulnerable to harassment: "Supporters of traditional marriage have received death threats and have had their personal property destroyed. . . . No one should have to endure the harassment that these individuals have endured . . . for standing up for what they believe in."[2]

The release of the signatures was initially delayed by Supreme Court Justice Anthony Kennedy in October 2009. The legal case, *Doe v. Reed*, was then considered by the Supreme Court.

The Court was nearly unanimous in its opinion: eight justices declared that those who signed petitions had no constitutional right to keep their identities private. The Court did suggest that in some cases there could be reason to allow these identities to remain private, and ordered a lower court to decide whether that was true in the case of Referendum 71. However, a majority of the Court appeared skeptical that anonymity was necessary in this case. In his opinion, Justice Antonin Scalia wrote: "Requiring people to stand up in public for their political acts fosters civic courage, without which democracy is doomed." If this belief holds sway on the Court, this adds an interesting wrinkle to direct democracy in the future. Even if people's votes on initiatives and referenda remain secret, their support of placing initiatives and referenda on the ballot may not be.

---

[1] Office of the Secretary of State. 2009, October 15. "Release of Initiative and Referendum Petitions." http://blogs.secstate.wa.gov/FromOurCorner/wp-content/uploads/2009/10/Acr65.pdf (accessed 5/4/11).

[2] Protect Marriage Washington. 2010, August 11. "Court Prohibits Release of Referendum Petitions." http://protectmarriagewa.com (accessed 5/4/11).

on the ballot, and media firms who produce radio and television ads promoting or denouncing the initiative, and pollsters who monitor the public opinion about the initiative, and direct mail firms who design and send letters to citizens about the initiative. Consultants often relish the opportunity to work on these campaigns, which offer them greater latitude to shape the campaign message than they might have working with an actual candidate. As one consultant said, "With ballot issues you build your own candidate."[38]

Judicial Elections

Thirty-eight states have judicial elections, of which there are three types.[39] Partisan elections pit opposing candidates identified with political parties against each other. Nonpartisan elections also feature opposing candidates, but they run without party labels (although political parties may endorse candidates). **Retention elections** allow voters to decide whether to allow seated judges to remain on the bench; these elections are simply referenda on the judges and do not select a replacement. In 2010, three justices from the Iowa State Supreme Court lost their retention elections after the court ruled in favor of gay marriage. This was the first time in Iowa's history that a sitting judge had ever lost a retention election. Moreover, while campaigns for these offices were once staid affairs that featured little actual electioneering, they have come to resemble campaigns for executive and legislative offices as well as many ballot initiatives.

Judicial campaigns have become increasingly costly: the total amount of money raised by state supreme court candidates across the country jumped from nearly $10 million in 1989–90 to almost $46 million in 2007–08, before falling somewhat to $27 million in 2009–10.[40] Partisan elections tend to be particularly expensive: they accounted for 74 percent of all spending in state supreme court elections from 2000 to 2009. Judicial campaigns also attract the efforts of various party organizations as well as interest groups such as chambers of commerce, trial lawyer groups, and the Business Council of America, who donate to judicial candidates or spend independently on their behalf. Finally, these campaigns feature a larger number

---

[38] Quoted in Johnson, *No Place for Amateurs*, p. 201.

[39] American Bar Association. "Fact Sheet on Judicial Selection Methods in the States." www.americanbar.org/content/dam/aba/migrated/leadership/fact_sheet.authcheckdam.pdf (accessed 5/3/11).

[40] James Sample, Adam Skaggs, Jonathan Blitzer, and Linda Casey. 2010. "The New Politics of Judicial Elections, 2000–2009." New York: Brennan Center for Justice and National Institute on Money in State Politics; Adam Skaggs, Maria da Silva, Linda Casey, and Charles Hall. 2011. "The New Politics of Judicial Elections 2009–2010." New York: Brennan Center for Justice and National Institute on Money in State Politics.

FIGURE 10.2 Contributions to State Supreme Court Candidates, 1989–2010

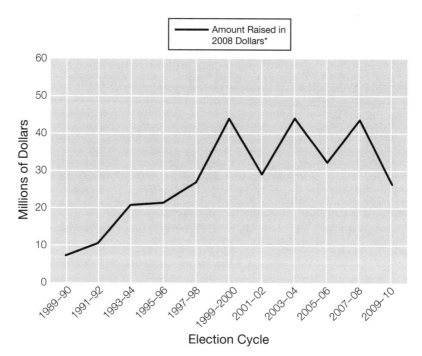

Election Cycle

*2008 dollar figures based on conversion rates from the even-numbered year of each two-year period.
Source: James Sample, Adam Skaggs, Jonathan Blitzer, and Linda Casey. 2010. "The New Politics of Judicial Elections, 2000–2009." Brennan Center for Justice and National Institute on Money in State Politics.

of television advertisements. State supreme court elections saw only about 23,000 ads in 2000, but more than 51,000 in 2012.[41] As in other sorts of campaigns, the ads are frequently hard-hitting, accusing judges of sleeping during trials, "putting criminals on the street," and the like.

One reason for the increased expense of state judicial elections is that, starting in the 1990s, business groups increasingly came into conflict with trial lawyers, consumer groups, and labor unions over tort reform. Tort reform typically entails limits to the awards that plaintiffs can win from corporations and businesses for, say, an allegedly faulty product. Business groups favored these reforms, but trial lawyers and consumer groups did not. This conflict then began to spill over into the judicial arena, since appellate

---

[41] Brennan Center for Justice. 2012. "New Data Shows Judicial Election Ad Spending Breaks Record at $29.7 Million." www.brennancenter.org/press–release/new-data-shows-judicial-election-ad-spending-breaks-record-297-million (accessed 4/17/13).

and state court justices would often hear tort cases on appeal and could adjust the amount of money awarded to plaintiffs. Thus, it made strategic sense for interest groups to insert themselves into state judicial campaigns. Judicial races had previously been so sleepy that these groups believed a sudden influx of spending could make a difference.

Whether the issue is tort reform, redistricting, or collective bargaining for state workers, in general it is cheaper to influence judicial elections than to help elect a favorable majority in the state legislature or a sympathetic gubernatorial candidate. As one Ohio union official put it, "We figured out a long time ago that it's easier to elect seven judges than to elect 132 legislators."[42] Needless to say, such sentiments do nothing to allay the fear that expensive campaigns compromise the integrity of judges. We return to this question below.

Activists in State and Local Campaigns

The entry of interest groups into state judicial elections hints at a broader feature of many state and local campaigns: without much voter or media interest, dedicated activists, whether from state and local party organizations or interest groups, can powerfully affect these races. In state and local elections, activists can often work to influence the outcome without attracting much attention or even competition. For them, it takes fewer resources to get a larger benefit: greater influence over state and local races than might be possible in more visible federal races.

Rules that dictate off-cycle elections can have a particularly strong effect on the influence of interest groups, because they result in lower voter turnout. For example, in school districts with off-cycle elections, teachers are typically paid more than in districts with on-cycle elections—that is, teachers unions are more likely to get their desired outcome: larger paychecks. Elections with low turnout help to empower interest groups whose members are likely to vote and thus produce policy outcomes closer to their preferences.[43] Small wonder, then, that parties and activists have routinely sought to manipulate the timing of elections to maximize their electoral or policy goals.[44]

---

[42] Quoted in Sample, Skaggs, Blitzer, and Casey, "The New Politics of Judicial Elections, 2000–2009," p. 9.

[43] Sarah Anzia. 2011. "Election Timing and the Electoral Influence of Interest Groups." *Journal of Politics*, 73, 2: 412–427.

[44] Sarah Anzia. 2010. "Partisan Power Play: The Origins of Local Election Timing as an American Political Institution." Working paper, Stanford University.

The history of political monopolies within American cities provides a second example. As discussed in Chapter 6, party machines have had sustained periods of influence in many cities, using a variety of rewards and punishments to choose candidates, mobilize voters, and ensure the continued loyalty of both. And although some of the most infamous machines no longer exist, urban politics still has its monopolies.[45] When Newark's Mayor Sharpe James was challenged by Cory Booker in 2002, Booker's campaign saw its signs disappear, its supporters harassed, and its headquarters robbed. Some of these actions were perpetrated by Newark police officers aligned with the James administration. Over his five terms, James had assembled a strong organization of party officials, activists, and even municipal employees who were willing to work on his behalf and, in this case, intimidate a challenger.

State legislative elections provide another example.[46] In many state legislative districts, the outcome is largely a foregone conclusion because the districts are so politically homogeneous. The majority party can essentially monopolize the district. This makes the primary election the most important election, since the majority party's nominee will almost always win the general election. If term limits are also in effect, primary elections to choose a new nominee occur more frequently, and term limited officials often compete in primaries for higher levels of office. Few, if any, state legislative primaries attract much attention from local news organizations or from voters, most of whom could not name their state representatives if asked.[47]

The result is that local party activists have considerable leeway to shape the outcome. As they do in city elections, local party organizations work to recruit candidates, influence the primary election, and ensure that the winner remains loyal to the activists' agenda while in the legislature. They are not machines but rather networks of like-minded officials and activists, sometimes with a de facto leader and sometimes not, who coordinate to influence the election. The power of this network will almost always trump that of potential candidates. Most candidates are not well known or personally wealthy, and thus they need the support of the local party to get on the ballot and to win. Because they must conform to the views of activists, these candidates will tend to be more

---

[45] Jessica Trounstine. 2008. *Political Monopolies in American Cities: The Rise and Fall of Bosses and Reformers.* Chicago: University of Chicago Press.

[46] Seth E. Masket. 2009. *No Middle Ground: How Informal Party Organizations Control Nominations and Polarize Legislatures.* Ann Arbor: University of Michigan Press.

[47] Samuel C. Patterson, Randall B. Ripley and Stephen V. Quinlan. 1992. "Citizens' Orientations toward Legislatures: Congress and the State Legislature." *Western Political Quarterly* 45, 2: 315–338

ideologically extreme than the voters that elect them, and the parties in the state legislature will be more polarized along ideological lines.

An example of how such a network matters comes from the rural Central Valley of California, where, for nearly twenty years until his retirement in 2007, Bill Thomas, a Republican member of the House of Representatives, held sway.[48] Thomas's support for a local candidate was considered crucial, and Republican office seekers curried his favor. His endorsement signaled others in the network, such as prominent donors, business leaders, and conservative groups, to support the chosen candidate. The network centered on Thomas was directly responsible for punishing a Republican state legislator, Mike Briggs, who disappointed conservatives by voting for a Democratic budget plan in 2001; the plan included a tax increase that conservatives opposed. Briggs found himself with a primary challenger, Devin Nunes, who was 28 years old, reliably conservative, and, perhaps most important, a former campaign staffer for Thomas. Nunes beat Briggs in the primary and went on to win the general election.

Conclusion

State and local elections may often seem like small potatoes. The candidates are typically anything but celebrities, and the campaigns are often unsophisticated. But they have considerable strategic importance. For politically ambitious people, state and local offices can be important for incubating political careers. Barack Obama and Jimmy Carter began their careers as state legislators. Some other presidents began their careers in elected office as governors, including Ronald Reagan, Bill Clinton, and George W. Bush.

State and local politics are especially important for candidates from groups that have traditionally been underrepresented in political office, such as women and ethnic minorities. Potential candidates from these groups face significant barriers if they want to start their political careers at higher levels of office, such as Congress. Success is more likely within state and local politics, where the barriers are lower and where they gain the experience, visibility, and viability needed to seek higher office.

State and local politics are also important to political parties and interest groups. Decision making at these levels affects a variety of policies that

---

[48] See Seth E. Masket. 2009. *No Middle Ground: How Informal Party Organizations Control Nominations and Polarize Legislatures.* Ann Arbor: University of Michigan Press, pp. 2, 31–32.

parties and groups care about, including taxation, schools, prisons, roads, and health care. Moreover, state and local elections offer parties and interest groups more opportunities for influence than do federal elections. They can work to choose and support candidates, knowing that the local candidates depend on this support. Parties and interest groups can work behind the scenes, because most state and local elections are rarely covered by the news media and thus largely invisible to voters.

The invisibility of many state and local campaigns gives rise to a paradox. State and local leaders are in some sense "closest" to citizens: these leaders are more intimately involved with the community they represent, and their decisions affect virtually every aspect of life in that community—from whether schools get new textbooks to whether potholes get filled. And yet state and local elections engage many fewer voters than federal and especially presidential elections. With little spending by the candidates and little attention from the media, voters are unfamiliar the candidates and do not learn much during the campaign. The weakening of party machines, whatever its benefits, has been associated with a decline in turnout. As a consequence, state and local elections see some of the lowest turnout rates among all American elections. One study of California municipal elections found that the average turnout in mayoral races was 28 percent, and in city council races 32 percent.[49] These rates are much lower than in federal elections: turnout even in midterm elections has been higher than 32 percent in every election since 1792. Moreover, even when state and local elections coincide with a presidential election, bringing more voters to the polls, voters sometimes fail to mark a choice for state and local offices (a phenomenon called "roll-off"). Voters may not get the information necessary to meet the standards of free choice and deliberation discussed in Chapter 1.

Some of this lack of voter involvement is because many state and local races are not competitive. State and local races are no different from congressional races in this sense. Many localities are not politically diverse. Republicans simply do not have much hope in Berkeley, California, while Democrats stand little chance in College Station, Texas. Incumbents have a considerable advantage, especially those who hold full-time, professionalized offices. They raise money, claim credit for legislative accomplishments, perform casework for constituents, and show up at every ribbon-cutting

---

[49] Zoltan L. Hajnal and Paul G. Lewis. 2003. "Municipal Institutions and Voter Turnout in Local Elections." *Urban Affairs Review* 38, 5: 645–68; Neal Caren. 2007. "Big City, Big Turnout? Electoral Participation in American Cities." *Journal of Urban Affairs* 29, 1: 39–46.

they can—all in the service of warding off potential challengers and defeating actual ones. The inequalities among candidates so frequently noted in congressional races are similarly prevalent in many state and local races.

The lack of competitiveness also stems from direct actions taken by leaders, parties, and interest groups. Gerrymandering is part of this story, of course: majority parties work, to the extent possible, to draw state legislative boundaries that will maximize the number of seats they hold. State and local politics also feature other strategies to reduce competitiveness. Political monopolies within cities promote one party's reign in part via strategies that render elections less competitive and reduce voter turnout.[50] Activist networks seek to control the nominations process and primary elections, often limiting the choices available to voters by "clearing the field" of opposing candidates.

None of this is necessarily problematic in terms of the goals of democratic political systems. Low voter turnout could at times reflect a degree of satisfaction with state and local representative and governments. The enhanced role of activists may be entirely appropriate, given that they feel much more strongly than the average voter about the issues that confront state and local governments. And representatives elected in uncompetitive races still may work to represent the interests of their constituents.

At the same time, a lack of competitiveness in state and local elections may create biases that have important effects on the process of governing. The power of activists, most of whom have strong ideological views, tends to produce leaders who are more ideologically extreme than voters. This bias toward ideologues creates polarization in government—whereby the two parties strongly disagree on policy and cannot reach effective compromises. The result of such polarization is that governments struggle to develop policy solutions to important problems. In California, which has one of the most polarized state legislatures, state budgets are routinely passed months after the ostensible deadline because Democrats and Republicans cannot agree on the appropriate levels of taxation and spending.

Low levels of turnout in local elections also create biases in terms of who wins elections and which groups are represented in government. In particular, racial and ethnic minorities are often affected—a situation exacerbated when local elections are conducted at large instead of in single-member districts. In low-turnout elections, minority candidates are more likely to lose mayoral elections, minorities are underrepresented on city councils, and the spending policies of local governments are out of step with

---

[50] Trounstine, *Political Monopolies in American Cities*, chapter 5.

the views of minorities.[51] Thus, the lack of competitiveness and the invisibility of many local races create another sort of political inequality: conditions that seem distinctly unfavorable to minority ethnic groups.

Unsurprisingly, then, many reformers seek to make state and local elections more competitive. As noted in Chapter 4, this is one goal of clean elections laws. Competitiveness produces more vigorous campaigns, which, on average, make voters more interested and willing to participate. Proponents of campaign finance reform and term limits often intend just that, although, as we have discussed, these reforms may have little impact. But there are important trade-offs in making campaigns more intense, ones highlighted by the trends in ballot initiative campaigns and judicial elections. Contested campaigns tend to be more professionalized and more expensive: more money is raised and spent, more consultants hired, and more advertisements aired. Competitive races also attract the energies of parties and interest groups, who may spend even more money independent of the candidates. All of this can make for mean and rowdy campaigns.

In the case of judicial elections, some believe that a bitter and expensive campaign can compromise the integrity of courts and judges, who may be inclined to rule in favor of campaign contributors rather than uphold the rule of law. A case in point involved a West Virginia Supreme Court justice, Brent Benjamin. In 2004, he defeated an incumbent justice, William McGraw. He did so with the help of Don Blankenship, the CEO of a West Virginia mining company, Massey Energy. Before the campaign, Massey Energy had been sued by another mining company, Harman Mining Company, for breach of contract. A jury ruled that Massey owed $50 million. Blankenship then spent $3 million in an attempt to defeat McGraw, establishing a group called "And for the Sake of the Kids," which aired ads accusing McGraw of "voting to let a child rapist out of prison." Three years after Benjamin won, the West Virginia Supreme Court heard Massey Energy's appeal of this $50 million verdict. Benjamin provided the swing vote in a 3–2 decision that overturned the verdict. Later, the U.S. Supreme Court threw out the West Virginia court's decision, arguing that Benjamin faced a conflict of interest so extreme that Harman Mining's due process rights may have been violated.[52] Such a scenario, however unusual, suggests that vigorous judicial campaigns may bring with them unintended consequences.

---

[51] Zoltan Hajnal. 2010. *America's Uneven Democracy: Race, Turnout, and Representation in City Politics.* New York: Cambridge University Press.

[52] *Caperton v. A.T. Massey Coal Co.*, 129 S. Ct. 2252. (2009).

To be sure, judges occupy a rarified office with unique responsibilities. We do not expect governors, legislators, mayors, and most other officeholders to be as impartial. But the same fears about the corrupting influence of campaigns donations occur at every level of office, as do concerns about other aspects of the campaign such as negative advertisements. This gets at the essence of the trade-off. Competitive elections provide more choices and more information for voters. They are also, absent a transformation in campaign finance, more expensive and often more negative. It is hard to have one without the other.

KEY TERMS

professionalism (p. 288)

citizen legislature (p. 289)

coattails effect (p. 291)

ballot initiatives (p. 297)

referenda (p. 297)

retention elections (p. 299)

FOR DISCUSSION

1. What is legislative professionalism and how does it affect the advantages of incumbents in state legislatures and the impact of the national economy on state legislative elections?

2. How do the strategies employed in state and local campaigns typically differ those in from federal campaigns?

3. Why do many state and local races give political party organizations and interest groups a particular opportunity to influence the election?

4. What are the possible advantages and disadvantages of having state and local elections become more competitive?

 Visit StudySpace for quizzes and other review material.
wwnorton.com/studyspace

CHAPTER 11

Voter Participation

In 2008, Barack Obama's campaign team created a Web site called MyBarackObama.com. This was neither the first candidate Web site nor the first attempt by campaigns to harness the power of the Internet. Eight years earlier, during the 2000 presidential primaries, John McCain demonstrated the fund-raising power of the Internet by raising more than $1 million in a single evening. In 2004, supporters of Howard Dean's primary campaign arranged meetings via Meetup.com. But in 2008, MyBarackObama.com took e-campaigning to a new level. It was not created to persuade people to vote for Obama; most people who signed on to the site had already decided to vote for him. Instead, it was created to get Obama supporters involved in the primary campaign against Hillary Clinton and John Edwards. One of the Web site's creators, Jascha Franklin-Hodge, explained that the Obama campaign "knew they didn't have the kind of political machine Clinton was going to come in with. They had to build their own machine, and the way to do this was with the online tools."[1]

People who logged on to MyBarackObama.com were immediately asked if they would be interested in canvassing neighborhoods, making calls on behalf of the candidate, or hosting a campaign event. They could even view the names of neighbors who were not registered to vote, print out their state's voter registration form, and read a script to help guide their conversations with those neighbors. On other parts of the site, supporters could make donations and commit to raising a certain amount of money for the campaign through friends and family. The Web site encouraged supporters to report what they were doing so the Obama campaign could keep track of their activity. If people reported engaging in an exceptionally high number of activities, field directors from the

---

[1] David Talbot. 2009. "The Geeks Behind Obama's Web Strategy." Boston.com., January 8. www.boston.com/news/politics/2008/articles/2009/01/08/the_geeks_behind_obamas_web_strategy/(accessed 6/6/11).

campaign would contact them and ask them to manage other volunteers. Thus, the Obama campaign used MyBarackObama.com to find volunteer staff and to recruit activists from communities across the country.

The Obama campaign in 2008 made use of other Internet tools as well, such as Facebook, Twitter, and YouTube, but it greatly expanded those efforts in 2012. For example, in 2012, Obama's campaign regularly posted short animated clips, or GIFs, on Tumblr, uploaded pictures from the campaign trail to Instagram and Flickr, and created playlists on Spotify. In 2012, the Obama campaign also took the novel step of using Facebook to replicate door-to-door canvassing on a mass scale. It sent supporters, who had downloaded an app, pictures of Facebook friends living in swing states and asked them to click a button to urge their friends to take important steps during the campaign, such as registering to vote or going to the polls.[2] Mitt Romney employed many of the same Internet tools to reach his supporters, but his campaign used these platforms far less than the Obama campaign. For example, one study found that across all platforms, during a two-week period, the Obama campaign published three times the number of posts than the Romney campaign did. Although it is unclear exactly how

Core of the Analysis

- The rules that govern elections determine who is eligible to vote and how easy it is for an individual to participate.
- Because of its rules, the United States has lower voter turnout than other developed democracies.
- Citizens' participation depends on three factors: ability, motivation, and opportunity.
- These factors create participatory distortions, whereby certain types of voters, such as those who are older, more educated, and white, are more likely to vote.
- Mobilization by political campaigns encourages people to participate and may be responsible for the recent increase in voter turnout.

---

[2] Jenna Wortham. 2012. "Campaigns Use Social Media to Lure Young Voters." *New York Times*, October 7.

Obama's and Romney's Internet activity affected the election outcome, it is clear that they believed the Internet could be used to encourage and facilitate electoral participation. One of the most important reasons people vote or volunteer to work for a campaign is because someone asks them to. Obama's campaigns in particular have demonstrated how the Internet can be used to find supporters and get them to participate merely by providing them with a little information and encouragement.

What Is Electoral Participation?

Political participation during the electoral season can take many forms. The most common form of participation is voting, but electoral participation encompasses other activities as well, such as trying to persuade a friend or coworker to vote for a particular candidate or writing a check to the candidate's campaign committee. **Electoral participation** refers to the range of activities by which individuals attempt to affect the outcome of an election, including not only partisan activities, which favor a particular candidate, but also nonpartisan activities, such as participation in voter registration drives.

Forms of electoral participation vary along two key dimensions: how often they can be performed and how much information they convey about citizens' preferences, needs, and desires. For example, citizens have only one vote, but they can volunteer as frequently as they like and donate as much money as laws regarding contribution limits will allow. This means that individuals can have an impact on the electoral process beyond their single vote if they have the interest, energy, and resources to get involved. For instance, people with more education and wealth are more likely to participate because they have such motivation and resources. This can create a **participatory distortion** whereby certain citizens have a greater impact on that process than others.[3] Another participatory distortion occurs when senior citizens vote at higher rates than young people. Participatory distortions can lead elected officials to give additional attention to the agendas of groups who participate more.

In addition, some forms of participation contain more information for elected representatives than other forms. Consider voting for a candidate versus writing to a newspaper to say why you support that candidate. Both actions are forms of electoral participation, but writing to a newspaper conveys more information than does voting. When citizens vote, their votes communicate their preference for one candidate over another, but not why they voted for that candidate. The winning candidates often claim a "mandate," suggesting that their victory means citizens support all of the policies they advocate. But in fact voters may disagree with many of the policy positions embraced by candidates but vote for them anyway because they seem more likeable or trustworthy than their opponent. When citizens engage in information-rich forms of electoral participation such as letter writing they provide candidates and elected officials with more specific guidance.

---

[3] Sidney Verba, Kay Lehman Schlozman, and Henry E. Brady. 1995. *Voice and Equality: Civic Voluntarism in American Politics.* Cambridge, MA: Harvard University Press, p. 15.

Trends in Participation in the United States

After the 2000 election, books with titles such as *The Vanishing Voter* and *Democracy at Risk* sought to explain declining levels of political participation in the United States.[4] A chief motivation for this was the trend in turnout in presidential elections between 1960 and 1996 (see Figure 11.1). With the exception of 1992, when the three-way race featuring George H. W. Bush, Bill Clinton, and Ross Perot piqued voters' interest, the turnout rate tended to decline during this period. Other forms of participation also declined, including displaying a candidate's button or bumper sticker, attending a

FIGURE 11.1 Voter Participation in Presidential Elections, 1952–2012

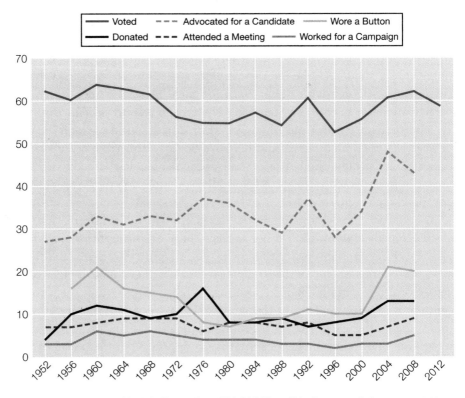

Source: Michael P. McDonald. 2012. "Turnout Data 1980–2012." http://elections.gmu.edu/voter_turnout.htm (accessed 3/13/13).
Note: Participation rates for non-voting activities in 2012 were unavailable at the time of press.

---

[4] Thomas E. Patterson. 2002. *The Vanishing Voter: Public Involvement in an Age of Uncertainty.* New York: Knopf; Stephen Macedo, et al. 2005. *Democracy at Risk: How Political Choices Undermine Citizen Participation.* Washington, DC: Brookings Institution Press.

meeting or rally for a candidate, or volunteering for a political campaign. The only form of electoral participation that defied the trend was advocating a candidate to family, friends, or coworkers.

Yet almost as soon as these books hit the shelves, the decline in electoral participation ended. Between 1996 and 2008, presidential election turnout increased from 53 to 62 percent, returning to the levels of the 1960s. In 2012, turnout decreased slightly to 59 percent, but remained high. Other forms of electoral participation increased as well. Between 1996 and 2004, the percentage of people reporting that they had tried to persuade another person to vote for a particular candidate increased from 28 to 48 percent, declining only slightly to 43 percent in 2008. The percentage reporting that they displayed a candidate's bumper sticker doubled from 10 percent in 1996 to 20 percent in 2008. The percentage saying they donated money to a candidate or party increased from 9 to 13 percent.

Levels of electoral participation in the United States decrease sharply in midterm years, when turnout hovers around 40 percent, or 10 to 20 points lower than in presidential election years (see Figure 11.2). All other forms of participation are less prevalent in midterm election years as well. There is a particular drop-off in the participation of young people, making the midterm electorate significantly older than the presidential electorate.[5]

Voter turnout in midterm elections has held steady since the mid-1970s. The decrease in turnout in presidential election years between 1960 and 1996 did not occur in midterm elections. One reason is that people who vote in midterm elections are typically "habitual voters"—people who vote in most elections. People who vote in presidential elections include habitual voters as well as those who become motivated by the excitement and media coverage generated by the election and who are mobilized by the campaigns. In fact, the decline in voter turnout in presidential elections between 1960 and 1996 may derive from unexciting elections due mainly to how uncompetitive they were and declining investment by candidates and parties in **get-out-the-vote (GOTV) efforts.**[6] Both factors have changed in recent presidential elections. Not only have voters been more interested in the elections, but candidates and parties have invested more in GOTV efforts. This investment appears to have produced results, as we will see later in this chapter.

---

[5] Raymond E. Wolfinger, Steven J. Rosenstone, and Richard A. McIntosh. 1981. "Presidential and Congressional Voters Compared." *American Politics Research* 9, 2: 245–56; Robert A. Jackson. 2000. "Differential Influences on Participation in Midterm versus Presidential Elections." *Social Science Journal* 37, 3: 385–402.

[6] Donald P. Green and Jennifer K. Smith. 2003. "Professionalization of Campaigns and the Secret History of Collective Action Problems." *Journal of Theoretical Politics* 15, 3: 321–39.

FIGURE 11.2 Voter Participation in Midterm Elections, 1958–2010

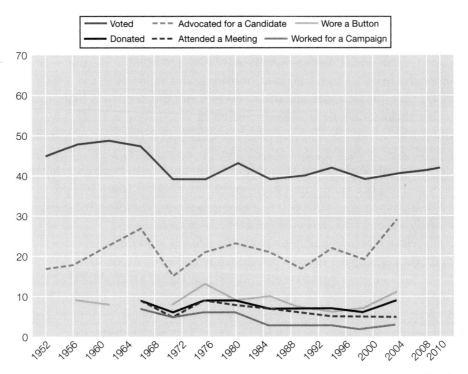

Sources: Popkin and McDonald, "The Myth of the Vanishing Voter"; McDonald, "Turnout Data 1980–2012"; and American National Election Study Cumulative File. The ANES did not ask questions about non-voting forms of electoral participation in 2006 and 2010.

Comparing Participation in the United States and Other Countries

Despite these recent increases in electoral participation, participation rates in the United States still lag behind those of many other countries, including many that are underdeveloped, such as Ghana, Nicaragua, and Sri Lanka. In terms of voter turnout rates, the United States ranked 46th out of the 76 countries that held presidential elections between 2000 and 2010 (see Figure 11.3).[7] Turnout rates in American midterm elections are even lower relative to those in other countries' parliamentary elections. Of the 81 countries

---

[7] The analysis was based on data obtained from the Institute for Democracy and Electoral Assistance. Only the most recent presidential election since 2000 was used for each country. Countries with populations smaller than one million or who were considered to be "not free" in the year of the election by Freedom House were excluded from the analysis.

FIGURE 11.3 Comparing Turnout in Presidential Elections, 2000–2010

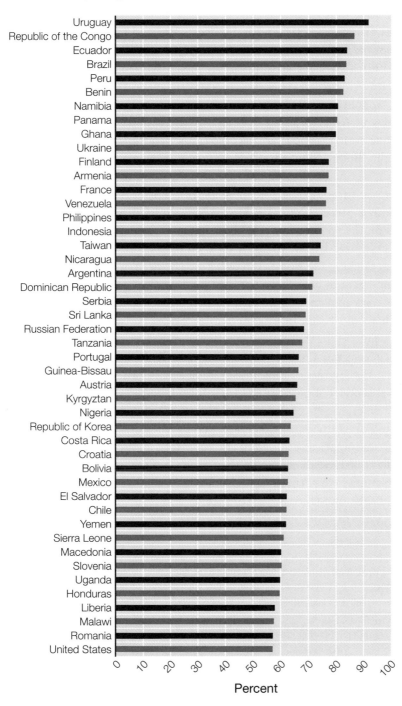

Source: Institute for Democracy and Electoral Assistance, Voter Turnout Database.

that held parliamentary elections between 2000 and 2010, the United States ranked 73rd in turnout.[8]

This difference between the United States and many other democracies does not mean that Americans are less politically engaged. Americans actually report a stronger attachment to their party than do citizens of other countries. Americans are also more likely to believe that what they say has an effect on politicians and government.[9] Instead, many of the rules that govern elections in America depress citizen participation. For one, the U.S. does not make voting compulsary, as do 32 other countries, including Argentina, Australia, Brazil, Singapore, and Turkey.[10] In many of these countries, citizens can be fined if they do not cast a ballot. Compulsory voting is estimated to increase turnout by 10–15 percentage points.[11] Second, Election Day in the United States occurs on a workday, while in many other countries it occurs on the weekend or a public holiday. Even though American employers are required by law to allow their employees to vote during work hours without docking their pay, employees may be hesitant to ask for the time off. It is important to note, however, that holding elections on "rest days" instead of workdays appears to have only a small effect on turnout.[12]

Perhaps most significant, the United States is distinguished from many other countries in that voting is a two-step process. As we noted in Chapter 2, citizens must register before they are allowed to vote, except in North Dakota. If they move, they must re-register in order to vote or else apply for an absentee ballot to vote at their former address. In most other western democracies, the government takes the responsibility for registering citizens to vote. For example, in Canada, when people turn 18 or become citizens, they are automatically added to the voter rolls and remain on the voter rolls regardless of how many times they move. By making citizens responsible for registering, the American system adds a significant cost to voting. As a result, nearly one-third of all Americans cannot vote on Election Day — even if they want to — because they are not registered.

---

[8] Only the most recent parliamentary election since 2000, which was not held at the same time as a presidential election, was used for each country.

[9] G. Bingham Powell, Jr. 1986. "American Voter Turnout in Comparative Perspective." *American Political Science Review* 80, 1: 17–43.

[10] Institute for Democracy and Electoral Assistance. "Voter Turnout Database." www.idea.int/vt/compulsory_voting.cfm (accessed 6/6/11).

[11] André Blais. 2007. "Turnout in Elections," *Oxford Handbook of Political Behavior*, eds. Russell J. Dalton and Hans-Dieter Klingemann. Oxford: Oxford University Press, pp. 621–35.

[12] Blais, "Turnout in Elections," p. 627.

Why Do People Participate in Campaigns and Elections?

People participate in politics because they derive some benefit from doing so. It can be a **material benefit**, meaning the person receives something tangible in exchange for their participation. For instance, individuals may receive payment for collecting petition signatures to help get a candidate's name on the ballot. Individuals also participate in order to receive **solidarity benefits**, which are the intangible rewards that come from being part of a collective effort, such as friendship with fellow volunteers or status in the community. Individuals participate in order to receive **purposive benefits**, which consist of satisfaction for having advanced an issue or ideological position, or for having fulfilled a duty. Ultimately, participating in a political campaign or election could bring all of these benefits, as participants benefit tangibly from getting paid for their work, enjoy the camaraderie among those working for the campaign, and feel good for having helped a worthy candidate.

Whatever the reasons for participation, people who regularly participate in campaigns and elections differ from those who do not. They possess a greater *ability, motivation,* and *opportunity* to participate. Ability is relevant because political participation requires a certain familiarity with the political process. For example, voting means knowing how to register and where the polling place is. Volunteering for a particular candidate means knowing how to contact the candidate's campaign and being comfortable with campaign work (such as talking to strangers about how they plan to vote). Even if people possess the abilities required to engage in such activities, they must have the motivation to do so. This can take many forms, such as having a sense of civic duty or being angry about the current political situation. To have an opportunity to participate, not only must people be legally eligible—to vote, for instance, one must be an American citizen and be over 18 years of age—the cost of participation must not be too high. As that cost increases, people will be less willing to participate.

Ability

The ability of individuals to participate in elections depends a great deal on their education and income. Although the reasons for this relationship might seem obvious, it is challenging to explain how and why education and income matter for participation in elections.

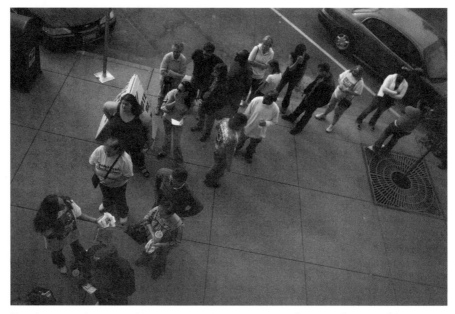

Despite recent increases in turnout, voter participation is lower in the United States than in many other advanced democracies.

Education People's level of formal education strongly predicts how much they participate in politics. This fact has been well documented in study after study. But it is difficult to determine why education matters and what kinds of education are most important. There is, for example, evidence that attaining a high school degree is more important for voting than obtaining a college degree.[13] Why would high school and earlier educational experiences matter more? For one, they help students understand how their democratic system functions, teach them the importance of participating in that system by voting, encourage students to discuss current events, and help them make sense of their political world. These are, for example, the functions of high school civics classes.[14] Primary and secondary education also increases students' aptitude as readers, writers, and speakers, which is

[13] Rachel Milstein Sondheimer and Donald P. Green. 2010. "Using Experiments to Estimate the Effects of Education on Voter Turnout." *American Journal of Political Science* 54: 174–89; Cindy D. Kam and Carl L. Palmer. 2008. "Reconsidering the Effects of Education on Political Participation." *Journal of Politics* 70: 612–31.

[14] Richard Niemi and Jane Junn. 1998. *Civic Education: What Makes Students Learn.* New Haven: Yale University Press.

associated with electoral participation.[15] Attending college, by contrast, has more muted effects because people who can and do attend college are often already politically involved. Thus, even college coursework that focuses on political science or other social sciences has only a small impact on the likelihood of voting.[16]

Does this mean that a formal education is the only way to learn the skills necessary for electoral participation? Absolutely not. They can be learned in workplaces, churches, and other institutions that provide opportunities to organize events, put together presentations, or develop any other skill that is useful in politics. For example, churches have long fostered political activism in the black community by mobilizing and teaching civic skills. This is one reason black churches provided the organizational backbone of the civil rights movement. At the same time, however, educational attainment increases the chances that an individual will have access to the kind of job that teaches civic skills. For example, teachers and lawyers are more likely than blue-collar workers to acquire civic skills on the job.[17]

Income Income is another resource that enables individuals to participate in politics, although it matters much less than education. Unsurprisingly, income is the strongest predictor of whether and how much individuals contribute to political causes. Perhaps more surprisingly, those with higher incomes are more likely to engage in every form of participation—even in protests, which are sometimes considered a "weapon of the weak." What is it about having a higher income that enables wealthier people to participate more than poor people? It is not that people with higher incomes have more free time. Careers that provide higher incomes, like doctor or lawyer, typically provide very little free time. Another possibility is that people who have low incomes must spend more of their time and energy simply trying to get by. Indeed, once people achieve a comfortable standard of living, increases in income no longer increase their participation rates. When people feel they no longer must live from hand to mouth, they are more able to focus on other things, including politics.[18]

[15] D. Sunshine Hillygus. 2005. "The Missing Link: Exploring the Relationship Between Higher Education and Political Engagement." *Political Behavior* 27: 25–47.

[16] Hillygus, "The Missing Link."

[17] Verba, Schlozman, and Brady, *Voice and Equality*, pp. 314–16.

[18] Raymond E. Wolfinger and Steven Rosenstone. 1980. *Who Votes?* New Haven, CT: Yale University Press, pp. 23–26.

Motivation

People who participate in an election not only possess the resources to do so but are motivated to get involved. Motivations can be loosely grouped into two categories: those that are individual—such as a general interest in politics—and those that are generated by the environment in which individuals live—such as a phone call from a campaign.

Individual Factors Two individual factors influencing electoral participation are political efficacy and political interest. **Political interest** is simply an ongoing interest in politics. Political efficacy, as described by political scientists, has two dimensions. **Internal efficacy** is being confident that one has the ability to understand and engage in politics, while **external efficacy** is the belief that the political system will be responsive to one's desires and needs. Political interest and internal efficacy are more stable over time than external efficacy: if people are interested in politics and believe that they can effectively participate in politics when they are young, they will tend to be interested and feel efficacious when they are older. External efficacy, by contrast, can fluctuate in response to one's experiences with government. For instance, if people vote for a particular candidate because they believe the candidate will enact certain policies, but the candidate fails to enact those policies once elected, then their external efficacy may drop.

Because political interest and internal efficacy are so stable over the lifespan, it is important to understand why some young people develop them and others do not. One source of political interest and efficacy may be personality. Our basic personality traits can have an impact on how we think and act politically. For example, people who are extroverted—that is, people who generally project their energy outward rather than inward—are more likely to participate in politics.[19] This makes sense because political participation other than voting requires social interaction. Our attitude toward conflict can also have an impact. Although voting or writing a check to a candidate is unlikely to involve conflict, participating in a campaign in virtually any other way does. People who canvass a neighborhood for a candidate may knock on the door of an opponent's supporter. Even supporters of the volunteer's candidate may be unfriendly if the knock interrupts their dinner. Participating in campaigns usually requires a person to have a thick skin and to be comfortable with the possibility of conflict.

Recently, political scientists have begun to explore whether genes play a role in electoral participation. For example, three studies have identified

---

[19] Jeffery J. Mondak and Karen D. Halperin. 2008. "A Framework for the Study of Personality and Political Behaviour." *British Journal of Political Science* 38: 335–62.

specific genes that are associated with turnout.[20] In two of these studies, the researchers argued that genes drive specific personality traits, such as patience and having a sense of duty, that in turn affect the chances that one will vote. Although it is too early to say how much genes matter and exactly how they interact with environmental factors to affect participation, this is an exciting new avenue of research for political scientists.

Environmental Factors

Although our own particular qualities or characteristics affect our willingness to participate politically, the broader environment in which we live also affects our political interest, efficacy, and, ultimately, participation. We consider two types of environmental effects: those related to an individual's social context and those related to campaign activities.

Social Contexts **Social context** refers to the people with whom one communicates and interacts—such as family, friends, classmates, coworkers, and neighbors. These people can affect the decision to participate by providing information, such as how to find the polling place where one is to vote. They also provide models from which individuals learn—either directly, as when a teacher educates students about American government, or indirectly, as when people become inspired by politically active role models and decide on their own to get involved in politics. Moreover, as we noted, people can decide to participate for the solidary benefits of participation: because they enjoy interactions with other people, such as their fellow volunteers on a campaign.

One of the most important social contexts for a child is the family. Parents can help to inculcate political interest and efficacy in their children. Some of this happens through mimicry. When children come of age politically, they may vote in part because they watched their parents vote. But besides providing modeling for their children, parents can deliberately try to instill political interest in their children. One important way they do this is simply by talking about politics. Conversations at the dinner table help to communicate parents' interest in politics to their children, who will then be more likely to become interested in politics themselves. Parents who adhere to the convention of not discussing politics at the dinner table

---

[20] Peter Loewen and Christopher T. Dawes. Forthcoming. "The Heritability of Duty and Voter Turnout." *Political Psychology*; Christopher T. Dawes and Peter Loewen. 2009. "The CHRNA6 Gene, Patience, and Voter Turnout." http://ssrn.com/abstract=1494509 (accessed 6/6/11); James H. Fowler and Christopher T. Dawes. 2008. "Two Genes Predict Voter Turnout." *Journal of Politics* 70, 3: 579–94.

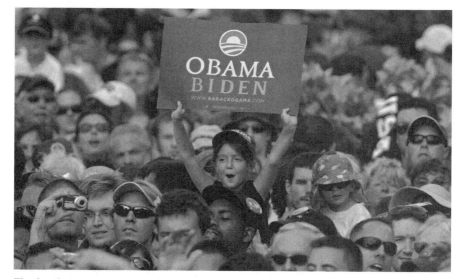

The family is an important influence on whether individuals participate in elections and politics in general. Children often follow the models provided by their parents' political participation.

might be decreasing the chances that their children will be interested in politics.[21]

Another important social context is schools, as we have already noted when discussing the role of formal education. Taking part in certain types of high school activities, particularly those that emphasize student government and community service, make young people more interested in politics and likely to participate as adults. Although participating in sports teams does not have the same effect, high school activities that emphasize public performance, such as debate and drama also appear to promote political participation.[22] The effects of nonathletic high school activities hold irrespective

[21] Verba, Schlozman, and Brady, *Voice and Equality*; Molly W. Andolina, Krista Jenkins, Cliff Zukin, and Scott Keeter. 2003. "Habits from Home, Lessons from School: Influences on Youth Civic Development." *PS: Political Science and Politics* 36, 2: 275–80; Hugh McIntosh, Daniel Hart and James Youniss. 2007. "The Influence of Family Political Discussion on Youth Civic Development: Which Parent Qualities Matter?" *PS: Political Science & Politics* 40, 3: 495–499.

[22] Daniel A. McFarland and Reuben J. Thomas. 2006. "Bowling Young: How Youth Voluntary Associations Influence Adult Political Participation." *American Sociological Review* 71, 3: 401–425; Jacquelynne S. Eccles and Bonnie L. Barber. 1999. "Student Council, Volunteering, Basketball, or Marching Band: What Kind of Extracurricular Involvement Matters?" *Journal of Adolescent Research* 14: 10–43; Paul A. Beck and M. Kent Jennings. 1982. "Pathways to Participation." *American Political Science Review* 76, 1: 94–108.

of a student's family income or the education level of their parents.[23] This suggests that cutting them from high school curriculums, as many school districts across the nation are doing, may have troublesome consequences for the future political participation of younger generations. Families and schools are particularly important because there is no formal way for children to participate in politics. They cannot vote until they are 18, for example, and generally lack other opportunities to participate meaningfully in political life.[24] It is no wonder that a recent survey of ninth graders found that they did not believe politics would affect them until they were older.[25] This may explain why the United Nations, as part of its 1989 Convention on the Rights of the Child, included a provision to promote children's active citizenship throughout the world. To that end, it held a Children's Forum in 2002 and invited a 13-year-old to address the General Assembly about the need to recognize children as political citizens.[26] Although it is difficult to imagine any country allowing children to vote, the United Nations' effort acknowledges the importance of social context in creating politically involved young people.

Later in life, social context continues to matter. Getting married can profoundly alter how often a person participates politically because the spouse becomes the central figure in that person's social context. In general, marital transitions (getting married or divorced, or becoming widowed) depress electoral participation in the short term as individuals adjust to their new personal circumstances. In the long term, the participation rates of married people converge, with spouses becoming more similar in, for example, whether and how often they vote.[27]

Social context also matters at the level of communities. In particular, people who feel as if they belong to a community are also likely to feel empowered and to participate. By contrast, those who feel alienated or marginalized may withdraw politically. For example, studies have found that poor individuals living in wealthy communities are less likely to vote than

---

[23] McFarland and Thomas, "Bowling Young."

[24] Virginia Sapiro. 2004. "Not Your Parents' Political Socialization: Introduction for a New Generation." *Annual Review of Political Science* 7: 1–23.

[25] James G. Gimpel, J. Celeste Lay, and Jason Shuknecht. 2003. *Cultivating Democracy: Civic Environments and Political Socialization in America*. Washington, DC: Brookings Institution Press.

[26] Daiva Stasiulis. 2002. "The Active Child Citizen: Lessons from Canadian Policy and the Children's Movement." *Citizenship Studies* 6, 4: 507–38.

[27] Laura Stoker and M. Kent Jennings. 1995. "Life-Cycle Transitions and Political Participation: The Case of Marriage." *American Political Science Review* 89, 2: 421–33.

those living in poor communities.[28] A number of studies have also shown that Democrats and Republicans living in "enemy territory"—communities dominated by the opposing party—are also less likely to participate and discuss politics than their counterparts living in friendlier areas.[29] Even young people living in areas that have a significantly older population are less likely to vote than young people living among a younger population.

Finally, a type of context that is even broader than community is the generation of which one is a part. Different **generational cohorts**—people who came of age politically at about the same time—can have distinctive patterns of electoral participation. This is not necessarily because of direct interaction with others in their generation. Instead, distinctive patterns arise from the norms of behavior and the levels of civic and political engagement that were pervasive when that generation came of age. For example, people who came of age during the Great Depression and World War II were part of what has sometimes been called the Greatest Generation, the most civically and politically active generation of the twentieth century—one that stayed politically involved throughout their lives, even long after the Great Depression and War World II had ended. In contrast, Baby Boomers—those born between 1946 and 1964—have been less engaged in civic life and politics, even though many of them came of age in the 1960s and witnessed the civil rights movement and the Vietnam War protests up close. Subsequent generations—those sometimes referred to as "Generation X," "Generation Y," and the "Millennials"—have continued the trend and are even less interested in politics than the Baby Boomers.[30]

Why were later generations less politically engaged than the "long civic generation" of the 1930s and '40s? One factor is technological change, beginning with the rapid arrival of television. In 1950, less than 10 percent of American households had a television set. By 1960, over 90 percent did. Between 1965 and 1995, the average number of hours Americans spent watching television per week increased from approximately 9 to 15 hours.[31] Television offers cit-

---

[28] R. Robert Huckfeldt. 1979. "Political Participation and Neighborhood Social Context." *American Journal of Political Science* 23, 3: 579–92.

[29] James Gimpel, Joshua Dyck, and Daron Shaw. 2004. "Registrants, Voters and Turnout Variability Across Neighborhoods." *Political Behavior* 26, 4: 343–75; Robert Huckfeldt and John Sprague. 1995. *Citizens, Politics, and Social Communication: Information and Influence in an Election Campaign.* New York: Cambridge University Press.

[30] Robert D. Putnam. 2000. *Bowling Alone: The Collapse and Revival of American Community.* New York: Simon & Schuster, p. 250–51.

[31] Putnam, *Bowling Alone*, p. 222.

izens alternative ways to spend their leisure time that often compete with other activities, such as volunteering for a local organization or participating in politics. One study estimates that every additional hour of television viewing per day is associated with a 10 percent reduction in civic activism.[32] The arrival and penetration of the Internet, mobile phones, video games, and personal audio devices, such as iPods, may be having a similar effect. Today, young people spend as much time with these new forms of media as they do watching television: more than 30 hours per week.[33]

What is more important than whether people have these technologies is how they use them. People who use the television and the Internet primarily for entertainment are indeed less likely to participate in politics. However, those who use the television and the Internet to follow politics are actually more participatory.[34] Moreover, the Internet itself can be a forum for engaging in political activity, for example by participating in online conversations about politics or donating to candidates.

Changes in values may also explain why more recent generations are less like to engage in politics than earlier ones. One value that has been embraced more broadly in recent generations is materialism.[35] Members of Generation X—those born between 1965 and 1979—are more likely than Baby Boomers or members of the World War II generation to say that having "a lot of money" is necessary for having a "good life."[36] They are also less likely to feel strong ties to their neighborhoods, churches, and local communities. Those with a preoccupation with earning money and a lack of connection to the community have little reason to become involved in civic activities or to vote.[37] The passing away of older, more participatory generations and their replacement by newer generations with different sets of priorities explains much of the decline in civic and electoral participation.

Mobilization Another environmental factor that promotes electoral participation is mobilization. **Mobilization** refers to the range of activities that

---

[32] Putnam, *Bowling Alone*, p. 228.

[33] Victoria Rideout, Ulla Foehr, and Donald Roberts. 2010. *Generation M2: Media in the Lives of 8- to 18-Year-Olds.* Menlo Park, CA: Kaiser Family Foundation, p. 2. www.kff.org/entmedia/upload/8010.pdf (accessed 4/12/11).

[34] Caroline J. Tolbert and Ramona S. McNeal. 2003. "Unraveling the Effects of the Internet on Political Participation." *Political Research Quarterly* 56, 2: 175–185.

[35] Wendy M. Rahn and John E. Transue. 1998. "Social Trust and Value Change: The Decline of Social Capital in American Youth, 1976–1995." *Political Psychology*, 19, 3: 545–65.

[36] Putnam, *Bowling Alone*, pp. 272–273.

[37] Putnam, *Bowling Alone*.

candidates, parties, activists, and interest groups engage in to encourage people to participate. These activities usually occur during a campaign, but groups can mobilize citizens at other times and for reasons besides electing a candidate. They can encourage citizens to support certain legislation by writing letters to their members of Congress, or to show up at a town hall meeting to oppose an action of their city council. To be sure, the goal of those who mobilize is not simply to increase civic participation. It is to use that participation to achieve certain ends, such as the election of a candidate. Thus, groups target their mobilization efforts at those who share their goals.

Individuals and groups seeking to mobilize citizens do so directly and indirectly. They mobilize directly when they contact citizens and encourage them to act. They mobilize indirectly by using the social networks in which citizens are embedded to reach them, including workplaces, churches, schools, labor unions, neighborhood associations, and large national organizations such as the National Rifle Association. During a campaign, for example, candidates seek the endorsement of community groups and national organizations in the hope that an endorsement will encourage group members to vote for the endorsed candidate. This saves the candidate some effort, not only because the groups assume some of the costs of communicating with their members, but because group members are more likely to trust recommendations from group leaders than direct appeals from candidates themselves.

Mobilization efforts often work because people respond when someone asks them to get involved. This may be because people are flattered by the request, like the idea of being involved in a collective effort, or find it difficult to say no and then feel they must follow through once they have committed. Groups seeking to mobilize members of a community are likely to focus their attention on individuals who are already active in their community. Active people have two qualities that mobilizers appreciate. First, they are easy to reach because they belong to a variety of organizations. Second, they are more likely to be influential when they do participate because they have a large social network and greater status in their community. Similarly, mobilization efforts are likely to target those with more education and higher incomes.

As we noted earlier, much of the decline in turnout in presidential elections between 1960 and 1996 occurred because campaigns abandoned traditional mobilization activities, such as neighborhood canvassing. Instead, they turned to television advertising to communicate with voters.[38] Television advertisements, however, are not particularly effective at mobilizing voters. For

---

[38] Steven J. Rosenstone and John Mark Hansen. 1993. *Mobilization, Participation, and Democracy in America*. New York: Macmillan.

example, eligible voters in media markets that witness a slew of presidential advertisements are no more likely to vote than those who live in markets that see no such advertisements. It does not make much difference whether the ads are predominantly positive (promoting a candidate) or negative (attacking a candidate). Although some commentators worry that negative advertising drives down turnout, as citizens' distaste for attacks makes them feel alienated from politics, the sum of the evidence suggests that negative advertising does not affect turnout in any consistent fashion.[39]

What are the most effective mobilization strategies? Research to date has found that the specific message used in mobilization activities does not matter a great deal. As yet, there seems to be no particular kind of appeal that works better than others. For example, reminding citizens that voting is their civic duty seems to be no more or less effective than reminding them that the election will be close and so "every vote counts." Instead, it is much more important how voters are contacted. One of the most effective strategies is in-person contact, as we noted in Chapter 5. Contacting eligible voters by having someone knock on their door and remind them to vote increases turnout by about 8 percentage points, according to one study. Telephone calls, which are somewhat less personal, have a smaller effect, and then only when the phone call seems "authentic"—a quality better provided by enthusiastic volunteers or trained professionals. A phone call that seems scripted or, worst of all, is merely a recorded message has little effect on turnout. Even more impersonal forms of communication, such as postal mail and e-mail, also seem to have little effect.[40]

The effects of campaign mobilization on citizens depend on the underlying ability and motivation of citizens. Citizens who are already very interested in politics are typically unaffected by mobilization because they are already highly likely to vote anyway. Citizens who have little interest in politics are also unaffected because no mobilization effort is likely to convince them to participate. Instead, it is citizens in the middle: those with some interest in politics who are often on the verge of voting but do not always end up making the effort. These citizens may need a reminder to vote, and campaigns can provide that.[41]

---

[39] Richard R. Lau, Lee Sigelman, and Ivy Brown Rovner. 2007. "The Effects of Negative Political Campaigns: A Meta-Analytic Reassessment." *Journal of Politics* 69, 4: 1176–1209.

[40] Donald P. Green and Alan S. Gerber. 2008. *Get Out the Vote!* 2nd ed. Washington, DC: Brookings Institution Press.

[41] Kevin Arceneaux and David Nickerson. 2009. "Who Is Mobilized to Vote? A Re-Analysis of Eleven Randomized Field Experiments." *American Journal of Political Science* 53, 1: 1–16.

Conducting Voter Mobilization Experiments During Campaigns

One challenge for political scientists studying the mobilizing effects of campaigns has been in gaining access to real campaigns where they can run experiments. In the 1998 midterm elections, Alan Gerber and Donald Green decided to test the effectiveness of campaign tools, such as mailing postcards, phone calls, and in-person visits, in getting voters to the polls. Partnering with the League of Women Voters, Gerber and Green split the residents of New Haven, Connecticut, into three groups that each received one of the following treatments: a postcard encouraging them to vote, a phone call with the same message, or an in-person visit. For comparison purposes, a fourth group received no contact. After the election, Gerber and Green examined voting records to see who had actually voted. They found that turnout among people who had received an in-person visit was 9.8 percent higher than among those receiving no contact. Postcards yielded less than a 1 percent boost in turnout, while telephone calls had no effect whatsoever.

When Gerber and Green's study was published in 2000, it attracted the attention of campaign practitioners. Hal Malchow and Mike Podhorzer, campaign consultants for the AFL-CIO, recognized the importance of the Gerber and Green study for their work and conducted experiments during the 2004 presidential election to test how different types of campaign appeals affect AFL-CIO members. After 2004, Malchow and Podhorzer invited other Democratic political operatives to meet at regular lunches to share research on campaign effects. They called their unofficial group the Analyst Institute. In 2007, the Analyst Institute became an official consulting firm, describing itself as "a clearinghouse for evidence-based best practices in progressive voter contact."[1]

Under the leadership of a new executive director, Todd Rogers, the Analyst Institute began to conduct research challenging some of the conventional wisdom among political practitioners. For example, they found that simply asking people about their voting plans significantly boosts turnout, especially among people living alone: their turnout jumps by 10 percent. Rogers speculates that the reason is that adults living together talk through their plans to vote with each other, which helps them envision it happening. A campaign worker can play the same role for people living alone, encouraging them to think through how they will get to the polls.

The Analyst Institute is not the only group running experiments in campaign mobilization these days. For instance, Rock the Vote has found that e-mail and text messages sent by well-known celebrities to young people encouraging them to vote are *less* effective than those with bland "senders," such as "Election Center."

Despite the utility of such findings for campaign practitioners, many are still resistant to running experiments during campaigns. Some are concerned that running experiments during a campaign might jeopardize its outcome. Others are concerned that the findings might jeopardize their careers. To understand this, consider how campaign phonebanking consultants felt after the first Gerber and Green study was published, which said that their calls had no effect on voters.

---

[1] Analyst Institute. http://www.analystinstitute.org/ (accessed 6/6/11).

Source: Sasha Issenberg. 2010. "Nudge the Vote." *New York Times*, October 31, p. MM28.

Starting in the 1998 midterm elections, the Democratic Party and its affiliated interest groups began to shift resources from advertising to voter outreach. The success enjoyed by the Democrats in the 1998 and 2000 elections led the Republican Party to focus more of their resources on voter outreach as well. As a result, 2004 saw unprecedented mobilization efforts by both parties—efforts that actually built on some of the mobilization research results we have described. This heightened focus on mobilization continued in 2008 and 2012. Thus, it is no accident that electoral participation has surged in recent presidential election years.

Opportunity

People may have the ability and motivation to participate, but still not do so because they lack the opportunity: they might not be eligible to participate, or the costs of their participating—how difficult and time-consuming it is—are too steep.

As we discussed in Chapter 2, one must be an American citizen of at least 18 years of age to vote. These current requirements for voting are far less stringent than in earlier periods of history, when women, African Americans, and other groups were barred from voting. The primary groups excluded today include the country's 75 million children and its 12 million permanent residents who work, live, and pay taxes here but are not citizens. Forty-seven states also bar felons from voting and 15 of these states bar ex-felons—those that have served their time in prison—from voting, which disenfranchises another 4 million individuals. Although these groups cannot vote, they can participate in elections in other ways, such as by volunteering for a campaign. For eligible Americans, the costs of voting depend on the costs entailed in each step—registering to vote and actually casting a ballot.

Voter Registration In most states, if one is not registered one cannot vote. As discussed earlier in this chapter, it is unusual for a developed democracy to make citizens responsible for registering, which adds an additional cost to voting. This extra burden, however, is no accident. Voter registration was enacted by Progressive era reformers in the early twentieth century. They sought to challenge the political machines, whose power derived from their ability to mobilize immigrants and the urban working poor. The Progressives believed—often with good reason—that these machines were corrupt and that the methods by which they achieved high rates of turnout among immigrants and the poor were corrupt as well. They also believed that the vote choices of uneducated and illiterate people were manipulated by party bosses. Requirements for voter registration were intended to help prevent fraud by requiring citizens to appear periodically before local officials to verify their eligibility.

Both the timing of registration and the magnitude of registration requirements affect the cost of voting. The earlier a person must register before an election, the more difficult the process becomes because it is easier to remember to register when Election Day is near. Furthermore, if a person must travel to a distant location to register, that also imposes a cost. At present, no state has a registration closing date more than 31 days before an election. Similarly, the National Voting Rights Act of 1993, also known as the **Motor Voter Act**, requires states to allow voters to register when they are applying for a driver's license and public assistance programs, such as food stamps, or to allow Election Day registration. As a result, the costs of registering are now lower than they have been at any time since registration laws were first enacted. However, the Motor Voter Act did not significantly increase turnout in presidential or midterm elections. This raises the question of whether further weakening registration laws would actually increase turnout, and whether voter registration laws can truly be blamed for lower turnout in the United States as compared to other countries.[42]

Convenience Voting There are other costs associated with actually casting a ballot. About 85 percent of the people who are registered typically vote; what prevents the remaining 15 percent from getting to the polls? One possibility is that they do not know where their polling place is. Some states mail citizens polling place information or sample ballots, and this is especially helpful in boosting the turnout rates for the less educated and the young.[43]

Many states have started experimenting with ways of making voting easier to boost turnout. **Convenience voting** refers to methods by which registrants can vote without actually casting a ballot at a polling place on Election Day. One way to make voting easier is to allow citizens to mail in their ballots. Every state now offers some form of **absentee voting**, which enables citizens to vote by mail-in paper ballot prior to Election Day. Twenty-one states, however, require individuals to state a reason for why they cannot vote in person, while the remaining states and the District of Columbia allow voters to apply for an absentee ballot without justifying their request.

---

[42] Benjamin Highton. 2004. "Voter Registration and Turnout in the United States." *Perspectives on Politics* 2: 507–15.

[43] Raymond E. Wolfinger, Benjamin Highton, and Megan Mullin. 2005. "How Postregistration Laws Affect the Turnout of Citizens Registered to Vote." *State Politics & Policy Quarterly* 5, 1: 1–23.

Seven of these states, as well as the District of Columbia, however, make it even easier to cast an absentee ballot by allowing any citizen to request to receive one for every future election.[44] Oregon and Washington have gone a step further by requiring all citizens to **vote by mail**. In these states, county administrators automatically mail out ballots to registered voters approximately three weeks before an election. Voters can either return the ballot by mail or drop it off at a designated location. Aside from absentee ballots and voting by mail, some states allow citizens to vote a week or two early at county elections offices or designated voting centers. A handful of other states allow voters to vote over the phone or to submit their ballot by fax. Currently, no state allows people to vote over the Internet.

Convenience voting is designed to make voting less costly and to increase turnout. Yet, early in-person voting and absentee voting have had little effect on turnout. Voting by mail is the only form of convenience voting that appears to increase turnout. Still, it does so not among the most unengaged eligible voters but among the "low-hanging fruit"—those who only need a nudge to actually cast a ballot.[45]

Electoral Competitiveness Thus far, our discussion of opportunity has focused on voting, but there are many other ways to participate, especially in campaigns. One factor that affects the opportunity to engage in these other forms of participation is the competitiveness of the election. When elections are close, candidates, parties, and interest groups have an incentive not only to encourage voters to participate but to create more opportunities for participation. For example, a person who lives in a battleground state during a presidential election has ample opportunity to attend candidate events, help canvass neighborhoods, and call friends, because presidential candidates set up campaign organizations in these states specifically to create such opportunities. Similarly, when a House or Senate race is competitive, candidates will provide the citizens of that district or state with more opportunities to participate.

Participating Online As mentioned at the start of the chapter, campaigns have been using the Internet to increase opportunities for participation. Candidates for major offices use their Web sites to provide supporters a

---

[44] National Conference of State Legislatures. "Absentee and Early Voting." www.ncsl.org/default.aspx?tabid=16604 (accessed 3/22/13).

[45] Adam J. Berinsky, Nancy Burns, and Michael W. Traugott. 2001. "Who Votes by Mail? A Dynamic Model of the Individual-Level Consequences of Voting-by-Mail Systems." *Public Opinion Quarterly* 65, 2: 178–97.

means to donate money, pledge their time and effort, and sign up for alerts about further opportunities to get involved. Candidate Web sites usually ask supporters to provide their zip codes so they will receive news about opportunities within their communities.

The Internet also allows citizens to connect and create participatory events on their own. One example is Howard Dean's use of Meetup.com to keep supporters connected during his campaign for the 2004 presidential election. Meetup made it possible for supporters to organize events at places, such as coffee shops and bars, where they could bring their friends and tell them about Dean. When Dean announced his candidacy in June 2003, he had just 3,000 supporters on Meetup, but by mid-November he had more than 140,000 supporters on the site and had raised over $15 million from them. Once the primaries began, supporters used Meetup to organize meetings where they would write letters to voters in key primary states, and to organize trips to those states to help campaign. Dean's campaign may have faltered in the end, but his innovative use of social networking set a precedent and multiplied the opportunities for Americans to participate by making it easier for citizens to customize and localize events.

Inequalities in Electoral Participation

The factors that encourage electoral participation reinforce one another. For example, people with more education are likely to have higher incomes and jobs where they can develop the confidence and skills that facilitate electoral participation.[46] Their education and jobs also ensure that they are embedded in social networks through which they are likely to be mobilized. In addition, their education and income make it more likely that they will access the Internet and learn about opportunities to participate in a campaign. Understanding how these factors reinforce one another illuminates why certain groups in America are more likely to participate and why others are not, creating participatory inequalities (see Figure 11.4). These inequalities magnify some voices while they mute the voices of others, potentially undermining democratic values.

The Racial Distortion

Over time, certain groups in the United States have become more likely to participate, demonstrating that participatory inequalities are not immutable. Before the adoption of the 1965 Voting Rights Act, African American

---

[46] Verba, Schlozman, and Brady, *Voice and Equality*.

FIGURE 11.4 Self-Reported Voting in the 2008 Presidential Election

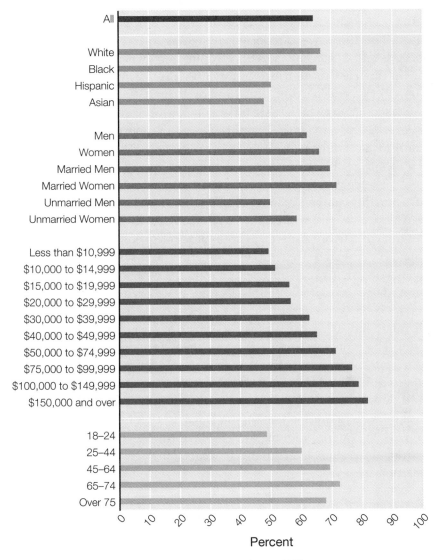

Source: Current Population Survey Voting and Registration Supplement, 2008.

turnout was understandably poor due to discriminatory laws that effectively disenfranchised black Americans, especially in the South. The Voting Rights Act empowered the federal government to take over voter registration in southern states to ensure that African Americans could vote. This legislation quickly yielded results. Within twenty years, the gaps in registration rates between blacks and whites in the South—which had been 50 percentage points or higher in Mississippi, North Carolina, and Alabama—dropped to less than 10 points.

Today, African Americans typically vote at rates just below those of whites. The difference in reported voting was 7 percent in 2004, 1 percent in 2008, and 3 percent in 2010. To put this in perspective, the difference in reported turnout between whites and Latinos was 20 percent in 2004, 16 percent in 2008, and 18 percent in 2010.[47] In 2008, the most recent election for which there is data on nonvoting forms of participation, blacks actually were *more* likely than whites to report attending a meeting or rally for a candidate, displaying a lawn sign or bumper sticker, or working for a campaign. Blacks continue to donate at lower rates than whites—in 2008, 17 percent of whites reported donating but only 10 percent of blacks did—but this can be accounted for by their lower incomes. It is remarkable that blacks and whites participate at virtually the same rate overall even though African Americans are typically less educated and have lower incomes than whites. Part of the explanation for black electoral activism is mobilization that occurs in black churches. Another part of the explanation is idiosyncratic to 2008: blacks were more excited than whites about Barack Obama's candidacy.

Latinos and Asian Americans participate at lower rates than blacks and whites. This is notable because these are the fastest growing minority groups in the country; in fact, Latinos are now the largest minority group (having surpassed African Americans). However, ethnicity per se does not explain this. Lower levels of education and income are more important, as are the struggles with mastering the English language that immigrants may face.[48] Many Asian American immigrants also hail from countries where political participation is not valued or encouraged, so they have not been socialized to participate.

The Gender Distortion

Women were excluded from voting in most American states until passage of the Nineteenth Amendment in 1920. Today, women vote at a slightly higher rate than men, again demonstrating that participatory inequalities can be

---

[47] The numbers from 2004 and 2008 are from Mark Hugo Lopez and Paul Taylor. 2009. "Dissecting the 2008 Electorate: Most Diverse in American History." Pew Research Center. The 2010 data is from Mark Hugo Lopez. 2011. "The Latino Electorate in 2010: More Voters, More Non-Voters." Pew Research Center.

[48] Wendy K. Tam Cho. 1999. "Naturalization, Socialization, Participation: Immigrants and (Non-) Voting," *Journal of Politics* 61: 1140–55.

erased. In 2008, 66 percent of women reported voting, compared to 62 percent of men. The gap is especially large between unmarried men and women in particular: in 2008, only 49 percent of unmarried men reported voting, compared to 58 percent of unmarried women.[49] There are few disparities between men and women in whether they attend political meetings or work for campaigns. The traditional gender gap emerges in other areas: men are more likely than women to report donating, discussing politics, and actually run for elected office. Men typically have higher salaries than women, which explains why they would donate more. The difference in engagement in political discussions may arise because men also report more interest in politics, demonstrate higher levels of political knowledge, and appear to be more comfortable engaging in the kinds of heated exchanges that political discussion often entails.[50] Another factor may be the perception that politics is a "man's world." When women do hold high-profile offices, girls become more interested in politics.[51] Thus, having few women in office may create a vicious cycle whereby young girls do not develop as great an interest in politics and then do not run for office themselves, perpetuating the underrepresentation of women in political office. We discussed some of the factors that lead women not to run for office in Chapter 5.

The Income Distortion

An especially large inequality exists between those with high and low incomes. For example, in 2008 turnout among citizens making more than $88,000 per year was 20 percentage points higher than those making less than $20,000. The only forms of participation that do not exhibit this disparity are attending political meetings and displaying a sign in favor of a candidate. From a certain perspective, this inequality makes little sense. The poor should be less satisfied with the political institutions and policies

---

[49] U.S. Census Bureau. 2008. "Table 11. Reported Voting and Registration, by Marital Status, Age, and Sex: November 2008." www.census.gov/hhes/www/socdemo/voting/publications/p20/2008/tables.html (accessed 6/6/11).

[50] Sidney Verba, Nancy Burns, and Kay Lehman Schlozman. 1997. "Knowing and Caring about Politics: Gender and Political Engagement." *Journal of Politics* 59: 1051–72; Stacy G. Ulbig and Carolyn L. Funk. 1999. "Conflict Avoidance and Political Participation." *Political Behavior* 21, 3: 265–82.

[51] David E. Campbell and Christina Wolbrecht. 2006. "See Jane Run: Women Politicians as Role Models for Adolescents." *Journal of Politics* 68: 233–47. See also Lonna Rae Atkeson. 2003. "Not All Cues Are Created Equal: The Conditional Impact of Female Candidates on Political Engagement." *Journal of Politics* 65, 4: 1040–61.

Young people are much less likely than older Americans to vote. In recent years, groups like Rock the Vote have sought to mobilize young voters. Here, Talib Kweli performs at a Rock the Vote event.

that make it so difficult for them to get ahead and thus participate more. Meanwhile the wealthy should be content with the status quo, since they have benefited from it. Yet the poor actually participate at lower rates than the rich. This is for the reasons we have discussed: wealthier people typically have more education and a professional career that provides them with skills that are useful in politics. They are also embedded in large social networks that encourage their participation and can be easily reached by those seeking to mobilize them.[52]

The Age Distortion

As discussed earlier, young people are much less likely to participate than older people. In 2008, 51 percent of people under the age of 30 voted, compared to 66 percent of those aged 30 to 64 and 70 percent of those 65 and over. This gap was somewhat smaller in 2008 than in a typical presidential election. In 2000, for instance, only 40 percent of people under the age of 30 reported voting. What explains this lower rate of participation among

---

[52] Verba, Schlozman, and Brady, *Voice and Equality.*

the young? First, young people move around a lot. With each move, they must re-register, which increases the cost of voting.[53] Their mobility also makes them more difficult to mobilize, because they are harder to track. Young people are also undergoing many other transitions — leaving school, getting married, starting new jobs, having children — that in the short term may depress participation because of the physical and psychological commitments they entail.[54] Of these, the first two — leaving school[55] and getting married[56] — appear to depress turnout the most. As people settle into their jobs and marriages, and as their children become less dependent on them, the costs associated with political participation decrease. Independent of such life transition effects, however, aging has a strong positive effect on political participation. Although scholars are still debating why this is the case, many believe it can be explained by pure learning, that is, as one ages one becomes more knowledgeable about the political system and how to engage with it, and an accumulation of life experience that spurs that engagement.[57]

Conclusion

As we've seen, political participation comes in a wide array of forms. Turnout in elections — as the most obvious and, in some ways, least demanding form of participation — captures the most attention. Turnout in the United States is low compared to other countries and actually declined from 1960 to 1996. In recent elections, however, turnout has increased, due in part to the mobilization efforts of presidential campaigns.

---

[53] Benjamin Highton. 2000. "Residential Mobility, Community Mobility, and Electoral Participation." *Political Behavior* 22, 2:109–120; M. Margaret Conway. 2000. *Political Participation in the United States*, 3rd ed. Washington DC: CQ Press.

[54] John M. Strate, Charles J. Parrish, Charles D. Elder, and Coit Ford III. 1989. "Life Span Civic Development and Voting Participation." *American Political Science Review* 83: 443–464; Philip E. Converse and Richard Niemi. 1971. "Non-Voting among Young Adults in the United States," in *Political Parties and Political Behavior*, ed. William J. Crotty et al., 2nd ed. Boston: Allyn & Bacon.

[55] Benjamin Highton. 2001. "The First Seven Years of the Political Life Cycle." *American Journal of Political Science* 45, 1: 202–209.

[56] Laura Stoker and M. Kent Jennings. 1995. "Life-Cycle Transitions and Political Participation: The Case of Marriage." *American Political Science Review* 89, 2:421–433.

[57] M. Kent Jennings and Laura Stoker. 1999. "The Persistence of the Past: The Class of 1965 Turns Fifty." Presented at the annual meeting of the Midwest Political Science Association; Steven J. Rosenstone and John Mark Hansen. 1993. *Mobilization, Participation, and Democracy in America*. New York: Macmillan.

Of course, one might ask why anyone participates in politics at all. Some would argue that the costs of electoral participation outweigh its benefits.[58] After all, the likelihood that a citizen's vote will decide the outcome of an election is infinitesimal. Part of the story is that citizens may value participation in politics for other reasons. As we discussed at the beginning of the chapter, citizens receive a variety of nontangible benefits from participation that make it enjoyable—such as the sense of satisfaction for fulfilling their civic duty or for helping a cause or candidate they believe in.

What affects the participation of those citizens who do involve themselves in campaigns and elections? We have suggested that ability, motivation, and opportunity are important factors. Ability is related to formal education, financial resources, and the civic skills acquired at work and through involvement in community groups. The motivation to participate stems from an interest in politics and the encouragement that one receives from the prevailing social context and from candidates, parties, and groups who engage in mobilization. The role of social context suggests that participation is, in a sense, contagious. Parents who care about politics and vote are more likely to have children who are politically engaged than are parents who do not care or vote. Politically active spouses spur their partners to participate. People who are politically active also encourage other people in their social networks to participate. The role of mobilization demonstrates that campaigns themselves can affect the decision to vote and the decision to participate in the election in other ways. In fact, even mobilization efforts are contagious: when campaigners knock on a door and remind someone to vote, it makes other eligible voters in that household more likely to vote.[59] As we noted at the outset of this chapter, campaigns can matter not simply by persuading people how to vote, but by persuading them to vote.

Finally, having the ability and motivation to participate is not enough if one does not have the opportunity. In the case of voting, one has the

---

[58]Andrew Gelman, Gary King, and W. J. Boscardin. 1998. "Estimating the probability of events that have never occurred: when is your vote decisive?" *Journal of the American Statistical Association* 93: 1–9; Donald Green and Ian Shapiro. 1994. *Pathologies of Rational Choice Theory.* New Haven, CT: Yale University Press, chap. 4; John Ferejohn and Morris Fiorina. 1974. "The Paradox of Not Voting: A Decision Theoretic Analysis." *American Political Science Review* 68: 525–536; William H. Riker and Peter C. Ordeshook. 1974. "A Theory of the Calculus of Voting." *American Political Science Review* 62: 25–42; Anthony Downs. 1957. *An Economic Theory of Democracy.* New York: Harper & Row.

[59] David Nickerson. 2008. "Is Voting Contagious? Evidence from Two Field Experiments." *American Political Science Review* 102, 1: 49–57.

opportunity to participate if one is eligible to vote and has registered. For other forms of participation, opportunities to participate are more likely to arise when elections are closer. Thus, citizens living in competitive jurisdictions will find themselves with ample opportunity to participate while those living in noncompetitive jurisdictions will find they have fewer opportunities to flex their democratic muscles.

As we first noted in Chapter 2, political participation is intrinsic to many conceptions of what "good" elections look like. One such conception privileges the ideal of political equality. Egalitarians lament participatory distortions because they can produce electoral outcomes and policies that are not representative of what the general population wants. Yet, studies that have examined such question argue that if all nonvoters participated, only some electoral outcomes and policies would change. The reason why only "some" would change is that an election must be close for the participation of nonvoters to make a difference and close elections are becoming rarer in the United States. In addition, only policies, about which there is significant disagreement between nonvoters and a substantial portion of voters, have the potential of changing if nonvoters participated. In other words, if nonvoters agree with voters about a given policy, the participation of nonvoters will not change an elected official's views about it.[60]

Beyond election outcomes, there is growing evidence that government is more responsive to those who participate than to those who do not. Thus, the way that members of Congress vote appears to reflect the preferences of voters more than the preferences of nonvoters, and the preferences of the wealthy more than the preferences of the poor.[61] The apparent influence of the wealthy may result from the greater frequency with which they contact their representatives, and the frequency and size of their donations to the representatives' campaigns.[62] Similarly, proposed government policies

---

[60] Jack Citrin, Eric Schickler, and John Sides. 2003. "What If Everyone Voted? Simulating the Impact of Increased Turnout in Senate Elections." *American Journal of Political Science* 47: 75–90; Michael D. Martinez and Jeff Gill. 2005. "The Effects of Turnout on Partisan Outcomes in U.S. Presidential Elections, 1960–2000." *Journal of Politics* 67, 4: 1248–74; Thomas L. Brunell and John DiNardo. 2004. "A Propensity Score Reweighting Approach to Estimating the Partisan Effects of Full Turnout in American Presidential Elections." *Political Analysis* 12, 1: 28–45.

[61] John D. Griffin and Brian Newman. 2008. "Are Voters Better Represented?" *Journal of Politics*. 67, 4: 1206–27; Larry Bartels. 2008. *Unequal Democracy: The Political Economy of the New Gilded Age.* New York and Princeton, NJ: Russell Sage Foundation Princeton University Press, chap. 9.

[62] Bartels, *Unequal Democracy.*

are much more likely to become law when they are supported by wealthy people than when they are supported by the poor or middle class.[63]

Such findings do raise important concerns about the quality of American democracy. At the same time, however, we must think critically about whether participatory equality is the most important ideal for elections and how it should be balanced with other ideals. Those who support imposing restrictions on voter registration claim they prevent voter fraud and corruption and mitigate how much political parties can manipulate the electoral process. Moreover, some argue that it is more important for citizens to vote in an informed manner than for all citizens to vote. In this view, it is actually worse if more people participate but do not know a lot about the candidates or the issues facing the country. Needless to say, these debates cannot be resolved easily, but as we try to understand them, it is useful to recognize that increasing electoral participation entails trade-offs between competing values.

KEY TERMS

electoral participation (p. 311)

participatory distortion (p. 311)

get-out-the-vote (GOTV) efforts (p. 313)

material benefit (p. 317)

solidarity benefits (p. 317)

purposive benefits (p. 317)

political interest (p. 320)

internal efficacy (p. 320)

external efficacy (p. 320)

social context (p. 321)

generational cohort (p. 324)

mobilization (p. 325)

Motor Voter Act (p. 330)

convenience voting (p. 330)

absentee voting (p. 330)

vote by mail (p. 331)

FOR DISCUSSION

1. How much does it matter for the quality of democracy if certain groups of citizens participate more in the political process than others?

---

[63] Martin Gilens. 2005. "Inequality and Democratic Responsiveness." *Public Opinion Quarterly* 69, 5: 778–896.

2. How can voting be made more convenient for young people?

3. Are you interested in politics? If so, who or what encouraged your interest?

4. Do you benefit from participating in politics? How?

 Visit StudySpace for quizzes and other review material.
wwnorton.com/studyspace

CHAPTER 12

Voter Choice

On December 23, 2012, the *Boston Globe* ran an extensive story analyzing the 2012 presidential election. The bottom line? "[Mitt] Romney's problems went deeper than is widely understood. His campaign made a series of costly financial, strategic, and political mistakes that, in retrospect, all but assured the candidate's defeat, given the revolutionary turnout tactics and tactical smarts of President Obama's operation." "Democrats," the article reported, "followed the trail blazed in 2004 by the Bush campaign which used an array of databases to 'microtarget' voters and a sophisticated field organization to turn them out. Obama won in part by updating the GOP's innovation." This praise for the strategic prowess of the Obama campaign was commonplace. It was easy for commentators to think of all the smart decisions that Obama had made, and equally important, the bad decisions that his opponent, Mitt Romney, had made—most notably, allowing the Democrats to define him as an out-of-touch millionaire during the late spring and early summer of 2012.

But two months before the elections, a group of political scientists offered models that attempted to forecast the election's outcome. The models are based on an understanding of how voters make choices and incorporate factors such as the state of the economy and presidential approval. As we discussed in Chapter 8, these factors are largely outside either candidate's control but still powerfully affect presidential election outcomes. The August 2012 models estimated that Obama would receive 51.9 percent, on average. In fact, he received 50.6 percent, so the average forecast, as well as the individual forecasts, were fairly close. More famously, former baseball statistics guru Nate Silver, blogging at fivethirtyeight .com for the *New York Times*, pegged Obama's vote at 50.8 percent in late August, calculating that the president's probability of re-election was about 70 percent. To be sure, election forecasting models are not always this accurate. In 2000, for example, the models predicted that Gore would receive about 56 percent of the vote, but in fact he received just over 50 percent. Still, more often than not, the political science models get it right — even though they fail to take account of the general election campaign.

That presidential elections are so predictable flies in the face of many media accounts of presidential campaigns. These accounts often portray the election's outcome as uncertain, which helps create a dramatic narrative, one in which crucial voters are on the fence and every twist and turn of the campaign — even a single misstatement in a debate — could make the difference between winning and losing. More to the point, the predictability of presidential elections calls into question the importance of the campaign itself. If the campaign matters, how can presidential elections be forecast with such accuracy, even months before the election? Do Americans cast their votes based largely on broader economic and political realities, and not on campaign messages and events?

In this chapter, we focus on voters and their decisions about which candidates to support. We begin by exploring the reasons behind voting decisions. Our starting point is a fact we have highlighted through this book: many Americans do not follow politics very closely. As a consequence, their voting decisions are not based on a wealth of information about the candidates. Instead, American voters are more likely to rely on shortcuts and rules of thumb when making a decision. They tend to vote for parties that are aligned with the social groups to which they belong. They develop an attachment to the party itself, one that serves as a standing decision in elections for all levels of office. They take stock of the performance of the incumbent party, especially with respect to the economy, and reward or punish it accordingly. Thus, voting decisions often

Core of the Analysis

- Many Americans are not especially attentive to election campaigns and tend to rely on simple strategies for deciding among candidates.
- Individuals tend to develop a psychological attachment to a political party, and this attachment colors opinions about political issues and candidates.
- Appraisals of national conditions (especially the state of the economy) are important factors for presidential vote choice.
- Campaigns can affect voters' decisions, but mainly when voters do not have preexisting views and when one candidate outspends another by a wide margin.
- Thus, campaigns are more likely to activate the partisan predispositions of voters than they are to persuade voters.

In 2000, models created by political scientists predicted that Al Gore would receive around 56 percent of the popular vote and win the election. However, he received just over 50 percent of the popular vote and lost in the Electoral College. What factors influence voters' decision, and how can we understand them?

depend on long-standing social and political identities or evaluations of things that the candidates themselves cannot change.

Does this mean, then, that political campaigns are irrelevant? Not at all. Campaigns remind people of their underlying attachments, thereby leading them to vote for the party or candidate they are naturally predisposed to support. But, as we discussed in Chapter 7, actual persuasion — changing someone's mind — is less common. Even still, under the right conditions, campaigns can move enough voters to shift the outcome of an election. We discuss several of those conditions, such as how familiar the candidates are to citizens, and the balance of resources among the competing candidates. We conclude by considering whether the voting decisions of Americans are in line with democratic ideals.

What Influences Vote Choice

By and large, Americans do not spend a great deal of time following politics. This is true even in presidential elections, when politics seems extraordinarily salient. In surveys conducted in every presidential election from 1952 to 2008, fewer than half of Americans said that they were "very interested in the current campaign" (Figure 12.1). This has two implications. First, as we have discussed, campaigns may have difficulty attracting the attention of potential voters, some of whom might prefer watching football or reality television, for example. This is one reason why many scholars are skeptical about the ability of campaigns to persuade voters and shape election outcomes. Second, Americans may not have a detailed understanding of the party platforms or the positions of the candidates running for office. Their choices in elections may therefore depend on more limited information, and especially on factors that enable them to make choices relatively quickly and easily. In the following sections, we consider five factors that influence vote choice: social identities, party identification, the performance of incumbents, policy issues, and candidate traits.

FIGURE 12.1 How Interested Are Americans in Political Campaigns?

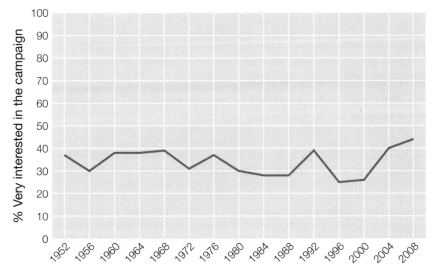

Source: Data are from the American National Election Studies Cumulative Files, 1952–2008. Data are available at www.electionstudies.org/nesguide/toptable/tab6d_6.htm (accessed 6/6/11).

Social Identities

In the aftermath of the wave of fascism that took hold in parts of Europe in the 1930s and 1940s, social scientists became fascinated with the potentially persuasive power of political communication. Some wondered, for example, whether people were easily swayed by propaganda, such as in a speech or radio broadcast, and whether propaganda might have allowed leaders like Adolf Hitler to gain and maintain power. In particular, scholars at Columbia University embarked on an innovative project, identifying a random sample of citizens in small communities—Elmira, New York, and Erie County, Ohio—and interviewing them multiple times during a presidential campaign.[1] These **panel studies** allowed researchers to understand how individuals changed their opinions in response to campaign activity.

In fact, the studies found that the campaign itself had little impact on citizens. Many citizens did not appear terribly knowledgeable about or interested in politics. They were not very responsive to the campaign or its mass media outreach. Instead, they maintained attitudes about the candidates that did not change much over time. Those whose attitudes did change—most often, from being undecided about the candidates to making a choice—tended to move in a predictable direction: toward the candidate that the individual was already predisposed to support.[2]

Why were voters predisposed to support a particular candidate in the first place? These studies revealed a crucial fact about voters' political attitudes: the attitudes depended on **social identities**. That is, voters were aligned with political parties because of class background, ethnicity, or religion. In part, this reflects the attention parties pay to group interests: the party that best serves the interests of a group may attract the enduring loyalty of its members. For example, in every election since the passage of the Voting Rights Act of 1965, about 90 percent of blacks have voted for Democrats. In 2012, 93 percent of black voters voted for the Democratic candidate Barack Obama. Similarly, the Republican Party's promotion of socially conservative policies—such as those limiting abortion—have garnered the support of most evangelical Christians. In 2012, 78 percent of

---

[1] Bernard R. Berelson, Paul F. Lazarsfeld, and William N. McPhee. 1954. *Voting: A Study of Opinion Formation in a Presidential Campaign.* Chicago: University of Chicago Press; Paul Lazarsfeld, Bernard Berelson, and Helen Gaudet. 1948. *The People's Choice.* New York: Columbia University Press.

[2] The same finding emerged in a later study of the 1980 presidential campaign. See Steven Finkel. 1993. "Reexamining the 'Minimal Effects' Model in Recent Presidential Campaigns." *Journal of Politics* 55: 1–21.

white born-again or evangelical Christians voted for Romney. Table 12.1 shows how various social groups voted in 2012. These numbers shift from election to election, but many of the basic demographic contours of the vote have been in place since the 1960s.

Of course, voters who identify with a social group will not always automatically vote for the political party most aligned with that group. They may need some sort of "reminder," one that essentially says: "People like you should vote for this candidate." The Columbia scholars argued that the degree to which those surveyed voted according to social identity often depended on their having contact and conversation with other members of their social group. Communication with other members of their church, workplace, school, and community often exposes them to more politically interested and engaged voters—so-called **opinion leaders**. As the election nears, these individuals talk about the election in ways that rekindle long-standing allegiances. In the 1948 presidential election, for example, some wavering Democrats came to support the Democratic nominee, Harry Truman, when opinion leaders within Catholic churches and labor unions explained how Truman was for the "little guy," while Thomas Dewey was just another business-friendly fat cat.[3]

For voters who do not always pay much attention to politics, social identities serve as a relatively easy way to reach a decision. It does not take much information to align one's vote with a social identity. Moreover, any information necessary to do so may come without any effort on the part of the voter, perhaps just a brief conversation with a coworker or friend. And because we often trust coworkers and friends more than, say, political candidates, we will view their opinions as particularly credible. Explanations of voting that emphasize the importance of social identities implicitly suggest that campaigns have minimal effects on how voters vote, except insofar as they supply information that helps voters connect their social identities to their choices in a particular election.

Party Identification

Perhaps social identities are not the most important identities when it comes to voting. It might be that a more influential factor is the identification that voters have not with social groups but with political parties themselves. This idea of a psychological attachment to a political party is called **party identification**. The concept was developed by scholars at the University of

---

[3] David McCullough. 1993. *Truman*. New York: Simon & Schuster.

TABLE 12.1 2012 Presidential Vote by Social Groups

	Obama	Romney	Obama Margin		Obama	Romney	Obama Margin
Northeast	58%	42%	16%	Protestant	42%	57%	–15%
Midwest	50%	47%	3%	Catholic	50%	48%	2%
South	43%	56%	–13%	Jewish	69%	30%	39%
West	55%	44%	11%	Other	74%	23%	51%
				None	70%	26%	44%
Male	45%	52%	–7%				
Female	55%	44%	11%	Weekly church attender	39%	59%	–20%
				Occasional	55%	43%	12%
White	39%	59%	–20%	Never	62%	34%	28%
Black	93%	6%	87%				
Latino	71%	27%	44%				
Asian	73%	26%	47%	Married	42%	56%	–14%
				Unmarried	62%	35%	27%
18–29	60%	37%	23%				
30–44	52%	45%	7%	Union member	58%	40%	18%
45–64	47%	51%	–4%	Not union member	49%	48%	1%
65+	44%	56%	–12%				
Less than $50,000	60%	38%	22%				
$50,000–$100,000	46%	52%	–6%				
More than $100,000	44%	54%	–10%				

TABLE 12.1 (continued)

	Obama	Romney	Obama Margin		Obama	Romney	Obama Margin
No high school	64%	35%	29%	Gay, lesbian, bisexual	76%	22%	54%
High school graduate	51%	48%	3%	Heterosexual	49%	49%	0%
Some college	49%	48%	1%	Urban	62%	36%	26%
College graduate	47%	51%	−4%	Suburban	48%	50%	−2%
Postgraduate	55%	42%	13%	Rural	37%	61%	−24%

Source: 2012 National Election Pool exit poll, conducted by Edison Media Research (N = 17,836 respondents).

Michigan drawing on nationally representative surveys conducted during the 1952 and 1956 elections.[4]

Party identification does not mean identification with particular political ideologies or opinions. For example, to identify as a Democrat is not the same as identifying as a liberal. Nor can party identification be equated with how you are registered to vote or even how you vote at the ballot box, although it is highly correlated with each. Instead, party identification is like other social identities. We feel that we are a member of a group ("I am a Democrat" or "I am a Republican") and we tend to feel positively about that group. So we cheer when our "team" wins and the other loses.

Where does party identification come from? It is learned relatively early in life, primarily from those who are closest to us for the most extended periods of time. Thus, our parents are the dominant influence on our party identification, although this tendency appears to be weakening (see Table 12.2). In 1992, a little less than 60 percent of citizens identified with the same party as their parents. Besides parents, other people and institutions—such as friends, schools, and churches—can also shape party identification.

---

[4] Angus Campbell, Philip E. Converse, Warren E. Miller, and Donald E. Stokes. 1960. *The American Voter*. Chicago: University of Chicago Press.

TABLE 12.2 Parent-Child Party Identification Correspondence			
	1958	**1976**	**1992**
Democrats	79%	62%	57%
Republicans	72%	56%	56%

Note: "Correspondence" refers to the percentage of partisan identifiers whose parents share their affiliation. The parental party identification question was last asked by ANES for the 1992 study.
Source: Data are from the American National Election Studies Cumulative Files, 1952–2008.

The prevailing political context at the time that one comes of age also matters: people who enter young adulthood when a president is popular will be more likely to identify with the president's party than people who come of age when the president is unpopular. For example, young people who came of age when Ronald Reagan was president are still more likely to be Republicans than those who came of age under the unpopular and scandal-ridden Richard Nixon.[5] Regardless of its sources, party identification is typically formed by young adulthood. Because it is learned so early, it is a durable attitude. People tend not to change much, even as they grow up, learn more, and see their circumstances evolve. In short, with party identification, where you end up depends in large part on where you start.

Of course, this discussion raises an important question: Does everyone develop a party identification? What about those people who identify as "independent"? To assess the true number of political independents, it is important to consider how party identification is typically measured. In a survey, respondents will be asked a question such as "Generally speaking, do you consider yourself a Republican, Democrat, or an Independent?" If respondents identify as Republican or Democrat, they are then asked, "Would you call yourself a strong or a not very strong Republican/Democrat?" Respondents who say they are "independent" or express no preference are then asked, "Do you think of yourself as closer to the Republican

---

[5] Scott Keeter, Juliana Menasce Horowitz, and Alec Tyson. 2008. *Gen Dems: The Party's Advantage Among Young Voters Widens.* Washington, DC: Pew Research Center for the People and the Press. http://pewresearch.org/pubs/813/gen-dems (accessed 7/22/10).

or Democratic Party?" These questions measure the direction and intensity of party identification and are used to create a seven-point scale:

1. Strong Democrat

2. Weak Democrat

3. Leans Democrat

4. Independent

5. Leans Republican

6. Weak Republican

7. Strong Republican

As measured by responses to the first in this series of questions, the number of independents (those who do not call themselves Republicans or Democrats) is rising: from 23 percent of Americans in 1952 to 40 percent in 2008.[6] But nearly all political independents think of themselves as closer to one party. Only 11 percent do not "lean" toward a party and could be considered "pure" independents—and, as Figure 12.2 shows, this percentage has actually declined in recent years. Moreover, independents who lean toward a party are almost as likely to support that party's candidates as those voters who call themselves Republicans or Democrats.

For those studying elections, party identification matters for three reasons. First, it functions as a filter or screen through which information must pass. In other words, we tend to accept information that comes from the party we identify with, or from sources closely identified with that party, and to discount information coming from sources on the other side.[7] This is why, as we noted in Chapter 8, partisans routinely think that their party's presidential nominee won every general election debate. Second, party identification also helps motivate people to vote; stronger partisans are more likely to vote than weak and leaning partisans, who in turn are more likely to vote than independents.

Finally, and perhaps most important, party identification is a powerful predictor of how citizens vote. In presidential elections, approximately 90 percent of Democrats and Republicans vote for their respective party's

---

[6] See American National Election Studies. 2010. "Party Identification 7-Point Scale, 1952–2008. www.electionstudies.org/nesguide/toptable/tab2a_1.htm (accessed 4/13/11).

[7] Philip Converse. 1962. "Information Flow and the Stability of Partisan Attitudes." *Public Opinion Quarterly* 26: 578–99.

FIGURE 12.2 Trends in Party Identification, 1952–2008

A. **Democratic Party Identification**

B. **Republican Party Identification**

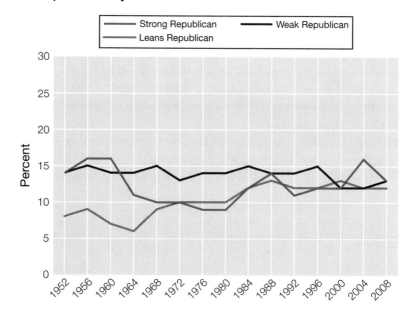

FIGURE 12.2 (**continued**)

C.   **Independent Party Identification**

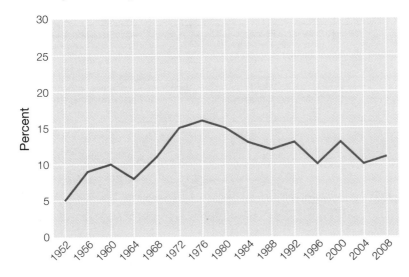

Source: Data are from the American National Election Studies Cumulative Files, 1952–2008. See www
.electionstudies.org/nesguide/toptable/tab2a_1.htm (accessed 6/6/11).

nominee. Many races at other levels of office, such as for the U.S. House and Senate, also see high levels of party loyalty. In fact, partisan loyalty has been increasing over time, as shown in Figure 12.3.[8] To be sure, party loyalty is not an absolute. From time to time, partisans defect and vote for a candidate of the opposite party—for example, because that candidate is a talented incumbent who has no credible challenger. But defections are the exception rather than the rule. Because of this, campaigns typically try to reinforce partisan loyalties among their followers and to persuade independents to vote for their candidate.

Like social identities, party identification functions as a useful shortcut for political decision making, especially when voters are not particularly well-informed about the candidates. Thus, party identification is particularly useful in races where voters know little about the candidates except for their party affiliation.

---

[8] Larry M. Bartels. 2000. "Partisanship and Voting Behavior." *American Journal of Political Science* 44, 1: 35–50.

FIGURE 12.3 Percentages of Self-Identified Partisans Voting for Their Party's Candidate in Presidential and House Elections, 1980–2008

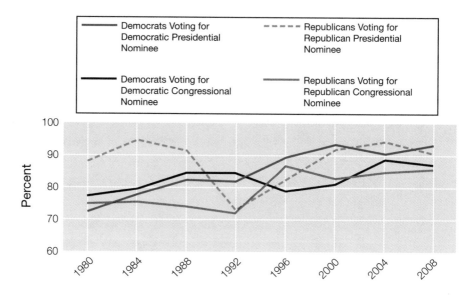

Source: Data are from the American National Election Studies Cumulative Files, 1952–2008.

Incumbent Performance

A third factor in many voters' decisions is the performance of the incumbent party or officeholder. The most important criterion in evaluating performance is the state of the economy. When the economy is growing, voters tend to reward the incumbent party.[9] For example, an incumbent president is more likely to be re-elected when the country is prosperous. But when the economy is growing slowly or not at all, voters tend to punish the incumbent president or, if that person is not running, the nominee of the incumbent party. As we discussed in Chapters 8 and 9, macroeconomic variables, such as changes in the average income of Americans, predict presidential and even congressional election outcomes. This lends credence to the idea that economic performance is a major factor when voters go to the polls.

How do voters use their perceptions about the economy to decide how to vote? For starters, voters rely more on their evaluations of how the economy

---

[9] See, for example, Ray C. Fair. 1978. "The Effect of Economic Events on Votes for President." *Review of Economics and Statistics* 60: 159–72; Michael Lewis-Beck and Thomas W. Rice. 1992. *Forecasting Elections*. Washington, DC: CQ Press; Edward R. Tufte. 1978. *Political Control of the Economy*. Princeton, NJ: Princeton University Press.

has performed in the past rather than how it might perform in the future. Using past performance to decide between candidates is called **retrospective voting**, and is often encapsulated by a single question: "Are we better off now than when the incumbent took office?" While basing one's voting decisions on the answer to this question may appear simpleminded, it is plausible that past performance predicts future performance.[10] In this way, retrospective voting provides an efficient shortcut for citizens looking to make choices about future leadership.

Previous research also indicates that voters rely more on their assessments of the national economy (**sociotropic voting**) than on assessments of their own financial situation (**pocketbook voting**).[11] Moreover, when voters assess the economy, they focus most on recent changes and, especially, changes in the election year itself.[12] Even if a president has presided over three years of a weak economy, if the economy shows strong growth in his fourth year, he is likely to be rewarded by the electorate. In this sense, voters are somewhat nearsighted: they see nearby, or more recent, economic events more clearly than events that occurred further in the past.

Finally, voters' evaluations of the economy are affected by their party identification. In this sense, party identification creates bias in evaluations. When a Democrat is president, Democrats evaluate the economy more positively than do Republicans. Republicans exhibit this same tendency when a Republican is president. And even if partisans do pick up on more objective information about the economy, this does not mean that negative economic assessments will cause them to defect from their party's candidates. Nearly 90 percent of Republicans voted for John McCain in 2008, even though the vast majority of them believed that the economy was weak under the incumbent Republican administration. Ultimately, because partisans tend to judge more generously the performance of their office-holders, it is independent voters whose vote choice is most influenced by the incumbent party's handling of the economy.

Policy Issues

In a typical campaign, candidates spend a great deal of time talking about issues relating to government policy, such the regulation of environmental pollution or the future solvency of Social Security and Medicare. When

---

[10] Morris P. Fiorina. 1981. *Retrospective Voting in American Elections.* New Haven, CT: Yale University Press.

[11] Donald Kinder, and D. Roderick Kiewiet. 1981. "Sociotropic Politics: The American Case." *British Journal of Political Science* 11:129–61.

[12] Larry Bartels. 2008. *Unequal Democracy.* Princeton, NJ: Princeton University Press.

voters make choices, do they factor these sorts of issue positions into their decision?

In Chapter 5, we introduced the median voter theorem, which posits that candidates take issue positions that are close to the hypothetical median voter, whose support is necessary to win the election. The median voter theorem assumes that voters make choices in a particular way: they evaluate the candidates' ideologies or their positions on issues and then choose the candidate who, on average, has positions most similar to their own. This strategy is called **proximity voting**—voters choose the candidates whose views are closest or most proximate to theirs.

Does proximity voting actually happen? Is voting really about "the issues"? In general, it is not. The strategy of proximity voting takes more time and effort than the other simple shortcuts that we have described. Voters do not often invest this kind of time and effort. To vote based on policy issues, voters first need to have opinions about those issues. But they often do not pay enough attention to politics to form opinions, especially about complex public policies. Even if they do have opinions, they may not pay enough attention to the campaign to discern where the candidates stand and which candidate is most proximate to them. Moreover, candidates do not always make their views clear. As we discussed in Chapter 5, candidates may have an incentive to be ambiguous.

One recent study estimated that less than half of the electorate has the requisite opinions on issues along with sufficient knowledge of candidates' views to engage in issue voting.[13] When issue voting does occur, it is usually limited to a particular group of voters within the broader electorate. These groups are called "issue publics," and consist of voters who are more likely to have strong opinions about the issue, to learn where the candidates stand, and to vote for a candidate only if that candidate agrees with them. An example would be senior citizens, who are especially attentive to protecting their current Medicare benefits. But this seems the exception and not the rule. Furthermore, there is some evidence that rather than voting based on policy, voters are more likely simply to adopt the policy positions of the candidates they already support based on party identification.[14]

---

[13] Michael Lewis-Beck, et al. 2008. *The American Voter Revisited*. Ann Arbor: University of Michigan Press, chap. 8.

[14] Gabriel Lenz. 2009. "Learning and Opinion Change, Not Priming: Reconsidering the Evidence for the Priming Hypothesis." *American Journal of Political Science* 53, 4: 821–37.

Candidate Traits

Candidates spend a great deal of time promoting not only their views but also their biographies and personal qualities. Do voters draw on their perceptions of candidates' personal qualities, such as appearance or personality, when making decisions in an election? At one level, this seems a simple strategy that would not demand much time or effort on the part of voters. They could merely get an impression of the candidates as people, perhaps from television advertising or candidate debates, and then use this impression to select the candidate that seems the stronger leader, more honest, better looking, and so on. Indeed, conventional accounts of political campaigns often draw attention to personal qualities. In 1960, Democrat John F. Kennedy was considered youthful, energetic, but perhaps a bit inexperienced. His Republican opponent, Richard Nixon, was considered experienced and knowledgeable, but not especially trustworthy. In 1992, Republican president George H. W. Bush was considered honest and experienced but out of touch with the problems of ordinary Americans. Many believe that Bush's image as a man detached from the people became fixed when he seemed perplexed by a price scanner in a grocery store during a campaign event. The Democratic challenger, Bill Clinton, on the other hand, was thought to be intelligent and compassionate (he told a crowd during the campaign: "I feel your pain") but not very honest. In 2008, Barack Obama was considered youthful, intelligent, and inexperienced (like his fellow Democrats Kennedy and Clinton), while John McCain's image as a maverick unafraid to buck the system was undermined by voter concerns about his age and temperament.

But do such qualities matter? There is some evidence that they do. For example, better-looking candidates appear to get more votes than less attractive opponents do. Similarly, the more positively people assess a candidate's personality—including traits such as honesty or capacity for leadership—the more likely they are to vote for the candidate.[15] Candidates also suffer when scandals, especially those involving allegations of official corruption, cast doubt on their character.[16]

---

[15] Chappell Lawson, Gabriel S. Lenz, Andy Baker, and Michael Myers. 2010. "Looking Like a Winner: Candidate Appearance and Electoral Success in New Democracies." *World Politics* 62, 4: 561–93; Donald R. Kinder, Mark D. Peters, Robert P. Abelson, and Susan T. Fiske. 1980. "Presidential Prototypes," *Political Behavior* 2, 4: 315–37.

[16] Tim Fackler and Tse-min Lin. 1995. "Political Corruption and Presidential Elections, 1929–1992." *Journal of Politics* 57, 4: 971–93; Daron R. Shaw. 1999. "A Study of Presidential Campaign Event Effects from 1952 to 1992." *Journal of Politics* 61: 387–422.

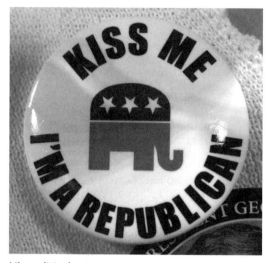

Like political scientists, campaign consultants recognize party identification as a strong influence on vote choice. Campaign strategists look at the partisan composition of the district as a starting point in determining whose votes they can count on and whose they can hope to win through persuasion.

At the same time, other evidence argues that a candidate's appearance and personality may matter much less, and may be dependent on the nature of the race. For instance, one recent study demonstrates that attractive candidates tend to run in races where they have a better chance of winning.[17] Thus, if attractive candidates get more votes than less attractive candidates, it is unclear whether it was because of attractiveness or because the race was simply easier to win. The same logic may extend to other attributes of candidates, such as their personalities. A candidate's appearance or personality will typically matter most when there is little other information to draw on, such as in smaller races that feature unfamiliar candidates and attract little media coverage. In races where there is much more information—such as a presidential race—it is less clear that people's evaluations of the candidates' personalities actually decide their vote. In such races, people may have a preferred candidate for other reasons—especially because of party identification—and thus evaluate their party's candidate more favorably. Such biases are not absolute, however. In 2012, many Republicans rated Obama as more likely to care about "people like me." And many Democrats rated Romney as a stronger leader than Obama. Nevertheless, 90 percent of both Democrats and Republicans voted for their party's nominee, despite any misgivings.

How Do Campaign Consultants Think about Vote Choice?

Consultants and academics have similar views about how voters decide between candidates. As we explained in Chapter 5, consultants share the belief that voters are not particularly interested in or knowledgeable about

---

[17] Matthew D. Atkinson, Ryan D. Enos, and Seth J. Hill. 2009. "Candidate Faces and Election Outcomes: Is the Face–Vote Correlation Caused by Candidate Selection?" *Quarterly Journal of Political Science* 4, 3: 229–49.

politics. This is why they advise candidates to repeat a basic message over and over—often via a barrage of television ads. Similarly, consultants often prefer emotional appeals over intellectual appeals, and negative appeals over positive appeals. Emotional appeals and negative appeals seem to be more likely to garner attention and more likely to be remembered.

Consultants, like academics, also believe that voters are strongly constrained by their partisanship and other predispositions. Recognizing these predispositions and acting accordingly is the hallmark of smart campaigns, which often have limited resources and thus need to focus their efforts on those voters most likely to help the campaign win. This is why consultants recommend not wasting time campaigning for the votes of opposing partisans, but instead focusing on delivering mobilizing messages to fellow partisans and persuasive messages to independents and weak partisans.

When Campaigns Matter

Although campaign consultants and political scientists share many beliefs about vote choice, they disagree over a key question: how much the campaign can affect voters' attitudes toward the candidates. Campaign consultants believe that their activities—television and radio advertisements, phone calls, direct mail, the Internet, social media, and person-to-person contact—help persuade voters and thus win elections. Political scientists are more skeptical but nevertheless acknowledge that campaigns can sometimes change voters' minds and even affect election outcomes. The crucial task is to identify *when* campaigns are likely to matter. Here we are particularly concerned about **persuasion**—a concept we introduced in Chapter 5 that means, in this context, convincing undecided voters to support a particular candidate or convincing the other party's supporters to defect. Later in this chapter we will also consider alternative ways that campaigns may matter.

Campaigns have their largest persuasive effects when two conditions are met: the candidates are relatively unfamiliar to voters, and one side is able to dominate by virtue of better resources. When candidates are not well known, voters are less likely to have opinions about them. Although party identification is likely to affect their initial assessments, they will still be more susceptible to persuasive appeals by the candidates because they will not have strongly held opinions about them.

Campaigns also matter more when one side can campaign more heavily than the other side. That is to say, campaigns matter more when one side dominates, typically when it has more money and thus a more extensive campaign organization, a larger presence on television and other media, and a better developed infrastructure for contacting and mobilizing voters. When opposing campaigns are more equally balanced in terms of resources, it is difficult for either campaign to get an edge. Television advertisements by one side can be matched with competing advertisements from the other side. The respective efforts of the two sides thus tend to cancel each other out. These two conditions suggest how much impact we should expect campaigns at different levels of office to have.

Presidential Elections

Despite the vast amounts of money that presidential candidates spend, presidential general election campaigns are less likely to decide election outcomes than campaigns at other levels of office. By the time the party conventions are over and the general election campaign has begun, the Democratic and Republican nominees are already relatively well known. They have been campaigning for months if not years, depending on when they began campaigning for the nomination. At the national party conventions, the parties spend several days promoting their nominees for a large television audience. Moreover, when incumbent presidents run for reelection, voters have had five or six years to get to know them, at least from the time their first campaign for president began.

Competing major-party presidential campaigns also tend to be roughly equal in terms of resources—including not only money but also motivation, information, and expertise. The assumption of equal resources has been valid since the passage of the Federal Election Campaign Act. As discussed in Chapter 4, from 1976 to 2004, presidential general election campaigns were publicly financed. That is, both major-party candidates accepted equal amounts of funding from the U.S. Treasury the morning after they accepted their party's nomination for president. In exchange for this money, candidates agreed not to raise or spend additional money on their own behalf.

It is obvious that the campaigns of the two major parties have equal motivation. The presidential election is, in the words of the Republican media consultant Stuart Stevens, "the big enchilada." Both parties try hard to win. It is only slightly less obvious that they are working with equal information. Both the Democratic and Republican presidential campaigns have ready access to information about the preferences of voters via polling and focus groups. Opposition research arms both campaigns with data on the relevant issue positions and backgrounds of the candidates. And teams of experts work with the candidates and their teams on issue positions and policy papers.

The assumption of equal expertise is based on the observation that both sides bring very talented people to the presidential election contest. Consider the main consultants in recent presidential elections. In 2000, George W. Bush relied on the direct mail whiz Karl Rove, while Al Gore relied on the veteran media consultant and speechwriter Bob Shrum. In 2004, Rove and Shrum were again pitted against each other, this time with Rove working for Bush's re-election and Shrum working for John Kerry. In 2008, Obama turned to the Chicago-based media communications consultant David Axelrod, while John McCain ultimately settled on a long-time GOP message consultant, Steven Schmidt. In 2012, Obama continued to rely on Axelrod, along with organizational guru Jim Messina, whereas Mitt Romney turned to longtime GOP consultant and television ad expert Stuart Stevens. It is, in fact, difficult to find a presidential race in which one side seemed overwhelmed by the expertise of the other side—even though after the election commentators are always willing to claim that the winners' team was that much smarter.

Taken in combination, these equalities lead to the possibility that presidential general election campaigns will fight to a draw. The winner will be determined not by the campaign but by the broader conditions in the country, especially the economy. Of course, even if this is true as a general rule, there are moments when the campaign itself appears crucial. It is possible, even in presidential campaigns, for one side to get a financial advantage over the other. In the 2000 presidential race, George W. Bush outspent Al Gore in the battleground states late in the campaign, and the resulting advantage in advertising may have cost Gore four points of the vote—a large number in states such as Florida where the race was close.[18] In 2008, when Obama bypassed public funding and outspent John McCain by an enormous margin, Obama did better in most areas of the country than John Kerry did in 2004. More importantly, Obama did particularly well the more he outspent McCain. Obama's largest campaign spending advantages were in Florida (+$28 million), Virginia (+$16.3 million), Indiana (+$11.4 million), and North Carolina (+$7.2 million), each of which went for the Democratic challenger; these states had gone for Bush in 2004 by five, eight, twenty-one, and twelve points, respectively. In general, however, a presidential candidate needs a fairly substantial advantage over an opponent to shift voters in his direction, and, even then, this shift will likely be small.[19] This is why presidential election outcomes are rarely decided by the

---

[18] Richard Johnston, Michael G. Hagen, and Kathleen Hall Jamieson. 2004. *The 2000 Presidential Election and the Foundations of Party Politics*. Cambridge: Cambridge University Press.

[19] Daron R. Shaw. 2006. *The Race to 270*. Chicago: University of Chicago Press.

campaign. One study of presidential campaigns from 1948 to 2000 found that in only 5 of the 14 presidential elections did the campaign appear to have changed the outcome.[20]

Although presidential general election campaigns often have only a small impact, presidential primary campaigns are much more important. The primaries often see much larger swings in the candidates' fortunes than the fall campaign does. Moreover, events during the campaign itself are responsible for these swings. Unlike candidates in the general elections, candidates for the presidential nomination vary greatly in their resources. Some are heavyweights: politicians with national visibility and the campaign war chests, media attention, and party endorsements to show for it. In the 2012 Republican presidential primaries, Mitt Romney and Texas governor Rick Perry fit this description. Other candidates, however, struggle for visibility and can rarely raise as much money or attract the same level of attention. In the 2012 Republican primaries, this describes candidates such as New Mexico governor Gary Johnson and Utah governor John Huntsman. These disparities in campaign resources help the heavyweights dominate the field, pulling voters to their side.

The candidates in presidential primaries are also much less well known than eventual nominees will be. Although some may be national figures, as was Hillary Clinton in 2008, many others are familiar only to the voters of the state or district that they actually represent as members of Congress or as governor. Thus, voters do not have well-formed opinions about many primary candidates, leaving more potential for the campaign to influence these opinions. Furthermore, voters cannot rely on their party identification to make decisions: all of the candidates in a party primary obviously share the same party identification. As we discussed in Chapter 8, the primary campaign often matters in this fashion: a candidate's victories in the early caucuses and primaries signals to voters that the candidate is viable. This creates a bandwagon effect, as voters gravitate toward successful candidates, believing them to be able to compete effectively in the general election. In 2008, Obama's standing in the polls increased by about 20 points between the first caucus in Iowa on January 3 and the Super Tuesday primaries on February 5. This is a much larger swing than presidential general election campaigns create. Thus, primary candidates know that by campaigning

---

[20] James E. Campbell. 2001. "When Have Presidential Campaigns Decided Election Outcomes?" *American Politics Research* 29, 5: 437–60.

effectively in these early primaries and caucuses, they build the momentum necessary to win the nomination.

Non-Presidential Elections

Campaigns for offices below the presidential level—for U.S. House and Senate, for state and local offices—are more likely to influence voters, relative to presidential general election campaigns. Again, familiarity with the candidates and resource disparities are reasons why. As we discussed in Chapters 9 and 10, citizens know much less about their representatives at lower levels of office. They often do not know the name of their congressional representative, to say nothing of their representatives in the state legislature, the state attorney general, and so on. Thus, their views about these people can be changed by a vigorous campaign. Oftentimes, this is what we see in the campaigns of challengers to incumbents in U.S. House elections. Campaign activity matters more for challengers because so few voters know them. Challengers with more money to spend become better known than poorer challengers over the course of the campaign.[21]

This makes campaign resource disparities all the more important. And, indeed, resource disparities are common in congressional, state, and local elections. One reason that incumbents often dominate these elections is because challengers cannot raise enough money to compete with them. This contrasts with presidential general elections, where, when the candidates both accept public funding, neither will be able to outspend the other overall. When challengers do raise money, it does move voters. In congressional elections from 1972 to 2006, no challenger who raised less than $100,000 won. By contrast, almost a third of those who raised at least $1 million won.[22] Campaign spending is arguably even more vital for challengers in elections for state legislature, state supreme court, and city council.[23] In these

---

[21] Gary C. Jacobson. 2006. "Measuring Campaign Spending Effects in U.S. House Elections," and Laurel Elms and Paul M. Sniderman, "Informational Rhythms of Incumbent Dominated Congressional Elections," both in *Capturing Campaign Effects*, eds. Henry E. Brady and Richard Johnston. Ann Arbor: University of Michigan Press.

[22] Gary Jacobson. 2009. *The Politics of Congressional Elections*, 7th ed. New York: Pearson Longman, p. 46. Amounts are in 2006 dollars and thus adjusted for inflation.

[23] Anthony Gierzynski and David Breaux. 1996. "Legislative Elections and the Importance of Money." *Legislative Studies Quarterly* 21, 3: 337–57; Chris W. Bonneau. 2007. "The Effects of Campaign Spending in State Supreme Court Elections." *Political Research Quarterly* 60: 489–99; Timothy B. Krebs. 1998. "The Determinants of Candidates' Vote Share and the Advantages of Incumbency in City Council Elections." *American Journal of Political Science* 42, 3: 921–35.

elections, which attract relatively little media coverage, voters are not likely to see, hear, or read anything about challengers unless it comes from their campaigns. Thus, campaigns can be crucial to the outcomes of such elections, even if the dollar amounts spent on them are miniscule compared to what is spent in higher-profile races.

How Campaigns Matter

The preceding discussion focused on the conditions under which campaigns can persuade voters. But it has said much less about *how* campaigns persuade voters, as well as other possible effects of campaigns. In Chapter 11, we described how campaigns can mobilize citizens. Now we continue to examine how campaigns affect voters' attitudes toward the candidates. Three types of effects are important: persuasion, reinforcement, and priming.

Persuasion

As we have discussed, campaigns are more likely to persuade voters when voters are unfamiliar with the candidates and when one side can outspend the other. But this observation only scratches the surface when it comes to analyzing how campaigns persuade. Although resource disparities are important, much of campaigning is not simply about spending more than the opponent, it is about crafting specific messages that are intended to persuade voters. This is what campaign consultants focus on, using polling data, focus groups, and their own experiences to design advertisements, write speeches, and produce other kinds of media. It is also about choosing the appropriate time to air those messages so that they will have the maximum impact on voters. Unfortunately, we do not know very much about what kinds of persuasion strategies consistently work. Campaign consultants sometimes have polls or focus groups, but often they rely on guesswork and interpretations of past elections. Free from the daunting prospect of an election looming, social scientists tend to put little stock in such evidence, but more rigorous data are usually difficult to come by.

One aspect of persuasive messages that has been studied extensively is tone—that is, whether the messages promote a candidate (positive campaigning), attack that candidate's opponent (negative campaigning), or offer some combination of the two (contrast campaigning). Campaign consultants tend to place great faith in the power of negativity. One Democratic consultant put it this way: "The big question in most campaigns . . . is whose negative campaign is better. If it's negative, it works. If it's positive, save it for your tombstone."[24] But is negativity really that powerful?

There is some evidence that negative advertising is more memorable than positive advertising. This is because negative information typically stands out in our daily lives, which generally consist of positive interactions.[25] For example, we are much more likely to remember the couple next to us in a restaurant if they are arguing than if they are conversing pleasantly. But there is much less evidence that negative campaigning actually helps the candidate who goes on the attack. On the whole, negative campaigning makes voters feel less favorable toward the candidate being attacked, which is the goal. However, it also makes voters feel less favorable toward the attacker, and this backlash may be stronger than the effect on views of the attacked candidate.[26] Negative advertising is thus a risky strategy at best.

Besides tone, another aspect of messaging is issue content. In fact, a strategy that campaigns often employ to persuade voters is to focus on **wedge issues**. These issues are designed to convince voters in the opposite party to defect from that party and vote for the other side. Here is one example of a wedge issue strategy. Latinos and African Americans tend to vote for Democratic candidates but at the same time maintain fairly conservative positions on social issues such as abortion and gay rights. In the 2004 elections, many believed that the Republican Party pursued a wedge issue strategy by sending anti–gay marriage direct-mail pieces to Latinos and blacks in the eleven states where "defense of marriage" initiatives were on the ballot. Some of these mail pieces linked Democratic candidates to support for "a gay agenda," thereby attempting to reduce the standing of these candidates among more socially conservative minority voters. Wedge issues are intended to take advantage of **cross pressures** within voters—that is, the fact that voters sometimes hold ideologically conflicting issue opinions (as in the case of a socially conservative Democrat). Voters who experience such cross pressures are more susceptible than other (non–cross pressured)

---

[24] Quoted in Richard R. Lau, Lee Sigelman, Caroline Heldman, and Paul Babitt. 1999. "The Effects of Negative Political Advertisements: A Meta-Analytic Assessment." *American Political Science Review* 93, 4: 852.

[25] Susan Fiske and Shelley Taylor. 1991. *Social Cognition*, 2nd edition. New York: McGraw-Hill.

[26] Richard R. Lau, Lee Sigelman, and Ivy Brown Rovner. 2007. "The Effects of Negative Political Campaigns: A Meta-Analytic Reassessment." *Journal of Politics* 69, 4: 1176–1209.

Campaign Strategy and the Persuasion Model

Sasha Issenberg, writing online for *Slate* magazine,[1] describes in fascinating detail how the Obama campaign identified and targeted persuadable votes for his re-election:

"Republican operatives around the country have noted with a mixture of curiosity and anxiety that nearby mailboxes are less crowded with mailers making the case for Obama than they were four years ago. This may be the result of a strategic imperative: In many states, Obama has a clearer path to victory than Romney solely by mobilizing existing supporters than by finding new ones. But it could also reflect the fact that Obama's strategists do not think they have to rely, as have most campaigns over the last generation, solely on the mail for their targeted efforts to win over voters.

"Earlier this year, Obama put his volunteers' ability to do that to the test. The campaign administered an experiment in several states in which phone-bank volunteers were given a script with a few talking points and broad instructions to open up a conversation with a potential voter. Before and after these interactions, a professional call center surveyed the targeted voters to identify which candidate they supported, and campaign analysts set to work developing a statistical portrait of those who moved in Obama's direction after talking with a volunteer.

"The result of that analysis is the campaign's so-called persuasion model, which generates a score predicting, from zero to 10, the likelihood that a voter can be pushed in Obama's direction. (The score also integrates a voter's likelihood of casting a ballot altogether, so that field organizers focus the attention on those with the best chances of turning out.) A zero designates a voter likely to be repelled by the interaction, and actually pushed toward Romney or a third-party candidate; a one projects a minimal possibility of persuasion; a nine someone who can be easily pushed.

"Campaign strategists have traditionally been so fearful of triggering a backlash that they rarely entrust volunteers with persuasion efforts. When placed at a phone or given a clipboard to knock on doors, volunteers usually are given tasks that do not require them to discuss sensitive or complex topics—their role has typically just been asking voters who they support, and reminding those who declare their support to turn out.

"(While in 2008 Obama encouraged volunteers to make the case for the Democratic candidate in their communities, the campaign never saw it as a replacement for their paid persuasion strategy. One adviser from that campaign mockingly describes the 2008 sensibility as 'building this utopian society where people talk with their neighbors.' Obama's strategists certainly didn't let up in traditional channels, like television ads and direct mail, where they can deploy language and imagery

---

delicately calibrated after polling and focus-group research.)

"'Persuasion calls are a more difficult thing for a volunteer to do because it's a lot easier to hang up on someone than slam a door in their face,' says Wisconsin Democratic Party chairman Mike Tate. 'You're not just asking someone who they're going to vote for or reminding them to vote—you're going to people who are undecided, who don't want to hear from you, and are often sick of politics.'

"Now, thanks to its experiments, the campaign feels confident enough in its ability to identify persuadable voters that it can direct well-trained volunteers to call them with pre-written scripts. (In an election year when so few voters are at all open-minded about the candidates, true persuasion targets are so dispersed that it is rarely efficient to send volunteers walking among their houses.) The messages are crafted for different kinds of persuadable voters. Obama's persuasion message for certain female targets threatens a 'return to an era when women didn't have control over own health choices.' Analytics are transforming the role, and value, of volunteers.

"Romney's campaign, meanwhile, appears to be selecting targets largely through the same method used in George W. Bush's 2004 campaign. After asking which candidate a respondent supports, the surveys that feed into Romney's microtargeting models also plumb for a voter's 'anger points.' *How angry does Obamacare make you? What about growing deficits?* With this data, Romney's targeters are able to model the likelihood that a voter will respond emotionally to one of its appeals—and if that person appears in the middle range between predicted support for Obama and Romney, the campaign will send a sequence of mail pieces on a related theme, like economics or social issues. While Republicans add modest pro-Romney 'advocacy' messages at the top of the scripts used at their Victory Center phone banks to identify potential supporters, they are relying on paid channels, not volunteers, to deliver persuasion messages."

voters to persuasion during a presidential campaign.[27] At the same time, given that most partisans vote loyally for their party's candidates, wedge issue strategies may not be as effective as the strategies that parties pursue to solidify their ranks.

Another aspect of persuasion is timing: When can persuasive campaigning most effectively be deployed? Typically, campaigns increase the volume of advertising and other activities as the election draws closer, believing that this is when most voters begin to focus. If so, the most important information is that which voters encounter immediately prior to casting their ballot. But there is a contrary point of view, which holds that candidates should start their campaigns early to define themselves and their opponents before all the noise of the general election begins.

Some evidence supports the first strategy — that of campaigning most heavily right before voters cast their ballots. A study of the 2006 Texas gubernatorial campaign of Rick Perry, which randomly assigned Perry's television advertisements to different media markets, found that the ads significantly improved Perry's vote share, but that the effect was temporary, fading within a week of the ads' airing.[28] A comparable analysis of other 2006 campaigns found a similarly rapid rate of "decay," suggesting again that campaign activities tend to have an immediate but short-lived impact.[29] Does this mean that early campaigning is always fruitless? Not necessarily. Moreover, given the substantial and increasing fraction of voters who cast their ballots before Election Day, campaigning "late" may actually mean campaigning at a consistently high level for weeks if not months.

Reinforcement

Because we have emphasized the challenges that campaigns face in persuading voters, it may seem as if campaigns only matter if they change people's attitudes. But campaigns can also be important by reinforcing attitudes. **Reinforcement** occurs when a campaign solidifies voters' preferences.

---

[27] D. Sunshine Hillygus, and Todd Shields. 2007. *The Persuadable Voter: Strategic Candidates and Wedge Issues in Political Campaigns*. Princeton, NJ: Princeton University Press.

[28] Alan S. Gerber, James G. Gimpel, Donald P. Green, and Daron R. Shaw. 2011. "The Size and Duration of Campaign Television Advertising Effects: Results from a Large-Scale Randomized Experiment." *American Political Science Review* 105, 1: 135–50.

[29] Seth J. Hill, James Lo, Lynn Vavreck, and John Zaller. 2007. "The Duration of Advertising Effects in Political Campaigns." Paper presented at the Annual Meeting of the American Political Science Association, Chicago.

Reinforcement is particularly likely to occur when most voters are already predisposed to support one party because of social group identities or identification with that party. For example, a voter may have a natural tendency to vote Republican but not know much about a particular Republican candidate and not feel strongly committed to this candidate. Campaign activity can increase this voter's level of commitment. Sometimes this is referred to as "rallying the base."

Although reinforcement is an important effect of campaigns, it is difficult to measure and thus somewhat underappreciated. Pre-election polls that simply ask voters whether they plan to vote Democratic or Republican will not capture how strongly voters feel or how certain they are. With further questioning, it might become clear that, early on in a campaign, many voters express a degree of uncertainty—one that disappears by late in the campaign, when voters have become devotees of their party's candidate and opponents of the other side's candidate. Of course, there is nothing automatic about reinforcement. A campaign might fail to rally its base. Such campaigns will naturally face long odds.

Priming

Not only can campaigns influence how people vote, they can also influence *why* they vote that way. That is, they affect the criteria that voters use in choosing a candidate, a process known as **priming** (Chapter 7). Why would campaigns be interested in priming? In any given election year, candidates know that they have some biographical details, personal experiences, and issue positions that give them an advantage, and some that do not. Campaigns will work to focus attention on issues that benefit them as well as issues that disadvantage their opponents. If the campaign ultimately focuses on issues beneficial to the candidate, this may help them win. Thus, campaigns are not simply about persuasion but about controlling the agenda and defining what the election is about.

Understanding priming helps answer an interesting question about elections, and presidential elections in particular: How can elections be so predictable and yet the polls fluctuate so much? We discussed in Chapter 8 (and alluded to at the outset of this chapter) how presidential elections can be forecast with considerable accuracy based on factors such as the state of the economy. And yet, during presidential campaigns, there can be notable swings in the polls; for example, in 2008, John McCain took the lead after the Republican National Convention, only to lose it two weeks later, never recovering it for the rest of the campaign. One explanation for why poll numbers eventually converge on the forecast is priming. As the election goes on, campaign activities tend to focus voters' attention on fundamental factors like the economy.[30] As these factors become more important criteria in voters' decisions, the polls move in the direction of the candidate favored by these fundamental factors—as, for example, an incumbent president would be if the economy were growing robustly. Of course, if the challenger to that incumbent president successfully changes the subject so that voters think of some other issue, the incumbent may lose. A systematic study of presidential elections since 1952 shows the importance of priming: when candidates who benefit from the state of the economy and other conditions emphasize these factors in their campaigns, they are more likely to win than similarly situated candidates who focus on some other issue.[31]

The 2000 election provides an illustration of the importance of priming. A pressing question after this election was why Al Gore did not win more of the popular vote, given how well the economy was doing in the year before the election and given his position as vice president under President Bill Clinton. One possible answer is that Gore's campaign agenda did not focus on the economy, and thus did not "prime" the economy in voters' minds. Gore was leery of associating himself even with positive aspects of the Clinton administration's record for fear that he would also be punished for Clinton's extramarital affair with Monica Lewinsky or other scandals. Thus, some voters may not have rewarded him for economic growth. Gore's strategy contrasts sharply with Obama's in 2008, which emphasized the weak economy.

Conclusion

The decisions Americans make about political candidates—and the campaign's role in influencing those decisions—are frequently the subject of concern. Commentators speculate about whether Americans make decisions that are well informed, which usually means that their decisions are based on specific knowledge of the candidates and especially their views about issues. This concern speaks to the standard of *deliberation* that we

---

[30] Andrew Gelman, and Gary King. 1993. Why Are American Presidential Election Polls So Variable When Votes Are So Predictable? *British Journal of Political Science* 23: 409–51; Thomas M. Holbrook. 1996. *Do Campaigns Matter?* Thousand Oaks, CA: Sage.

[31] Lynn Vavreck. 2009. *The Message Matters: The Economy and Presidential Campaigns.* Princeton, NJ: Princeton University Press.

introduced in the first chapter. Typically, that standard is applied to how candidates are campaigning or how the media covers campaigns. But the same standard could be applied to citizens. For one, healthy deliberation implies that citizens are themselves paying attention, willing to learn, and willing to contribute to the national conversation that happens in and around elections. Moreover, if the news media and candidates are expected to provide detailed information to voters but voters simply are not paying attention, then perhaps the voters bear as much or more responsibility as the quality of media coverage or campaign messages.

This perspective may give voters far less credit than they deserve. We have emphasized throughout this chapter that voters often rely on simple decision rules that do not require detailed information. For example, Americans often rely on long-standing psychological attachments to one of the two major political parties. They also draw on appraisals of the economy to evaluate incumbent performance. These strategies may be simple, even simplistic, but they may also be good shortcuts. What does it mean to say that something is a good shortcut? The question is whether voters who choose a Democratic or Republican candidate based on party identification would be likely to choose that same candidate if they had received and digested reams of information about the candidates. In other words, did the shortcut get voters to the same place that they would have reached had they devoted considerable time and energy to researching the alternatives? In many cases, the answer is probably yes. Some research has demonstrated that voting based on issue proximity calculations often gets citizens to the same vote choice they would have made had they relied solely on their partisanship. This is why social identities and party identification in particular may be reliable shortcuts. If so, then we might be slightly less concerned if voters do not follow the campaign closely.

A second concern raised about voters' behavior in elections concerns the impact of the campaign itself. Commentators sometimes worry that voters— particularly those who are not paying close attention to the campaign—could be unduly affected by clever television advertisements or other kinds of campaign appeals. This speaks to the standard of *free choice* that we have discussed previously. If campaigns can influence voters by airing ads that play on voters' fears with exaggerated attacks of the opponent, or ads that contained misleading information or even outright falsehoods, then perhaps voters' choices are not quite free but are instead being manipulated by the candidates.

By and large, such fears seem unfounded. Campaigns can be important for the voting process. They reinforce the views of partisans and occasionally persuade some voters who are on the fence. But their effects appear to stop well short of manipulation. Indeed, political reality—objective factors and conditions—significantly constrains how much campaigns can influence voters. Campaigns are hard-pressed to overcome political reality and voters' partisan habits, particularly when the efforts of one candidate are countered and offset by the efforts of the opponent. This is especially true for presidential election campaigns. The result is that presidents presiding over prosperous times typically win (for example, Reagan in 1984 and Clinton in 1996), and those presiding over recessions almost always lose (for example, Carter in 1980 and Bush in 1992). Only when voters know little about the candidates or when they cannot rely on shortcuts like party identification do campaigns appear more influential—and even then only when one candidate can outspend the other.

We are not suggesting that campaigns do not matter at all. For one, they might be important even if they do not persuade many voters. They provide information, mobilize voters, and force candidates to articulate policy positions that become the basis for subsequent accountability. Furthermore, in some cases, they do persuade enough voters to affect the outcome. Thus the campaign can be the difference between winning and losing—certainly in at lower levels of office and perhaps even in presidential elections from time to time.

This basic understanding of voters and vote choice is shared by political scientists and campaign professionals. Understandably, the people inside the campaigns tend to think their actions are important to voters, more so than academics viewing proceedings from afar. But consultants and campaign workers comprehend, perhaps better than anyone else, how difficult it is to capture the attention of voters and score points. Ironically, it is precisely because it is so difficult to move voters that campaigns often develop a strong belief in how important it is to allocate resources effectively, message coherently, and win the daily battle with the news media.

KEY TERMS

panel study (p. 346)

social identities (p. 346)

opinion leaders (p. 347)

party identification (p. 347)

retrospective voting (p. 355)

sociotropic voting (p. 355)

pocketbook voting (p. 355)

proximity voting (p. 356)

persuasion (p. 359)

wedge issues (p. 365)

cross pressures (p. 365)

reinforcement (p. 368)

priming (p. 369)

FOR DISCUSSION

1. What is party identification and how does it influence the behavior of voters?

2. Why do scholars believe that most voters do not engage in issue voting?

3. Identify and briefly describe three ways in which campaigns might "matter" for voters.

4. Why is it that political scientists are particularly skeptical about the ability of presidential campaigns to determine election outcomes?

 Visit StudySpace for quizzes and other review material.
wwnorton.com/studyspace

CHAPTER 13

Democracy in Action or a Broken System?

It is easy to imagine political campaigns as wars in which the candidates are generals and the people they direct — staff and volunteers — are the loyal troops that engage in combat. This conception of political campaigns is evident among practitioners and scholars. For example, Mary Matalin and James Carville called their book about the 1992 presidential election *All's Fair: Love, War and Running for President*, while the Republican consultant Ed Rollins called his autobiography *Bare Knuckles and Back Rooms*.[1] Lee Atwater, a consultant for Presidents Ronald Reagan and George H. W. Bush, claimed that his favorite book was Sun Tzu's *Art of War* because "Everything in it you can relate to my profession, you can relate to the campaign."[2] It is not surprising, then, that Matalin's epigraph for *All's Fair* was the Vietnamese battle cry, "Follow me if I advance. Kill me if I retreat. Avenge me if I die."[3] Scholars are no less likely to use the war metaphor, as evidenced by book titles such as *The Battle for Congress, Campaign Warriors,* and *Air Wars*.[4]

To a certain extent, it is understandable why campaigns are depicted as wars. The word *campaign* itself derives from the Latin word *campus* ("field"), which originally referred to the period of time when an army was in the field. There are two problems with conceiving of political campaigns as battles, however.

---

[1] Ed Rollins. 1997. *Bare Knuckles and Back Rooms: My Life in American Politics*. New York: Broadway.

[2] John R. Pitney. 2001. *The Art of Political Warfare*. Norman: University of Oklahoma Press, p. 13.

[3] Mary Matalin and James Carville. 1995. *All's Fair: Love, War, and Running for President*. New York: Simon & Schuster.

[4] James Thurber. 2001. *The Battle for Congress: Candidates, Consultants and Voters*. Washington, DC: Brookings Institution Press; James Thurber and Candice Nelson. 2000. *Campaign Warriors: Political Consultants in Elections*. Washington, DC: Brookings Institution Press; Darrell M. West. 2005. *Air Wars: Television Advertising in Election Campaigns 1952–2004*. Washington, DC: CQ Press.

First, doing so makes it seem like there are no limits to the actions that political actors can take in pursuit of victory. What else could Matalin and Carville mean by the title *All's Fair*? Second, while the metaphor might be helpful for imagining the roles of political candidates and campaign workers, it is not very helpful for imagining the role of citizens. Are they soldiers? Civilians? Most citizens do not get involved in political campaigns beyond voting, so the soldier metaphor seems inapt. Civilians, on the other hand, can be viewed either as the people who stay behind to tend the home front and support the troops or as those who dodge sniper fire as they scrounge for food and water. Needless to say, these are poor ways to conceive of citizens in a democracy. Understanding campaigns means moving beyond martial metaphors and examining the role that campaigns play in a democracy.

Throughout this book, we have emphasized that campaigns in the United States reflect the country's laws and institutions, the strategic motivations of candidates, the choices that voters make, and the broader economic and historical context in which elections take place. In other words, campaigns make sense when one understands the incentives and constraints political actors face. The fact that there is an intelligible logic to how campaigns and elections function, however, does not mean that they are serving our democracy well. The challenge of evaluating campaigns animates this chapter. The discussion starts with the assumption that the most important role political campaigns play in a democracy is to provide citizens with information to help them make a choice on Election Day. We then ask how campaigns might promote the democratic values of free choice, political equality, and deliberation that we discussed at the beginning of the book. The discussion concludes that although campaigns in the United States are not perfect, they do facilitate important democratic processes. How they might be improved is a complicated matter, both in theory and in practice.

Core of the Analysis

- American campaigns and elections can be evaluated in terms of key democratic values, especially free choice, equality, and deliberation.
- The American tradition of free speech makes it difficult to reform political campaigns and further these three values.
- American campaigns generally uphold the free choices and equality of citizens.
- Some proposed campaign reforms have promise, but it is not always clear whether those reforms would work and whether citizens and politicians would agree to them.

Campaigns and Democratic Values

To help visualize the role that political campaigns play in democratic elections, imagine an election without them, that is, one with no television and radio advertisements, no phone calls from campaign volunteers, no glossy mailers, and no debates. Because the candidates would not be making appearances and speeches, news outlets would rarely cover the election. On Election Day, only the most politically engaged citizens would be aware that there was even an election going on, let alone know where they needed to go to cast their ballot. Only the most motivated of those citizens would actually vote. And those who did would know very little about the candidates.

This short exercise reveals that political campaigns provide voters with information. Yet it is plainly clear to any observer that the quality of campaign information can range wildly. The goal of the following discussion is to use democratic theory to create a set of standards by which citizens can evaluate political campaigns. These standards are summarized in Table 13.1.

Free Choice

In a representative democracy, such as the United States, elections allow citizens to choose who will represent them in government. By definition, a choice involves selecting one of a number of alternatives. This means voters must be allowed to choose between at least two parties or candidates.

TABLE 13.1 What Free Choice, Equality, and Deliberation Require of Campaigns and Elections	
Free Choice	• A choice of at least two candidates • No intimidation, manipulation, or coercion of citizens
Equality	• The votes of citizens should have an equal impact on election outcomes • All candidates should be able to disseminate similar amounts of information • The rules governing campaigns and elections must apply equally to all candidates
Deliberation	• Candidates and citizens must have opportunities to deliberate before an election • Citizens must have a high volume of campaign information from a diverse range of sources • Candidates must offer reasons for the positions they take • Candidates should not be required to refrain from criticizing one another

If an election is uncontested, voters have no real choice. Yet, even when this minimal requirement has been met, free choice is not guaranteed. For example, voters can be coerced or manipulated into voting a particular way. When this happens, voters are no longer free or autonomous.

Political Equality

Political equality has always been a central value in the American political system. The principle of "one person, one vote" is a natural extension of the belief that "all men are created equal." Equal access to the ballot box, however, is not sufficient to ensure equality. Inequalities can also arise during the campaign.

In *A Preface to Democratic Theory*, the political scientist Robert Dahl argues that preserving equal political influence requires that voters possess identical information about the choices confronting them on Election Day.[5] Here, "identical" means that candidates should be able to disseminate similar amounts of information to voters so that no one candidate or party can monopolize the avenues of communication in a campaign. The constitutional scholar Ronald Dworkin arrives at the same conclusion by arguing that citizens are equals not only as voters but as candidates for office as well.[6] In fact, Dworkin contends that we should be just as concerned about the equality of candidates for office as we are about the equality of voters. He argues that all citizens—including elected officials, candidates for office, and organized groups—should have a fair and equal opportunity to publish, broadcast, or otherwise command attention for their views. A candidate who controls the flow of political communication has disproportionate influence over citizen opinion.

Political equality also requires that election rules and regulations apply equally to all candidates. In his book *Just Elections*, Dennis Thompson argues that in a truly fair election candidates would have "comparable opportunities to raise resources, unbiased rules for conducting primaries and elections, and impartial procedures for resolving disputes."[7] Some would argue that this is too demanding, because candidates may not be able to raise resources for good reasons, for example because their views are unpalatable to potential donors.

---

[5] Robert Dahl. 1956. *A Preface to Democratic Theory*. Chicago: University of Chicago Press.

[6] Ronald Dworkin. 2002. *Sovereign Virtue: The Theory and Practice of Equality*. Cambridge: Harvard University Press.

[7] Dennis Thompson. 2002. *Just Elections*. Chicago: University of Chicago Press.

Republican candidates for president in the 2012 election participated in numerous debates beginning in 2011. Did these debates and other early campaign events provide voters with the information they needed to deliberate and make a considered decision?

Deliberation

Like political equality, deliberation has long been associated with democracy. In his eulogy of democratic Athens, Pericles called the period of discussion preceding a political decision "an indispensable preliminary to any wise action at all." But political decisions, and even elections, are not inherently deliberative. The side with the most votes wins, whether or not there has been discussion. The possibility that political decisions are made without such a discussion is particularly bothersome to those in the minority. They would prefer a more deliberative campaign process so that they can try to persuade the majority. And even if they lose, such a process would leave them with the sense that they had a fair hearing.

How can we evaluate the deliberative quality of a campaign? First, there must be a large volume of information to ensure that citizens receive at least a portion of it. Second, voters must be exposed to information from diverse sources, including candidates, parties, and interest groups, so that their views are not biased because they received information from only one side. Third, campaigns should provide reasons for supporting or opposing a particular candidate. If a candidate for office says "I oppose abortion," citizens may know where the candidate stands but not know the candidate's reasoning. When candidates offer reasons for their beliefs—for example, "I oppose abortion because I believe life begins at conception and that it is immoral to end a life"—it helps citizens understand their views and encourages more discussion. Finally, deliberation demands accountability. Earnest and honest discussion requires that candidates identify themselves and take responsibility for their words.

It is important to understand that deliberation does not require that candidates refrain from criticizing one another. Because deliberation requires candidates to be honest, attacks are a concern when candidates mislead voters, but deceitful attacks must be distinguished from valid criticisms. For one, even if positive advertisements are more appealing than negative ads, politics inevitably involves disagreement, and it is important to clarify the disagreements among opposing candidates. Negative advertisements can actually be more informative in this regard than positive ads, which often mask differences and rely on innocuous images of flags, sunshine, and smiling children.

Freedom of Speech

The First Amendment of the Constitution of the United States says that "Congress shall make no law . . . abridging the freedom of speech. . . ." The First Amendment is normally interpreted as giving American citizens the legal right to speak freely and openly, without government regulation. Because free speech is a fundamental right in our country, it is difficult to regulate campaigns in ways that might promote some of the values just discussed, because such reforms would entail limits on speech and expression. For example, if political equality requires that candidates provide equivalent amounts of information to citizens, Congress could create a law that established spending limits in campaigns to prevent one candidate from spending more and thus providing more information than the other candidates. It could also create a law that prevented political candidates from spending their own money in campaigns to ensure that a wealthy candidate does not have an advantage over a less wealthy competitor. In fact, as we discussed in Chapter 4, Congress did pass a law that did both things: the Federal Election Campaign Act of 1971. However, in *Buckley v. Valeo* (424 U.S. 1, 1976), the Supreme Court ruled that these provisions were unconstitutional because they violated the free speech protections of the First Amendment.

As a result of this commitment to free speech, the United States has one of the least regulated campaign systems in the world.[8] In fact, many of the

---

[8] Bruce I. Buchanan. 2001. "Mediated Electoral Democracy: Campaigns, Incentives, and Reform," *Mediated Politics: Communication in the Future of Democracy*, eds. Lance Bennett and Robert M. Entman. New York: Cambridge University Press, p. 366.

laws and regulations that other countries have adopted to improve campaign discourse would very likely be overturned by the U.S. Supreme Court. For instance, political parties in Japan can use television advertising only to discuss policy positions and must refrain from mentioning the name or record of any individual candidate. Some other countries limit the duration of the campaign, or prohibit the publication of public opinion polls for a certain period of time before an election so that their results do not discourage people from voting. Even if Americans wanted to adopt such restrictions—which is by no means clear—they would likely violate the principle of free speech, at least as it is interpreted by contemporary U.S. courts.

In sum, the political values of free choice, equality, and deliberation require political campaigns and elections to have certain characteristics. First, free choice requires contestation, meaning that an election must feature at least two candidates. It also requires that a citizen's vote choice not be coerced or manipulated and that citizens have information about all of their vote choices. Political equality requires that citizens receive equivalent amounts of information about candidates and that the rules and regulations governing campaigns apply equally to all candidates. The value of deliberation concerns both the quantity and quality of information. Citizens must have access to a large amount of campaign information from a variety of sources. Deliberation also demands that candidates offer clear reasons for their positions and engage the arguments of their opponents. Even if Americans' commitment to free speech conflicts with some of these values, they are important values to keep in mind when evaluating campaigns.

The Reality of Political Campaigns

Is it realistic to expect campaigns to live up to all of the ideals discussed in the previous section? As we have emphasized, even if we agree that certain democratic values are important, there might be trade-offs among values, or limits on what we can reasonably expect from candidates and citizens. Thus, it is important to consider the "reality" of American campaigns.

What Do Citizens Want from Campaigns?

Do citizens want the kind of campaign that these values imply—one that focuses on substantive comparisons of the candidates and asks citizens to deliberate and participate in the electoral process? If not, then there arises a dilemma: Should campaigns be modeled on abstract values, even if citizens do not necessarily endorse these values, or should campaigns simply give citizens what they want?

What exactly do citizens say they want from political campaigns? It depends on how interested in politics they are.[9] Those who are interested in and informed about politics tend to favor more substantive and interactive campaigns—including candidate debates, town hall meetings where candidates interact with citizens, and, in general, more discussion of policy issues. Those who are less interested in politics, however, tend to favor campaigns that demand less of them, providing them with simple cues that enable them to make choices with minimal time and effort. For example, citizens who are not very interested in politics may be more interested in each candidate's résumé, including information about the candidate's political career, such as voting records, and personal life, such as credit scores and DMV records. Citizens who do not follow politics closely are thus most interested in getting a sense of who the candidates are as people. They do not necessarily want detailed analyses about where the candidates stand on the issues. Nor are they necessarily interested in investing time and energy in campaign events, such as town hall meetings, that provide venues for deeper discussion of the issues and the choices before voters in the election.

The fact that citizens do not necessarily agree about the "ideal" campaign makes it complicated to reform campaigns. That some citizens prefer less substantive campaigns does not necessarily mean that reforms aimed at making campaigns more substantive or deliberative should be abandoned. Instead, it may suggest that reformers should also look for ways to make campaigns more appealing to those who are not political sophisticated—for instance, by finding ways to provide voters with simple, digestible information, such as a short description of the candidates' issue positions next to their names on a ballot.

How Do American Campaigns Measure Up?

Americans love to hate political campaigns. They complain about negative ads but rarely tune them out. They bemoan the tactics of candidates but rarely seem to punish candidates who push the envelope of campaigning. As a result, Americans may actually create incentives for candidates to do the things that Americans claim to dislike. James Madison referred to the "the vicious arts"[10] by which candidates win elections;

---

[9] Keena Lipsitz, Christine Trost, Matthew Grossman, and John Sides. 2005. "What Voters Want from Political Campaign Communication." *Political Communication* 22: 337–54.

[10] Alexander Hamilton, James Madison, and John Jay. 1961. *The Federalist Papers.* New York: Penguin, p. 82.

but a phrase like "vicious arts" is too strong. Evaluating campaigns by the standards of free choice, equality, and deliberation reveals a more mixed portrait.[11]

Free Choice Most campaigns and elections in the United States promote free choice. In general elections, citizens usually have two or more candidates from which to choose, as well as access to information about their choices. Coercion or intimidation of voters in American is now quite rare. Although candidates do make misleading claims, it is difficult for them to lie outright without an opposing candidate or the news media challenging them. It is quite common for television news programs to include **ad watch** segments in which they dissect candidate advertising. In addition, organizations such as FactCheck.org monitor the accuracy of campaign advertisements, speeches, and interviews.

Certain aspects of American elections, however, do undermine individual free choice. Although citizens have access to an abundance of information about presidential candidates and candidates for statewide office, they have much less information about candidates in local races. Motivated citizens can learn about the candidates if they make the effort, but most lack such motivation. At best, they "accidentally" pick up information through advertisements and local media coverage. A competitive election can help citizens learn because the candidates have more money to buy advertisements and the media have more of an incentive to cover the election. The problem is that many elections are not competitive.

Indeed, as we noted in Chapters 9 and 10, a surprising number of elections in the United States are not even contested—that is, there is only one candidate, or at least only one major-party candidate, running for office. Uncontested elections occur more often in local races and state legislative races, but some U.S. House and Senate elections are also uncontested. For example, one Senate race and twelve House races were uncontested in the 2010 midterm election. Many other races are contested but feature only one major-party candidate. In recent years, there have often been fifty or more U.S. House races with only one major-party candidate. Most primaries for House, Senate, and statewide offices are uncontested. In fact, on average, just 30 percent of primaries featuring an incumbent are contested. Although one might argue that it is more important for the general election to be contested than a primary, keep in mind that many jurisdictions in the United

---

[11] This approach is advocated by and elaborated upon in Keena Lipsitz. 2011. *Competitive Elections and the American Voters*. Philadelphia: University of Pennsylvania Press, chap. 2.

States are dominated by one of the two major parties. In such jurisdictions, where the outcome of the general election is a foregone conclusion, one can argue that the choice voters make in the primary election is as important as in the general election, if not more so.

Even when races are contested by two major-party candidates, they are often not competitive. Although presidential elections remain consistently competitive, electoral competitiveness is declining in House and Senate races, in state legislative elections, and in most primary elections.[12] The level of electoral competition in local races is stable, but that is only because it is and has long been quite low. A recent study of mayoral races in 38 large cities from 1979 to 2003 found that the average margin of victory was 22 percentage points.[13] Most scholars consider a margin of less than 10 percent to be competitive. In short, a skeptic might argue that while citizens have a choice of candidates even when an election is uncompetitive, they do not really have much of a choice if one of the candidates is certain to win.

Political Equality Competitive elections in the United States produce the highest levels of political equality. Competitive races attract Democratic and Republican donors, allowing both major party candidates to get their messages out. This is because political parties, PACs, and individual contributors funnel their limited resources to races where they have the best chance of affecting the outcome. As discussed in Chapter 8, presidential elections exhibit the equalizing effects of true competition. These races are always well funded, so that major party presidential candidates invariably compete with one another on roughly equal terms. Yet, in virtually every other type of election in the United States, the lack of competitiveness means that opposing candidates compete on very unequal terms.

But is this a reason to condemn the American system? Not necessarily. First, it is important to consider whether strict equality of resources is required. The standard of strict equality makes sense when applied to voters. In a democracy, there is no legitimate basis for claiming that one person's

---

[12] Gary C. Jacobson. 2009. *The Politics of Congressional Elections.* 7th ed. New York: Pearson/Longman; Richard G. Niemi, Lynda W. Powell, William D. Berry, Thomas M. Carsey, and James M. Snyder, Jr. 2006. "Competition in State Legislative Elections, 1992–2002," in *The Marketplace of Democracy*, eds. Michael P. McDonald and John Samples. Washington, DC: Brookings Institution Press, pp. 53–73; Stephen Ansolabehere, John M. Hansen, Shigeo Hirano, and James M. Snyder, Jr. 2006. "The Decline of Competition in U.S. Primary Elections, 1908–2004," in *The Marketplace of Democracy*, eds. Michael P. McDonald and John Samples. Washington, DC: Brookings Institution Press, pp. 74–101.

[13] Neal Caren. 2007. "Big City, Big Turnout? Electoral Participation in American Cities." *Journal of Urban Affairs* 29, 1: 31–46.

vote should count more than another's. Political candidates, however, might not deserve equal resources: one of the candidates might actually be better for the job. The amount of money that candidates are able to raise reflects, in part, the confidence that citizens have in them. If citizens believe certain candidates to be untrustworthy or out of step with the district, they will not contribute to their campaigns. Likewise, PACs contribute to candidates who they believe will best represent their interests in Congress. As a result, some inequality in campaign resources may be natural.

But citizens and PACs give to candidates for other reasons that are less legitimate from the standpoint of political equality. For instance, PACs contribute to incumbents because they know they are likely to win, and the PACs want to ensure access and perhaps influence the way a politician will vote on a particular piece of legislation. Citizens may decide not to donate to candidates that they like simply because they do not think the candidates will win, thereby giving an advantage to the likely victor—who, in many cases, is also an incumbent. When campaign resource inequalities result from these kinds of calculations, they are more of a concern. It is impossible to say how much of the campaign resource inequality we see in campaigns today is due to legitimate and illegitimate reasons. Below we discuss some campaign finance reforms that might discourage giving to candidates for the illegitimate reasons described.

Another requirement of political equality is that the rules and regulations governing our electoral processes apply to all candidates equally. In one sense, our system reflects and promotes the goal of political equality: major-party candidates who run for any office in this country must abide by the same rules and regulations. But minor parties are uniquely burdened by a host of laws and regulations.[14] Consider the situation of minor-party presidential candidates. Whereas the names of the Democratic and Republican candidates automatically appear on the ballot in every state, minor-party candidates must petition state election officials to get their names on the ballot. As we noted in Chapter 2, this usually requires collecting a certain number of signatures from citizens, which can range from as few as 25 in states such as Tennessee to as many as 5 percent of a state's registered voters in states such as Montana and Oklahoma.[15] In addition, as detailed in

---

[14] Steven J. Rosenstone, Roy L. Behr, and Edward H. Lazarus. 1996. *Third Parties in America*, 2nd ed. Princeton, NJ: Princeton University Press; Samuel Issacharoff and Richard H. Pildes. 1998. "Politics as Markets: Partisan Lockups of the Democratic Process." *Stanford Law Review* 50: 643–717; Ian Shapiro. 2003. *The Moral Foundations of Politics*. New Haven, CT: Yale University Press.

[15] Rosenstone, Behr, and Lazarus, *Third Parties in America*, p. 21.

Chapter 4, presidential candidates from the two major parties are automatically eligible for public funds to finance their general election campaigns. Minor parties, on the other hand, receive public funding *after* the general election, and then only if they receive at least 5 percent of the national popular vote and appear on the ballot in at least 10 states. Minor-party candidates are also not invited to participate in televised presidential debates unless polls show that at least 15 percent of the population supports their candidacy. Of course, an election system with no barriers to ballot access or public financing would be inordinately expensive and potentially confusing for voters. Still, the current system does not treat all candidates equally.

True political equality also requires that electoral disputes be settled by a neutral arbiter. In this country, elections are administered by individuals who are affiliated with political parties. In 33 states, the secretary of state or chief election official is chosen through a partisan election. In the remaining states, the position is usually filled by gubernatorial appointment. No state uses a nonpartisan election process. The most obvious consequence of having party loyalists occupying such positions is the potential for political bias. Most rules governing elections have consequences that benefit one party more than the other. For example, making it harder to vote by limiting voting hours or requiring voters to present a photo identification typically helps Republican candidates. Conversely, making it easier to vote usually helps Democrats. Since most people do not want to wait in long lines, reducing the number of polling places in an area dominated by an opponent can lower turnout among her supporters.[16]

In addition, when there are election disputes, such as in Florida after the 2000 presidential election, this bias has the potential to affect the outcome of an election by swaying the decisions of election officials. The lack of neutral election officials creates the problem of "foxes guarding henhouses."

Deliberation American campaigns do offer opportunities for deliberation, but critics contend that they could offer more. Deliberation depends on both the quantity and quality of information provided to citizens. As we have discussed, the quantity of information depends on the competitiveness of the election. Because the majority of races in the United States are not competitive, citizens are arguably receiving less information than deliberation demands.

---

[16] Heather Gerken. 2009. *The Democracy Index*. Princeton, NJ: Princeton University Press, p. 16.

The quality of information depends on whether candidates address similar issues, offer specific positions on those issues, and provide the reasoning for their positions. Deliberative events such as debates offer an opportunity for candidates to communicate this kind of information. Debates require candidates to address the same topics—typically, those posed by a moderator—and give them time to explain and defend their thinking. But debates are not necessarily the best forums for deliberation. For one, their occurrence usually depends on the whims of candidates. Candidates who believe that their interests are not served by participating in a debate can avoid them. Moreover, the format of debates may reflect the strategic goals of the candidate more than what is "good" for the electorate. The format and rules governing debates are agreed upon in advance by the candidates. For example, candidates participating in presidential debates usually sign a binding contract that lays out the debate rules. In the past, these rules have stipulated that candidates have no more than thirty seconds to respond to a question and that the candidates cannot ask each other direct questions. These rules reduce uncertainty for the candidates and limit the possibility that they will make mistakes, both of which are desirable from the perspective of campaign consultants. Such restrictions could, however, undermine the "give and take" between the candidates and limit the deliberative value of the debate.

Outside of debates, candidates have much more flexibility and freedom in how they communicate with voters. Here again, competition is crucial in whether campaigns will live up to deliberative values. In competitive elections, candidates are much more likely to talk about the same issues—and thus engage in a true dialogue—during the campaign.[17] They are also more likely to offer specific statements of their issue positions.[18] For example, competition might make the difference between a candidate's saying "I want to improve education" and "I want to improve education by giving students and their parents education vouchers so they can leave a failing public school." Obviously the latter statement provides voters with a better sense of the policies a candidate will pursue if elected. Increased competition leads to greater issue specificity because candidates in tight races must be clear about their issue positions to attract money and to aggressively confront their opponents. When races are not competitive, however, candidates are more likely to offer bland statements that convey little information to voters.

---

[17] Noah Kaplan, David K. Park, and Travis N. Ridout. 2006. "Dialogue in American Political Campaigns? An Examination of Issue Convergence in Candidate Television Advertising." *American Journal of Political Science* 50, 3: 724–36.

[18] Kim Fridkin Kahn and Patrick J. Kenney. 1999. *The Spectacle of U.S. Senate Campaigns.* Princeton, NJ: Princeton University Press.

There have been efforts to increase the quality of information provided by American campaigns. The Bipartisan Campaign Reform Act of 2002 included a "stand by your ad" provision that requires candidates to state their approval of their advertisements—for example, "I am John Smith and I approve this message." In radio advertisements, this requires an audio statement by the candidate that offers identification and approval. In television advertisements, candidates must also personally approve of the ad through either a visual appearance or an audio voice-over. In addition, the candidate's name must appear at the end of the advertisement in "a clearly readable manner" for at least four seconds. Failure to comply with these provisions can result in a fine by the Federal Election Commission. More important, candidates who fail to comply with this requirement can lose their "lowest unit rate" status— political candidates are typically charged the lowest advertising rate possible for a time slot—for the duration of their campaign. This provision in the law is intended to reduce negativity, but it also forces candidates to take visible responsibility for their advertising, which contributes to deliberation.

Reforming Campaigns

The preceding discussion highlighted some strengths and weakness of American campaigns. For the most part, American campaigns protect the free choice and political equality of citizens, but they do not create equal opportunities for candidates. The resulting inequalities can undermine the deliberative quality of elections. Are there reforms that might make political campaigns better? As we have discussed throughout this book, identifying effective reforms is not easy. A reform may further one value while undermining another. For example, limiting candidate spending to help ensure that citizens have more balanced information from competing candidates would restrict freedom of speech. A reform may also simply not work. Consider televised ad watches, in which news programs evaluate the truthfulness of campaign advertisements. Ad watches have been shown to have the perverse effect of reinforcing the advertisement's content rather than countering it because viewers can only remember the ad, not the critique of it.[19] Or consider the idea that candidates and campaign consultants should pledge publicly not to campaign negatively. Such a pledge may fail because

---

[19] Lori Melton McKinnon and Lynda Lee Kaid. 1999. "Exposing Negative Campaigning or Enhancing Advertising Effects: An Experimental Study of Ad Watch Effects on Voters' Evaluations of Candidates and their Ads." *Journal of Applied Communication Research* 27, 3: 217–36.

few candidates and consultants are willing to adopt or respect it and because citizens actually learn as much or more from negative campaigning as from positive campaigning.[20]

In this section, we examine seven reforms whose advocates believe would improve the content and conduct of campaigns in the United States (see Table 13.2). We discuss their effectiveness, as measured by current research, as well as whether the public is likely to support the reforms. If citizens are not enthusiastic about a reform and do not understand its importance, then its chances of being adopted are slim.

Making All Elections Publicly Financed

Although presidential candidates have access to public financing, most other candidates for political office in the United States do not. Providing candidates with public financing would enhance political equality because it would help underfunded challengers compete with well-heeled incumbents. It would also improve electoral competitiveness, which encourages candidates to provide voters with the kinds of information that facilitate deliberation.[21] Public financing may also improve individual free choice by encouraging more people to run for office and ensure that more elections are contested. But the effects depend on the amount of public funding provided. For example, Hawaii and Wisconsin provide only a small amount of public money to state legislative candidates, rendering their programs less effective. Other states, such as Minnesota and Arizona, provide more money and appear to have had greater success with respect to enhancing competitiveness.[22]

Citizens must therefore be prepared to fund public financing programs generously to make them work. There is little evidence, however, that Americans are willing to do so. For example, fewer than 12 percent of U.S. citizens filing federal tax returns typically check the box on their tax form indicating that they would like to donate $3 to the Presidential Election Campaign Fund (the source of public funding for presidential candidates).[23] Citizens

---

[20] L. Sandy Maisel, Darrell M. West, and Brett M. Clifton. 2007. *Evaluating Campaign Quality: Can the Electoral Process Be Improved?* New York: Cambridge University Press; Richard R. Lau, Lee Sigelman, and Ivy Brown Rovner. 2007. "The Effects of Negative Political Campaigns: A Meta-Analytic Reassessment." *Journal of Politics* 69, 4: 1176–1209.

[21] Lipsitz, *Competitive Elections.*

[22] Kenneth R. Mayer, Timothy Werner, and Amanda Williams. 2006. "Do Public Financing Programs Enhance Competition?" in *The Marketplace of Democracy*, eds. Michael P. McDonald and John Samples. Washington, DC: Brookings Institution Press, pp. 245–67.

[23] Tax Foundation. 2008. "Presidential Election Campaign Fund Untapped by Obama Claims Little Support from Taxpayers." News Release. www.taxfoundation.org/press/show/23306.html (accessed 6/7/11).

TABLE 13.2 Reforming American Campaigns and Elections

Reform	Free Choice	Equality	Deliberation	Support among public?
Publicly finance campaigns	✓	✓		Medium[a]
Make campaign donations anonymous		✓		None
Adopt the national popular vote		✓		Medium[b]
Reform the redistricting process		✓		Low[c]
Create neutral election administration positions		✓		None
Use deliberative polls			✓	None
Create a national day of deliberation			✓	None
Use citizen juries to make recommendations			✓	None

[a] Primo, "Reformers vs. Reality."
[b] Level of support based on number of newspapers endorsing the National Popular Vote, including the *New York Times, Chicago Sun-Times,* and *Los Angeles Times,* among others. Polls conducted for the National Popular Vote also indicate a high level of support, although it unclear how much of a priority the reform is.
[c] Pew, "Lack of Competition."
Note: Support among the public is categorized as "low" support or "some" support, but could theoretically range higher. In the cases where we have indicated "None" we mean that most people have never heard of the reform, which is why there is no support for it.

are reluctant to check this box even though the tax form assures them that doing so does not increase the amount of tax they pay. As we noted in Chapter 4, even if a majority of citizens do support publicly financed campaigns in the abstract, they do not necessarily consider campaign finance reform an important priority.[24] Moreover, incumbent politicians have little incentive to pass a reform that would essentially give campaign funds to their opponents.

---

[24] David M. Primo. 2002. "Reformers vs. Reality." *The Independent Review* 7, 2: 202–19.

Making Campaign Donations Anonymous

Another way to reform campaigns would be to make all donations anonymous. This reform accepts the role of private donations; there may be nothing inherently wrong with citizens contributing to a candidate who they feel will represent them effectively. The potential problem is that some citizens may contribute to candidates because they want access or a favor in return. Making donations anonymous would eliminate this possibility, since candidates could never learn who had given them money. Candidates and political parties would no longer be able to accept checks directly from individuals and PACs. Instead, an individual or PAC would give to a blind trust established in the candidate's or political party's name. It is possible that individuals could tell a candidate or party that they made a large contribution, but talk is cheap, and under this system anyone could make such a claim. Supporters call this idea the **donation booth**: just as ballots are cast in secret in the voting booth, donations would be made in secret as well.[25]

A relevant question is whether anonymous donations would reduce the amount of money—and, hence, the amount of communication—in campaigns. Many contributors might not give money if they do not think candidates will acknowledge their donations. Moreover, few Americans have heard of this reform so its advocates will have the additional burden of explaining to citizens what it is.

Limiting Campaign Spending

Although U.S. citizens are ambivalent about public financing, they do support limits on campaign spending. Even so, there is considerable debate about how spending limits would affect elections. Although some contend that spending limits hurt challengers—who need to spend a lot to successfully compete against incumbents—spending limits actually have little effect on challenger success.[26] Moreover, the Supreme Court has ruled that

---

[25] Ian Ayres and Jeremy Bulow. "The Donation Booth." http://faculty-gsb.stanford.edu/bulow/articles/The%20donation%20booth.pdf (accessed 6/7/11).

[26] Alan S. Gerber. 1998. "Estimating the Effect of Campaign Spending on Senate Election Outcomes Using Instrumental Variables." *American Political Science Review* 92, 2: 401–11; Steven D. Levitt. 1994. "Using Repeat Challengers to Estimate the Effect of Challenger Spending on Election Outcomes in the U.S. House." *Journal of Political Economy* 102, 4: 777–98; Donald P. Green and Jonathan S. Krasno. 1990. "Rebuttal to Jacobson's 'New Evidence for Old Arguments'." *American Journal of Political Science* 34, 2: 363–72; Donald P. Green and Jonathan S. Krasno. 1988. "Salvation for the Spendthrift Incumbent: Reestimating the Effects of Campaign Spending in House Elections." *American Journal of Political Science* 32, 4: 884–907. But see Gary C. Jacobson. 1990. "The Effects of Campaign Spending in House Elections: New Evidence for Old Arguments." *American Journal of Political Science* 34, 2: 334–62; Gary C. Jacobson. 1978. "The Effects of Campaign Spending in Congressional Elections." *American Political Science Review* 72: 769–83.

spending limits are a violation of free speech and, consequently, cannot be imposed on candidates. Candidates can, however, volunteer to limit their spending in exchange for public funding (see Chapters 4 and 8). Thus, public financing and spending limits are usually linked in our political system. This means that the fate of the latter depends on the fate of the former.

Reforming the Redistricting Process

As we discussed in Chapter 2, states typically redraw the boundaries of congressional and state legislative districts after the decennial national census. State legislatures are most often responsible for determining these boundaries, and their plans must be approved by the state's governor. This process means that any party that controls the legislature and governor's mansion can draw district lines in a manner that protects its members, as well as incumbents more generally. Thus, redistricting has been linked to two trends: the increase in the incumbency advantage and the decrease in electoral competitiveness. Both of these limit free choice and political equality. As discussed in Chapter 9, the proposals for reforming the redistricting process involve either bypassing the state legislatures and giving power to independent commissions, or officially adopting redistricting guidelines that mandate enhanced competition.

There is some evidence that such measures do, in fact, work against incumbents to enhance electoral competitiveness, although there is a considerable debate about how large a factor it is.[27] However, there is little

---

[27] Michael P. McDonald. 2006. "Drawing the Line on District Competition." *PS: Political Science and Politics* 39, 1: 91–94; Michael P. McDonald. 2006. "Re-Drawing the Line on District Competition." *PS: Political Science and Politics* 39, 1: 99–102; Michael P. McDonald. 2006. "Redistricting and Competitive Districts," in *The Marketplace of Democracy*, eds. Michael P. McDonald and John Sample. Washington, D.C.: Brookings Institution Press, pp. 222–44; Bruce E. Cain, Karin MacDonald, and Michael P. McDonald. 2005. "From Equality to Fairness: The Path of Political Reform," in *Party Lines: Competition, Partisanship, and Congressional Redistricting*, eds. Thomas E. Mann and Bruce E. Cain. Washington D.C.: Brookings Institution Press, pp. 6-30; Michael Lyons and Peter F. Galderisi. 1995. "Incumbency, Reapportionment and U.S. House Redistricting." *Political Research Quarterly* 48, 4: 857–71. Edward R. Tufte. 1973. "The Relationship Between Seats and Votes in Two-Party Systems." *American Political Science Review* 67, 2: 540–55. But see Gary C. Jacobson. 2006. "Competition in U.S. Congressional Elections," in *The Marketplace of Democracy*, eds. Michael P. McDonald and John Samples. Washington, D.C.: Brookings Instititution Press, pp. 27–52; Alan I. Abramowitz and Kyle Saunders. 2005. "Why Can't We All Just Get Along? The Reality of a Polarized America." *Forum: A Journal of Applied Research in Contemporary Politics* 3, 2; Alan I. Abramowitz, Brad Alexander, and Matthew Gunning. 2006. "Incumbency, Redistricting, and the Decline of Competition in U.S. House Elections." *Journal of Politics* 68, 1: 75–88. Alan I. Abramowitz, Brad Alexander, and Matthew Gunning. 2006. "Don't Blame Redistricting for Uncompetitive Elections." *PS: Political Science and Politics* 39, 1: 87–90; Alan I. Abramowitz, Brad Alexander, and Matthew Gunning. 2006. "Drawing the Line on District Competition: A Rejoinder." *PS: Political Science and Politics* 39, 1: 95–98.

evidence that American citizens care about redistricting. In 2006, the Pew Research Center for the People and the Press conducted the first survey dedicated to assessing the public's level of knowledge of (and concern about) the declining competitiveness of House elections.[28] Survey respondents did not share the concerns of politicians and political experts about declining electoral competitiveness and were not aware of redistricting debates. Nor were they aware of whether the elections in their own congressional district tended to be competitive. Perhaps more important, most respondents did not see any benefits to increased competitiveness. When asked about how a tough election affects a politician, 22 percent said it "makes them work harder to represent their district better," while 62 percent said tough campaigns make politicians "focus too much on fund-raising and campaigning instead of being a good representative." Such numbers suggest that the impetus for redistricting reform is unlikely to come from the public any time soon. As was the case with public financing, politicians often have little incentive to support redistricting reform, especially if they believe it would alter the boundaries of their own districts or cost their party seats in Congress or the state legislature.

Reforming or Abolishing the Electoral College in Presidential Elections

The Electoral College undermines citizen equality because the manner in which it functions makes the vote of citizens in battleground states worth more than those of citizens in non-battleground states. We have also discussed how the Electoral College creates incentives for campaigns to allocate more time, money, and attention to citizens in battleground states. Electoral College reformers tend to fall into one of two categories: those who would abolish or effectively bypass it; and those who would simply eliminate the "winner-take-all" rule—where the winner takes all of the state's electors—in exchange for a more representative allocation of electoral votes. As mentioned in Chapter 8, some reformers in the first category advocate requiring states to allocate their state's electoral votes to the winner of the national popular vote (this is the so-called National Popular Vote movement). This reform is more likely to take effect than the constitutional amendment, which would be required to eliminate the Electoral College, because it requires the support of only the legislatures in states with a total of 270 electoral votes. The second class of reforms usually involves

---

[28] Andrew Kohut, Scott Keeter, and Carroll Doherty. 2006. "Lack of Competition in Elections Fails to Stir Public." Pew Research Center for the People and the Press, the Brookings Institution, and the Cato Institute. http://people-press.org/reports/pdf/294.pdf (accessed 6/7/11).

exchanging the winner-take-all rule for either a proportional allocation or an allocation of electoral votes based on electoral outcomes in individual congressional districts. Because basing electoral votes on candidate performance in congressional districts would politicize the redistricting process even more than it already is, most reformers prefer allocating electoral votes according to a system of proportional representation.

Although many Americans have a sense of what it means to live in a battleground state during a presidential election, only the most politically astute understand how the Electoral College works and why the National Popular Vote might be desirable.[29] Despite the lack of widespread popular support, NPV bills have been introduced in virtually every state. Eight states, including California, Hawaii, Illinois, Maryland, Massachusetts, New Jersey, Vermont, and Washington, as well as the District of Columbia, have passed an NPV measure, which will take effect only when enough states have adopted the reform to provide the winner with an Electoral College majority (270). At this point, the law has been enacted by states with a total of 132 electoral votes. NPV supporters have been dealt a setback, however, by the New York State Assembly, which refuses to hear an NPV law passed by the state senate. Without the state's 29 electoral votes, it will be difficult for the NPV to reach 270.

Furthermore, adopting a national popular vote for president would not necessarily enhance citizen equality. Candidates who currently campaign in battleground states because of the Electoral College would not allocate their resources evenly across the nation if there were a national vote. Instead, they would focus on areas of the country where large concentrations of swing voters reside. The bottom line is that candidates have finite resources and, as we have stressed throughout this book, will be strategic about how they use them.

Making Election Administration Neutral

Political equality requires that the rules and regulations governing elections be enforced in a neutral manner, but most election officials in the United States are party loyalists. One way to reform the system is to create nonpartisan, professional election administrators. Election administrators could be chosen by a commission that would include representatives from major and minor parties to ensure that the enforcement of election laws did not discriminate against minor parties or the non-incumbent party. Once

---

[29] Darshan Goux. 2006. "A New Battleground? Media Perceptions and Political Reality in Presidential Elections, 1960–2004." Paper presented at the American Political Science Association Annual Meeting, Philadelphia, PA.

selected by the commission, members could serve for a relatively long term to further insulate them from partisan politics.

In the wake of the 2000 presidential election, many hoped that Congress or the courts would address election administration reform. Their hopes have met with disappointment. As a result, election law scholars have offered alternative methods to enhance democracy. One scholar proposed the creation of a **Democracy Index** that would rank all states and localities based on election performance.[30] Such indices are quite common for ranking how democratic countries are. The ranking for states and localities in the United States would take into account a variety of factors, including whether the state has a neutral election official, whether eligible citizens can easily register and vote, whether every vote is counted properly, and whether registered voters rolls are accurate. The Democracy Index is intended to influence through embarrassment; its proponents believe that states ranked at the bottom will want to improve their marks. Other scholars recommend a more conventional approach of pushing election reform packages through Congress and the state legislatures. History shows that election reforms can be passed when there is unified party control of the executive and legislative branches.[31]

Irrespective of the path to reform, the fair and neutral administration of American elections is likely to improve political equality. But reformers face an "invisibility" problem when pushing for election reform. Citizens become concerned about election administration problems only when the election is close. Once the election is over, they quickly forget about the problems. Furthermore, the practical consequences of administering elections in a partisan manner are not always obvious. If a Democratic administrator fails to provide a sufficient number of ballots to a Republican precinct, it may or may not influence who wins the election. Improving the administration of elections would be good for democracy, but this reform may seem less important unless citizens see that it affects election outcomes.

Increasing Opportunities for Deliberation

A final set of reforms is intended to improve opportunities for voter deliberation within campaigns. Many proposals focus on increasing the frequency of candidate debates and town hall meetings, the two most obvious forums in which candidates and voters interact. There are also some more innovative

---

[30] Gerken, *The Democracy Index*

[31] Richard Hansen. 2010. "Election Administration Reform and the New Institutionalism." *California Law Review* 98, 3: 1075–1100.

ideas for enhancing deliberation. One is the **deliberative poll.**[32] Deliberative polls, which were developed in the United States and have been used
around the world, begin by identifying and interviewing a random sample of
citizens about some set of issues or candidates. Then respondents to the poll
are asked to travel (all expenses paid) to some location for two or three days,
where they listen to a range of different speakers and arguments about the
same issues or candidates. They are then reinterviewed, and changes in their
opinions are taken as evidence of the impact of deliberation. Ideally, these
deliberative polls are aired on television so that other citizens can watch
what happens when fellow citizens are given the time and space to think
deeply about issues or electoral choices. A companion proposal would have
the federal government sponsor a national **Day of Deliberation**, in which
citizens are given paid time off from work to attend meetings to discuss the
upcoming election.[33]

Another proposal is to convene **citizen juries**—randomly selected panels
of people who would deliberate for several days about the choices in the
election—to develop recommendations on which ballot measures and candidates to support.[34] Voters would learn about the recommendations and
endorsements of these citizen panels through voting guides or sample ballots. This would simultaneously increase deliberation and lessen the costs of
voting for individual citizens.

Despite their potential benefits, it is unclear whether citizens would
participate in deliberative forums or accept the recommendations of those
who have. Furthermore, individuals who are exposed to disagreement—a
natural part of these deliberative exercises—can become ambivalent about
politics and less likely to participate in elections.[35] Thus, achieving the goal
of increased deliberation in campaigns and elections might come at the cost
of lower participation.

There are some practical concerns as well. Deliberative forums are relatively expensive and place substantial demands upon the participants. These
forums also require that the candidates or their representatives take an
active part in the process, something they may be reluctant to do. Moreover,

---

[32] James S. Fishkin. 1995. *The Voice of the People: Public Opinion and Democracy.* New
Haven, CT: Yale University Pres.

[33] Bruce Ackerman and James S. Fishkin. 2005. *Deliberation Day.* New Haven, CT: Yale
University Press.

[34] John Gastil. 2000. *By Popular Demand: Revitalizing Representative Democracy Through
Deliberative Elections.* Berkeley: University of California Press.

[35] Diana Mutz. 2006. *Hearing the Other Side: Deliberative vs. Participatory Democracy.*
Cambridge: Cambridge University Press.

publicizing the results or recommendations of deliberative forums requires collaboration with the news media or the state governments, and it is unclear whether such collaborations would take place.

Conclusion

Campaigns in the United States are heavily influenced by rules and institutions, by the broader political reality, by strategic considerations, and by the voters themselves. The larger point is the manner in which campaigns function is logical, given the context of the American political system. This is not to say that they are perfect or should not be improved. It is simply to say that they are neither inherently bad nor somehow irrational. They can be analyzed systematically and judged on their own terms.

But campaigns also play a vital role in democracy. So while they can be judged and analyzed on their own terms, they should also be measured against the standards of democratic theory. We have evaluated American campaigns in terms of three standards: free choice, political equality, and citizen deliberation. In some ways, American campaigns live up to these standards. When contested, campaigns force incumbent politicians to account for themselves, provide voters with information about their electoral choices, and encourage citizens to become politically involved. In other ways, American campaigns fall short, particularly because they are often uncompetitive, and competition directly facilitates each of these three values.

There are reforms that could improve the democratic performance of election campaigns in the United States, but it is not clear whether enough citizens or politicians support these reforms or whether reforms would withstand challenges on free-speech grounds. Perhaps the most practical and effective reforms would be establishing neutral election administration and increasing the frequency of candidate debates and town hall meetings. Neutral election administration would help guarantee that election rules apply to all candidates and parties equally. Encouraging candidates to engage in more debates and town hall meetings would create more opportunities for deliberation. And while parties and candidates will surely resist these reforms due to the increased uncertainty and risk that they would bring, they are less opposed to these reforms than many others, such as public financing and redistricting reform.

These changes will not make American campaigns perfect. In fact, even if all of the reforms considered here were to be adopted tomorrow, citizens would almost certainly still have reservations about their politicians and the election process. Some of this reflects partisan reactions to a competitive system: when your side loses, you tend to question the process. Some of this reflects the long and honorable American tradition of complaining about politics and politicians. But despite Americans' avowed distaste for election campaigns, surveys show that they still believe that their democratic system is the best in the world. Furthermore, campaigns in other parts of the world are beginning to look more like those in the United States. The question, then, is how to preserve and expand the engaging, entertaining, and creative aspects of the American experiment in mass democracy. The answer is critical to the long-term health of the American system of government.

KEY TERMS

ad watch (p. 382)

donation booth (p. 390)

Democracy Index (p. 394)

deliberative poll (p. 395)

Day of Deliberation (p. 395)

citizen juries (p. 395)

FOR DISCUSSION

1. Which of the values discussed in this chapter—free choice, equality, deliberation, or free speech—do you think is most important for campaigns in democratic elections? Why?

2. Given the challenges facing this country, how important do you think it is to reform our political campaigns?

3. Would you participate in a town hall meeting about local candidates? Why or why not?

4. The authors of this book argue that political campaigns receive a passing grade in terms of how they serve democracy. Have they convinced you?

 Visit StudySpace for quizzes and other review material.
wwnorton.com/studyspace

GLOSSARY

501(c) organizations—Organizations that are exempt from federal taxation and may be able to engage in political activity, subject to certain restrictions

527 organization—Officially designated political organization under the tax code, and required to disclose its contributors to the Internal Revenue Service. These organizations came to the fore in 2004, the first election after BCRA's ban on soft money for parties.

absentee voting—The process by which citizens who cannot vote in person on Election Day request that ballots be mailed to their homes, and then vote by mailing those ballots to election officials

ad watch—A feature in media outlets in which journalists study campaign ads and comment on their content and truthfulness

agenda setting—The news media's ability to influence the issues that the public regards as important by selecting which stories to cover

at-large elections—Geographic units that elect multiple members as their representatives

attack ads—Advertisements in which supporters of one candidate question the character, ethics, and/or integrity of their candidate's opponent

Australian ballot—A method of voting by secret ballot, widely adopted in the United States in the early part of the 1900s, that made it impossible for casual observers or party workers to determine for whom a citizen had cast a vote

ballot initiatives—Measures that affect laws or public policy and that are proposed by interested citizens and then voted on by citizens in elections

battleground/swing states—States that are competitive between the major party candidates and whose outcome may decide the presidential election

Bipartisan Campaign Reform Act (BCRA)—2002 law that prohibited soft money spending by national, state, and local parties, limited soft money spending by outside groups, and increased individual contribution limits

blanket/jungle primary—Election in which all candidates for each office are listed on the ballot, and anyone registered to vote in that election may vote for any one candidate; typically, the top two vote-getters advance to a second, runoff election

blogs—Web sites with regularly updated stories that often have a more personalized and conversational style; originally short for web logs

Buckley v. Valeo—1976 decision overturning the Federal Election Campaign Act's limits on spending by federal candidates as a violation of the First Amendment

Bush model—Campaign strategy focusing efforts on identifying partisans and getting them to the polls

campaign—An organized effort to persuade and mobilize voters to support or oppose a party or candidate

campaign strategy—A campaign's understanding of how its candidate is going to win the election, who will vote for the candidate, and why

casework—The work performed by members of Congress or their staff to help constituents deal with government bureaucracies

caucuses—Relatively closed affairs in which registered partisans attend meetings at election precinct locations and vote to select delegates to the county or state party conventions

citizen juries—Randomly selected panels of people who deliberate about the choices in the election to develop recommendations for other citizens

citizen legislature—A legislature in which serving as a legislator is a part-time position that comes with relatively little salary or staff support

Citizens United v. Federal Election Commission—2010 decision holding that under the First Amendment, corporate funding of independent political broadcasts in candidate elections cannot be limited

civil service—Government jobs or positions in which employment and promotions are based on professional qualifications and performance

clean elections systems—A system of campaign finance whereby candidates who raise a minimum amount of private donations qualify for public funding from the government. Once they accept public funding, they cannot spend any more money raised from private donors.

Clinton model—Campaign strategy focusing on identifying persuadable voters and reaching out to them with poll-tested, popular issue positions

closed primary—Election for the party's nominee in which only those registered as party members can vote

coattails effect—When a popular high-profile candidate is on the ballot, lesser known candidates in that candidate's party benefit from that candidate's appeal to voters—they "ride the coattails" of the high-profile candidate

communities of interest—Redistricting principle that districts should attempt to keep together citizens in areas that share a political history or set of interests

contrast advertisements—Advertisements in which supporters of a candidate seek to favorably compare their candidate's record and positions to their opponents' record and positions

convenience voting—Absentee, early, or mail-in voting conducted before Election Day to facilitate turnout

convention bump/convention bounce—Increased support for a candidate resulting from the party's national convention

coordinated expenditures—Money that political parties spend to help cover a candidate's campaign costs in a federal election. Such expenditures are limited by law.

cross pressures—Two or more beliefs, identities, or issue positions that pull a voter in different partisan directions

Day of Deliberation—A paid day for citizens to take time off from work to attend meetings to discuss an upcoming election

delegates—People chosen to vote for the presidential nominee of the party at the national convention

deliberative poll—A type of survey in which a random sample of citizens are asked about some set of issues or candidates, then attend a meeting in which they think about or discuss these issues more, and then answer a second set of questions to see if their opinions have changed

Democracy Index—A ranking of all states and localities based on how democratic their elections are

Democratic Party (1828–present)—Political party associated with Andrew Jackson, representing interests suspicious of entrenched commercial class; the first party to embrace mass democratic participation

donation booth—A blind trust established in a candidate's or political party's name into which individuals or PACs can make anonymous donations

Duverger's Law—Single-member, simple plurality election systems tend to produce two major political parties

earned media/free media—The publicity that candidates get by engaging in promotional activities

election—The selection of persons to hold public office by means of a vote

electoral participation—The range of activities by which individuals attempt to affect the outcome of an election

era of pre-democratic campaigns—Time between the ratification of the U. S. Constitution in 1788 and the widespread expansion of elected public offices in the 1820s

express advocacy—Specifically advocating the election or defeat of a candidate

external efficacy—The belief that the political system will be responsive to one's desires and needs

Federal Election Campaign Act (FECA)—1971 law, substantially amended in 1974, that set limits on contributions to federal campaigns, provided for public funding of presidential election campaigns, mandated contribution disclosure and finance report filings, established the Federal Election Commission to oversee finance laws, and set limits on candidate spending. The last of these provisions was overturned by the Supreme Court.

Federal Election Commission (FEC)—The regulatory agency that enforces the laws governing federal elections

Federalist Party (1796–1828)—Political party associated with Alexander Hamilton, representing a more expansive view of federal governing power, especially with respect to regulating commercial interests; support was strongest in the northeastern states

focus groups—A form of qualitative research in which a group of people are asked about their perceptions, opinions, beliefs, and attitudes toward a product, service, concept, advertisement, idea, or packaging. Questions are asked in an interactive group setting where participants are free to talk with other group members. In campaigns, small groups of persuadable voters interviewed in depth to gather additional data and test specific issue positions.

framing—Choosing the language to define a debate and fitting individual issues into the contexts of broader story lines. The news media's ability to influence what the public thinks is at stake in a debate by categorizing issues into one of many possible interpretations.

franking privilege—The ability of members of Congress to send mail to constituents without postage

front-loading—Moving statewide nominating contests earlier in the calendar to increase their influence

front-porch campaign—Tactic whereby the candidate stays at home and allows his campaign team to arrange for select meetings with news media outlets

front-runner—Candidate perceived to have the money, experience, and popular support to win

generational cohort—A group of people who came of age politically at about the same time

gerrymandering—Drawing district lines to maximize some political interest

get-out-the-vote (GOTV) efforts—The efforts of candidates, parties, and interest groups to get citizens to vote

hard money—Money raised in accord with campaign finance laws

Hill Committees—A term used to refer to the four major party campaign committees involved in congressional elections

horse race journalism—News reporting that focuses on which candidates are becoming more or less likely to win an election as well as what each candidate is doing to improve their standing in the polls

incumbency advantage—The vote share earned by an incumbent compared to what a non-incumbent would have earned if he or she had run

incumbent—The candidate in an election who already occupies the office

independent candidates—Persons running for office who are not affiliated with any particular political party

independent expenditure committees—Political action committees that can raise unlimited donations from various sources and then spend money to advocate for or against candidates

independent expenditures—A piece of campaign communication by an independent group that engages in express advocacy; party expenditures made without consulting or coordinating with a candidate

infotainment—Media content that provides a combination of information and entertainment, such as comedy news programs or coverage of celebrities

interest group—A collection of people with the shared goal of influencing public policy that does not run its own candidates for office

internal efficacy—Confidence that one has the ability to understand and engage in politics

interpretive journalism—News reporting that includes analysis of the reasons why events happen and the likely effects that the events will have

issue advocacy—Advocating a position on a political issue without explicitly advocating for the election or defeat of a candidate

issue ownership—Concept that political parties have differential credibility on certain issues, and that their candidates try to win elections by convincing voters that issues they "own" are the most important for a given election

literacy tests—Knowledge questions asked by election officials at the polls; used to prevent blacks from voting in southern states, and were suspended in states where turnout was less than 50 percent of the age-eligible population by the Civil Rights Act (1965)

magic words—Words that make an advertisement subject to campaign finance laws and regulations

majority-minority districts—Districts in which racial or ethnic minorities form a majority of the population

malapportionment—Any significant differences in the number of citizens across districts

material benefit—A reward or payment received in exchange for political participation

median voter theorem—In a majority election, if voter policy preferences can be represented as a point along a single dimension, and if all voters vote for the candidate who commits to a policy position closest to their own preference, and if there are only two candidates, then a candidate maximizes her votes by committing to the policy position preferred by the median voter

microtargeting—Rating the voting behavior of every individual on the registered voter list

based on a statistical model of the vote estimated from a large random sample

mobilization—The range of activities that candidates, parties, activists, and interest groups engage in to encourage people to participate

Motor Voter Act—A federal law requiring states to allow voters to register when they are applying for a driver's license and public assistance programs or to allow Election Day registration

narrow-casting—Targeting a message to a small audience using e-mail, direct mail, and telephone calls

negative campaigning—Campaign messages that consist of criticism leveled by one candidate against another during a campaign

new media—Communication outlets designed to reach online audiences developed after the rise of the Internet

news values—The criteria reporters and editors use to determine what is newsworthy, such as how recently an event occurred and whether is was unexpected

one person, one vote—The principle that each person's vote should have equal weight in determining representation; first articulated in *Reynolds v. Sims* (1964)

open primary—Election for the parties' nominees in which registrants are allowed to vote in any primary they choose (but only in one)

open seat—An election in which no incumbent is running

opinion leaders—Individuals who follow politics and help inform other members of the group about issues and candidates

pack journalism—The tendency of reporters to read and discuss each other's stories and converge on a similar narrative about the campaign

panel study—Survey that interviews respondents at one point in time and then re-interviews at a later point in time in order to measure change in their opinions

participatory distortion—Occurs when certain groups of citizens have a greater impact on the political process than other groups

party-as-organization—The institutions, professionals, and activists that administer party affairs, including the official bodies that raise funds and create the rules for the party

party identification—A citizen's allegiance to one of the political parties, including both party preference and level of commitment

party-in-government—The members of a party who hold public office

party-in-the-electorate—The group of citizens who identify with a political party or regularly support candidates from one party

permanent campaign—The notion that candidates never stop campaigning because of the constant need to raise money for the next election cycle

personal vote—That portion of an elected official's vote share that can be attributed to their relationship with constituents

persuadable/swing votes—The number of voters in a given election who are not committed to supporting a particular candidate. This is usually estimated by the percentage point difference between the maximum and minimum vote for a major party's candidates across recent elections.

persuasion—Convincing undecided voters to support a particular candidate or convincing the other party's supporters to defect

plurality rule—A way of determining who wins elections in which the candidate with the most votes wins (even if they do not get a majority of the votes)

pocketbook voting—Choosing between candidates based on how one's personal finances have faired during the incumbent party's rule

political action committee (PAC)—Private group organized to elect political candidates

political amateur—A candidate with no political experience

political interest—Having an ongoing interest in politics

political machines—Party organizations that mobilized lower status citizens to win office, and then used government to reward party

workers and bestow services and benefits to their constituents

political parties—Group of people with the shared interest of electing public officials under a common label

poll taxes—Fee requirements for voting; typically used to keep blacks from voting in southern states, and outlawed by the Voting Rights Act (1965)

positive campaigning—Campaign messages in which candidates make an affirmative case for their election based on their background, experience, record, or issue positions

primary election—Election in which voters select the candidate that will run for the party in the general election

priming—The news media's ability to influence the criteria that citizens use to make judgments about people by selecting which stories to cover

probability sample—Some number of individuals from a certain population randomly selected and asked a set of questions; the key is that every individual in the population of interest has a known probability of being selected

professionalism—A quality of legislatures that captures how much work legislators perform and status they receive. In a more professionalized legislature, serving as a legislator is a full-time job with a substantial salary and staff support.

Progressive/"Bull Moose" Party (1912–1914)—A political party, associated with Theodore Roosevelt, and representing disaffected Republicans who favored greater power and democratic prerogatives for the "little man" and regulation of major industries

proportional representation—System in which seats are allocated based on the percentage of the vote won by each party

proximity voting—Choosing a candidate based on how close the candidate's views are to one's own views across a range of relevant issues

public funding—Campaign funds provided by the government

purposive benefits—The satisfaction one derives from having advanced an issue or ideological position, or from having fulfilled a duty

quality challenger—A candidate with the experience and backing necessary to run a competitive campaign

reapportionment—Process of determining the number of representatives allotted to each state after the decennial census count

Reconstruction—Era immediately after the Civil War in which policies were enacted to protect the freedoms and rights of black citizens. Reconstruction policies were particularly important in the southern states, where Union troops were stationed to enforce these policies. The Reconstruction era ended at different times for different states, but many believe that the Compromise of 1877 effectively ended Reconstruction.

redistricting—Drawing new district lines after the decennial census count

referenda—Measures that affect laws or public policy that allow citizens to vote on a statute already passed by state legislatures

reinforcement—The notion that news consumers interpret information as giving added strength or support to their existing views. The process of solidifying voters' support for a candidate.

Republican-Democratic Party (1796–1824)—Political party associated with Thomas Jefferson, representing a more limited view of federal governing power, preferring state and local governing authority; support was strongest in the southern and western states

Republican L—The pattern formed by Republican-leaning states in the mountain west and southern states

Republican Party (1860–present)—Political party originally associated with Abraham Lincoln and representing interests opposed to slavery and favoring the continuation of the Union

retail politics—Face-to-face communication between candidates and voters of political positions and arguments

retention elections—Judicial elections in which voters decide whether a sitting judge should continue in that position; these elections do not feature a competition between the sitting judge and an opponent

retrospective voting—Choosing between candidates according to broad appraisals of whether things have improved or gotten worse under the incumbent

right to equal time—A Federal Communications Commission rule that requires most radio and television broadcasters to treat candidates equally when selling or giving away airtime

roll-call vote—At a party convention, the aggregation of state-by-state votes of delegates

same-day/election-day registration—System in which eligible citizens may register to vote as late as Election Day itself

semi-closed primary—Election for the party's nominee in which party registrants and those unaffiliated with any party are allowed to vote

single-member districts—Geographic units that elect only one person to represent the entire unit

social context—The people with whom one communicates and interacts, such as family, friends, classmates, coworkers, and neighbors

sociotropic voting—Choosing between candidates based on how one thinks the country has faired under the incumbent party's rule

soft money—Money raised outside the limits normally established by campaign finance laws

solidarity benefits—An intangible reward for participation that comes from being part of a collective effort

sorting—People's partisan preferences have become more closely aligned with their political views

sound bite—A short segment of sound or video used in a news report as an excerpt of an event or interview

strategic voting—In an election with more than two candidates, voting for a candidate other than one's first choice in order to prevent an undesirable outcome

Super PACs—PACs that can collect unlimited amounts of donations as a consequence of a recent Supreme Court decision, *Citizens*

United v. FEC. Super PACs are required to disclose their donors.

survey research—A research method involving the use of questionnaires and/or statistical surveys to gather data about people and their thoughts and behaviors

term limits—Legal restrictions on the maximum time a person can hold a specific office

Tillman Act—1907 law banning corporate contributions to political campaigns

traditional media—Communication outlets designed to reach large audiences that developed prior to the advent of the Internet. Broadcast and cable television, radio, newspapers, and magazines are the common forms.

viability—Ability to win the nomination

vote by mail—When jurisdictions conduct elections by ballots that are automatically mailed to voters instead of using polling stations

vote targets—Estimates of how many votes a candidate will need to win the election.

These are based on calculations of how many people will vote in a particular election, what percentage of the vote will be needed to win, how many votes can be counted on, and how many votes are persuadable.

voter identification/voter ID calls—Calls, usually via telephone, to every person on the voter list to ask about the candidates and issues in the upcoming election

Voting Rights Act (of 1965)—Congressional legislation designed to end discriminatory practices disenfranchising blacks, especially in the South

wedge issues—Political issues intended to persuade voters to abandon the party they traditionally support and support the opposite party

Whig Party (1832-1852)—Political party that rose in response to the Democratic Party in the 1830s, representing voters concerned by Jackson's expansive view of the presidency and his attacks on commercial interests

wire services—A news agency that collects and distributions news stories to many outlets

CREDITS

Chapter 1: p. 8 Tom Williams / Roll Call via Getty Images; **p. 11** Ethan Miller / Getty Images; **p. 16** Justin Sullivan / Getty Images

Chapter 2: p. 22 Mario Tama / Getty Images; **p. 28** Patrick Andrade / The New York Times / Redux; **p. 35** © Bettmann / Corbis; **p. 42** Ad Hoc Collection / The Georgia Archives

Chapter 3: p. 59 The Granger Collection; **p. 61** The Granger Collection; **p. 63** The Granger Collection

Chapter 4: p. 91 Chris Keane / Getty Images; **p. 97** YouTube

Chapter 5: p. 129 Bob Child / AP; **p. 147 (LEFT)** Tom Williams / Roll Call / Getty Images; **p. 147 (RIGHT)** Jason Reed / Reuters / Corbis; **p. 148** YouTube

Chapter 6: p. 154a Tom Williams / Roll Call / Newscom; **p. 154b** Kevin Dietsch / UPI / Newscom; **p. 154c** Micah Walter / Reuters / Corbis; **p. 154d** Mike Eliason / Santa Barbara News-Press / Zuma / Newscom; **p. 158** Pete Marovich / Zuma / Newscom; **p. 168** Archie Carpenter / UPI / Newscom; **p. 170** YouTube

Chapter 7: p. 182 Trinity United Church of Christ / AP; **p. 203** CBS / Landov; **p. 208** Mark Cowan / UPI / Landov

Chapter 8: p. 216 Harry Hamburg / NY Daily News Archive via Getty Images; **p. 227** Marc Piscotty / Rapport / Newscom; **p. 244** AP Photo

Chapter 9: p. 252 Ethan Hyman / Raleigh News & Observer / MCT via Getty Images; **p. 264** YouTube; **p. 265** Douglas Graham / Roll Call via Getty Images; **p. 274** Nick Pickles / Getty Images

Chapter 10: p. 282 Kevin Winter / Getty Images; **p. 283** Sharon Cantillon / Buffalo News; **p. 295** Courtesy Travis County Clerk Elections Division

Chapter 11: p. 318 Chris Hondros / Getty Images; **p. 322** Chris Fitzgerald / CandidatePhotos .com / Newscom; **p. 336** KG / Splash News / Newscom

Chapter 12: p. 344 JEFF MITCHELL / REUTERS / Landov; **p. 358** Mark Avery / Orange County Register / Corbis

Chapter 13: p. 378 Xinhua / Photoshot / Newscom

INDEX